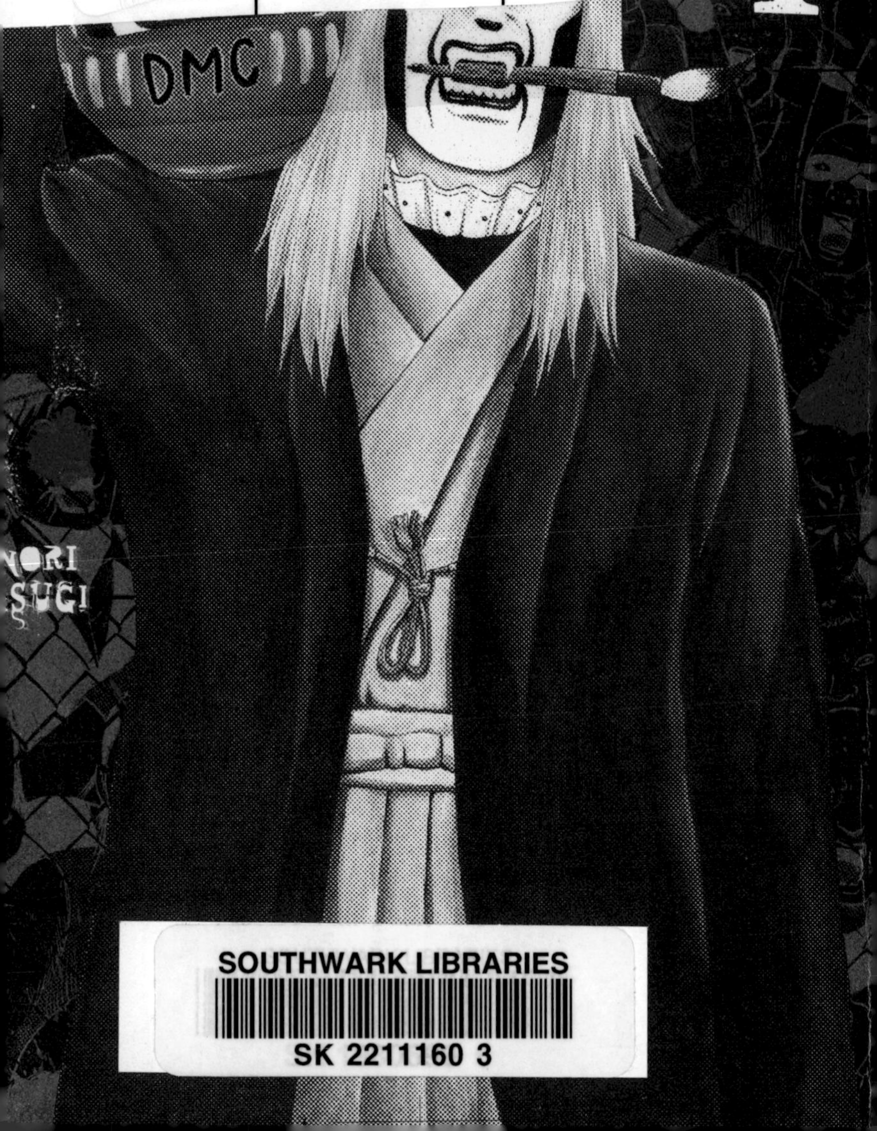
4
DMC

Detroit Metal City

DMC

DETROIT METAL CITY IS
KRAUSER II (LEAD GUITAR, VOCALS) CAMUS (DRUMS) JAGI (VOCALS AND BASS)

WARNING!
THIS ALBUM CONTAINS NOTHING BUT THE MOST PROFANE OF PROFANITIES! LISTEN AT THE RISK OF YOUR IMMORTAL SOUL.

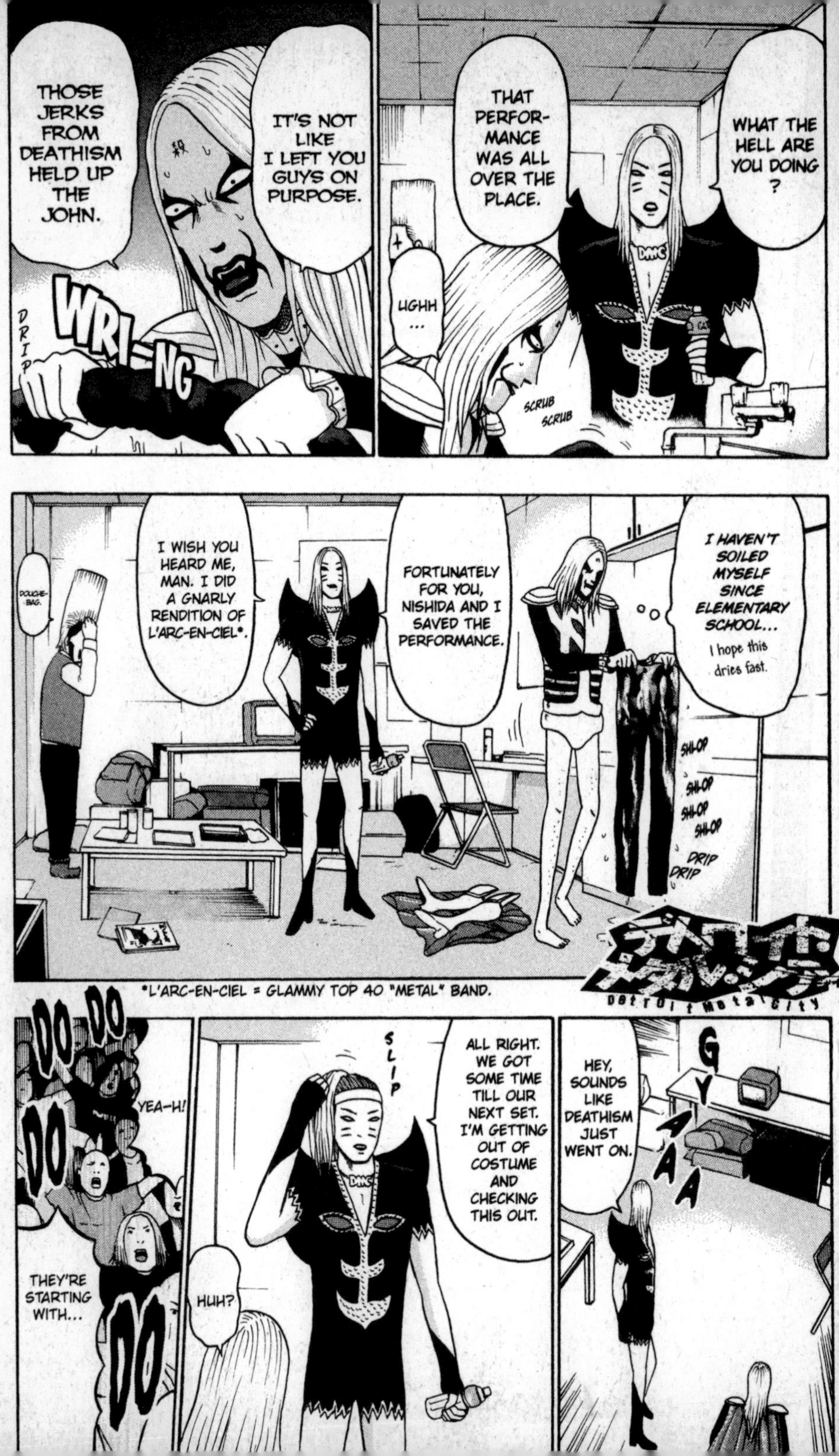
WHAT THE HELL ARE YOU DOING?
THAT PERFORMANCE WAS ALL OVER THE PLACE.
UGHH...
SCRUB SCRUB
IT'S NOT LIKE I LEFT YOU GUYS ON PURPOSE.
THOSE JERKS FROM DEATHISM HELD UP THE JOHN.
WRI-NG
DRIP
I HAVEN'T SOILED MYSELF SINCE ELEMENTARY SCHOOL...
I hope this dries fast.
SHLOP SHLOP SHLOP SHLOP
DRIP DRIP
FORTUNATELY FOR YOU, NISHIDA AND I SAVED THE PERFORMANCE.
I WISH YOU HEARD ME, MAN. I DID A GNARLY RENDITION OF L'ARC-EN-CIEL*.
DOUCHE-BAG.
GYAAAA
HEY, SOUNDS LIKE DEATHISM JUST WENT ON.
SLIP
ALL RIGHT. WE GOT SOME TIME TILL OUR NEXT SET. I'M GETTING OUT OF COSTUME AND CHECKING THIS OUT.
HUH?
DO DO DO DO
YEA-H!
THEY'RE STARTING WITH...

*L'ARC-EN-CIEL = GLAMMY TOP 40 "METAL" BAND.

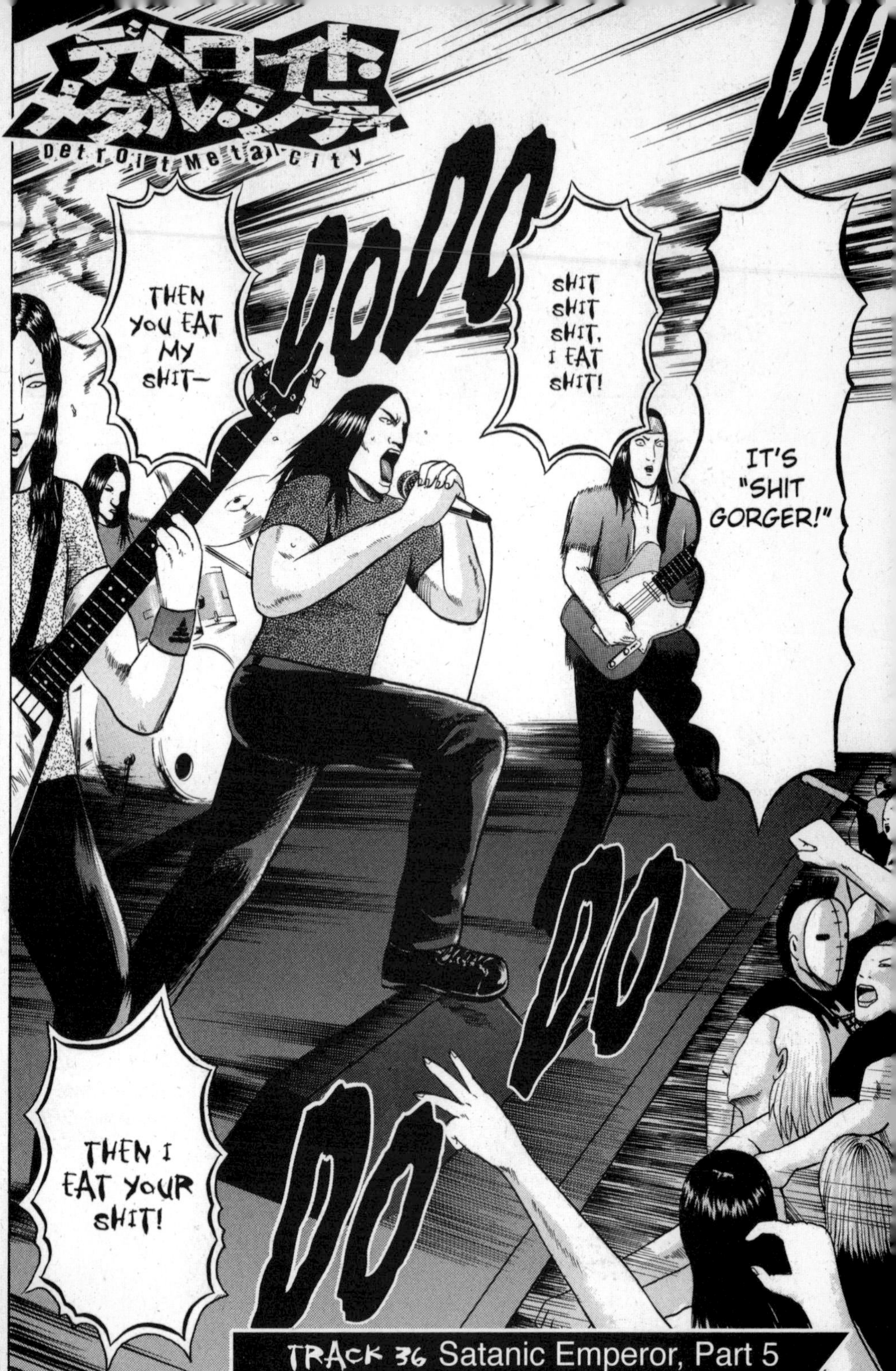
Detroit Metal City
DO
IT'S "SHIT GORGER!"
SHIT SHIT SHIT, I EAT SHIT!
DODO
THEN YOU EAT MY SHIT-
DODO
DODO
THEN I EAT YOUR SHIT!

TRACK 36 Satanic Emperor, Part 5

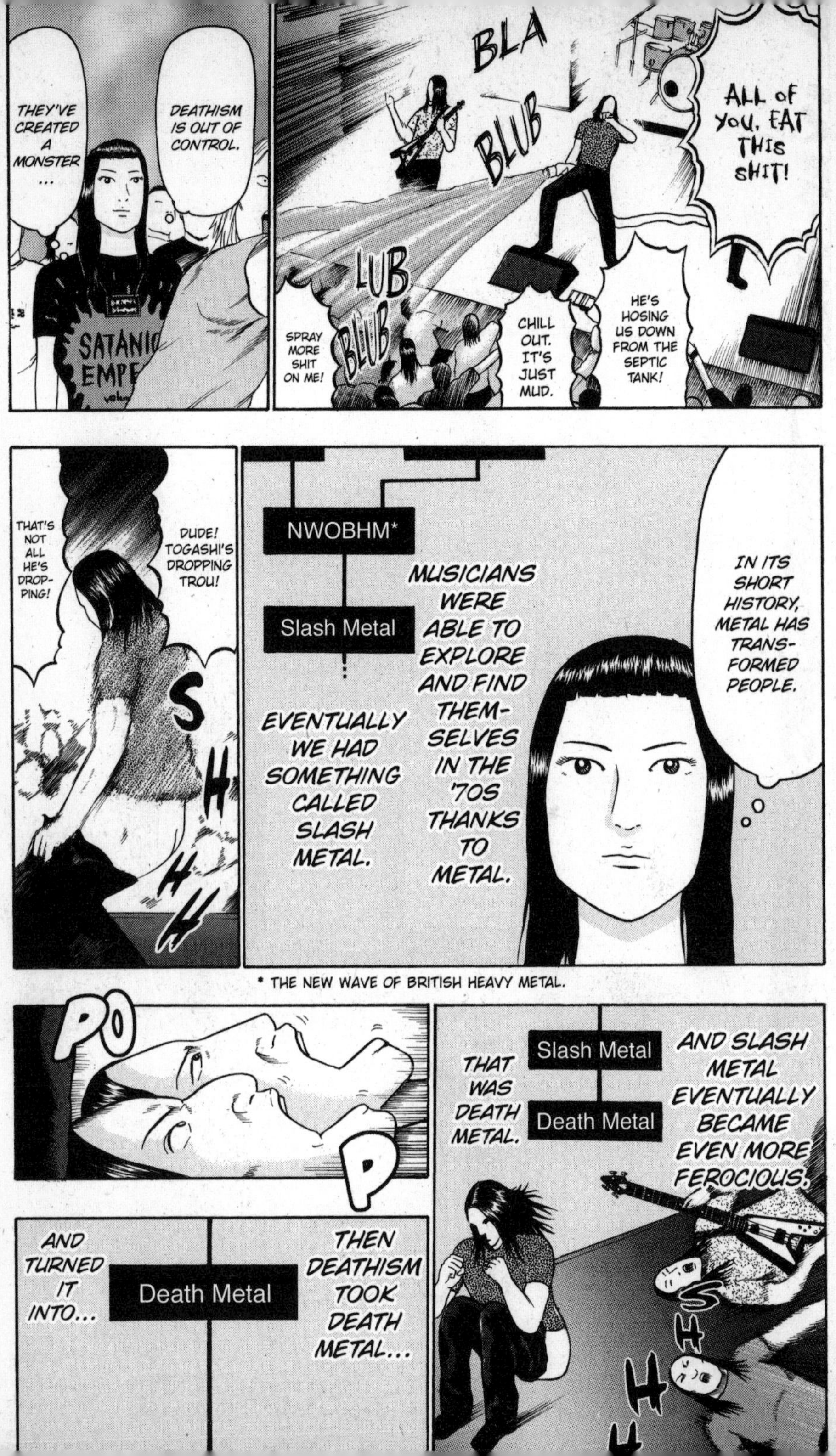
ALL OF YOU. EAT THIS SHIT!
BLA
BLUB
HE'S HOSING US DOWN FROM THE SEPTIC TANK!
CHILL OUT. IT'S JUST MUD.
LUB
BLUB
SPRAY MORE SHIT ON ME!
DEATHISM IS OUT OF CONTROL.
THEY'VE CREATED A MONSTER ...
SATANIC EMPE
IN ITS SHORT HISTORY, METAL HAS TRANS-FORMED PEOPLE.
MUSICIANS WERE ABLE TO EXPLORE AND FIND THEM-SELVES IN THE '70S THANKS TO METAL.
NWOBHM*
Slash Metal
EVENTUALLY WE HAD SOMETHING CALLED SLASH METAL.
DUDE! TOGASHI'S DROPPING TROU!
THAT'S NOT ALL HE'S DROP-PING!
SHHH
AND SLASH METAL EVENTUALLY BECAME EVEN MORE FEROCIOUS.
Slash Metal
Death Metal
THAT WAS DEATH METAL.
SHHH
PO
P
THEN DEATHISM TOOK DEATH METAL...
Death Metal
AND TURNED IT INTO...
* THE NEW WAVE OF BRITISH HEAVY METAL.

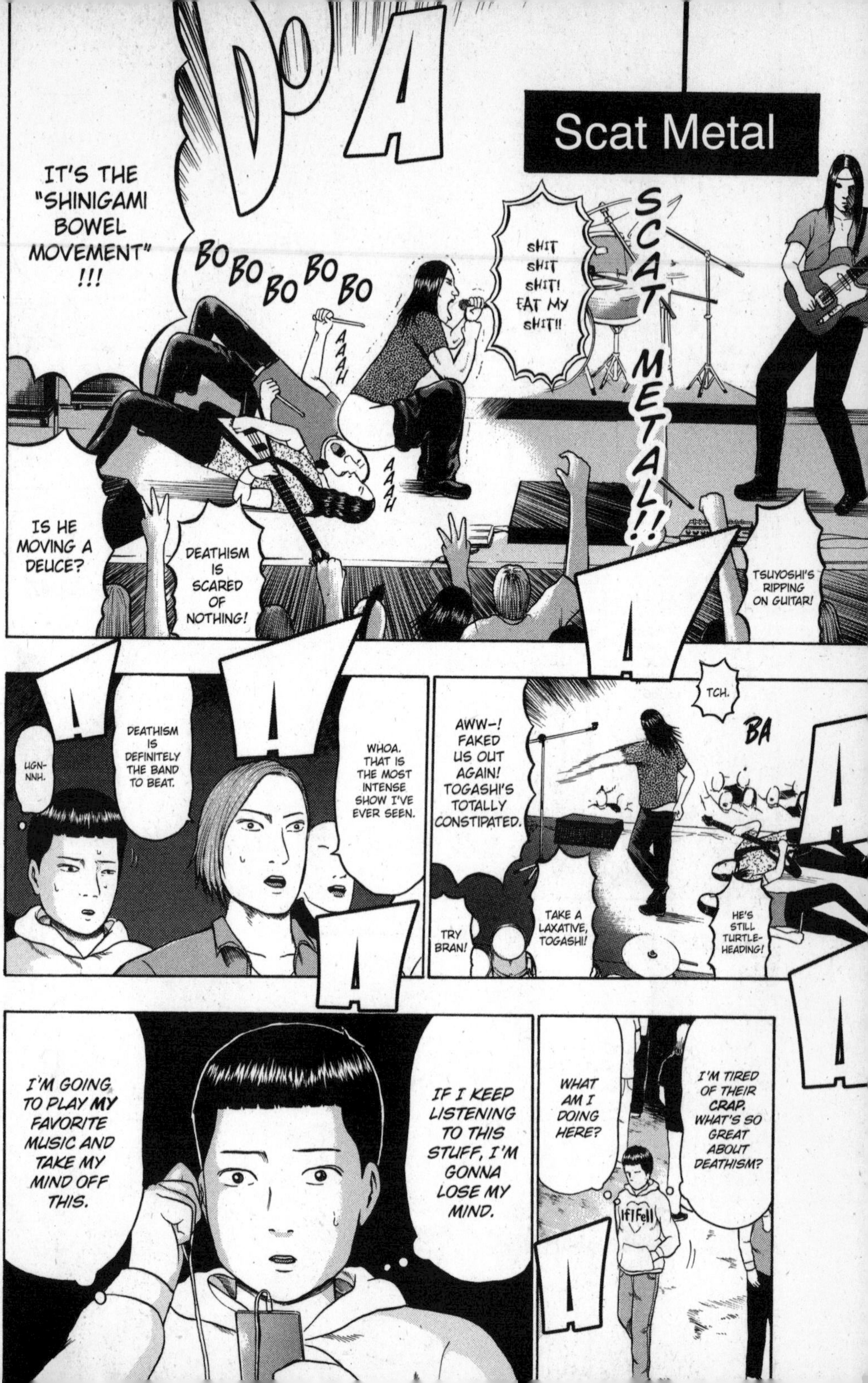

Scat Metal
SCAT METAL!!
SHIT SHIT SHIT! EAT MY SHIT!!
DA
BO BO BO BO BO
IT'S THE "SHINIGAMI BOWEL MOVEMENT"!!!
AAAH
AAAH
TSUYOSHI'S RIPPING ON GUITAR!
DEATHISM IS SCARED OF NOTHING!
IS HE MOVING A DEUCE?
TCH.
BA
AWW-! FAKED US OUT AGAIN! TOGASHI'S TOTALLY CONSTIPATED.
HE'S STILL TURTLE-HEADING!
TAKE A LAXATIVE, TOGASHI!
TRY BRAN!
WHOA. THAT IS THE MOST INTENSE SHOW I'VE EVER SEEN.
DEATHISM IS DEFINITELY THE BAND TO BEAT.
UGN-NNH.
I'M TIRED OF THEIR CRAP. WHAT'S SO GREAT ABOUT DEATHISM?
WHAT AM I DOING HERE?
If I Fell
IF I KEEP LISTENING TO THIS STUFF, I'M GONNA LOSE MY MIND.
I'M GOING TO PLAY MY FAVORITE MUSIC AND TAKE MY MIND OFF THIS.

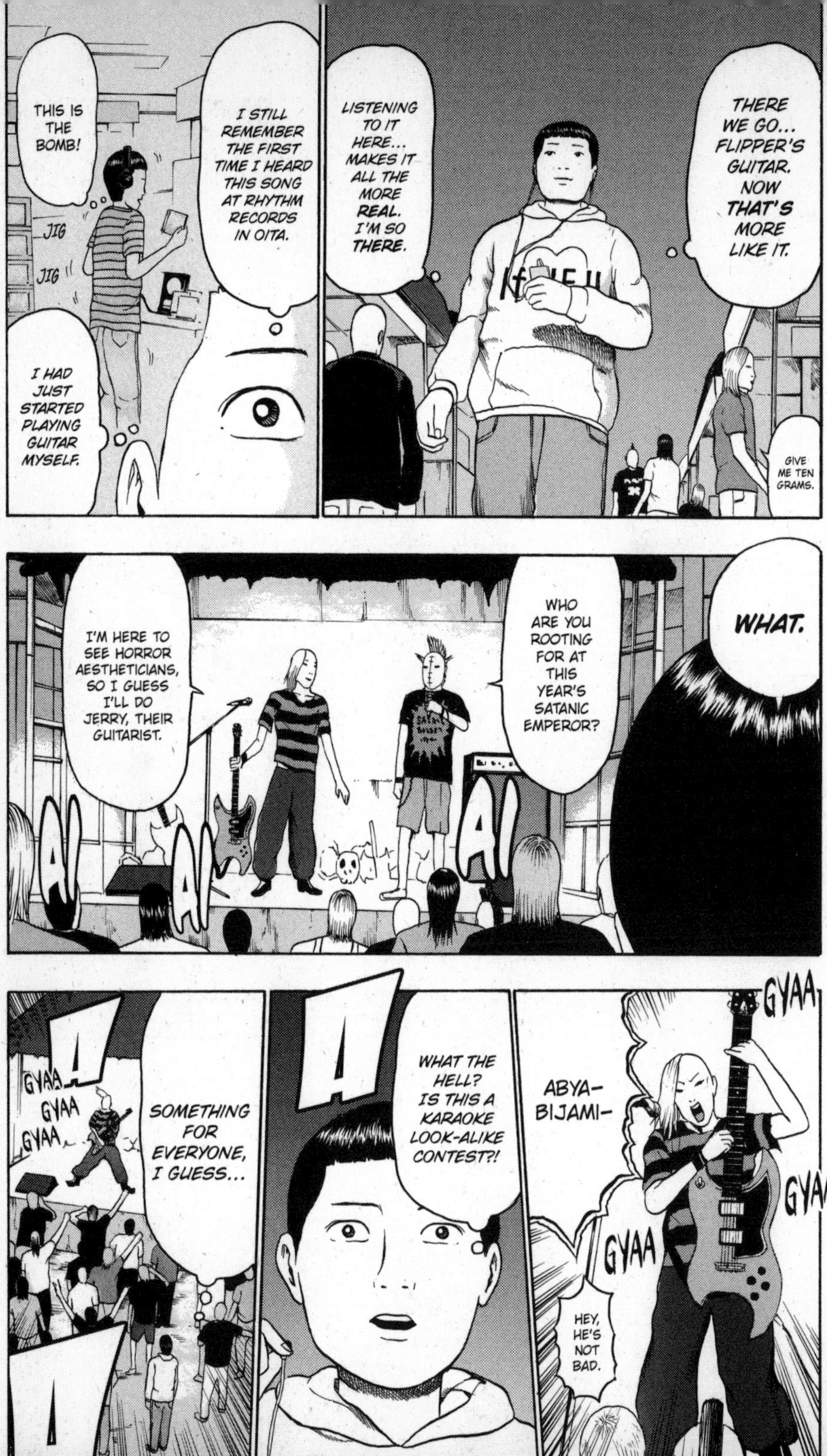

THERE WE GO... FLIPPER'S GUITAR. NOW THAT'S MORE LIKE IT.
LISTENING TO IT HERE... MAKES IT ALL THE MORE REAL. I'M SO THERE.
GIVE ME TEN GRAMS.
I STILL REMEMBER THE FIRST TIME I HEARD THIS SONG AT RHYTHM RECORDS IN OITA.
THIS IS THE BOMB!
JIG
JIG
I HAD JUST STARTED PLAYING GUITAR MYSELF.
WHAT.
WHO ARE YOU ROOTING FOR AT THIS YEAR'S SATANIC EMPEROR?
I'M HERE TO SEE HORROR AESTHETICIANS, SO I GUESS I'LL DO JERRY, THEIR GUITARIST.
A!
A!
A!
GYAA
ABYA-BIJAMI-
GYAA
GYAA
HEY, HE'S NOT BAD.
WHAT THE HELL? IS THIS A KARAOKE LOOK-ALIKE CONTEST?!
A
SOMETHING FOR EVERYONE, I GUESS...
A
GYAA
GYAA
GYAA
A

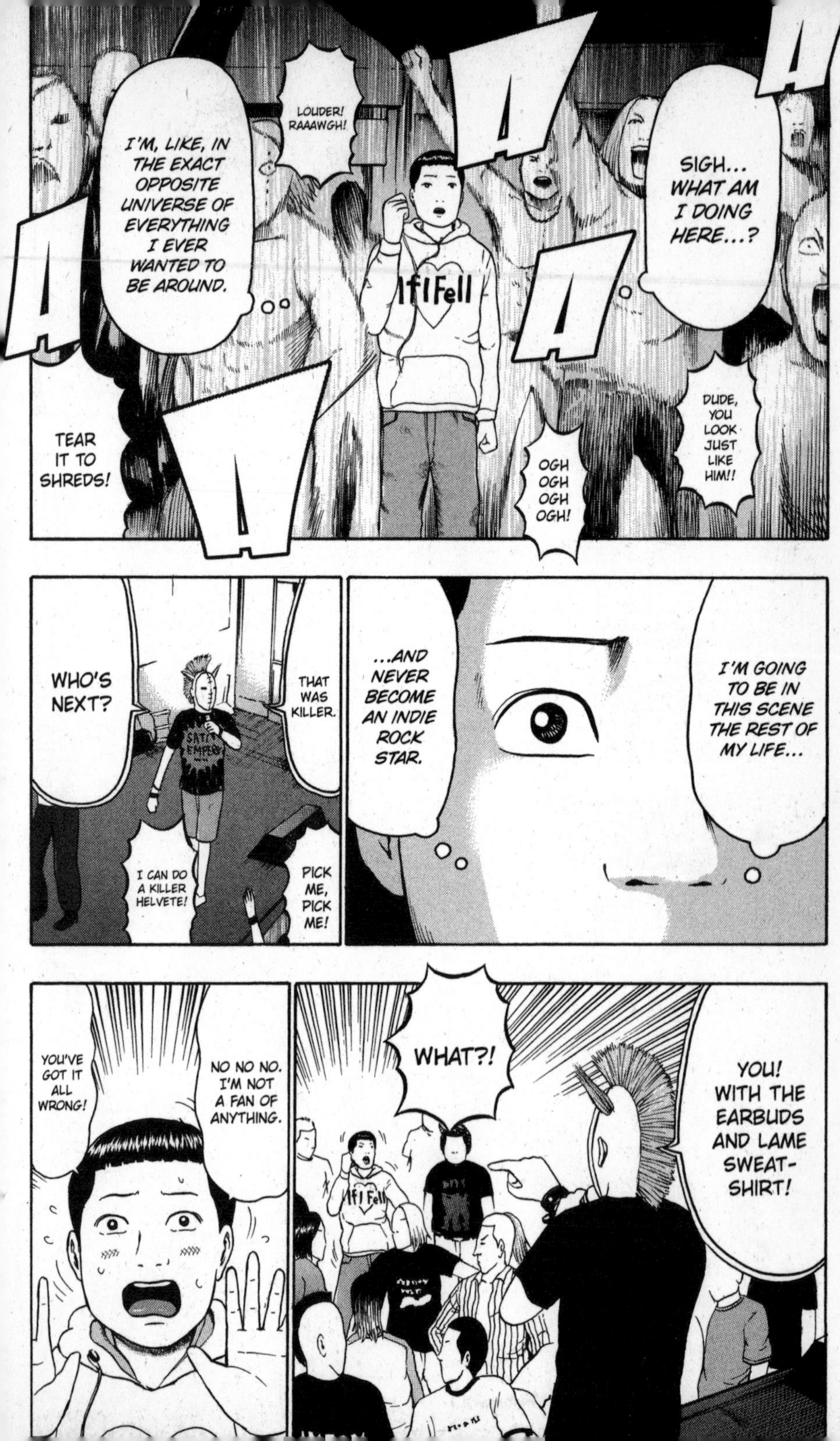
AAAAAA
SIGH... WHAT AM I DOING HERE...?
LOUDER! RAAAWGH!
I'M, LIKE, IN THE EXACT OPPOSITE UNIVERSE OF EVERYTHING I EVER WANTED TO BE AROUND.
DUDE, YOU LOOK JUST LIKE HIM!!
OGH OGH OGH OGH!
TEAR IT TO SHREDS!
I'M GOING TO BE IN THIS SCENE THE REST OF MY LIFE...
...AND NEVER BECOME AN INDIE ROCK STAR.
THAT WAS KILLER.
WHO'S NEXT?
PICK ME, PICK ME!
I CAN DO A KILLER HELVETE!
YOU! WITH THE EARBUDS AND LAME SWEAT-SHIRT!
WHAT?!
NO NO NO. I'M NOT A FAN OF ANYTHING.
YOU'VE GOT IT ALL WRONG!

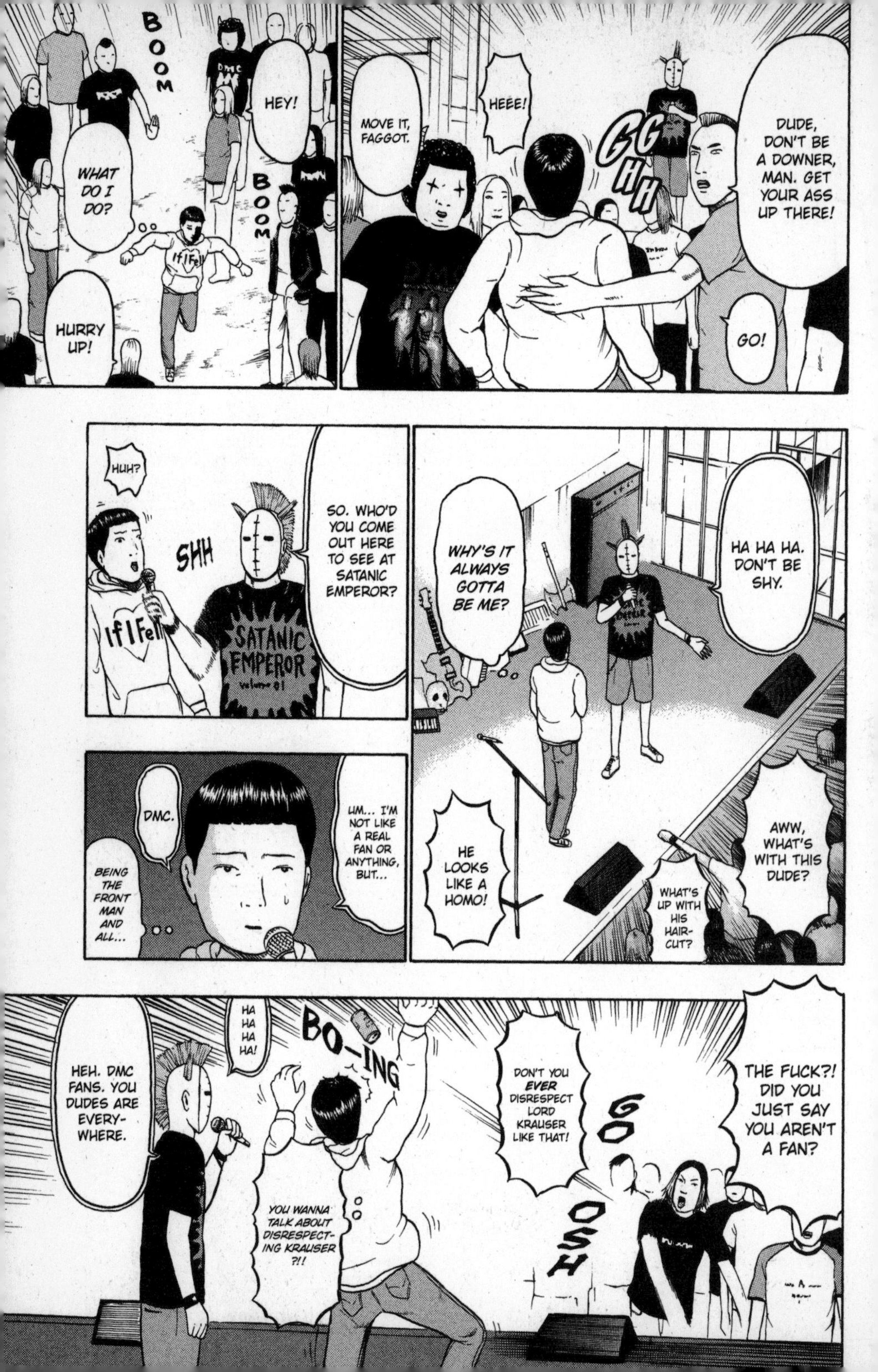
DUDE, DON'T BE A DOWNER, MAN. GET YOUR ASS UP THERE!
GGHH
HEEE!
MOVE IT, FAGGOT.
GO!
HEY!
BOOM
BOOM
WHAT DO I DO?
HURRY UP!
HA HA HA. DON'T BE SHY.
WHY'S IT ALWAYS GOTTA BE ME?
AWW, WHAT'S WITH THIS DUDE?
WHAT'S UP WITH HIS HAIR-CUT?
HE LOOKS LIKE A HOMO!
SO. WHO'D YOU COME OUT HERE TO SEE AT SATANIC EMPEROR?
HUH?
SHH
SATANIC EMPEROR
UM... I'M NOT LIKE A REAL FAN OR ANYTHING, BUT...
DMC.
BEING THE FRONT MAN AND ALL...
THE FUCK?! DID YOU JUST SAY YOU AREN'T A FAN?
DON'T YOU EVER DISRESPECT LORD KRAUSER LIKE THAT!
GOOSH
BO-ING
HA HA HA HA!
HEH. DMC FANS. YOU DUDES ARE EVERY-WHERE.
YOU WANNA TALK ABOUT DISRESPECT-ING KRAUSER ?!!

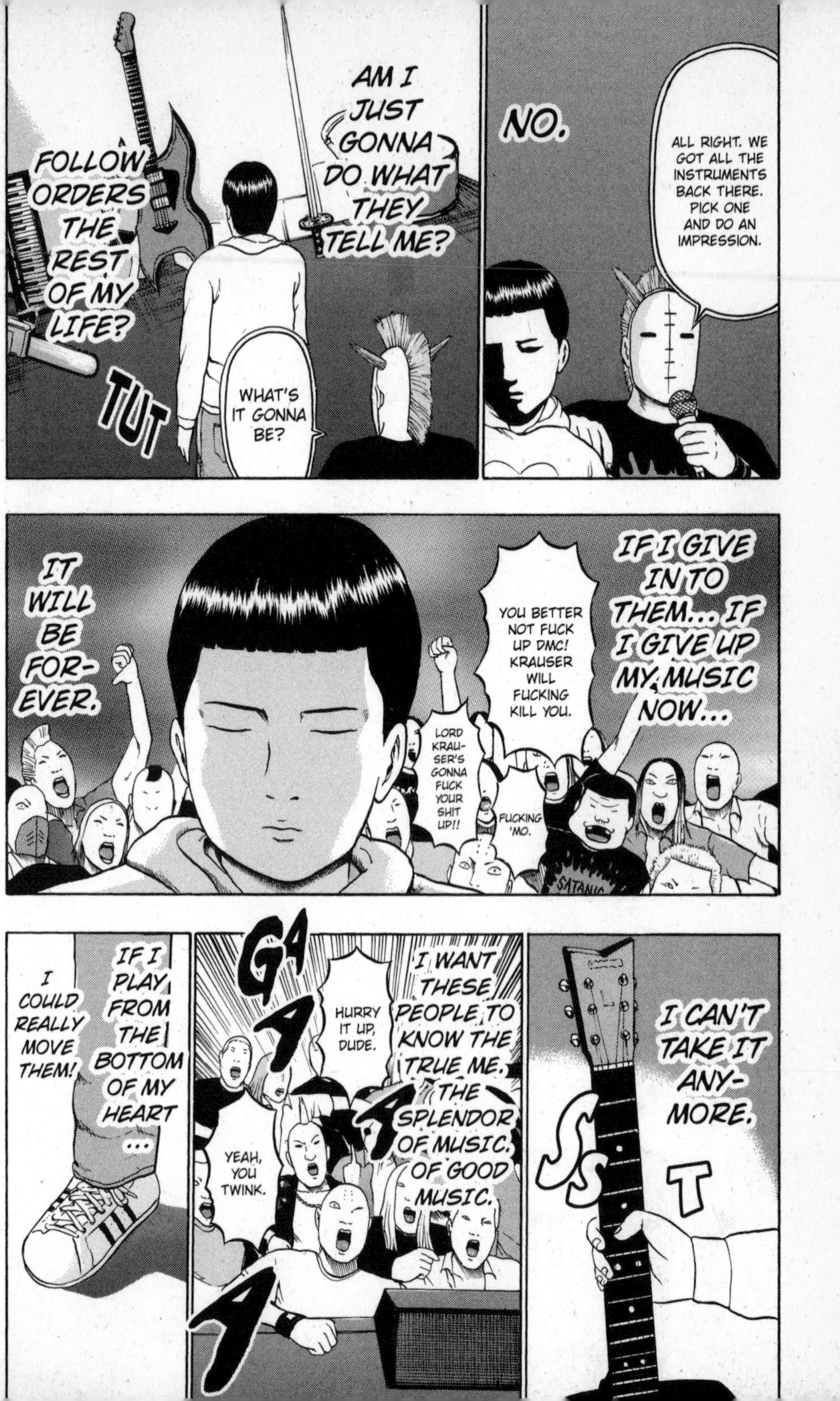
ALL RIGHT. WE GOT ALL THE INSTRUMENTS BACK THERE. PICK ONE AND DO AN IMPRESSION.
NO.
AM I JUST GONNA DO WHAT THEY TELL ME?
FOLLOW ORDERS THE REST OF MY LIFE?
WHAT'S IT GONNA BE?
TUT
IF I GIVE IN TO THEM... IF I GIVE UP MY MUSIC NOW...
YOU BETTER NOT FUCK UP DMC! KRAUSER WILL FUCKING KILL YOU.
LORD KRAU-SER'S GONNA FUCK YOUR SHIT UP!!
FUCKING 'MO.
SATANIC
IT WILL BE FOR-EVER.
I CAN'T TAKE IT ANY-MORE.
SST
I WANT THESE PEOPLE TO KNOW THE TRUE ME. THE SPLENDOR OF MUSIC. OF GOOD MUSIC.
HURRY IT UP, DUDE.
GAAA
YEAH, YOU TWINK.
IF I PLAY FROM THE BOTTOM OF MY HEART...
I COULD REALLY MOVE THEM!

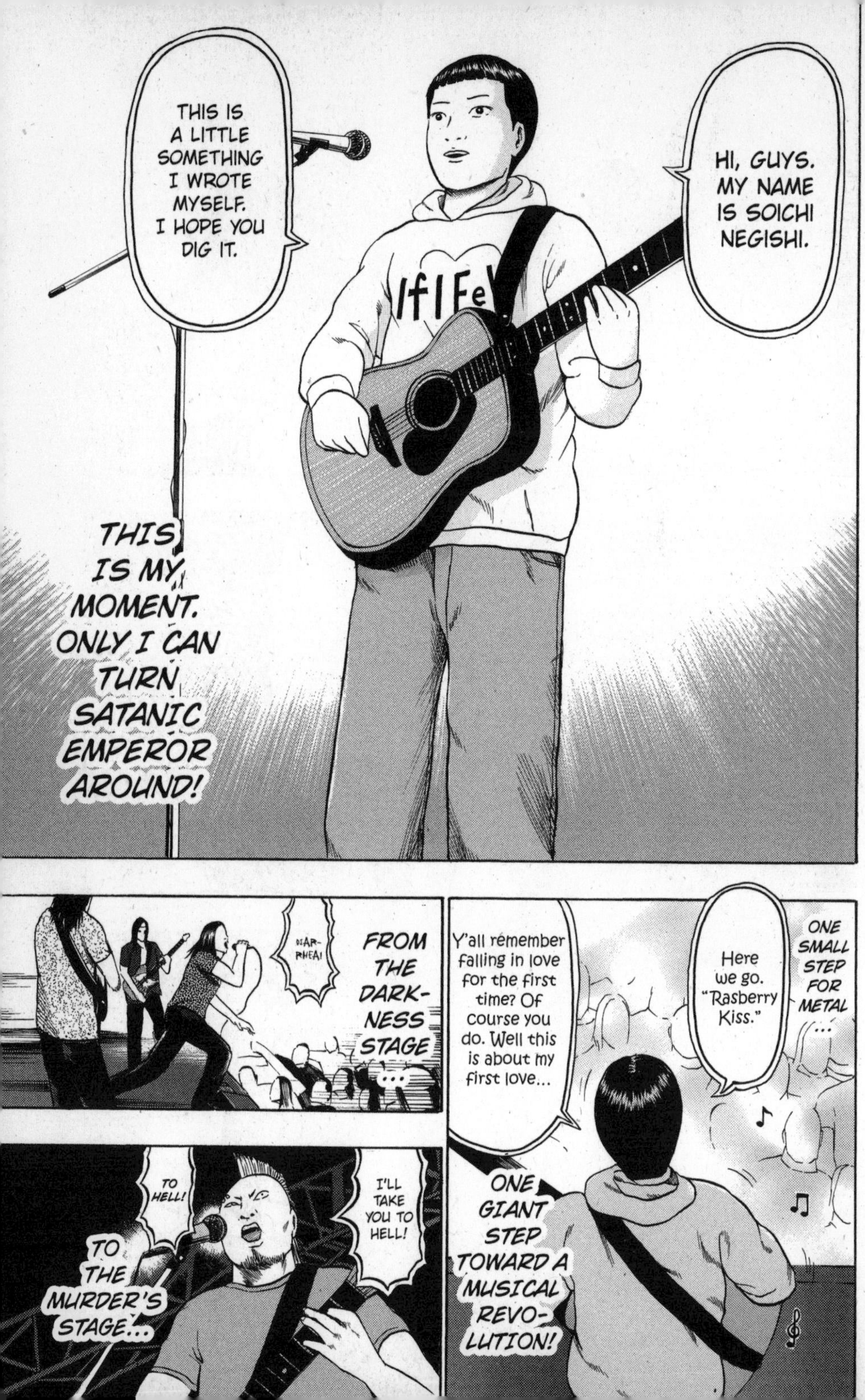
HI, GUYS. MY NAME IS SOICHI NEGISHI.
THIS IS A LITTLE SOMETHING I WROTE MYSELF. I HOPE YOU DIG IT.
THIS IS MY MOMENT. ONLY I CAN TURN SATANIC EMPEROR AROUND!
ONE SMALL STEP FOR METAL…
Here we go. "Rasberry Kiss."
Y'all remember falling in love for the first time? Of course you do. Well this is about my first love…
ONE GIANT STEP TOWARD A MUSICAL REVO-LUTION!
FROM THE DARK-NESS STAGE…
DIAR-RHEA!
I'LL TAKE YOU TO HELL!
TO HELL!
TO THE MURDER'S STAGE…

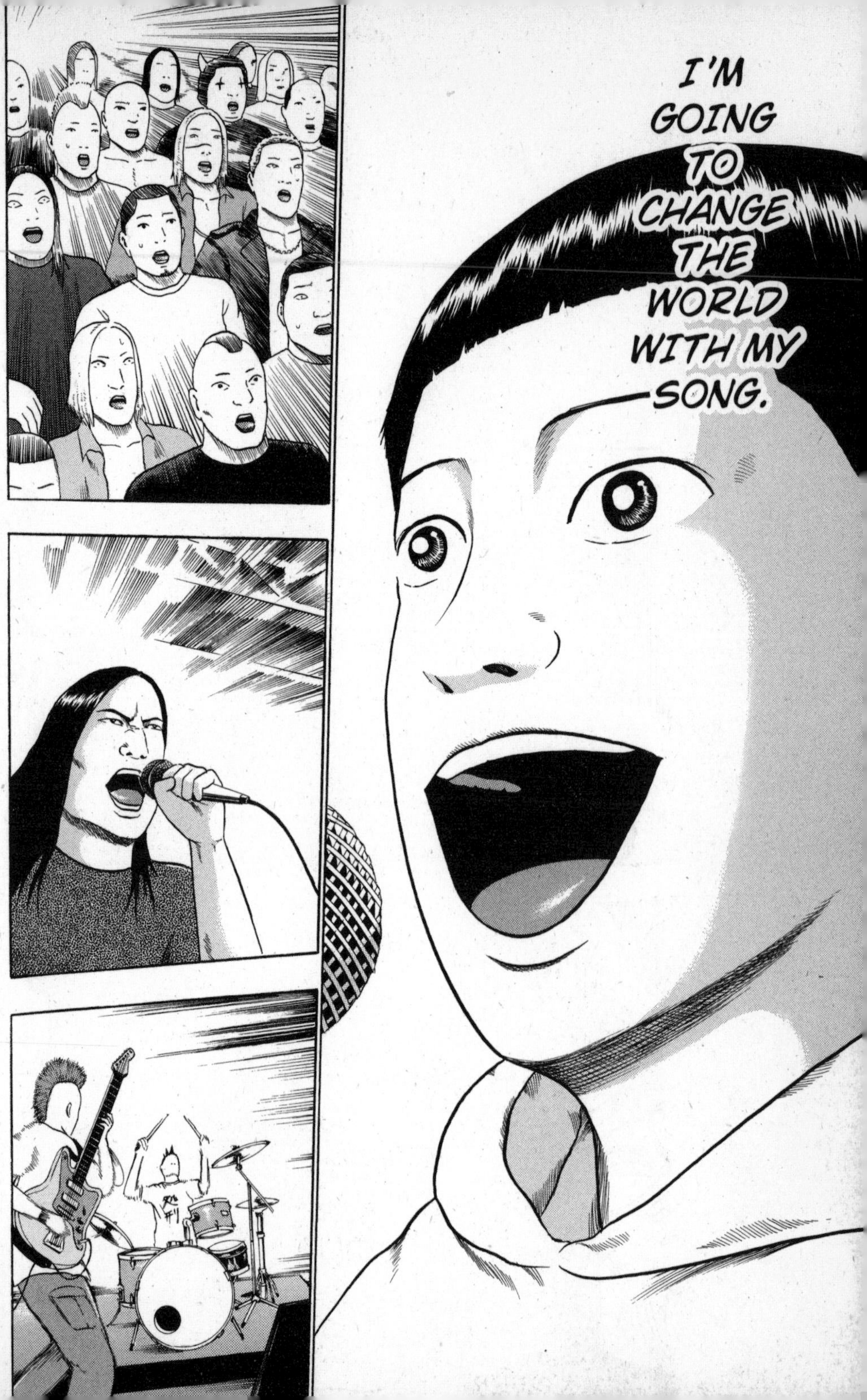
I'M GOING TO CHANGE THE WORLD WITH MY SONG.

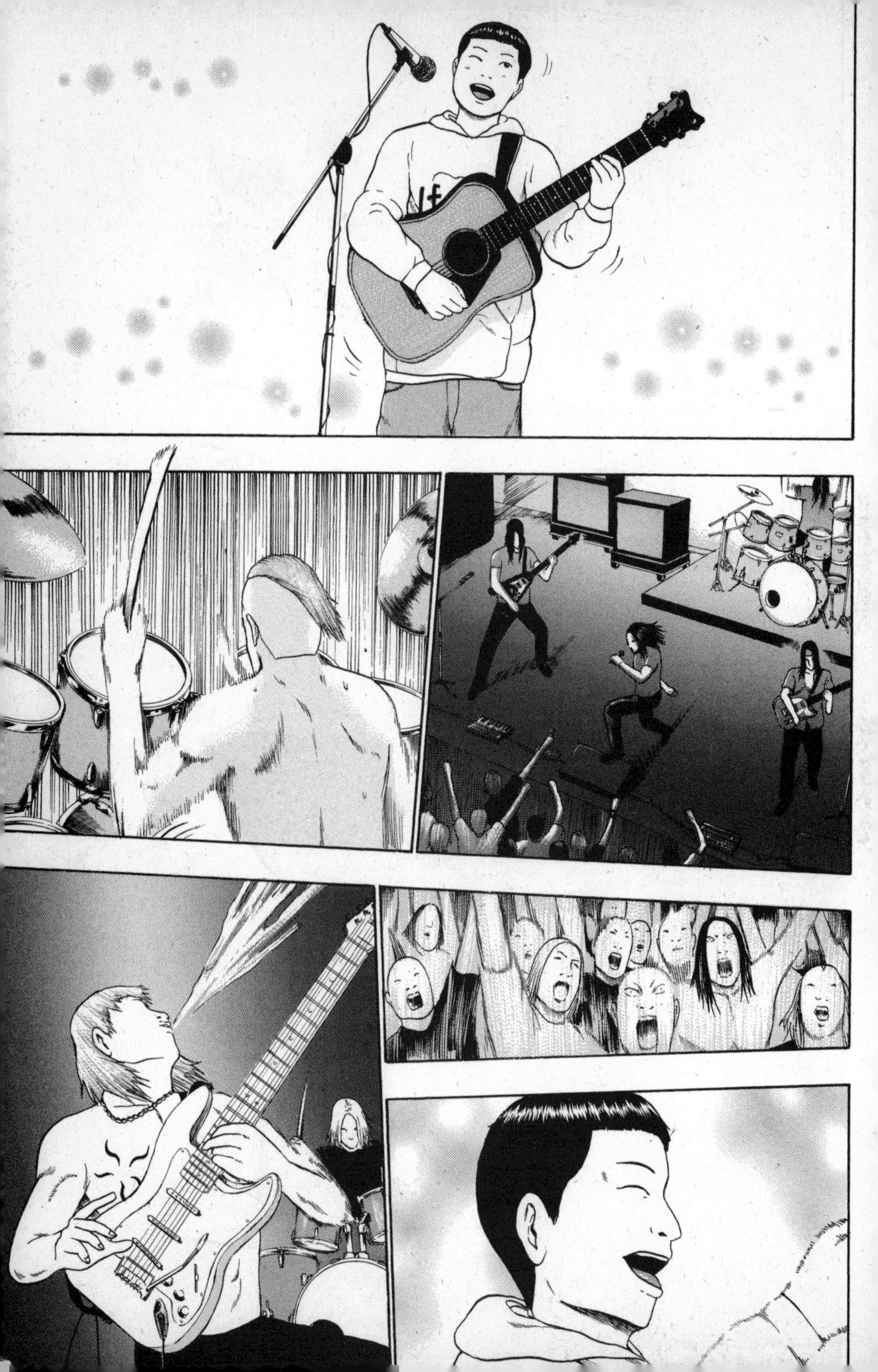

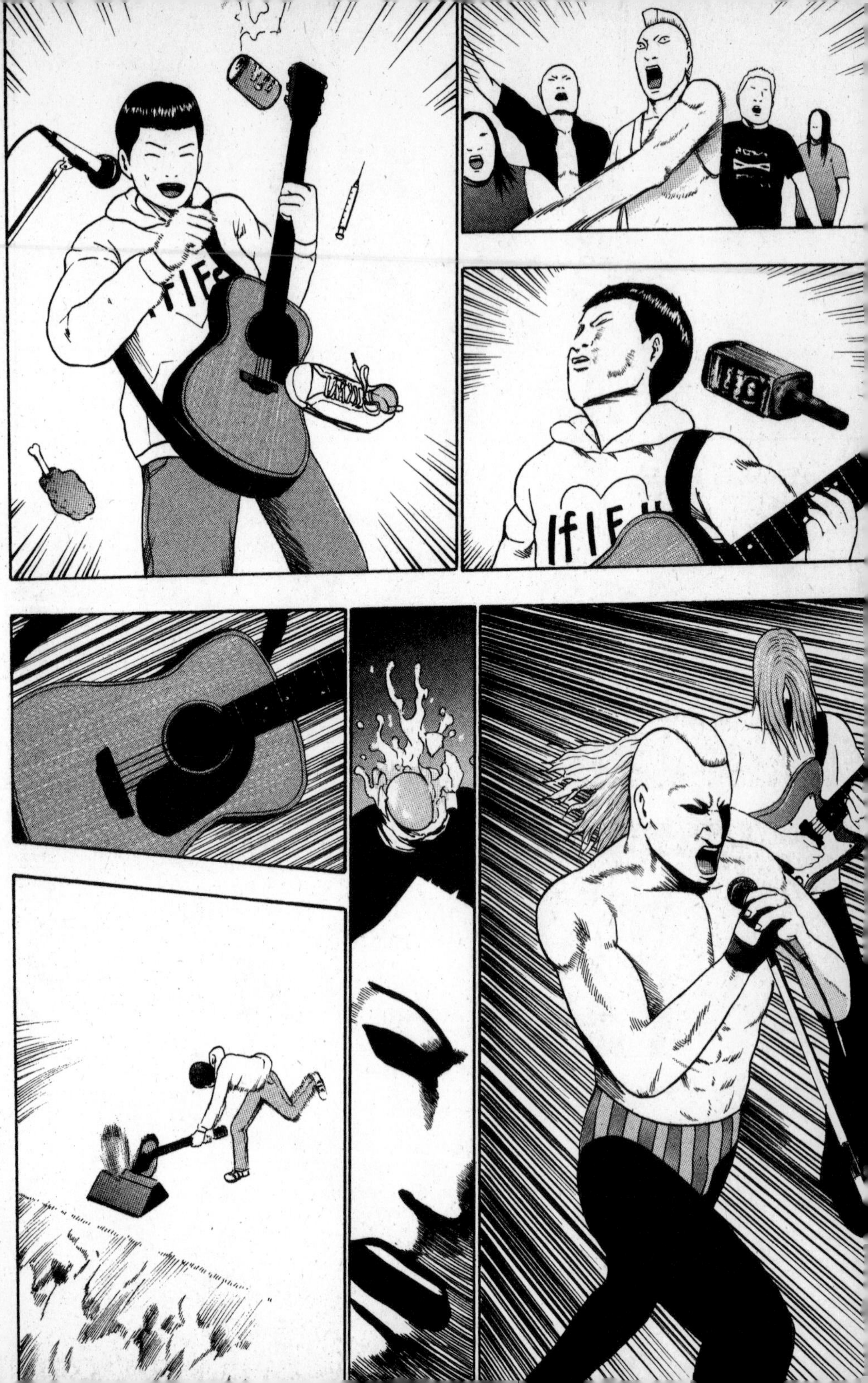

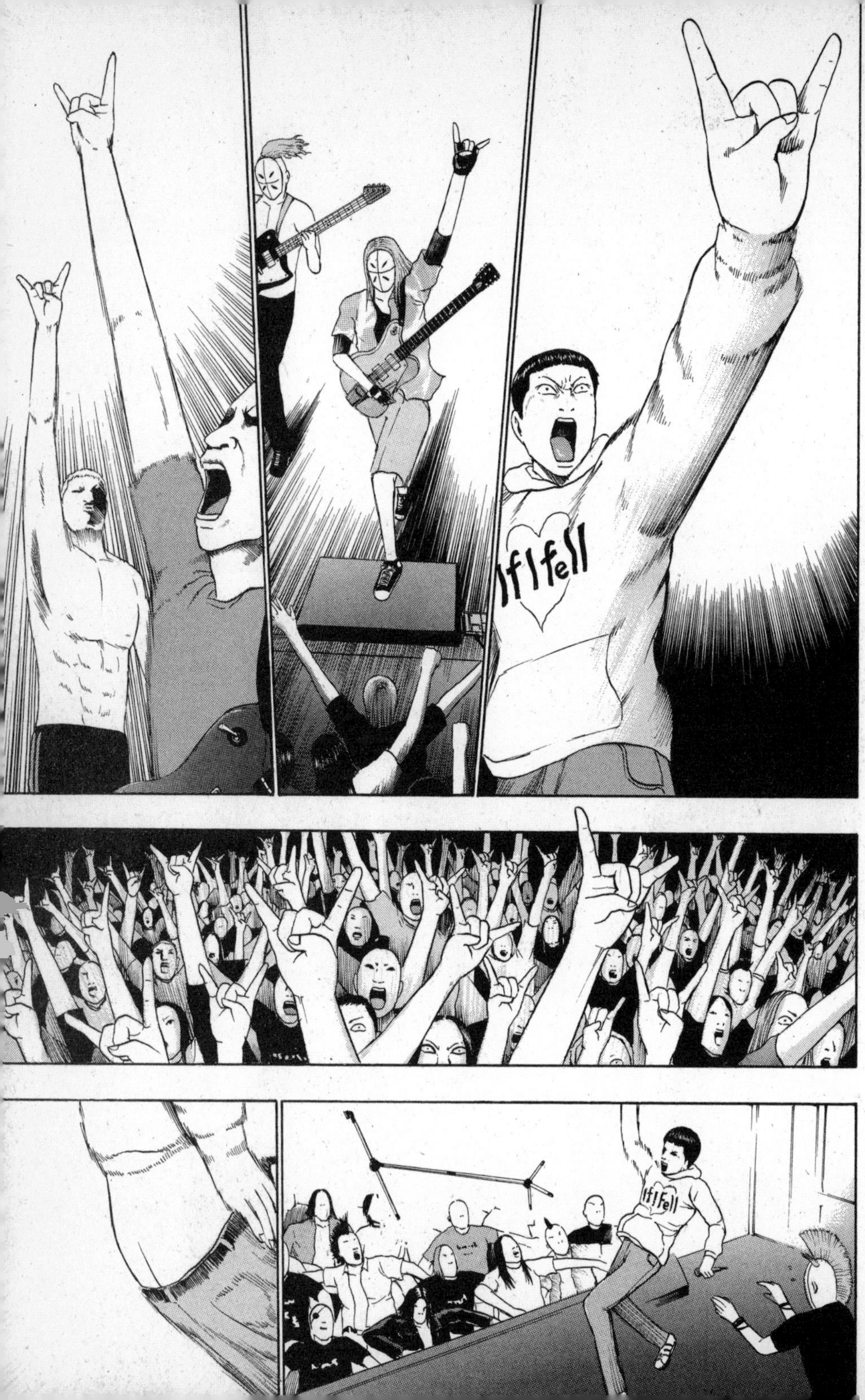
If I fell
If I fell

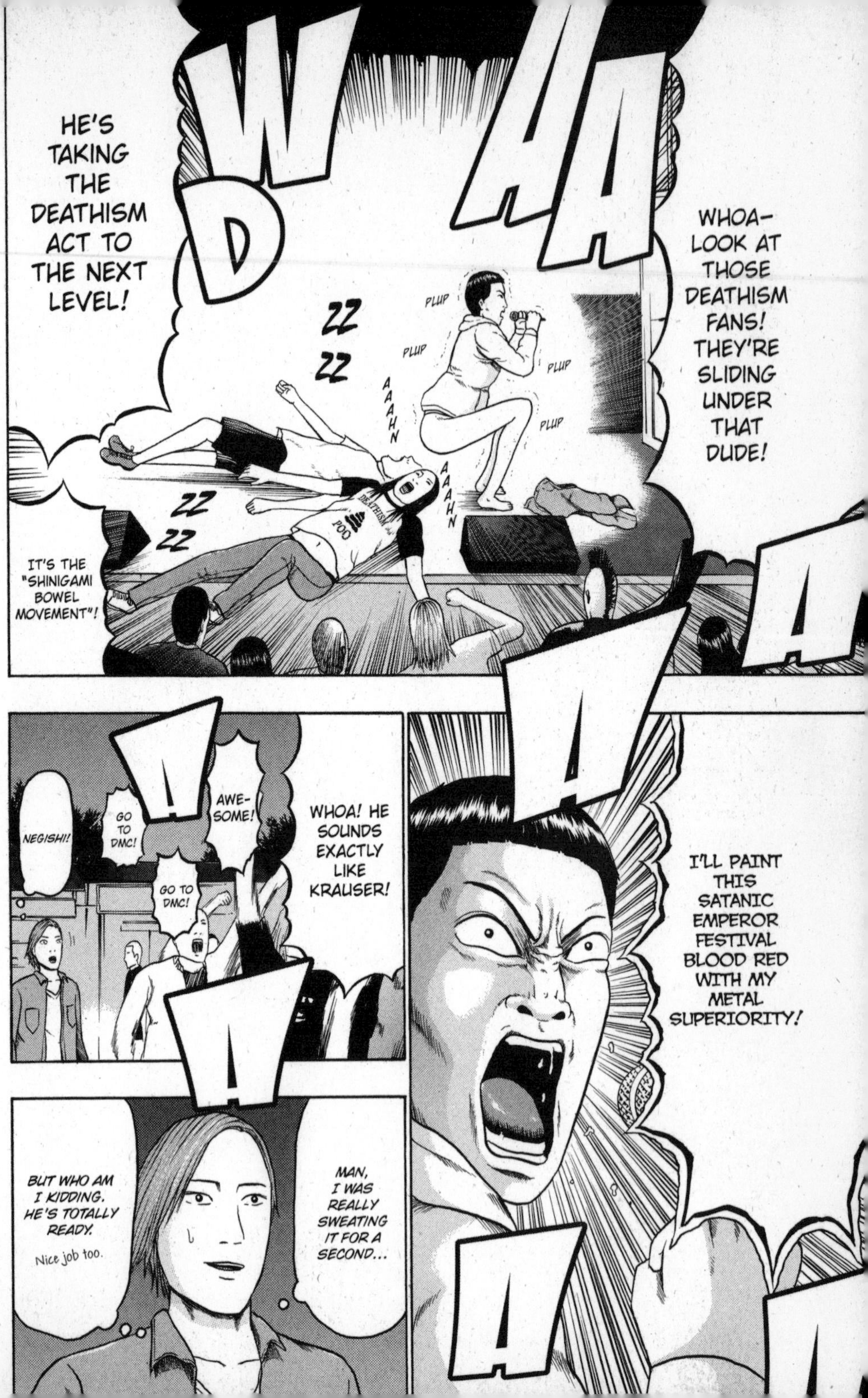
WHOA- LOOK AT THOSE DEATHISM FANS! THEY'RE SLIDING UNDER THAT DUDE!
HE'S TAKING THE DEATHISM ACT TO THE NEXT LEVEL!
PLUP
PLUP
PLUP
PLUP
AAAAHN
AAAAHN
ZZ ZZ
ZZ ZZ
DEATHISM POO
IT'S THE "SHINIGAMI BOWEL MOVEMENT"!
I'LL PAINT THIS SATANIC EMPEROR FESTIVAL BLOOD RED WITH MY METAL SUPERIORITY!
WHOA! HE SOUNDS EXACTLY LIKE KRAUSER!
AWE-SOME!
GO TO DMC!
NEGISHI!
GO TO DMC!
MAN, I WAS REALLY SWEATING IT FOR A SECOND...
BUT WHO AM I KIDDING. HE'S TOTALLY READY.
Nice job too.

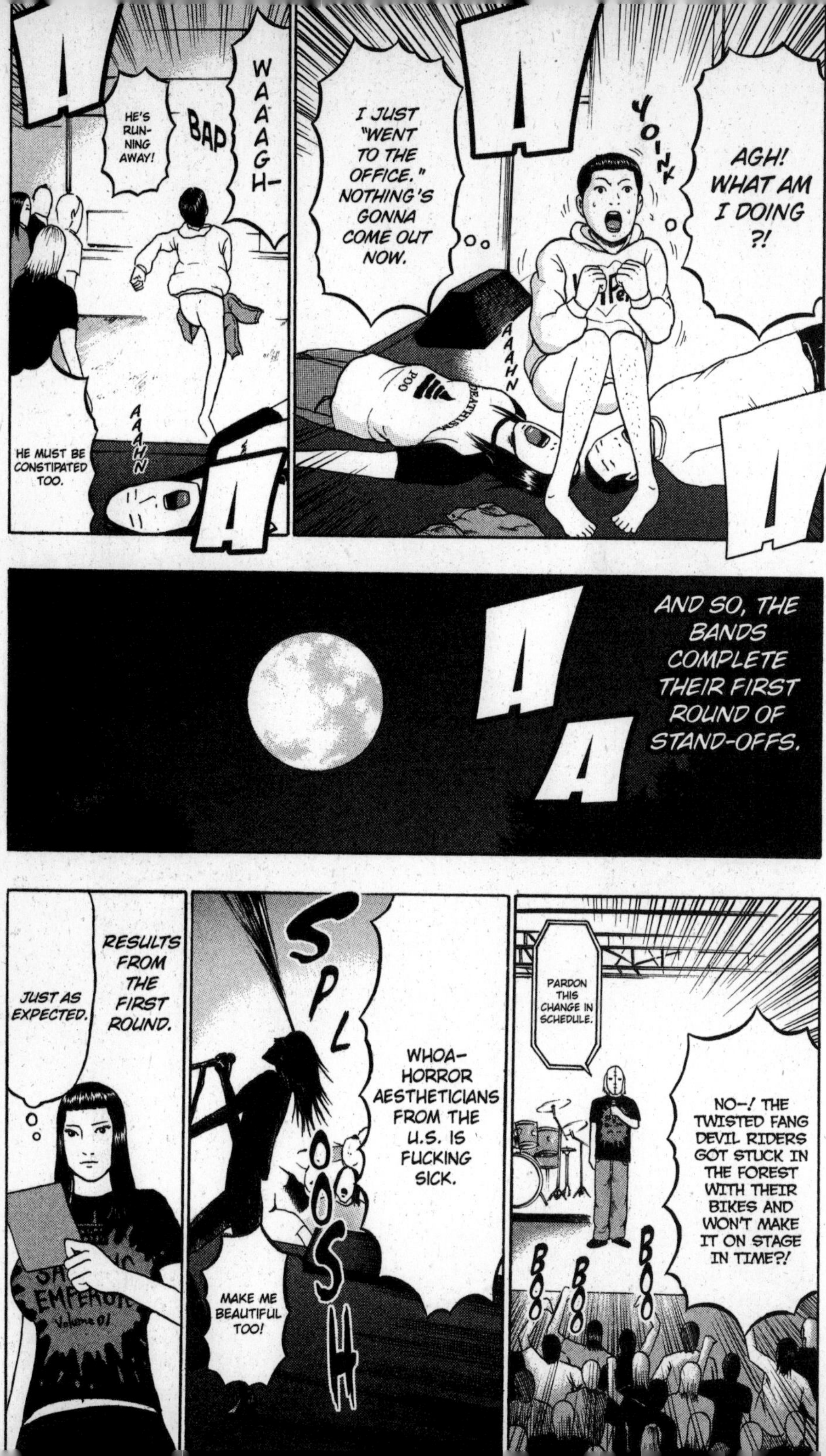
A
YOINK
AGH! WHAT AM I DOING?!
I JUST "WENT TO THE OFFICE." NOTHING'S GONNA COME OUT NOW.
AAAHN
A
A
WAAAAGH—
BAP
HE'S RUN-NING AWAY!
AAAHN
HE MUST BE CONSTIPATED TOO.
A
AND SO, THE BANDS COMPLETE THEIR FIRST ROUND OF STAND-OFFS.
A
A
PARDON THIS CHANGE IN SCHEDULE.
NO—! THE TWISTED FANG DEVIL RIDERS GOT STUCK IN THE FOREST WITH THEIR BIKES AND WON'T MAKE IT ON STAGE IN TIME?!
BOO
BOO
BOO
SPLOOSH
WHOA-HORROR AESTHETICIANS FROM THE U.S. IS FUCKING SICK.
MAKE ME BEAUTIFUL TOO!
RESULTS FROM THE FIRST ROUND.
JUST AS EXPECTED.

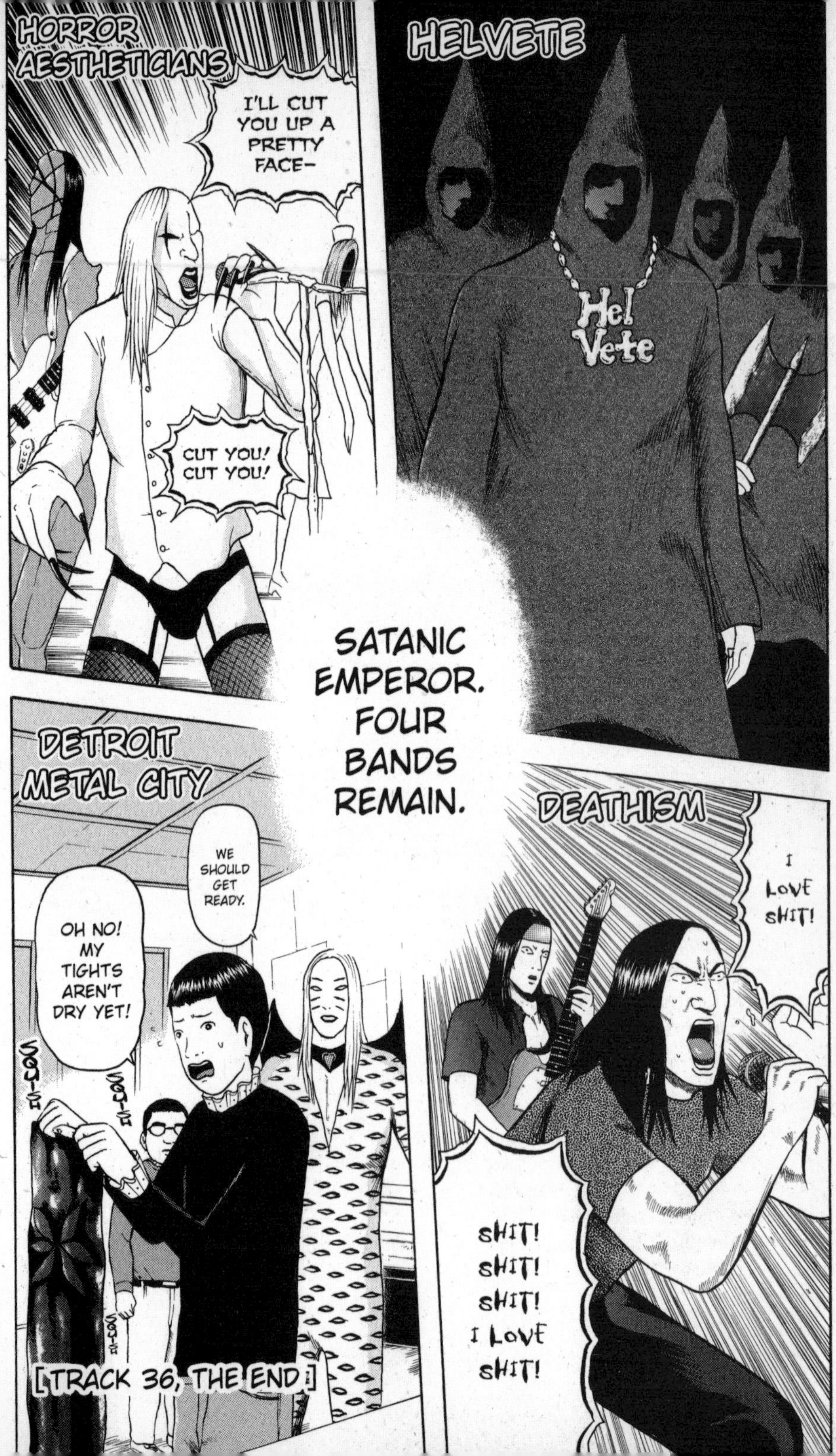
HELVETE
Hel Vete
HORROR AESTHETICIANS
I'LL CUT YOU UP A PRETTY FACE-
CUT YOU! CUT YOU!
SATANIC EMPEROR. FOUR BANDS REMAIN.
DEATHISM
I LOVE SHIT!
SHIT! SHIT! SHIT! I LOVE SHIT!
DETROIT METAL CITY
WE SHOULD GET READY.
OH NO! MY TIGHTS AREN'T DRY YET!
SQUISH
SQUISH
SQUISH
[TRACK 36, THE END]

DMC LEXICON

 RHYTHM RECORDS IN OITA

An independently run record store in the center of Oita City, Known and loved by youngsters for 35 years. The store closed down on March 4, 2007, resulting in this part of Japan being left ten years behind the rest of the world when it comes to contemporary music.

Usage: Rhythm Records closed down? Oita can't let this just happen!

デトロイト・メタル・シティ
Detroit Metal City

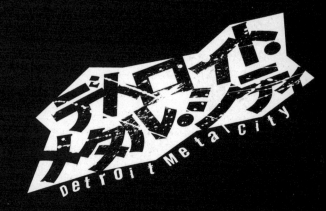

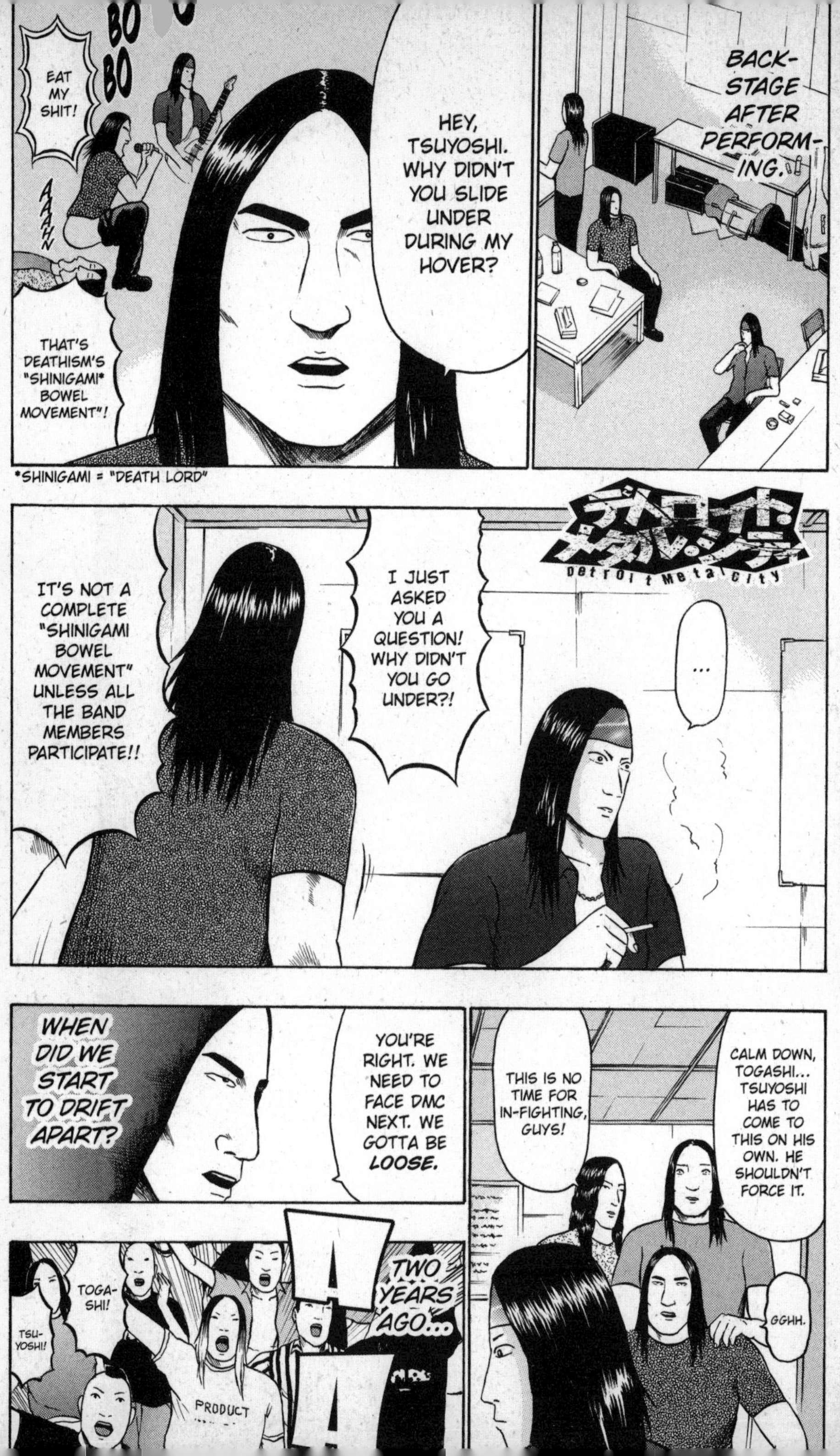
BACK-STAGE AFTER PERFORMING.
HEY, TSUYOSHI. WHY DIDN'T YOU SLIDE UNDER DURING MY HOVER?
BO BO
EAT MY SHIT!
AAAAHN
THAT'S DEATHISM'S "SHINIGAMI* BOWEL MOVEMENT"!
*SHINIGAMI = "DEATH LORD"
Detroit Metal City
…
I JUST ASKED YOU A QUESTION! WHY DIDN'T YOU GO UNDER?!
IT'S NOT A COMPLETE "SHINIGAMI BOWEL MOVEMENT" UNLESS ALL THE BAND MEMBERS PARTICIPATE!!
CALM DOWN, TOGASHI… TSUYOSHI HAS TO COME TO THIS ON HIS OWN. HE SHOULDN'T FORCE IT.
THIS IS NO TIME FOR IN-FIGHTING, GUYS!
GGHH.
YOU'RE RIGHT. WE NEED TO FACE DMC NEXT. WE GOTTA BE LOOSE.
WHEN DID WE START TO DRIFT APART?
TWO YEARS AGO…
TOGA-SHI!
TSU-YOSHI!
PRODUCT

TRACK 37 Satanic Emperor, Part 6

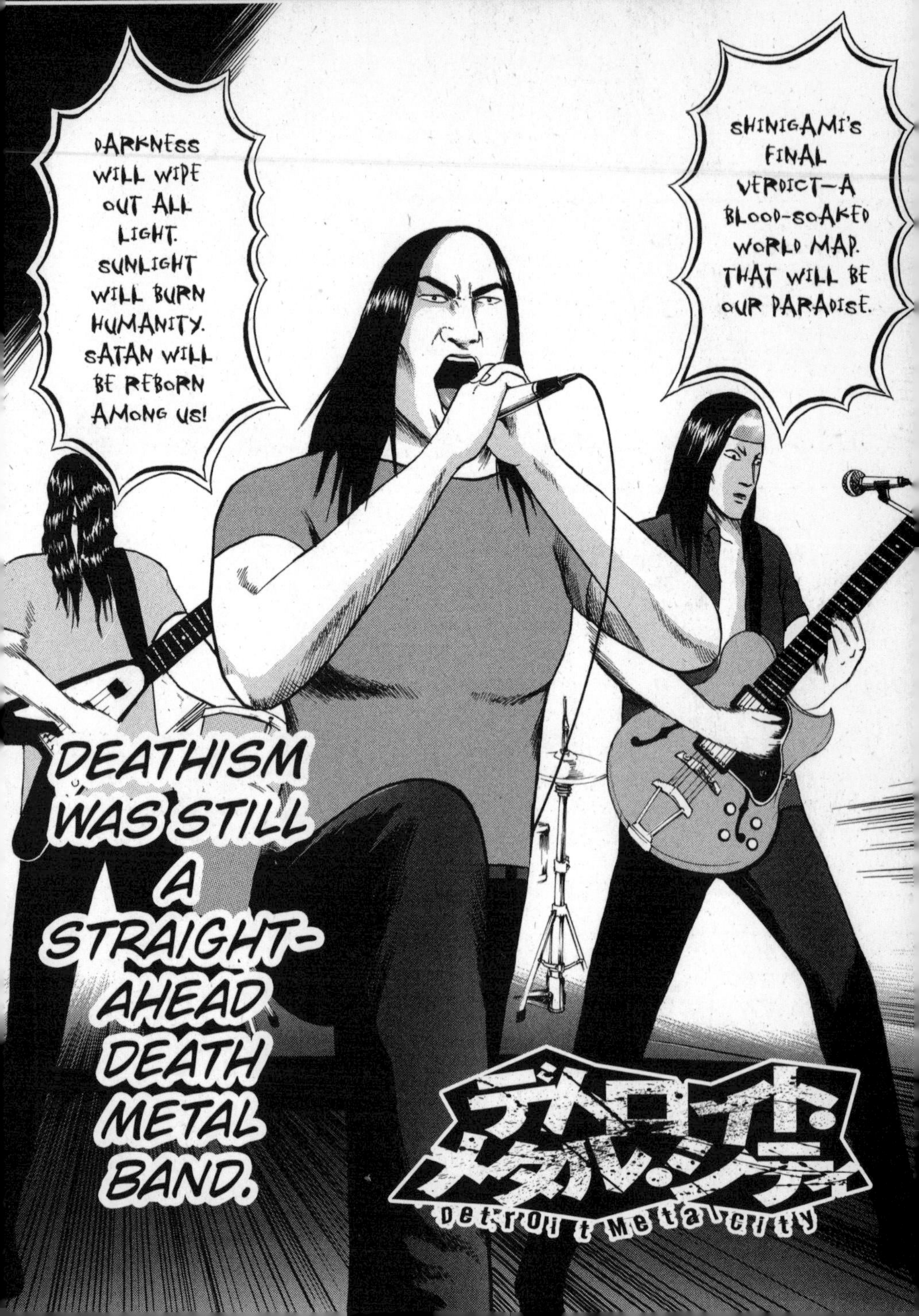

SHINIGAMI'S FINAL VERDICT—A BLOOD-SOAKED WORLD MAP. THAT WILL BE OUR PARADISE.
DARKNESS WILL WIPE OUT ALL LIGHT. SUNLIGHT WILL BURN HUMANITY. SATAN WILL BE REBORN AMONG US!
DEATHISM WAS STILL A STRAIGHT-AHEAD DEATH METAL BAND.
Detroit Metal City

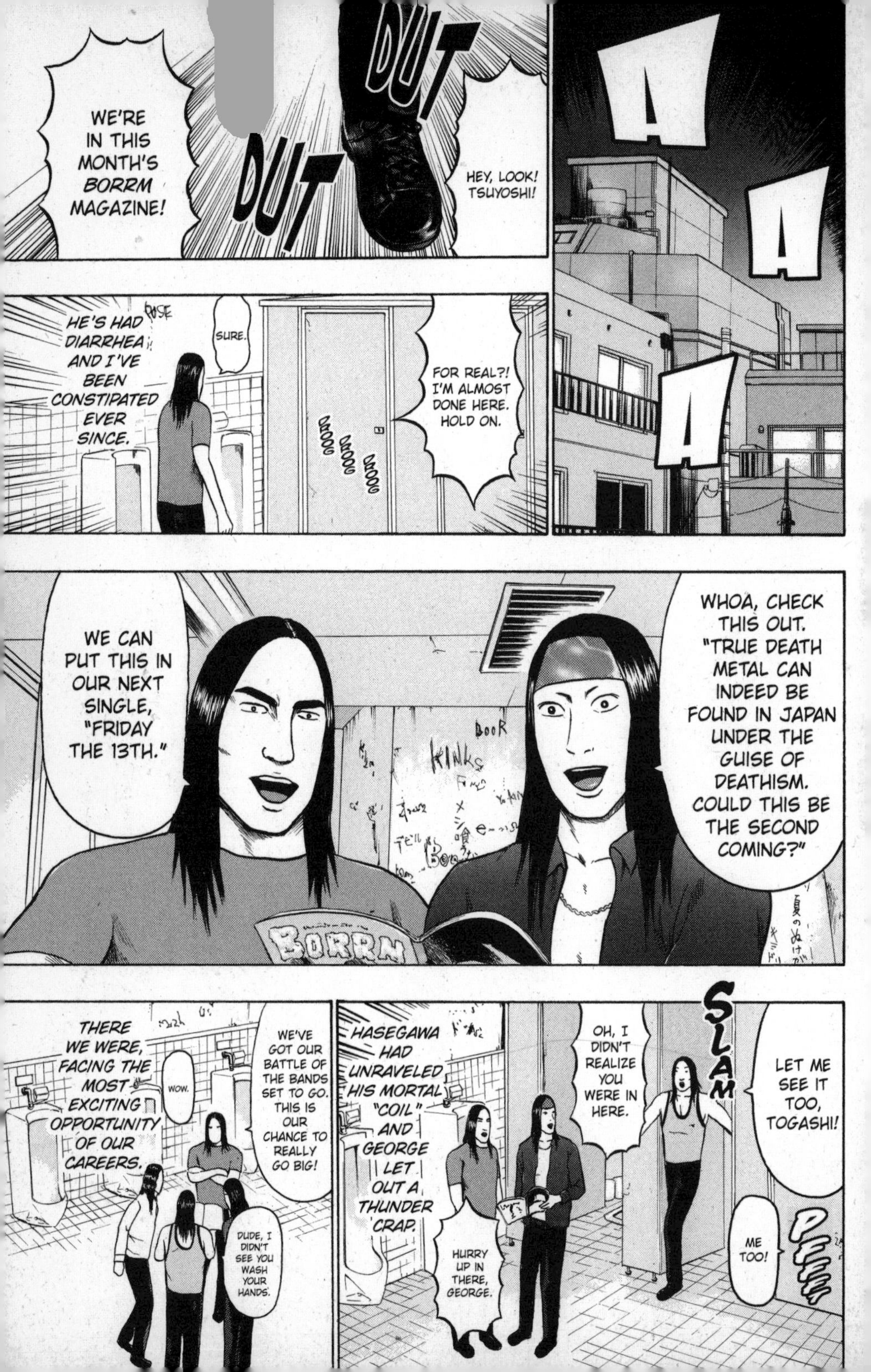
A
A
A
DUT
DUT
HEY, LOOK! TSUYOSHI!
WE'RE IN THIS MONTH'S *BORRM* MAGAZINE!
FOR REAL?! I'M ALMOST DONE HERE. HOLD ON.
DROOG DROOG DROOG
SURE.
HE'S HAD DIARRHEA AND I'VE BEEN CONSTIPATED EVER SINCE.
WHOA, CHECK THIS OUT. "TRUE DEATH METAL CAN INDEED BE FOUND IN JAPAN UNDER THE GUISE OF DEATHISM. COULD THIS BE THE SECOND COMING?"
WE CAN PUT THIS IN OUR NEXT SINGLE, "FRIDAY THE 13TH."
BORRM
SLAM
LET ME SEE IT TOO, TOGASHI!
OH, I DIDN'T REALIZE YOU WERE IN HERE.
PFFFF
ME TOO!
HASEGAWA HAD UNRAVELED HIS MORTAL "COIL" AND GEORGE LET OUT A THUNDER CRAP.
HURRY UP IN THERE, GEORGE.
WE'VE GOT OUR BATTLE OF THE BANDS SET TO GO. THIS IS OUR CHANCE TO REALLY GO BIG!
WOW.
THERE WE WERE, FACING THE MOST EXCITING OPPORTUNITY OF OUR CAREERS.
DUDE, I DIDN'T SEE YOU WASH YOUR HANDS.

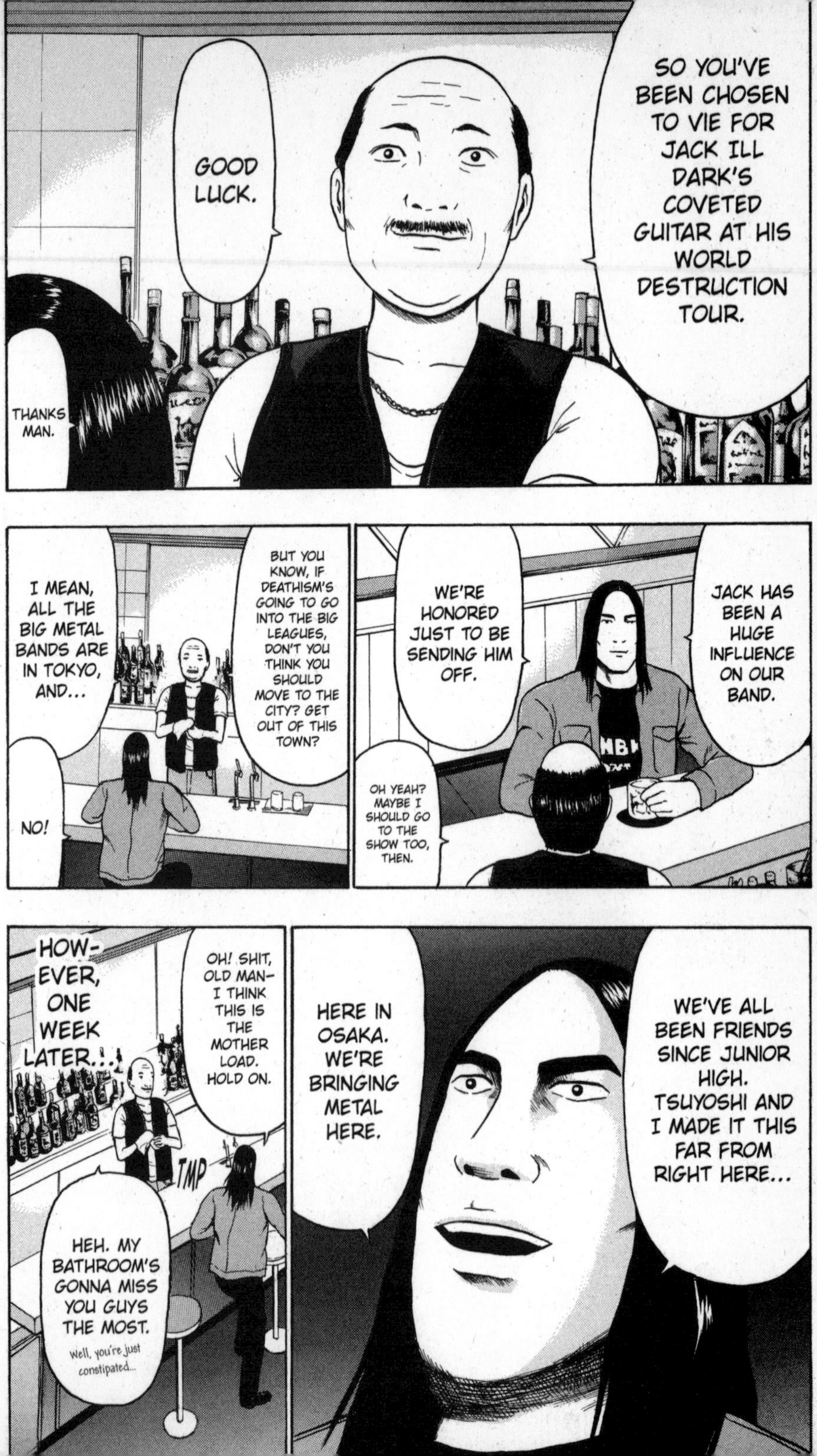
SO YOU'VE BEEN CHOSEN TO VIE FOR JACK ILL DARK'S COVETED GUITAR AT HIS WORLD DESTRUCTION TOUR.
GOOD LUCK.
THANKS MAN.
JACK HAS BEEN A HUGE INFLUENCE ON OUR BAND.
WE'RE HONORED JUST TO BE SENDING HIM OFF.
OH YEAH? MAYBE I SHOULD GO TO THE SHOW TOO, THEN.
BUT YOU KNOW, IF DEATHISM'S GOING TO GO INTO THE BIG LEAGUES, DON'T YOU THINK YOU SHOULD MOVE TO THE CITY? GET OUT OF THIS TOWN?
I MEAN, ALL THE BIG METAL BANDS ARE IN TOKYO, AND...
NO!
WE'VE ALL BEEN FRIENDS SINCE JUNIOR HIGH. TSUYOSHI AND I MADE IT THIS FAR FROM RIGHT HERE...
HERE IN OSAKA. WE'RE BRINGING METAL HERE.
HOW-EVER, ONE WEEK LATER...
OH! SHIT, OLD MAN- I THINK THIS IS THE MOTHER LOAD. HOLD ON.
TMP
HEH. MY BATHROOM'S GONNA MISS YOU GUYS THE MOST.
Well, you're just constipated...

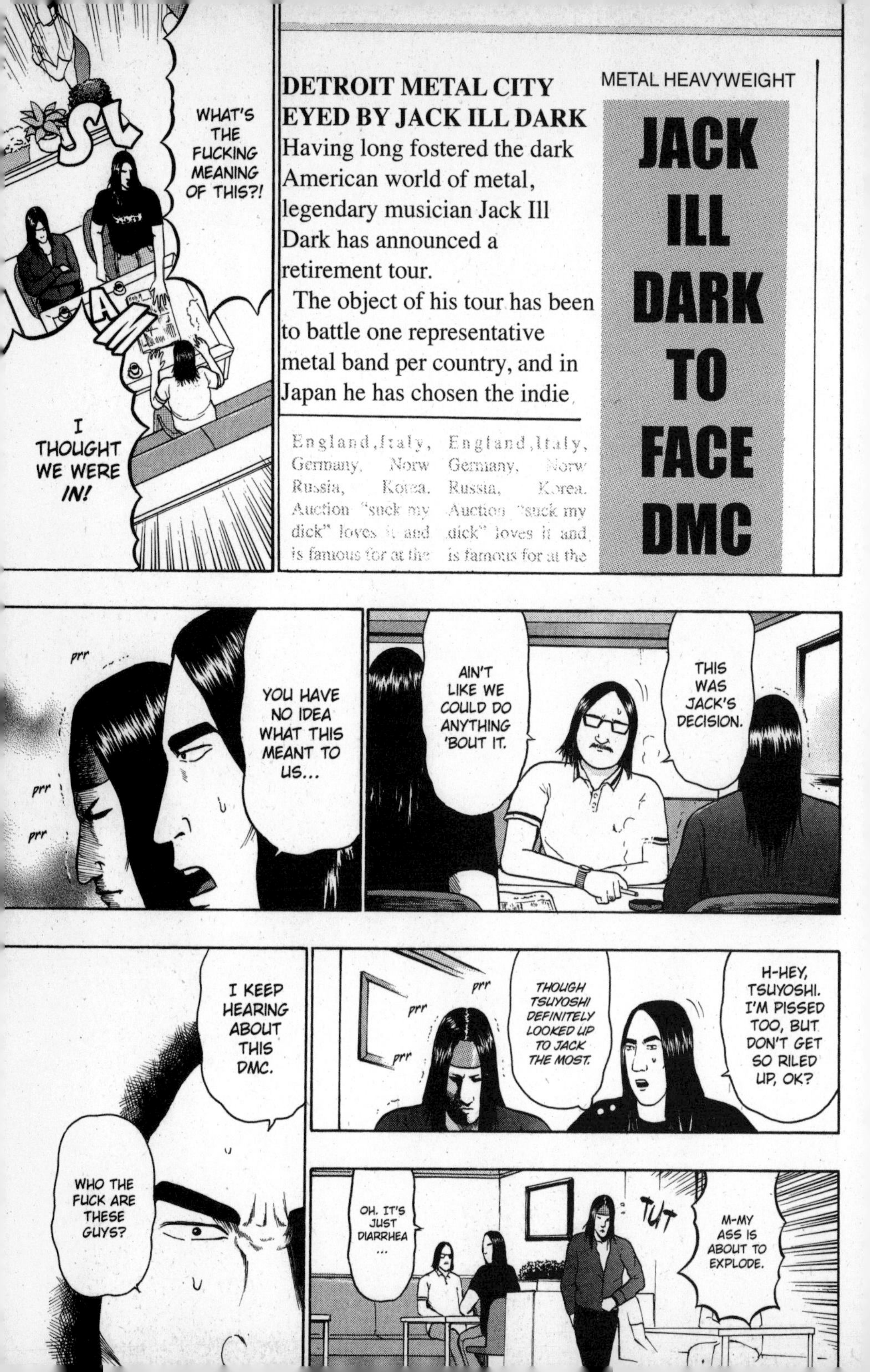

METAL HEAVYWEIGHT
JACK ILL DARK TO FACE DMC
DETROIT METAL CITY EYED BY JACK ILL DARK
Having long fostered the dark American world of metal, legendary musician Jack Ill Dark has announced a retirement tour.
The object of his tour has been to battle one representative metal band per country, and in Japan he has chosen the indie
England, Italy, Germany, Norw Russia, Korea. Auction "suck my dick" loves it and is famous for at the
England, Italy, Germany, Norw Russia, Korea. Auction "suck my dick" loves it and is famous for at the
SLAM
WHAT'S THE FUCKING MEANING OF THIS?!
I THOUGHT WE WERE *IN!*
THIS WAS JACK'S DECISION.
AIN'T LIKE WE COULD DO ANYTHING 'BOUT IT.
prr
YOU HAVE NO IDEA WHAT THIS MEANT TO US...
prr
prr
H-HEY, TSUYOSHI. I'M PISSED TOO, BUT DON'T GET SO RILED UP, OK?
THOUGH TSUYOSHI DEFINITELY LOOKED UP TO JACK THE MOST.
prr
prr
prr
M-MY ASS IS ABOUT TO EXPLODE.
TUT
OH. IT'S JUST DIARRHEA ...
I KEEP HEARING ABOUT THIS DMC.
WHO THE FUCK ARE THESE GUYS?

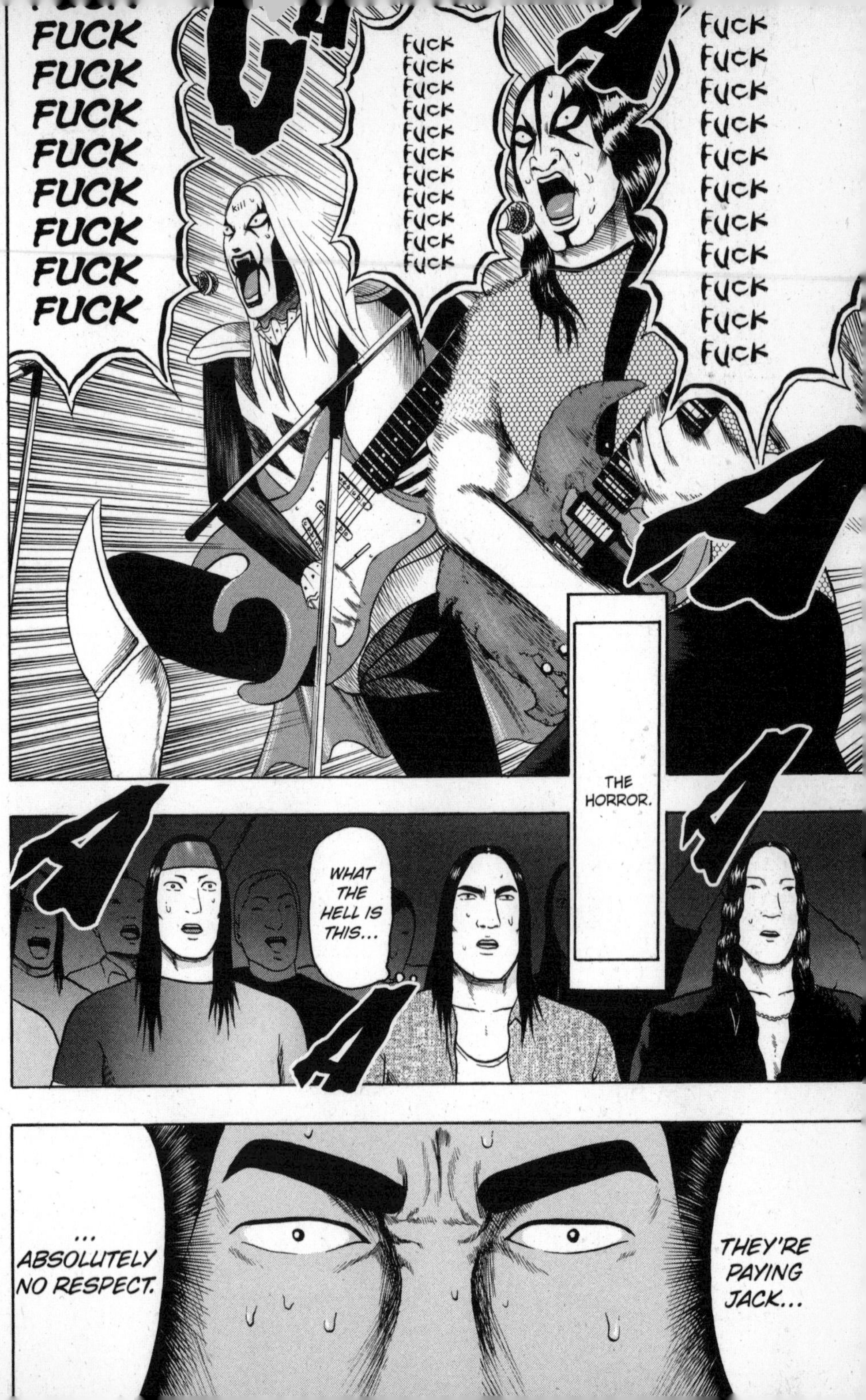

FUCK FUCK FUCK FUCK FUCK FUCK FUCK FUCK FUCK FUCK FUCK
FUCK FUCK FUCK FUCK FUCK FUCK FUCK FUCK FUCK FUCK FUCK
FUCK FUCK FUCK FUCK FUCK FUCK FUCK FUCK
THE HORROR.
WHAT THE HELL IS THIS...
THEY'RE PAYING JACK...
...ABSOLUTELY NO RESPECT.

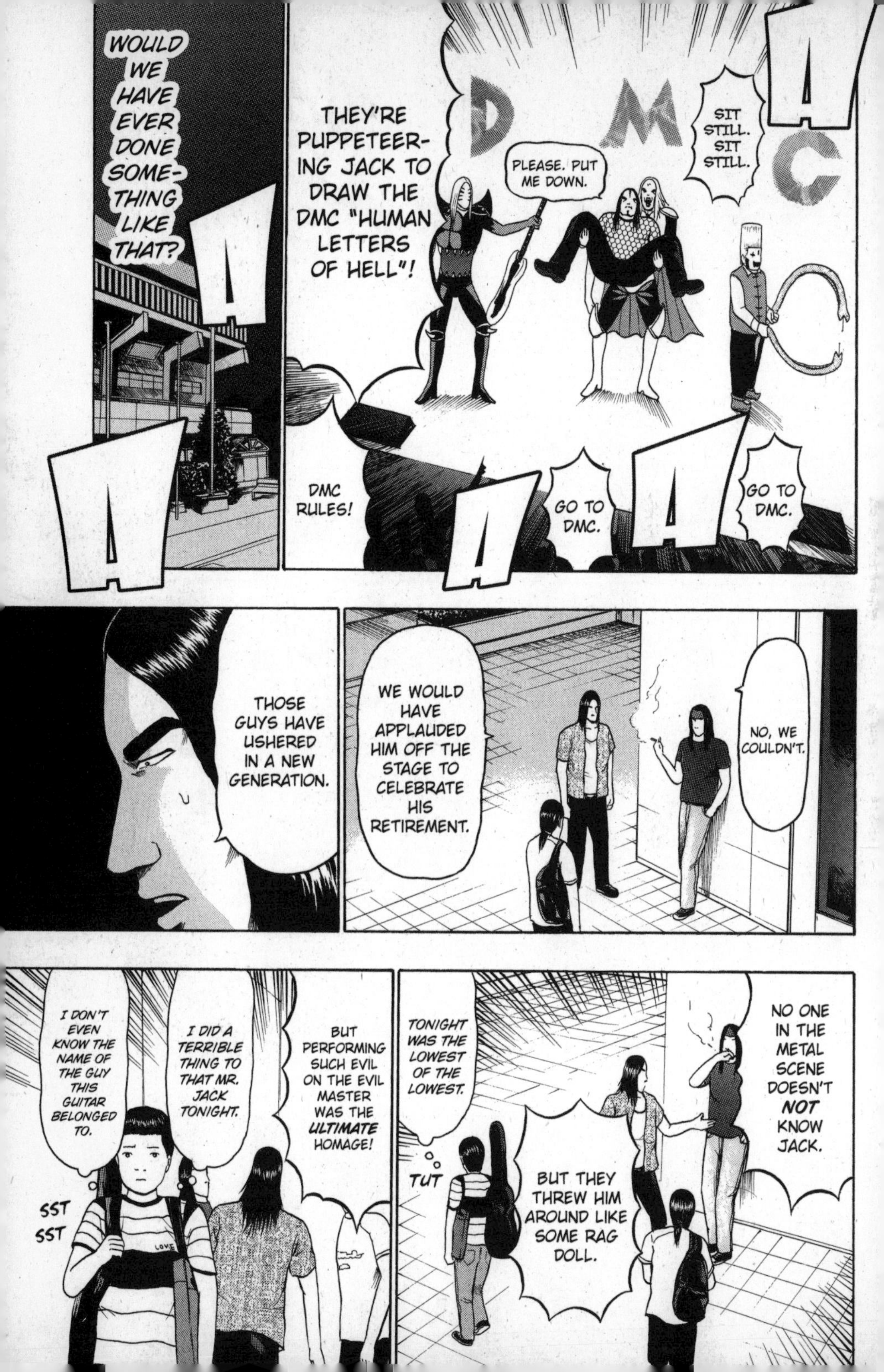

A
C
M
D
SIT STILL. SIT STILL.
PLEASE. PUT ME DOWN.
THEY'RE PUPPETEERING JACK TO DRAW THE DMC "HUMAN LETTERS OF HELL"!
A
GO TO DMC.
A
GO TO DMC.
A
DMC RULES!
WOULD WE HAVE EVER DONE SOMETHING LIKE THAT?
A
A
NO, WE COULDN'T.
WE WOULD HAVE APPLAUDED HIM OFF THE STAGE TO CELEBRATE HIS RETIREMENT.
THOSE GUYS HAVE USHERED IN A NEW GENERATION.
NO ONE IN THE METAL SCENE DOESN'T **NOT** KNOW JACK.
BUT THEY THREW HIM AROUND LIKE SOME RAG DOLL.
TONIGHT WAS THE LOWEST OF THE LOWEST.
TUT
BUT PERFORMING SUCH EVIL ON THE EVIL MASTER WAS THE ***ULTIMATE*** HOMAGE!
I DID A TERRIBLE THING TO THAT MR. JACK TONIGHT.
I DON'T EVEN KNOW THE NAME OF THE GUY THIS GUITAR BELONGED TO.
SST SST

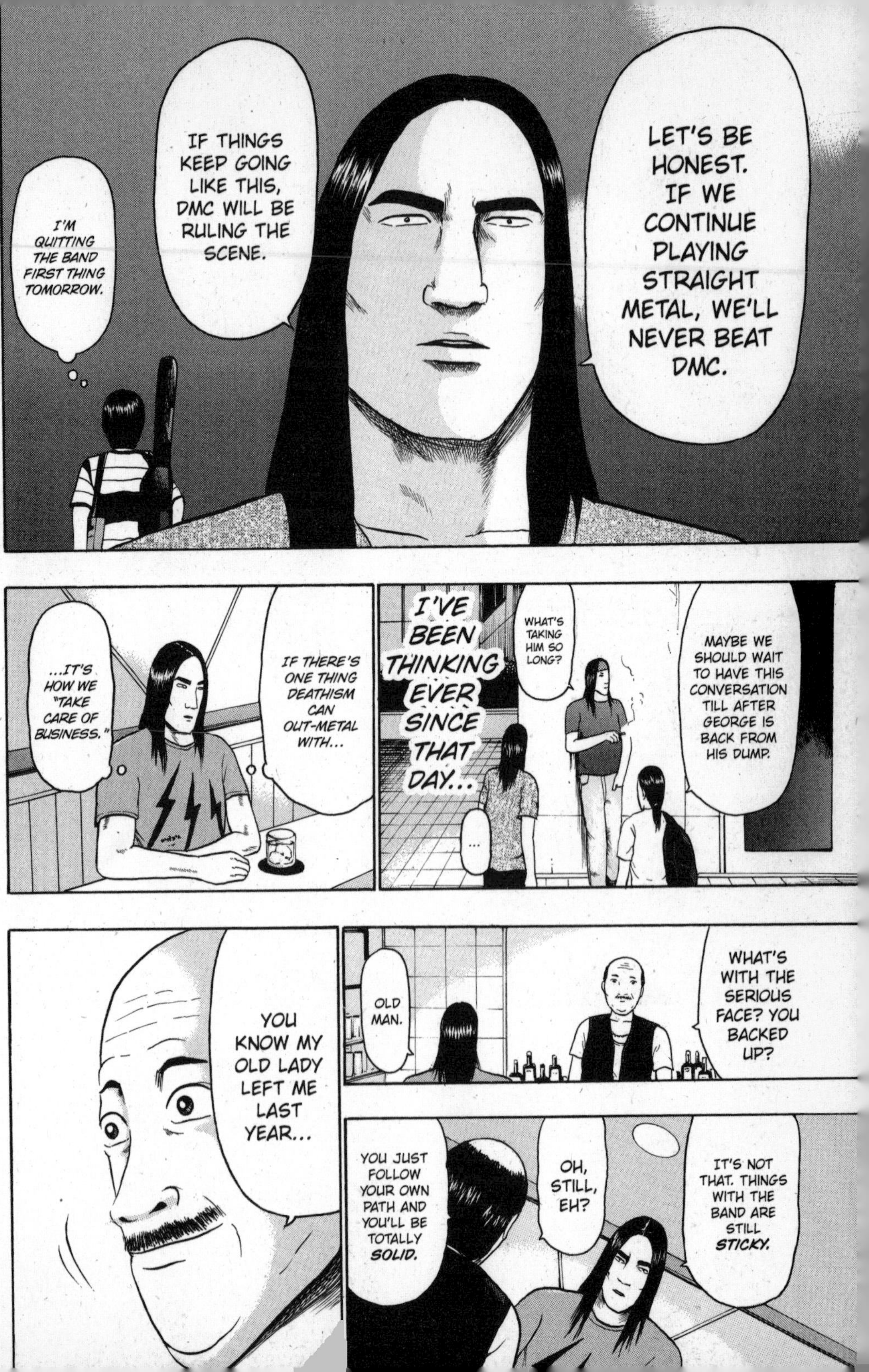
LET'S BE HONEST. IF WE CONTINUE PLAYING STRAIGHT METAL, WE'LL NEVER BEAT DMC.
IF THINGS KEEP GOING LIKE THIS, DMC WILL BE RULING THE SCENE.
I'M QUITTING THE BAND FIRST THING TOMORROW.
MAYBE WE SHOULD WAIT TO HAVE THIS CONVERSATION TILL AFTER GEORGE IS BACK FROM HIS DUMP.
WHAT'S TAKING HIM SO LONG?
I'VE BEEN THINKING EVER SINCE THAT DAY...
...
IF THERE'S ONE THING DEATHISM CAN OUT-METAL WITH...
...IT'S HOW WE "TAKE CARE OF BUSINESS."
WHAT'S WITH THE SERIOUS FACE? YOU BACKED UP?
OLD MAN.
IT'S NOT THAT. THINGS WITH THE BAND ARE STILL *STICKY.*
OH, STILL, EH?
YOU JUST FOLLOW YOUR OWN PATH AND YOU'LL BE TOTALLY *SOLID.*
YOU KNOW MY OLD LADY LEFT ME LAST YEAR...

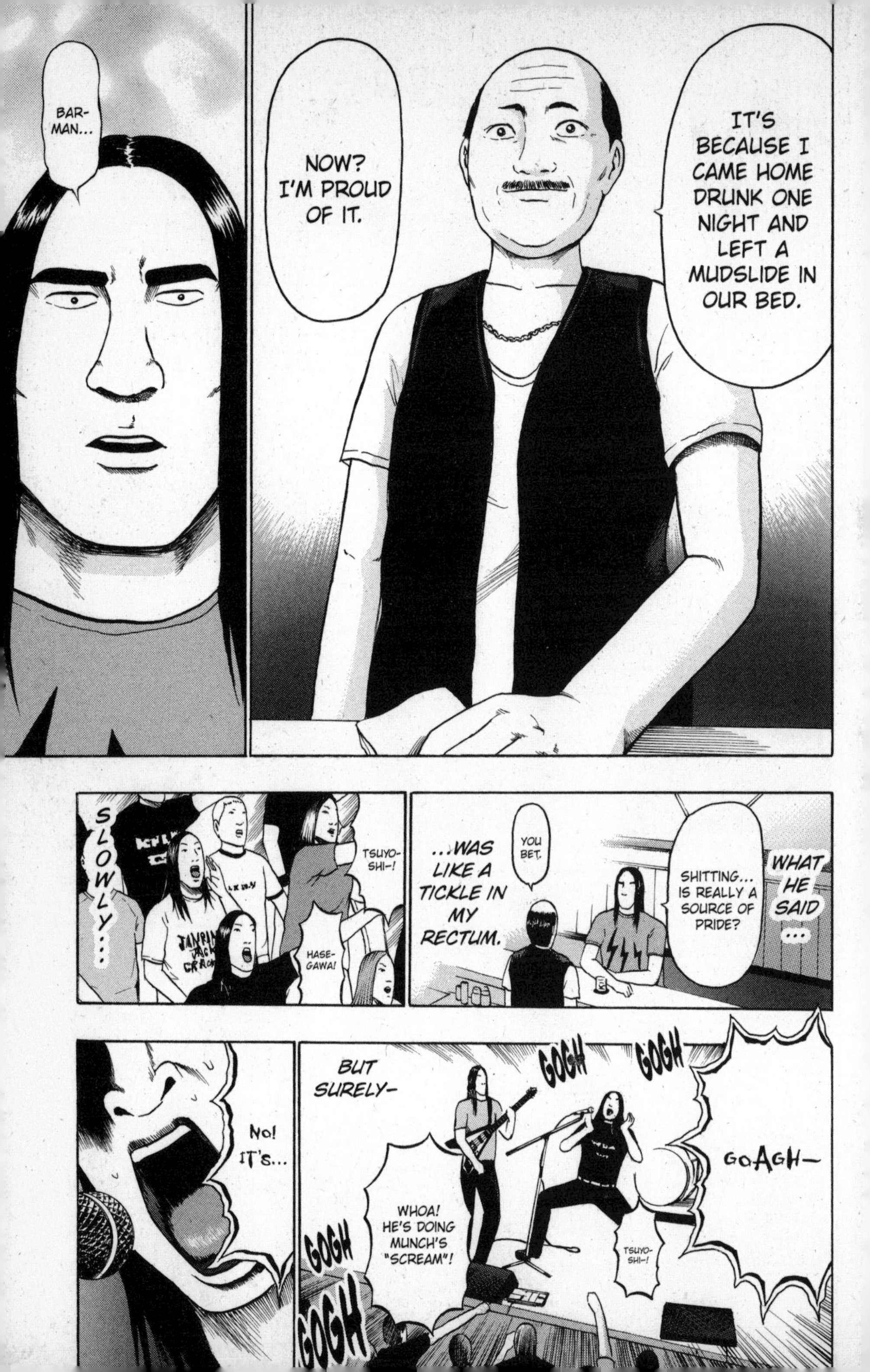
IT'S BECAUSE I CAME HOME DRUNK ONE NIGHT AND LEFT A MUDSLIDE IN OUR BED.
NOW? I'M PROUD OF IT.
BAR-MAN...
WHAT HE SAID...
SHITTING... IS REALLY A SOURCE OF PRIDE?
YOU BET.
...WAS LIKE A TICKLE IN MY RECTUM.
TSUYO-SHI-!
SLOWLY...
HASE-GAWA!
GOGH
GOGH
BUT SURELY-
GOAGH-
WHOA! HE'S DOING MUNCH'S "SCREAM"!
TSUYO-SHI-!
GOGH
GOGH
NO! IT'S...

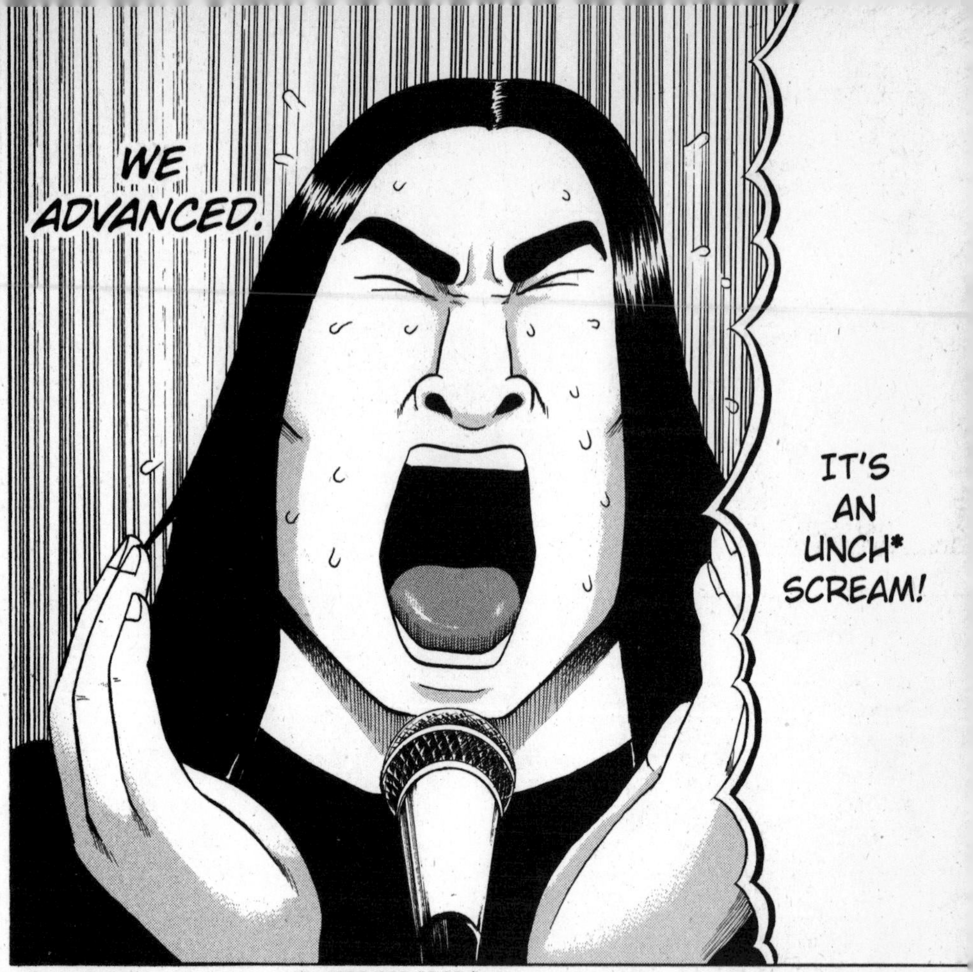
IT'S AN UNCH* SCREAM!
WE ADVANCED.

*UNCH IS SHORT FOR *UNCHI*, JAPANESE FOR "POO."

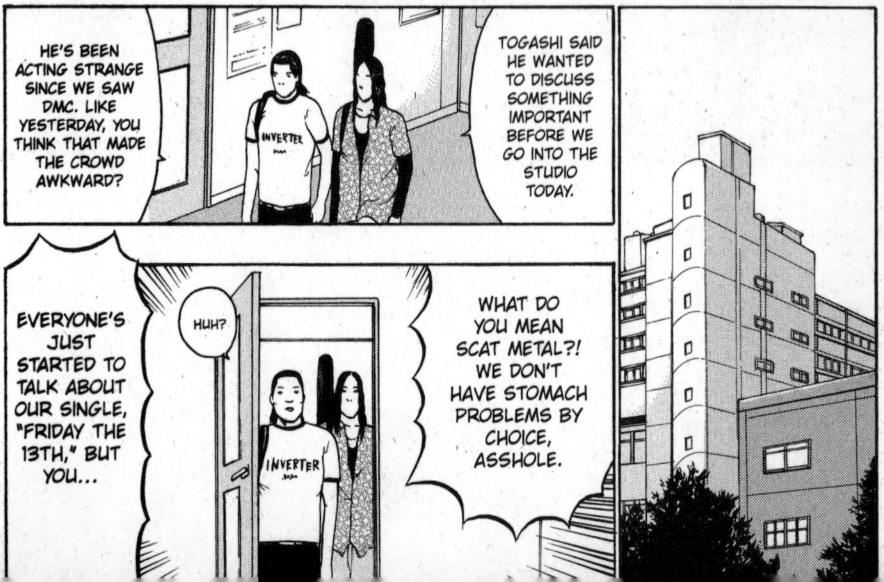
TOGASHI SAID HE WANTED TO DISCUSS SOMETHING IMPORTANT BEFORE WE GO INTO THE STUDIO TODAY.
HE'S BEEN ACTING STRANGE SINCE WE SAW DMC. LIKE YESTERDAY, YOU THINK THAT MADE THE CROWD AWKWARD?
INVERTER
WHAT DO YOU MEAN SCAT METAL?! WE DON'T HAVE STOMACH PROBLEMS BY CHOICE, ASSHOLE.
HUH?
EVERYONE'S JUST STARTED TO TALK ABOUT OUR SINGLE, "FRIDAY THE 13TH," BUT YOU...
INVERTER

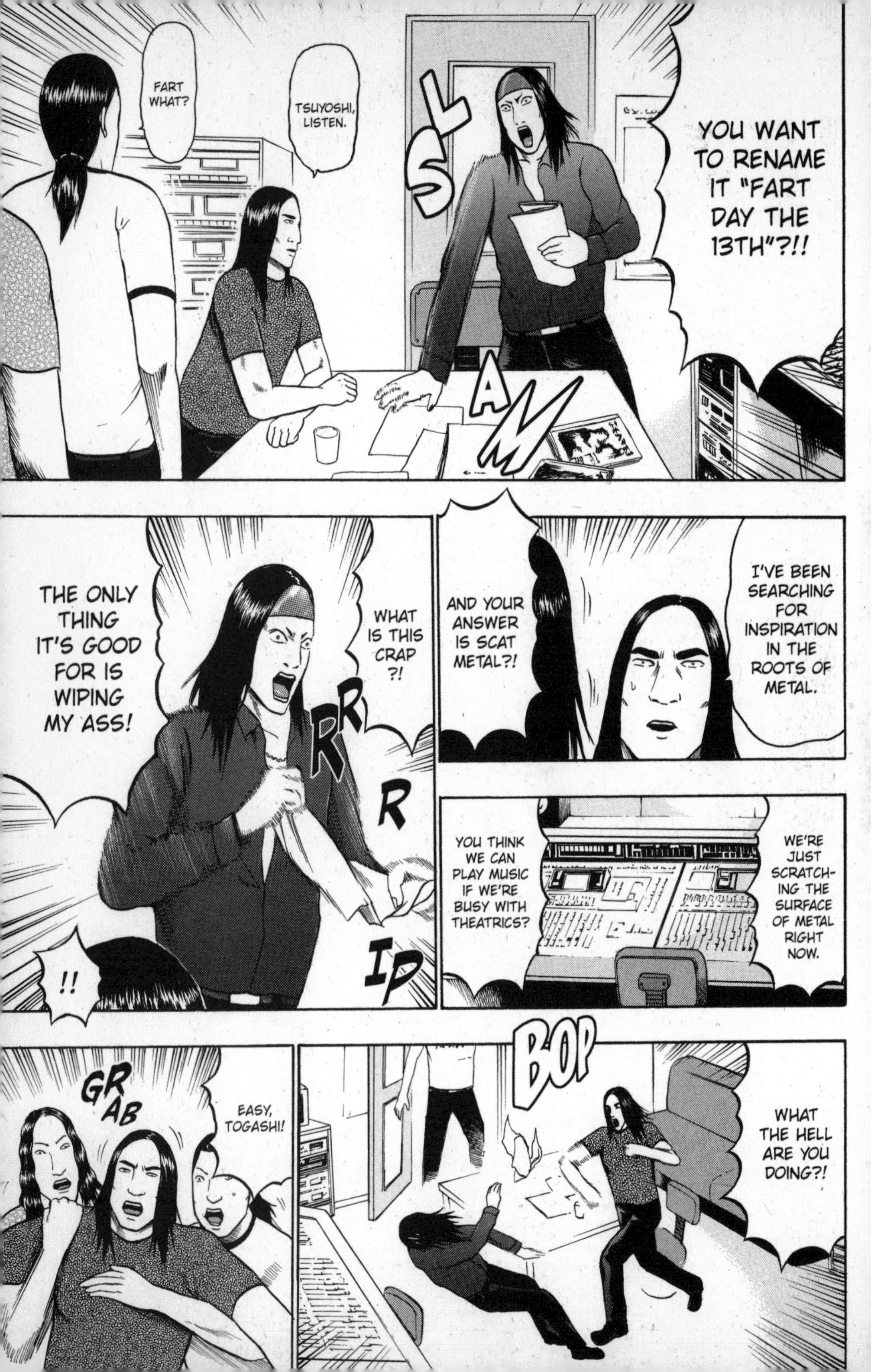
YOU WANT TO RENAME IT "FART DAY THE 13TH"?!!
SLAM
TSUYOSHI, LISTEN.
FART WHAT?
I'VE BEEN SEARCHING FOR INSPIRATION IN THE ROOTS OF METAL.
AND YOUR ANSWER IS SCAT METAL?!
WE'RE JUST SCRATCHING THE SURFACE OF METAL RIGHT NOW.
YOU THINK WE CAN PLAY MUSIC IF WE'RE BUSY WITH THEATRICS?
WHAT IS THIS CRAP?!
THE ONLY THING IT'S GOOD FOR IS WIPING MY ASS!
RRRIP
!!
BOP
WHAT THE HELL ARE YOU DOING?!
GRAB
EASY, TOGASHI!

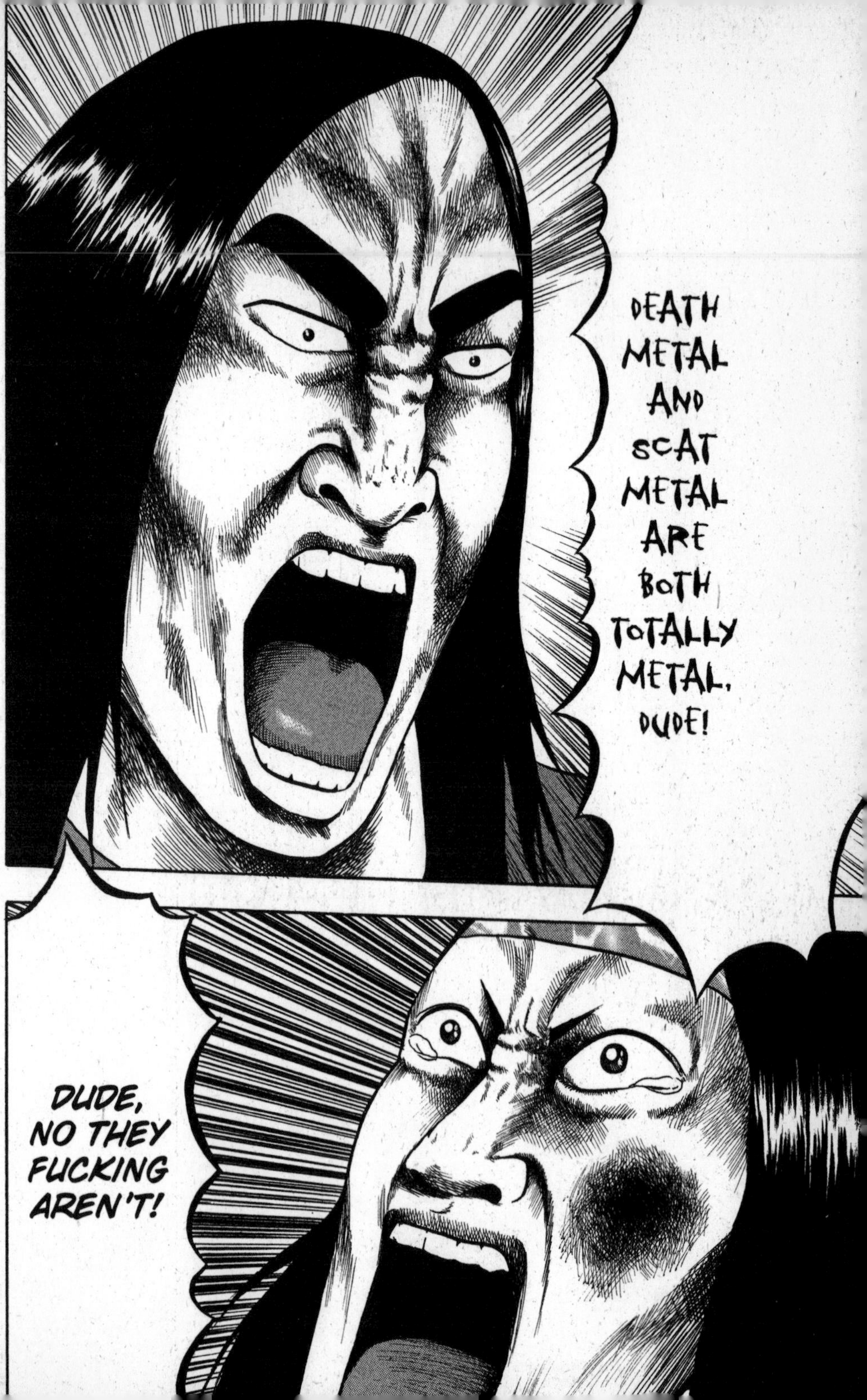
DEATH METAL AND SCAT METAL ARE BOTH TOTALLY METAL, DUDE!
DUDE, NO THEY FUCKING AREN'T!

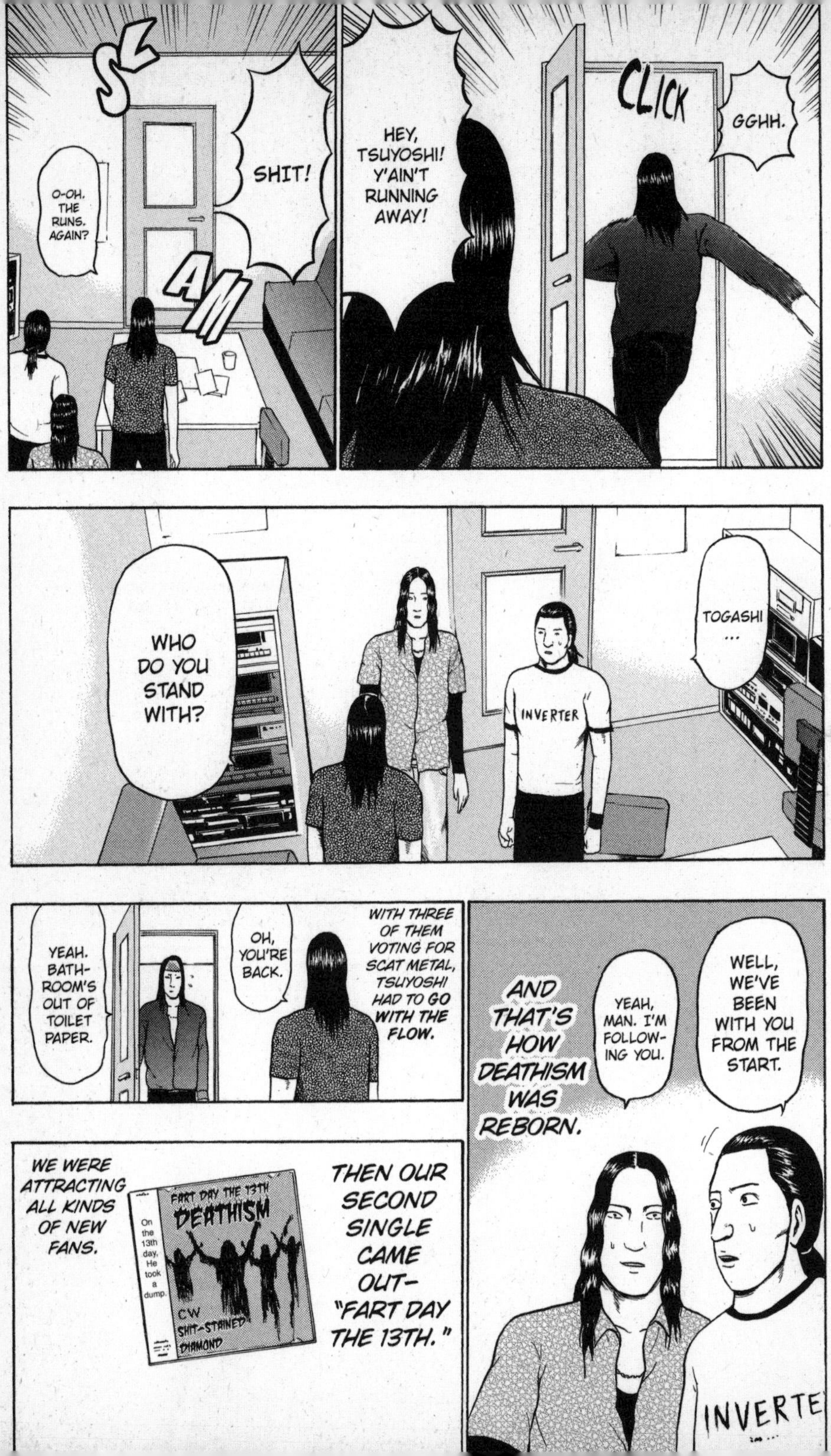
CLICK
GGHH.
HEY, TSUYOSHI! Y'AIN'T RUNNING AWAY!
SHIT!
SLAM
O-OH. THE RUNS. AGAIN?
TOGASHI ...
INVERTER
WHO DO YOU STAND WITH?
WELL, WE'VE BEEN WITH YOU FROM THE START.
YEAH, MAN. I'M FOLLOW-ING YOU.
AND THAT'S HOW DEATHISM WAS REBORN.
INVERTE
WITH THREE OF THEM VOTING FOR SCAT METAL, TSUYOSHI HAD TO GO WITH THE FLOW.
OH, YOU'RE BACK.
YEAH. BATH-ROOM'S OUT OF TOILET PAPER.
THEN OUR SECOND SINGLE CAME OUT— "FART DAY THE 13TH."
FART DAY THE 13TH
DEATHISM
On the 13th day, He took a dump.
CW SHIT-STAINED DIAMOND
WE WERE ATTRACTING ALL KINDS OF NEW FANS.

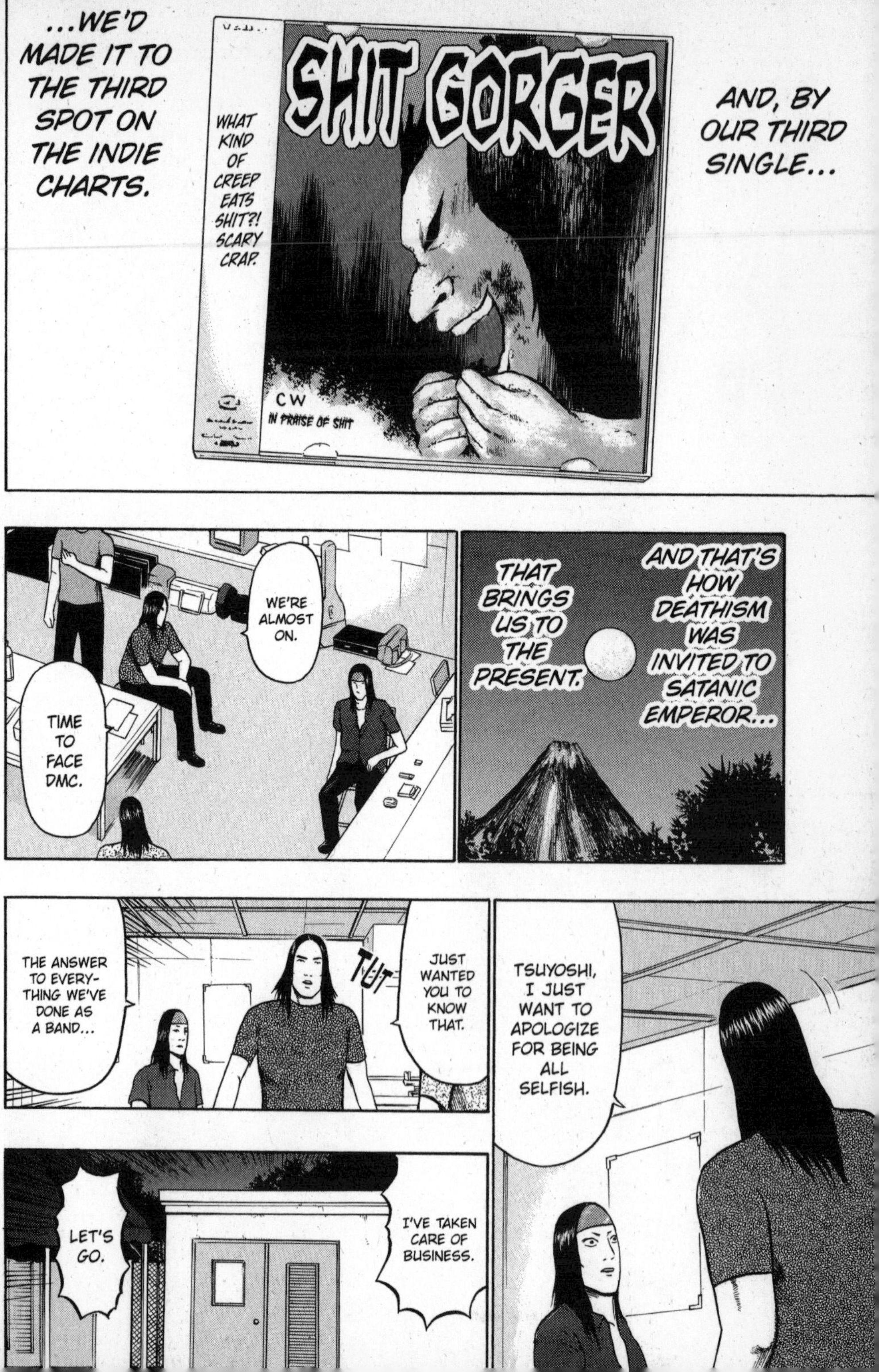
AND, BY OUR THIRD SINGLE...
SHIT GORGER
WHAT KIND OF CREEP EATS SHIT?! SCARY CRAP.
CW
IN PRAISE OF SHIT
...WE'D MADE IT TO THE THIRD SPOT ON THE INDIE CHARTS.
AND THAT'S HOW DEATHISM WAS INVITED TO SATANIC EMPEROR...
THAT BRINGS US TO THE PRESENT.
WE'RE ALMOST ON.
TIME TO FACE DMC.
TSUYOSHI, I JUST WANT TO APOLOGIZE FOR BEING ALL SELFISH.
JUST WANTED YOU TO KNOW THAT.
TUT
THE ANSWER TO EVERY-THING WE'VE DONE AS A BAND...
I'VE TAKEN CARE OF BUSINESS.
LET'S GO.

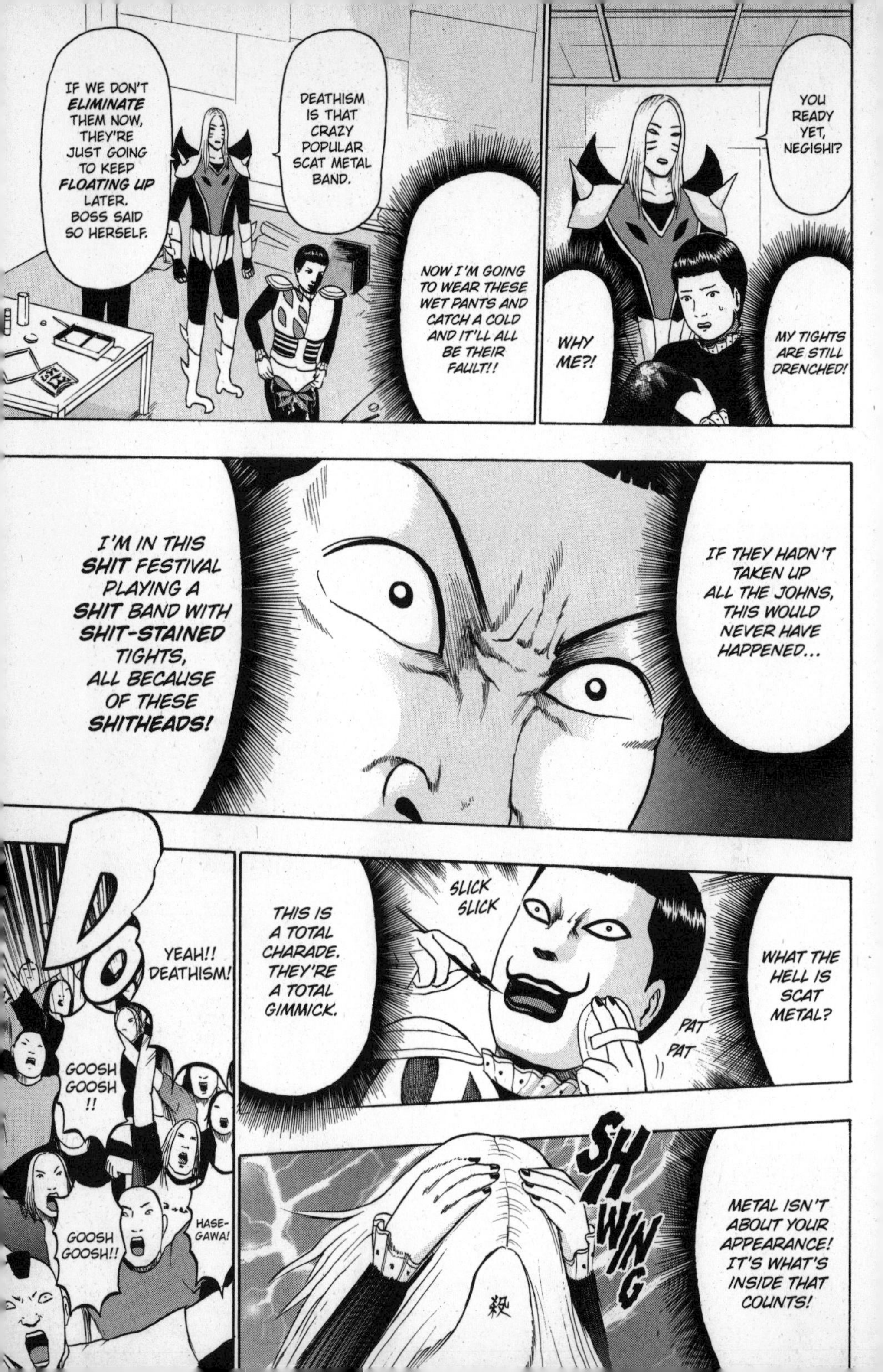

YOU READY YET, NEGISHI?
MY TIGHTS ARE STILL DRENCHED!
WHY ME?!
DEATHISM IS THAT CRAZY POPULAR SCAT METAL BAND.
IF WE DON'T ELIMINATE THEM NOW, THEY'RE JUST GOING TO KEEP FLOATING UP LATER. BOSS SAID SO HERSELF.
NOW I'M GOING TO WEAR THESE WET PANTS AND CATCH A COLD AND IT'LL ALL BE THEIR FAULT!!
IF THEY HADN'T TAKEN UP ALL THE JOHNS, THIS WOULD NEVER HAVE HAPPENED...
I'M IN THIS SHIT FESTIVAL PLAYING A SHIT BAND WITH SHIT-STAINED TIGHTS, ALL BECAUSE OF THESE SHITHEADS!
WHAT THE HELL IS SCAT METAL?
PAT PAT
SLICK SLICK
THIS IS A TOTAL CHARADE. THEY'RE A TOTAL GIMMICK.
METAL ISN'T ABOUT YOUR APPEARANCE! IT'S WHAT'S INSIDE THAT COUNTS!
SHWING
殺
DO
YEAH!! DEATHISM!
GOOSH GOOSH !!
HASE-GAWA!
GOOSH GOOSH!!

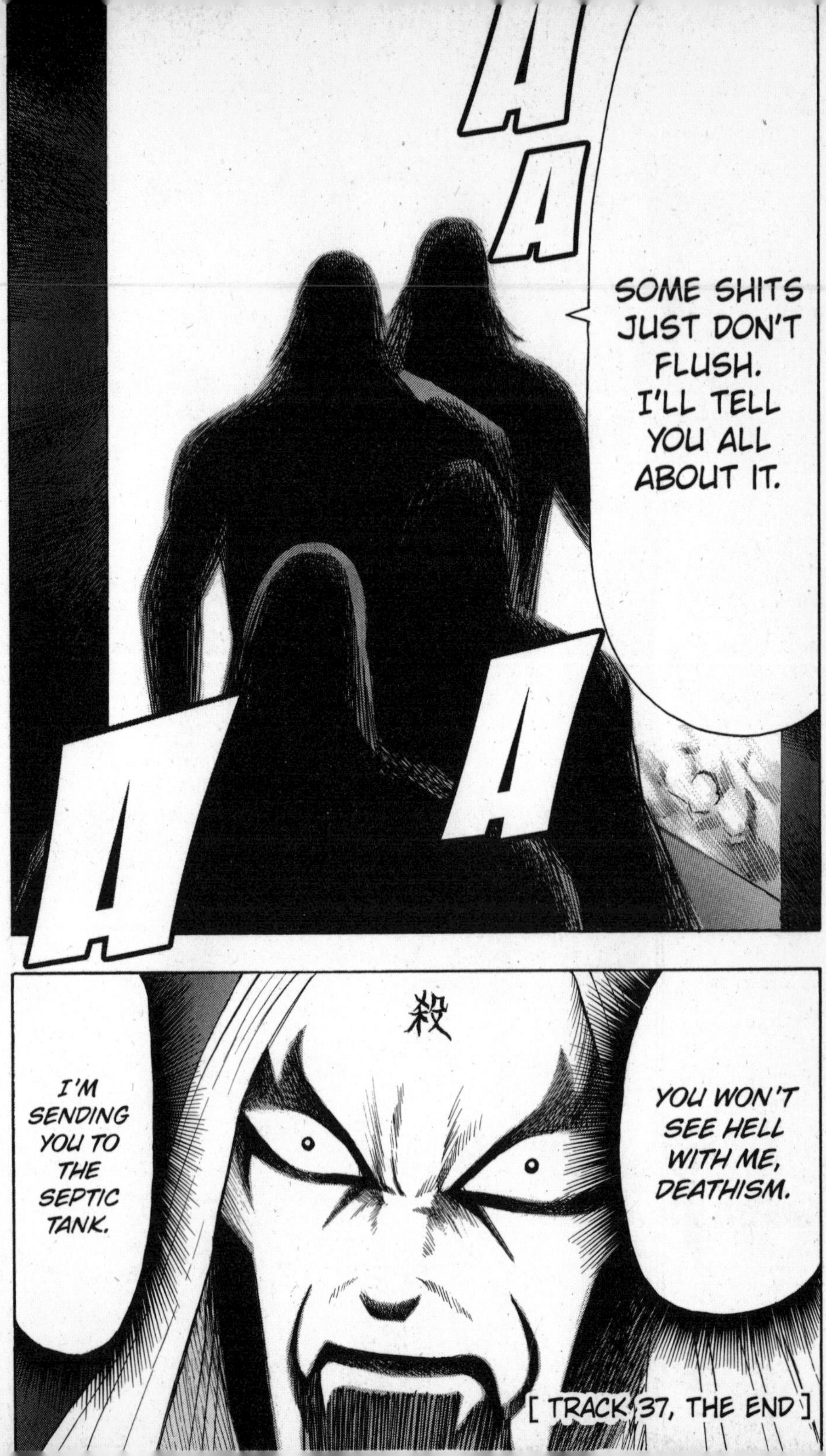
AAAAA
SOME SHITS JUST DON'T FLUSH. I'LL TELL YOU ALL ABOUT IT.
殺
YOU WON'T SEE HELL WITH ME, DEATHISM.
I'M SENDING YOU TO THE SEPTIC TANK.
[TRACK 37, THE END]

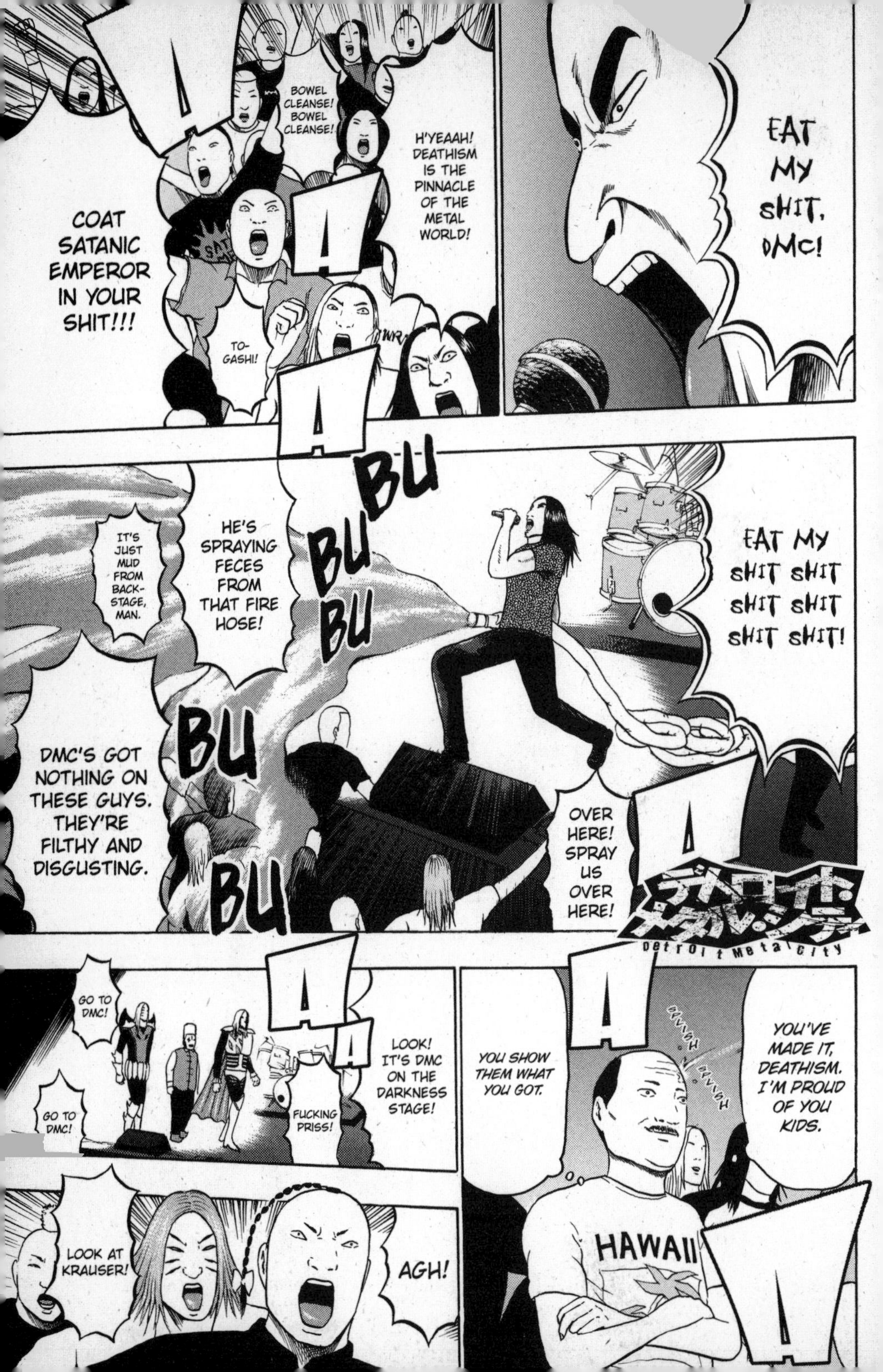
EAT MY SHIT, DMC!
A
BOWEL CLEANSE! BOWEL CLEANSE!
H'YEAAH! DEATHISM IS THE PINNACLE OF THE METAL WORLD!
A
COAT SATANIC EMPEROR IN YOUR SHIT!!!
TO-GASHI!
A
EAT MY SHIT SHIT SHIT SHIT SHIT SHIT!
BU
BU
BU
HE'S SPRAYING FECES FROM THAT FIRE HOSE!
IT'S JUST MUD FROM BACK-STAGE, MAN.
A
OVER HERE! SPRAY US OVER HERE!
BU
DMC'S GOT NOTHING ON THESE GUYS. THEY'RE FILTHY AND DISGUSTING.
BU
Detroit Metal City
A
YOU'VE MADE IT, DEATHISM. I'M PROUD OF YOU KIDS.
YOU SHOW THEM WHAT YOU GOT.
HAWAII
A
A
A
LOOK! IT'S DMC ON THE DARKNESS STAGE!
FUCKING PRISS!
GO TO DMC!
GO TO DMC!
AGH!
LOOK AT KRAUSER!

TRACK 38 Satanic Emperor, Part 7

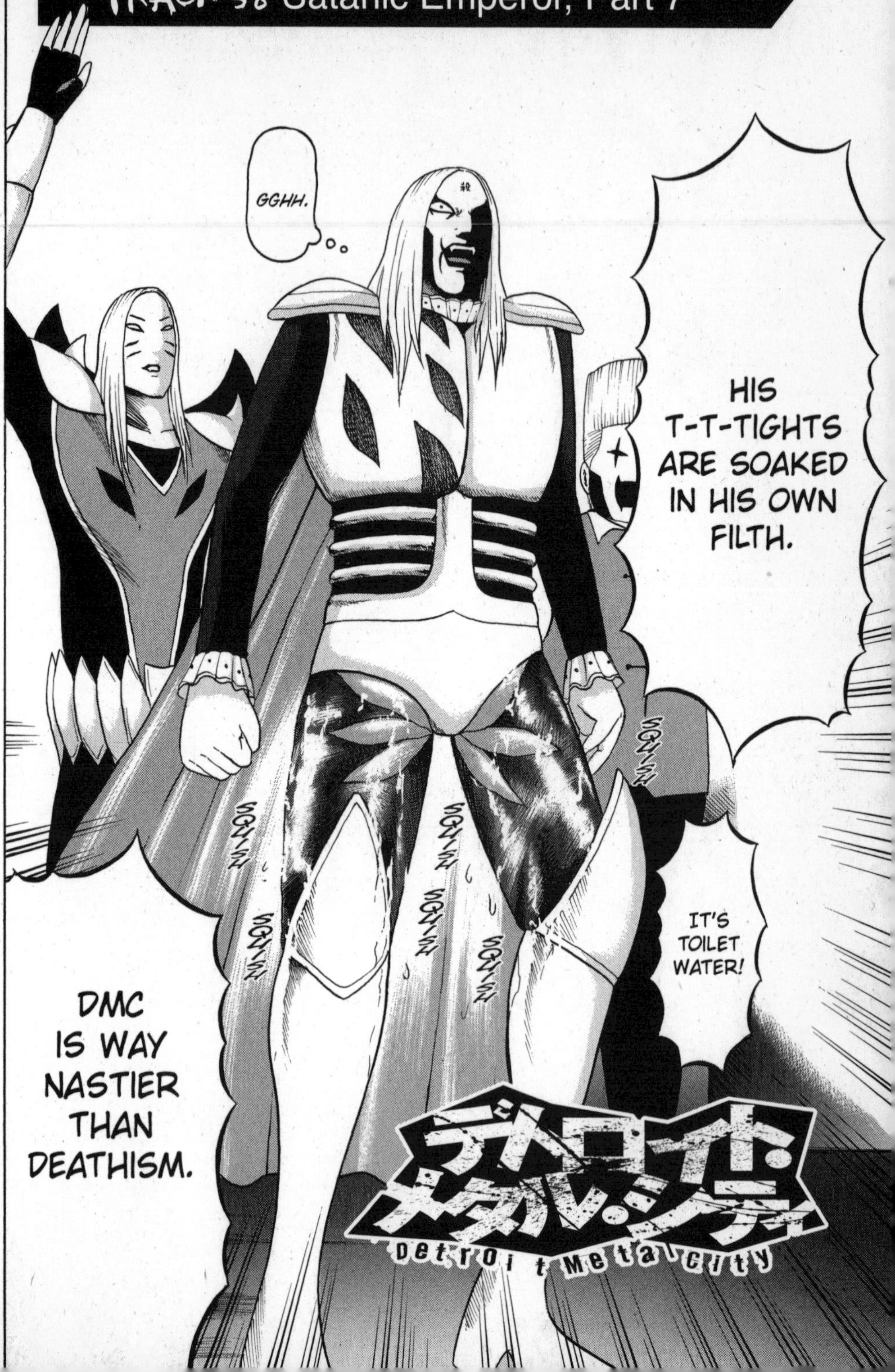
HIS T-T-TIGHTS ARE SOAKED IN HIS OWN FILTH.
GGHH.
SQUISH
SQUISH
SQUISH
SQUISH
SQUISH
SQUISH
IT'S TOILET WATER!
DMC IS WAY NASTIER THAN DEATHISM.
Detroit Metal City

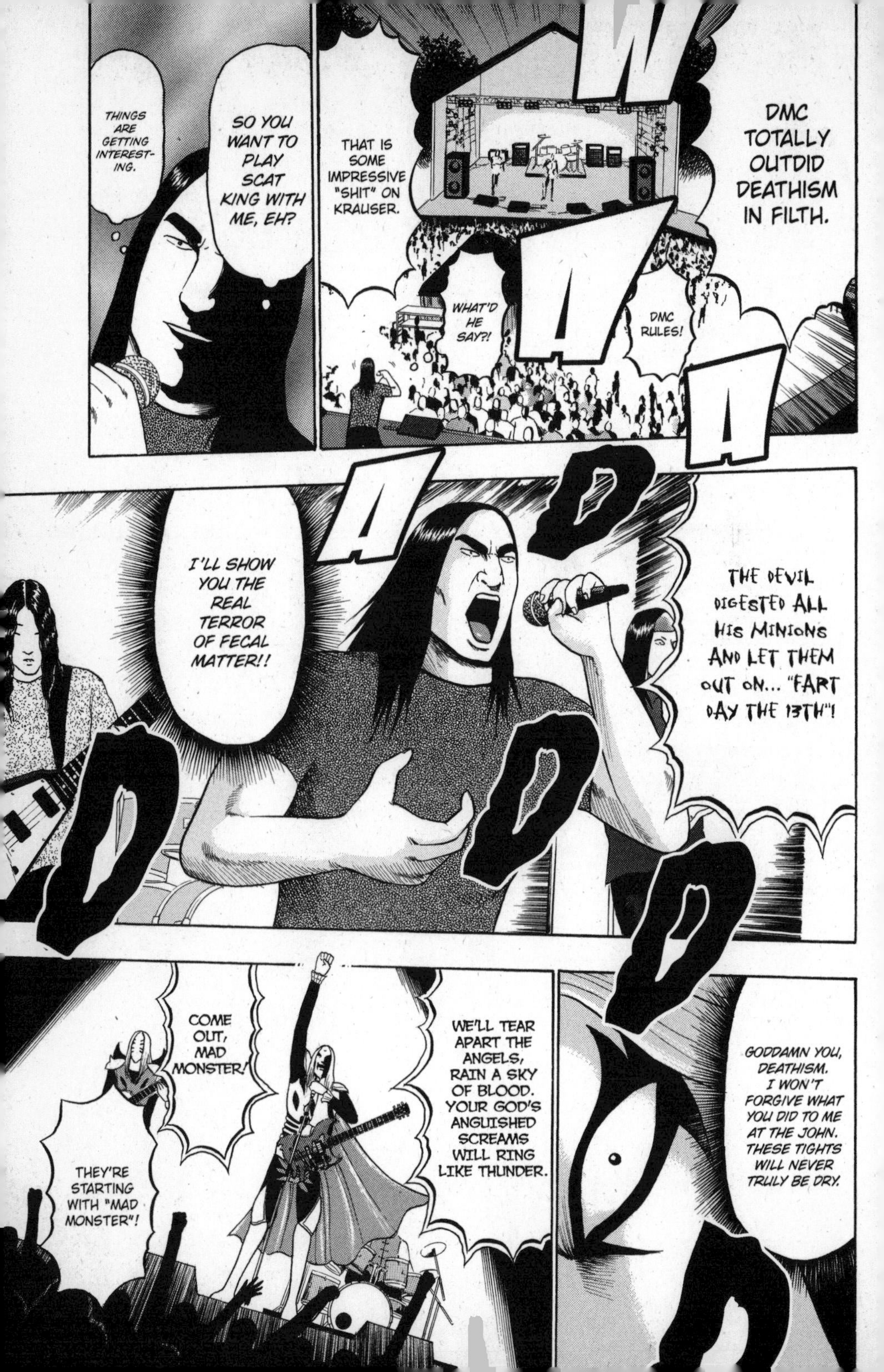
DMC TOTALLY OUTDID DEATHISM IN FILTH.
THAT IS SOME IMPRESSIVE "SHIT" ON KRAUSER.
WAAAA
DMC RULES!
WHAT'D HE SAY?!
SO YOU WANT TO PLAY SCAT KING WITH ME, EH?
THINGS ARE GETTING INTERESTING.
THE DEVIL DIGESTED ALL HIS MINIONS AND LET THEM OUT ON... "FART DAY THE 13TH"!
A
DDDDD
I'LL SHOW YOU THE REAL TERROR OF FECAL MATTER!!
GODDAMN YOU, DEATHISM. I WON'T FORGIVE WHAT YOU DID TO ME AT THE JOHN. THESE TIGHTS WILL NEVER TRULY BE DRY.
WE'LL TEAR APART THE ANGELS, RAIN A SKY OF BLOOD. YOUR GOD'S ANGUISHED SCREAMS WILL RING LIKE THUNDER.
COME OUT, MAD MONSTER!
THEY'RE STARTING WITH "MAD MONSTER"!

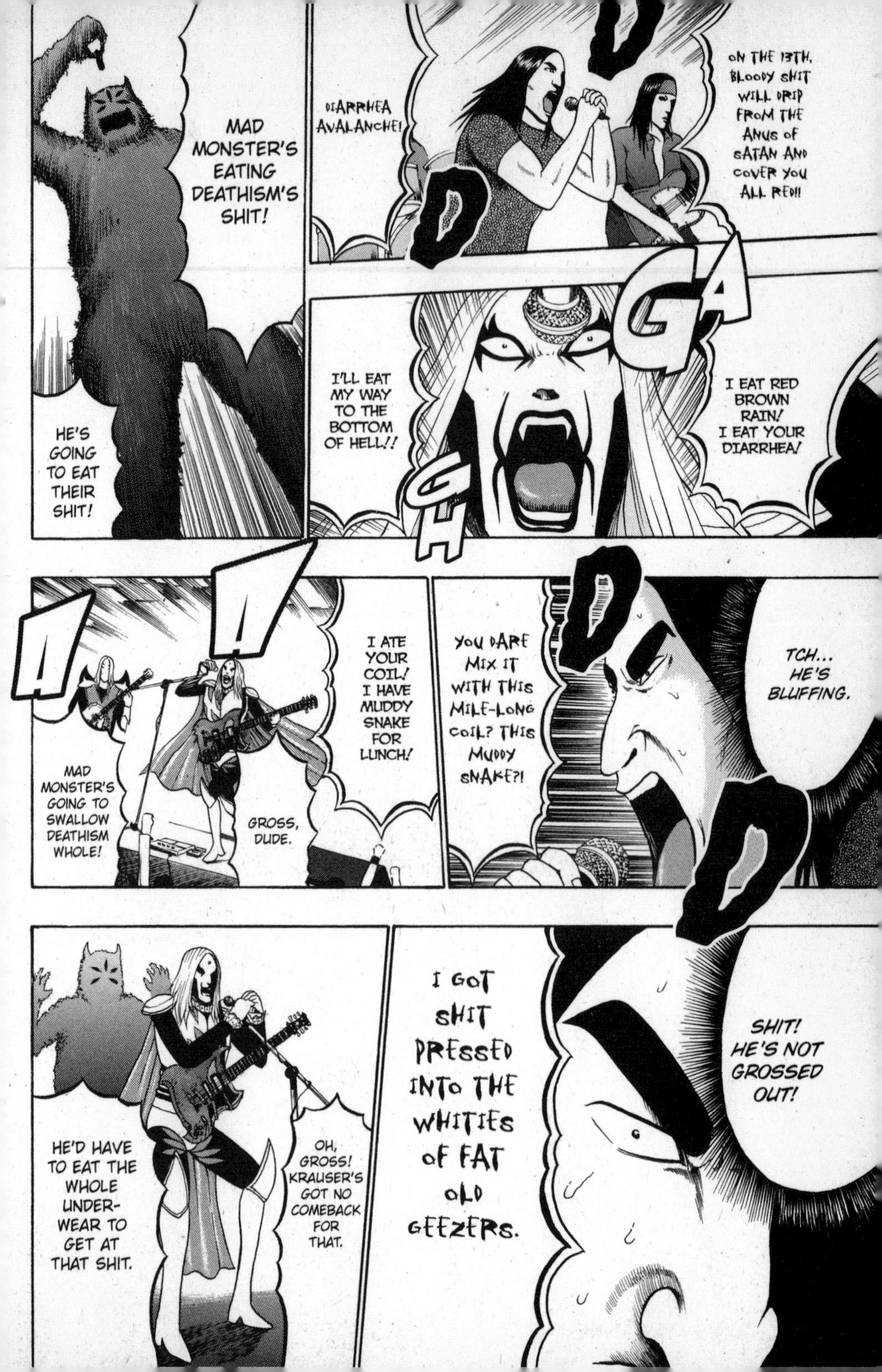
ON THE 13TH, BLOODY SHIT WILL DRIP FROM THE ANUS OF SATAN AND COVER YOU ALL RED!!
DIARRHEA AVALANCHE!
D
D
GA
I EAT RED BROWN RAIN! I EAT YOUR DIARRHEA!
I'LL EAT MY WAY TO THE BOTTOM OF HELL!!
GH
MAD MONSTER'S EATING DEATHISM'S SHIT!
HE'S GOING TO EAT THEIR SHIT!
TCH... HE'S BLUFFING.
D
YOU DARE MIX IT WITH THIS MILE-LONG COIL? THIS MUDDY SNAKE?!
D
I ATE YOUR COIL! I HAVE MUDDY SNAKE FOR LUNCH!
A
A
GROSS, DUDE.
MAD MONSTER'S GOING TO SWALLOW DEATHISM WHOLE!
SHIT! HE'S NOT GROSSED OUT!
I GOT SHIT PRESSED INTO THE WHITIES OF FAT OLD GEEZERS.
OH, GROSS! KRAUSER'S GOT NO COMEBACK FOR THAT.
HE'D HAVE TO EAT THE WHOLE UNDER-WEAR TO GET AT THAT SHIT.

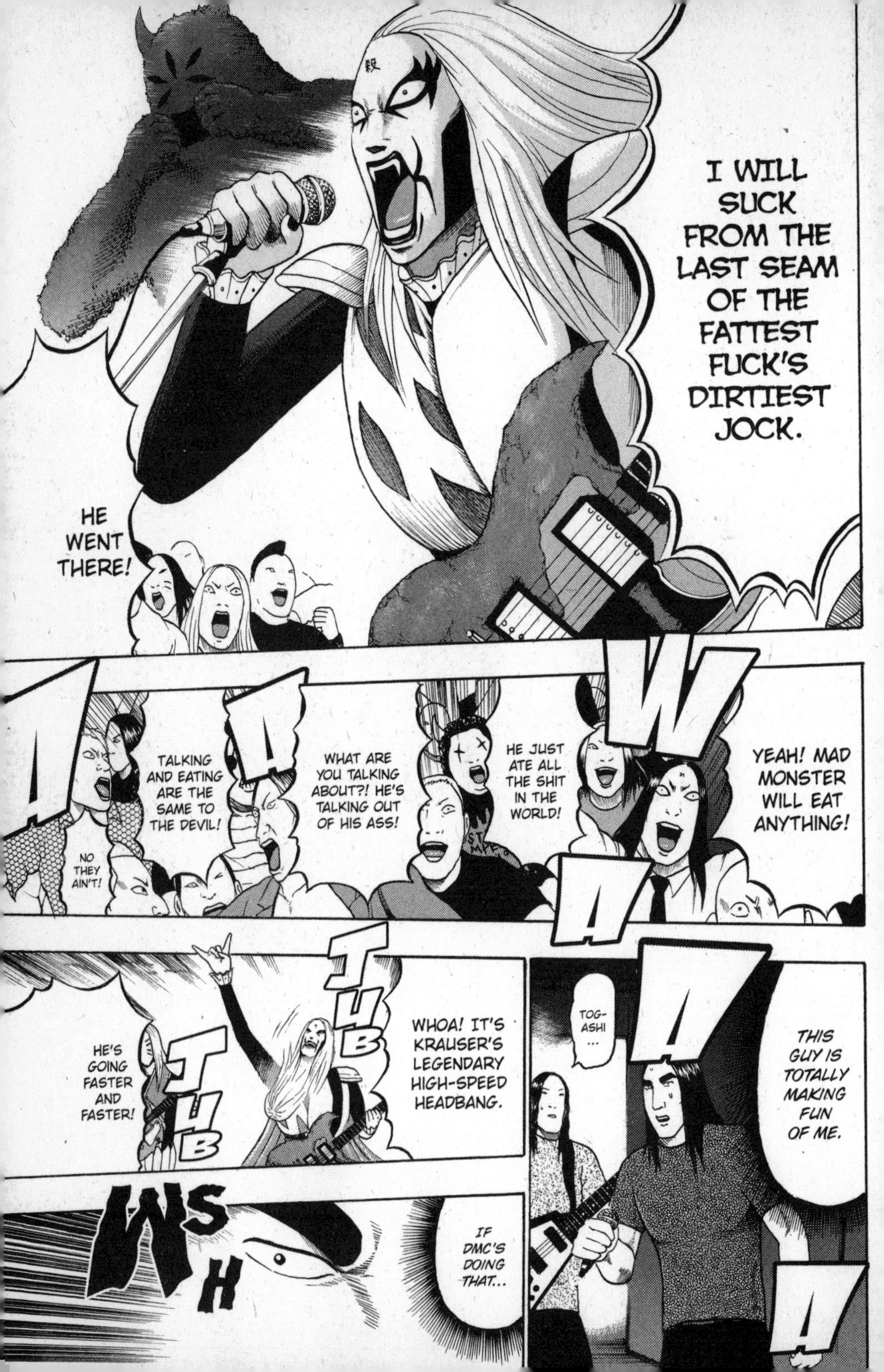
I WILL SUCK FROM THE LAST SEAM OF THE FATTEST FUCK'S DIRTIEST JOCK.
HE WENT THERE!
W
YEAH! MAD MONSTER WILL EAT ANYTHING!
A
HE JUST ATE ALL THE SHIT IN THE WORLD!
WHAT ARE YOU TALKING ABOUT?! HE'S TALKING OUT OF HIS ASS!
A
TALKING AND EATING ARE THE SAME TO THE DEVIL!
NO THEY AIN'T!
A
!
THIS GUY IS TOTALLY MAKING FUN OF ME.
TOG-ASHI...
!
TUB
WHOA! IT'S KRAUSER'S LEGENDARY HIGH-SPEED HEADBANG.
TUB
HE'S GOING FASTER AND FASTER!
IF DMC'S DOING THAT...
WSH

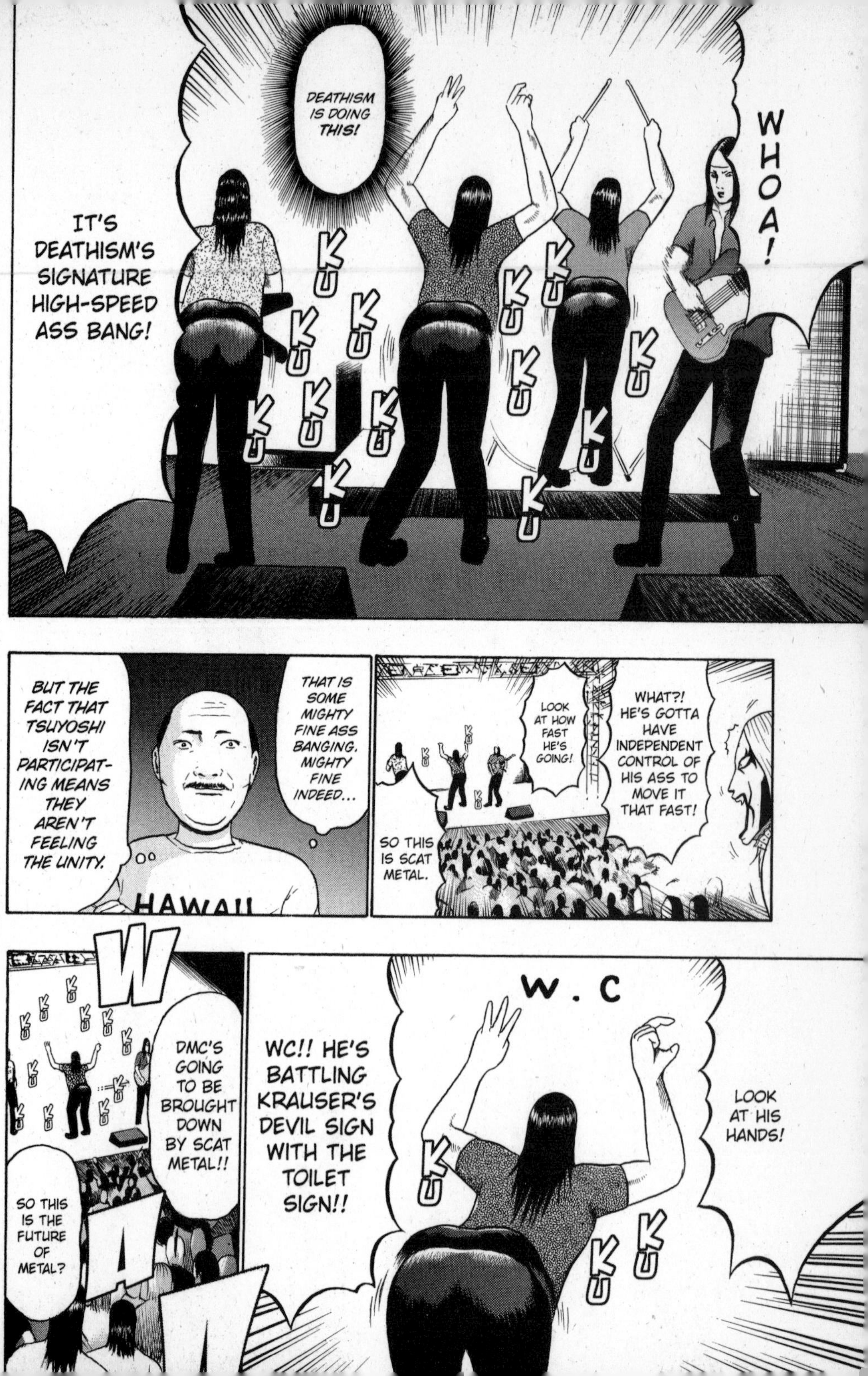
WHOA!
DEATHISM IS DOING THIS!
IT'S DEATHISM'S SIGNATURE HIGH-SPEED ASS BANG!
KU
WHAT?! HE'S GOTTA HAVE INDEPENDENT CONTROL OF HIS ASS TO MOVE IT THAT FAST!
LOOK AT HOW FAST HE'S GOING!
SO THIS IS SCAT METAL.
THAT IS SOME MIGHTY FINE ASS BANGING. MIGHTY FINE INDEED...
BUT THE FACT THAT TSUYOSHI ISN'T PARTICIPAT-ING MEANS THEY AREN'T FEELING THE UNITY.
W . C
LOOK AT HIS HANDS!
WC!! HE'S BATTLING KRAUSER'S DEVIL SIGN WITH THE TOILET SIGN!!
W
DMC'S GOING TO BE BROUGHT DOWN BY SCAT METAL!!
SO THIS IS THE FUTURE OF METAL?

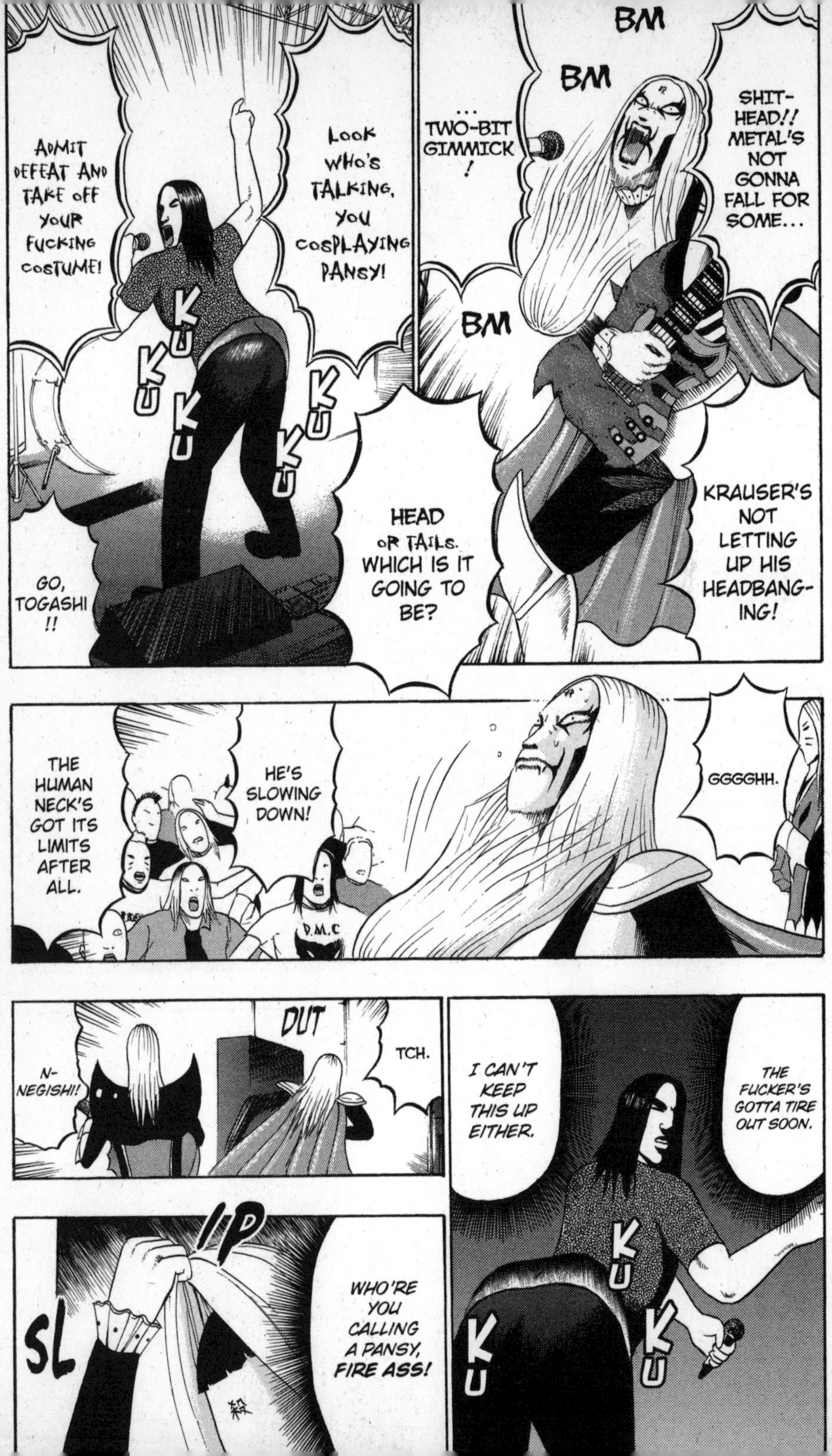
BM
BM
SHIT-HEAD!! METAL'S NOT GONNA FALL FOR SOME...
... TWO-BIT GIMMICK!
BM
KRAUSER'S NOT LETTING UP HIS HEADBANGING!
HEAD OR TAILS. WHICH IS IT GOING TO BE?
LOOK WHO'S TALKING, YOU COSPLAYING PANSY!
ADMIT DEFEAT AND TAKE OFF YOUR FUCKING COSTUME!
KU KU KU KU KU
GO, TOGASHI!!
GGGGHH.
HE'S SLOWING DOWN!
THE HUMAN NECK'S GOT ITS LIMITS AFTER ALL.
D.M.C
THE FUCKER'S GOTTA TIRE OUT SOON.
I CAN'T KEEP THIS UP EITHER.
KU KU KU
TCH.
DUT
N-NEGISHI!
SLIP
WHO'RE YOU CALLING A PANSY, FIRE ASS!

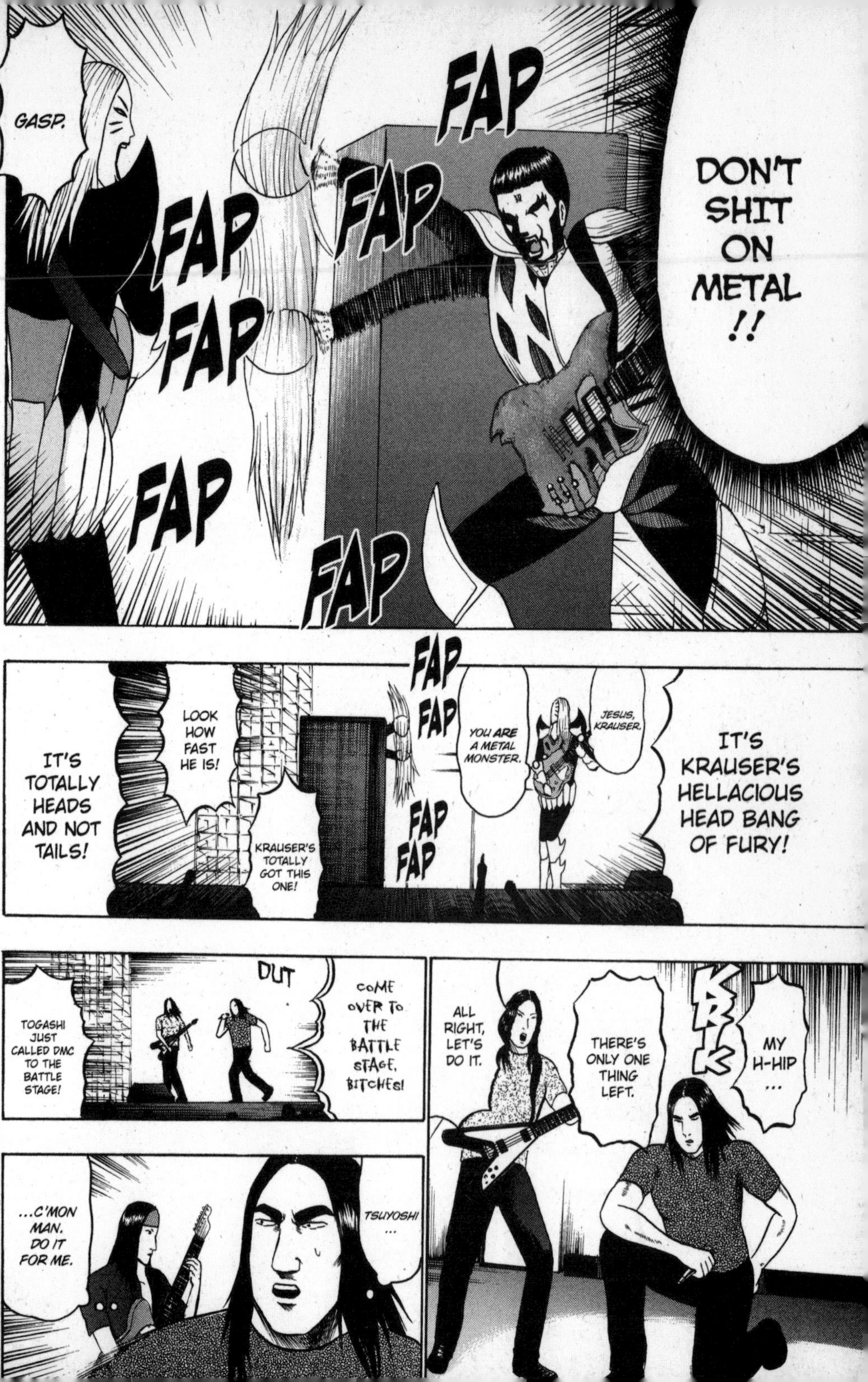
DON'T SHIT ON METAL !!
FAP
FAP
FAP
FAP
FAP
FAP
GASP.
IT'S KRAUSER'S HELLACIOUS HEAD BANG OF FURY!
JESUS, KRAUSER.
YOU ARE A METAL MONSTER.
FAP FAP
FAP FAP
KRAUSER'S TOTALLY GOT THIS ONE!
LOOK HOW FAST HE IS!
IT'S TOTALLY HEADS AND NOT TAILS!
MY H-HIP ...
KRK
THERE'S ONLY ONE THING LEFT.
ALL RIGHT, LET'S DO IT.
DUT
COME OVER TO THE BATTLE STAGE, BITCHES!
TOGASHI JUST CALLED DMC TO THE BATTLE STAGE!
TSUYOSHI ...
...C'MON MAN. DO IT FOR ME.

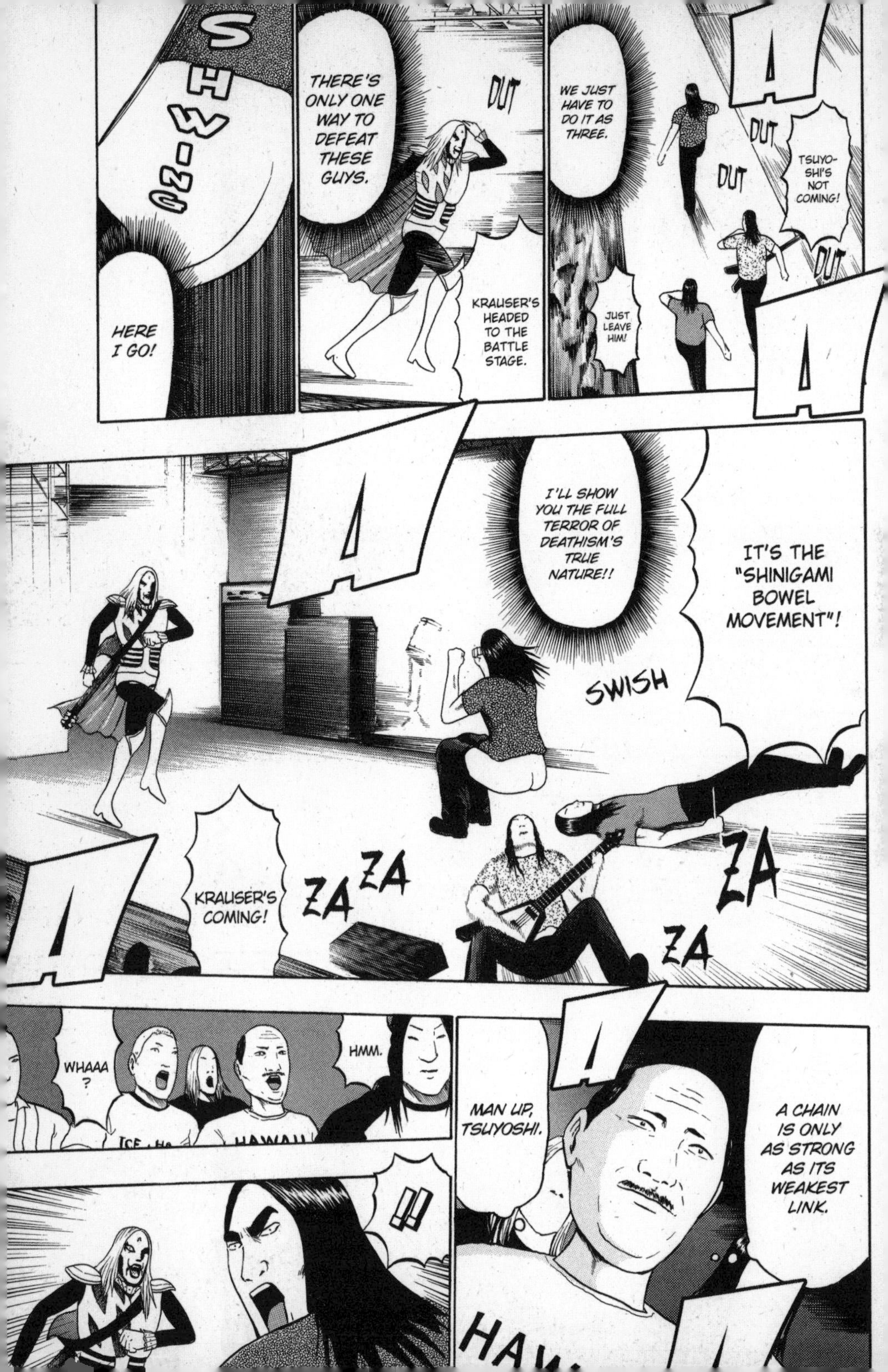

A
DUT
TSUYO-SHI'S NOT COMING!
DUT
DUT
WE JUST HAVE TO DO IT AS THREE.
DUT
JUST LEAVE HIM!
A
THERE'S ONLY ONE WAY TO DEFEAT THESE GUYS.
DUT
KRAUSER'S HEADED TO THE BATTLE STAGE.
SHWING
HERE I GO!
A
IT'S THE "SHINIGAMI BOWEL MOVEMENT"!
I'LL SHOW YOU THE FULL TERROR OF DEATHISM'S TRUE NATURE!!
SWISH
ZA
ZA
ZA
ZA
KRAUSER'S COMING!
A
A
A CHAIN IS ONLY AS STRONG AS ITS WEAKEST LINK.
MAN UP, TSUYOSHI.
HMM.
WHAAA?
!!

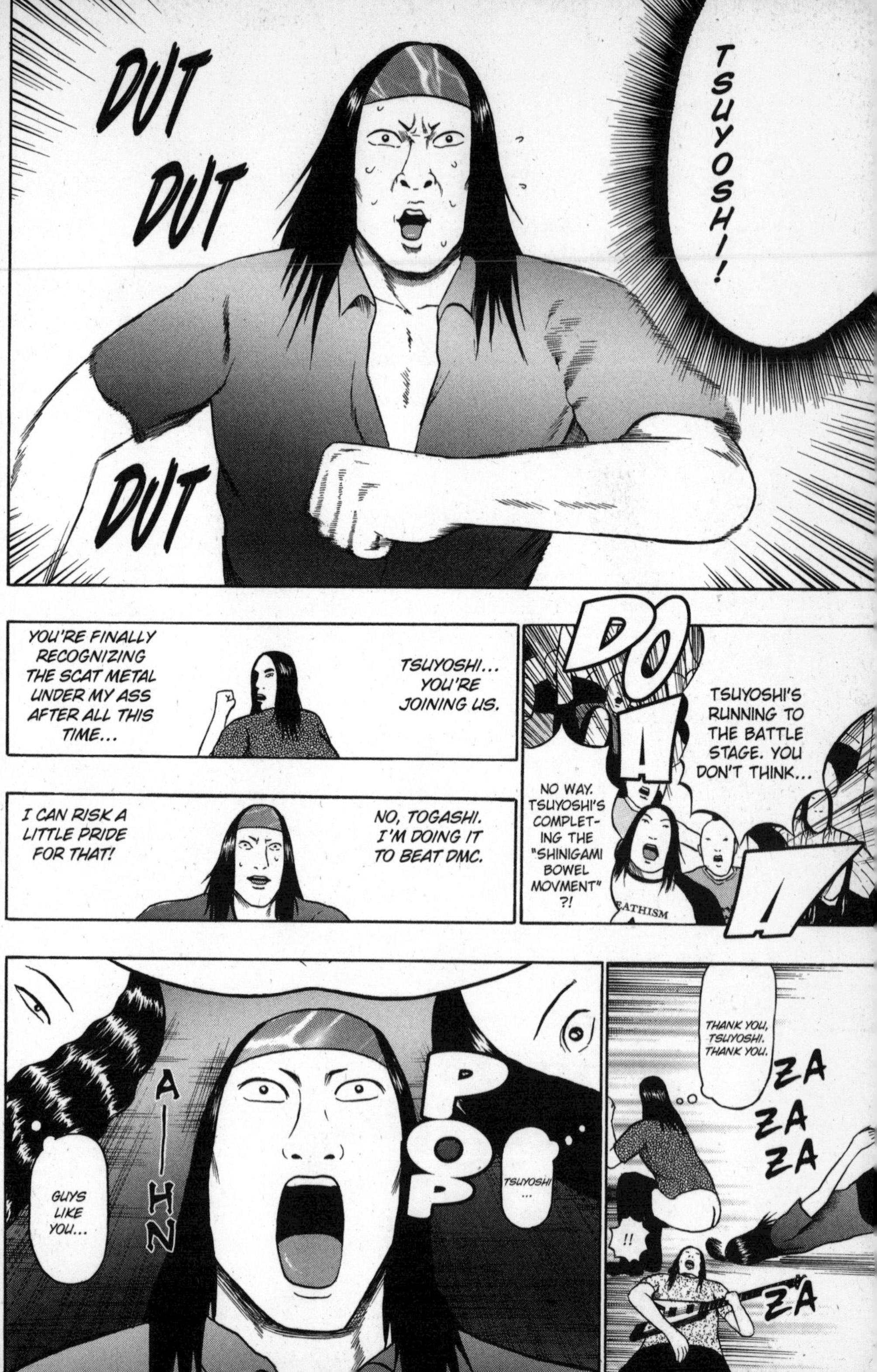
TSUYOSHI!
DUT
DUT
DUT
DOA
TSUYOSHI'S RUNNING TO THE BATTLE STAGE. YOU DON'T THINK...
NO WAY. TSUYOSHI'S COMPLETING THE "SHINIGAMI BOWEL MOVMENT"?!
A
TSUYOSHI... YOU'RE JOINING US.
YOU'RE FINALLY RECOGNIZING THE SCAT METAL UNDER MY ASS AFTER ALL THIS TIME...
NO, TOGASHI. I'M DOING IT TO BEAT DMC.
I CAN RISK A LITTLE PRIDE FOR THAT!
THANK YOU, TSUYOSHI. THANK YOU.
ZA ZA ZA
!!
ZA
POP
TSUYOSHI...
A-HN
GUYS LIKE YOU...

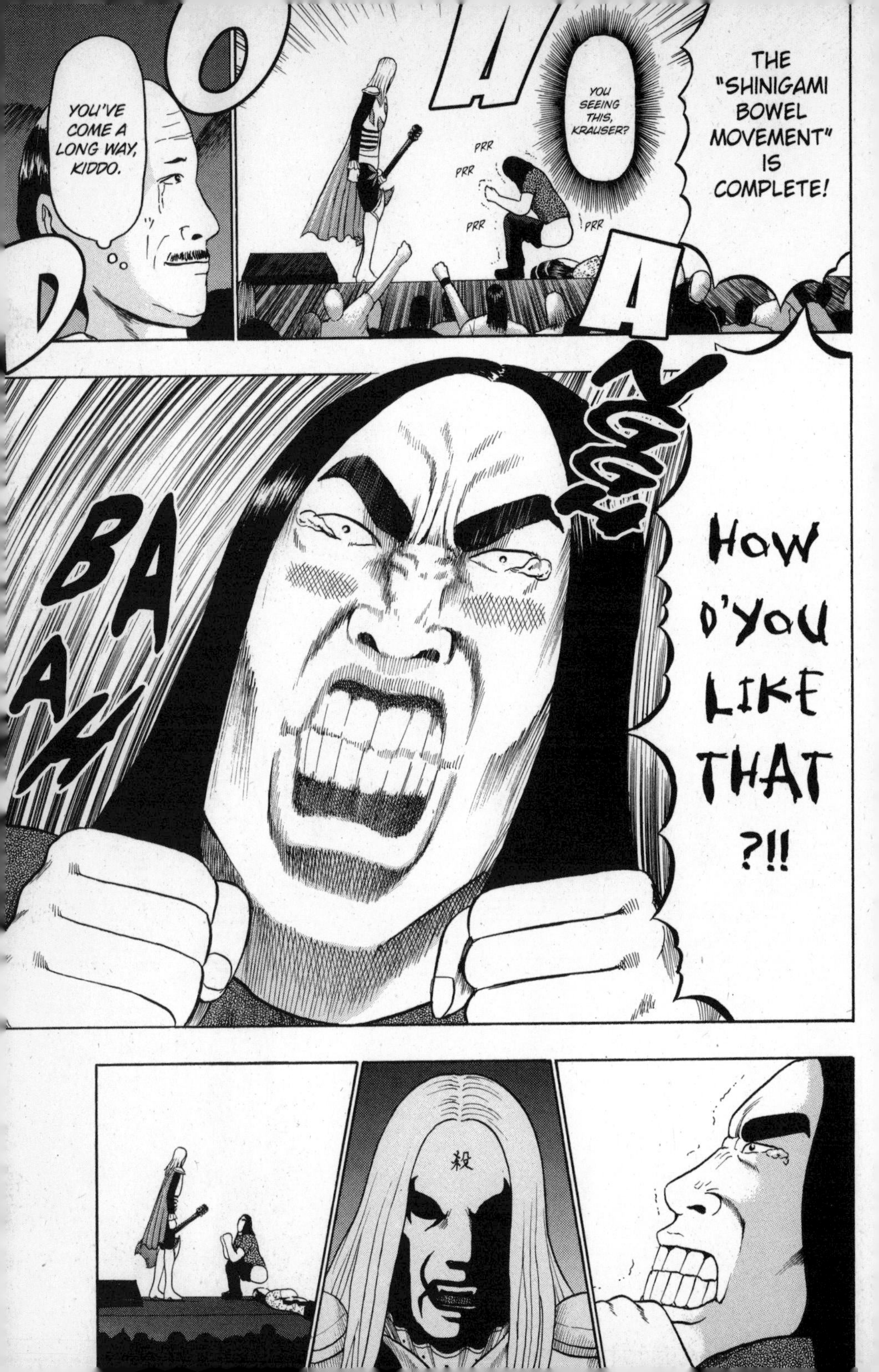
THE "SHINIGAMI BOWEL MOVEMENT" IS COMPLETE!
YOU SEEING THIS, KRAUSER?
PRR
PRR
PRR
PRR
YOU'VE COME A LONG WAY, KIDDO.
HOW D'YOU LIKE THAT ?!!
BAAH

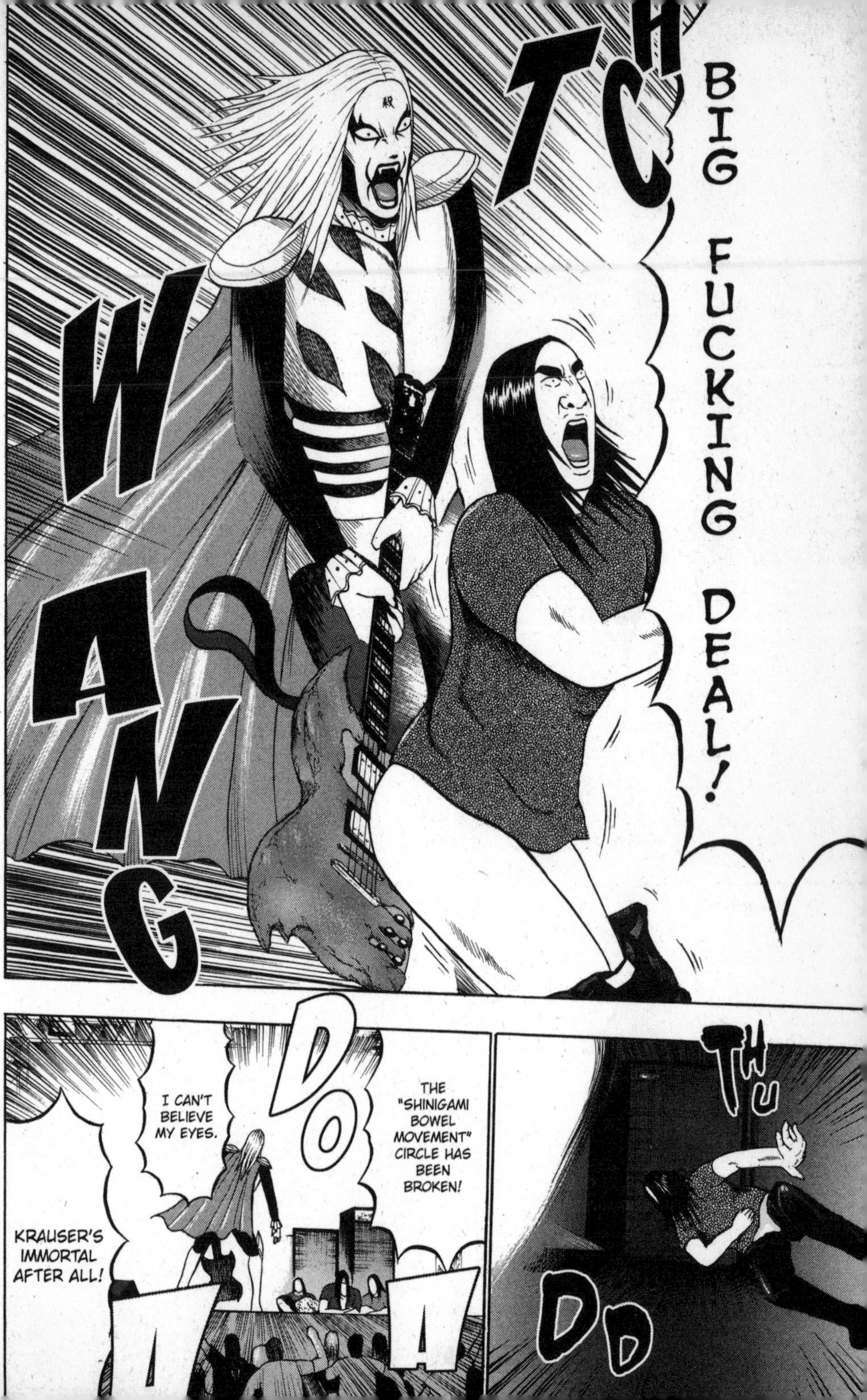
BIG FUCKING DEAL!
TCH
WANG
THU
DD
DO
THE "SHINIGAMI BOWEL MOVEMENT" CIRCLE HAS BEEN BROKEN!
I CAN'T BELIEVE MY EYES.
KRAUSER'S IMMORTAL AFTER ALL!

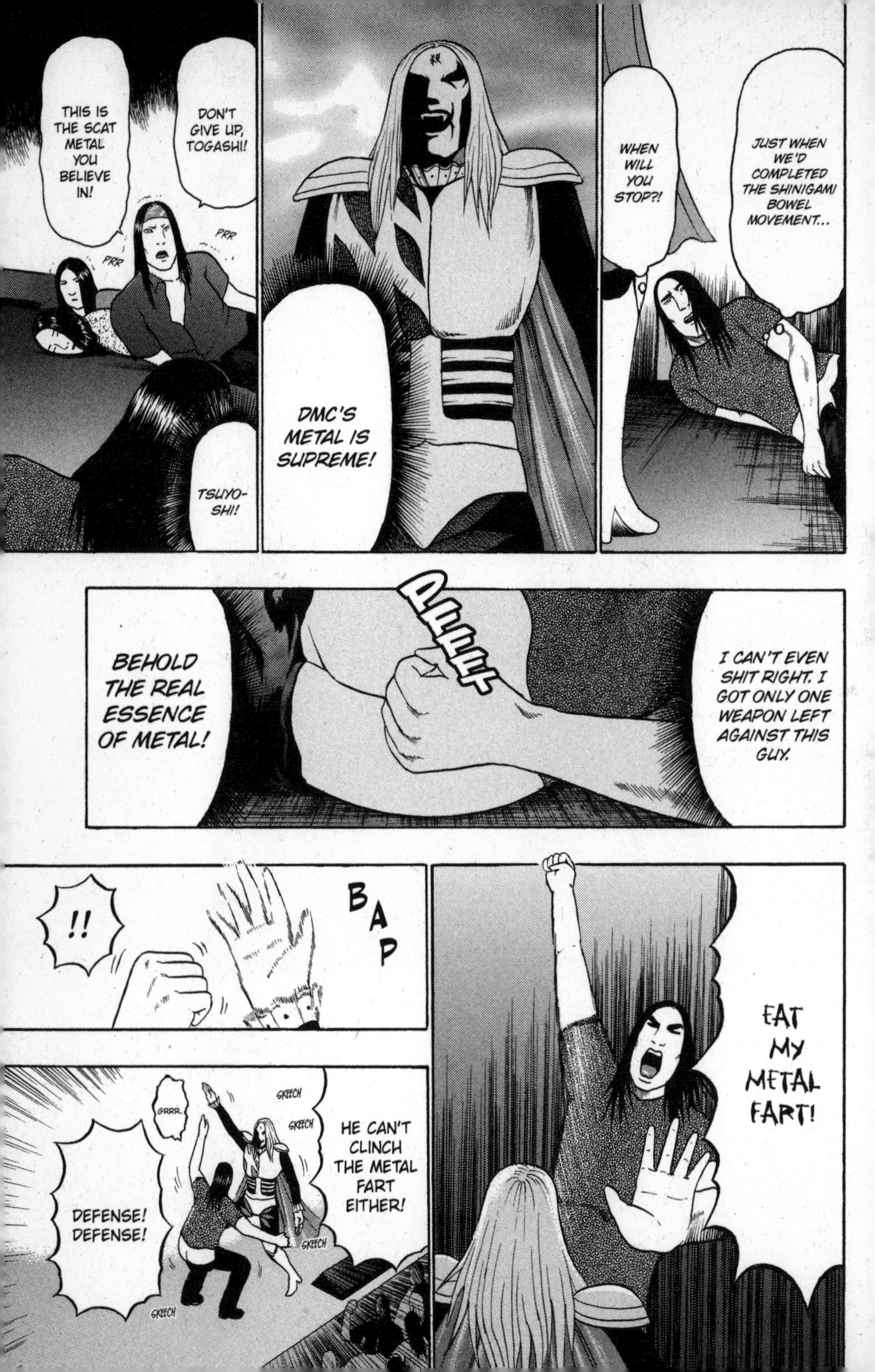
JUST WHEN WE'D COMPLETED THE SHINIGAMI BOWEL MOVEMENT...
WHEN WILL YOU STOP?!
DMC'S METAL IS SUPREME!
DON'T GIVE UP, TOGASHI!
THIS IS THE SCAT METAL YOU BELIEVE IN!
PRR
PRR
TSUYOSHI!
I CAN'T EVEN SHIT RIGHT. I GOT ONLY ONE WEAPON LEFT AGAINST THIS GUY.
BEHOLD THE REAL ESSENCE OF METAL!
EAT MY METAL FART!
BAP
!!
HE CAN'T CLINCH THE METAL FART EITHER!
SKEECH
SKEECH
GRRR
DEFENSE! DEFENSE!
SKEECH
SKEECH

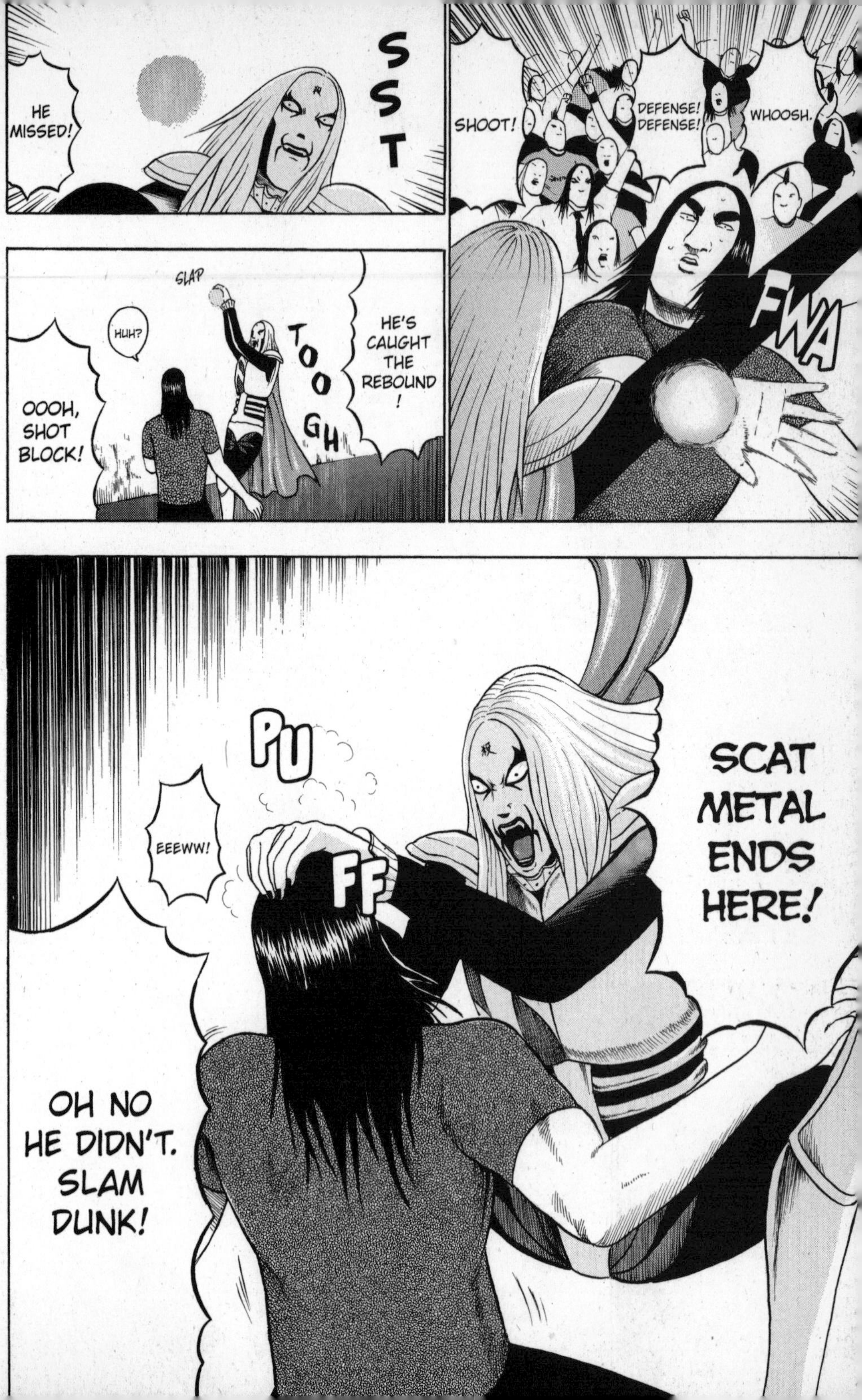
WHOOSH.
DEFENSE! DEFENSE!
SHOOT!
FWA
SST
HE MISSED!
HE'S CAUGHT THE REBOUND!
TOOGH
SLAP
HUH?
OOOH, SHOT BLOCK!
SCAT METAL ENDS HERE!
PUFF
EEEWW!
OH NO HE DIDN'T. SLAM DUNK!

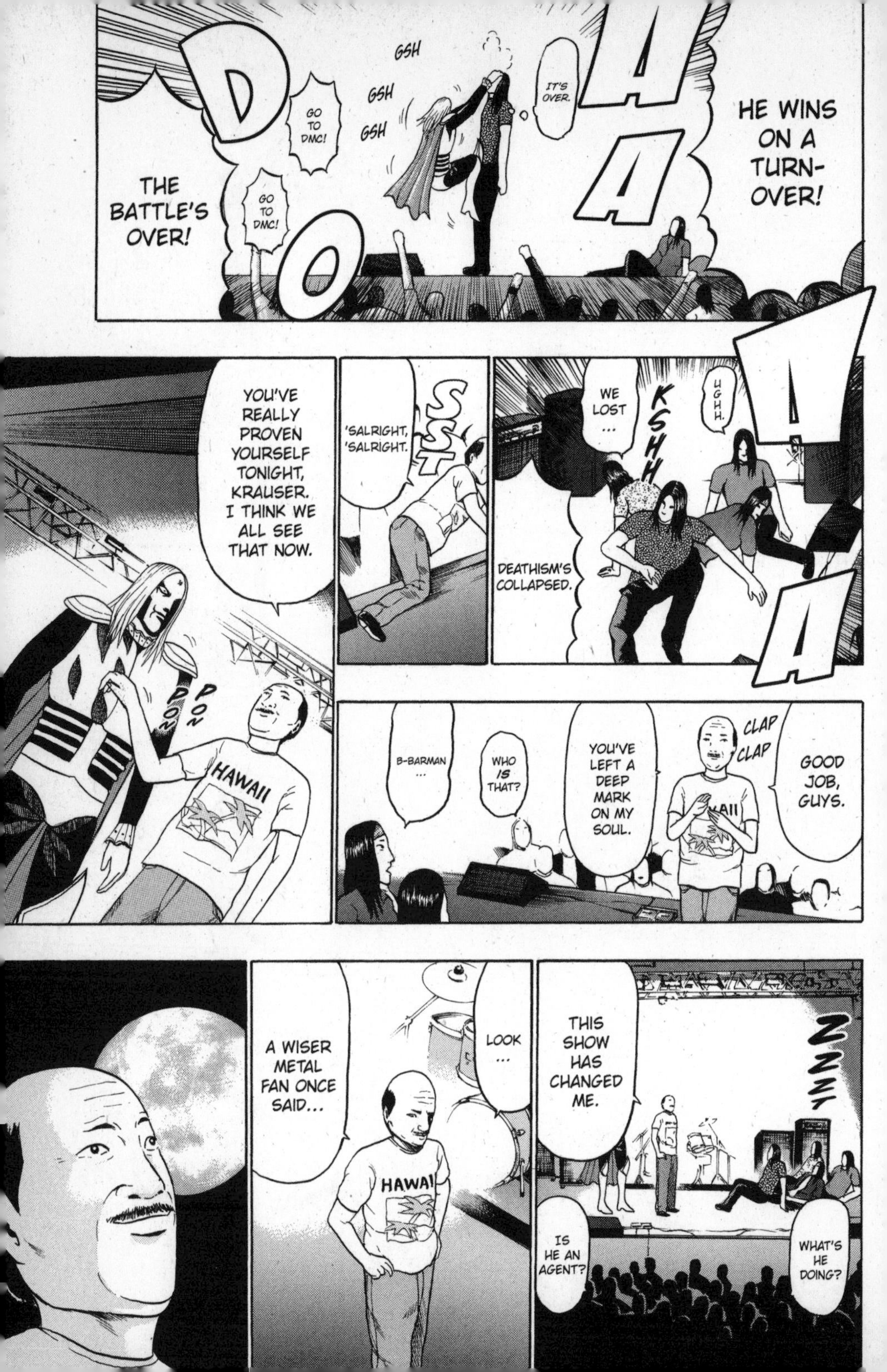
HE WINS ON A TURN-OVER!
IT'S OVER.
GSH
GSH
GSH
GO TO DMC!
GO TO DMC!
THE BATTLE'S OVER!
UGHH.
KSHHH
WE LOST ...
DEATHISM'S COLLAPSED.
SST
'SALRIGHT, 'SALRIGHT.
GOOD JOB, GUYS.
CLAP CLAP
YOU'VE LEFT A DEEP MARK ON MY SOUL.
WHO IS THAT?
B-BARMAN ...
YOU'VE REALLY PROVEN YOURSELF TONIGHT, KRAUSER. I THINK WE ALL SEE THAT NOW.
PON PON
ZZZ
THIS SHOW HAS CHANGED ME.
WHAT'S HE DOING?
IS HE AN AGENT?
LOOK ...
A WISER METAL FAN ONCE SAID...

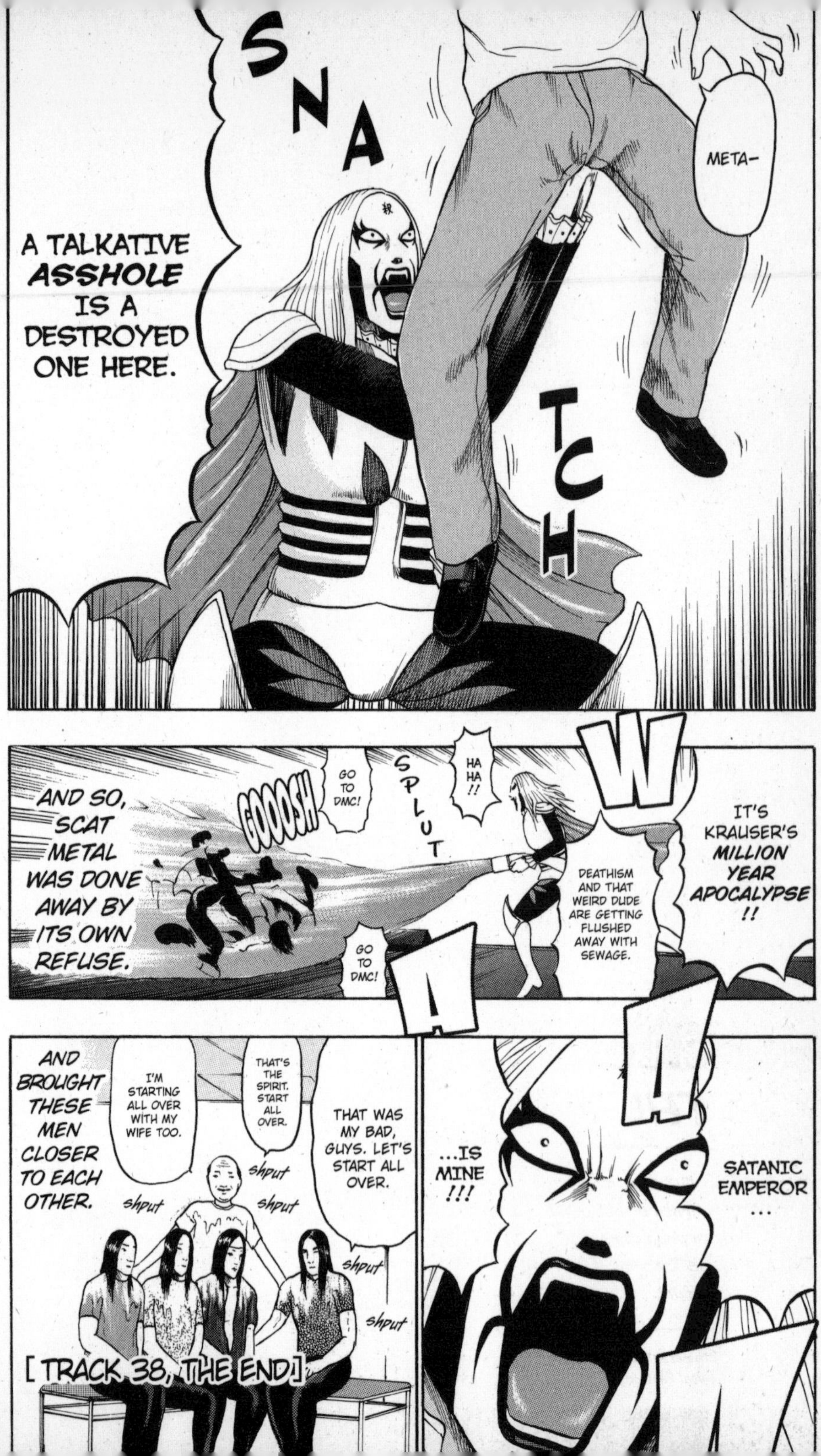
META-
SNATCH
A TALKATIVE ASSHOLE IS A DESTROYED ONE HERE.
IT'S KRAUSER'S MILLION YEAR APOCALYPSE!!
W
DEATHISM AND THAT WEIRD DUDE ARE GETTING FLUSHED AWAY WITH SEWAGE.
HA HA!!
SPLUT
GO TO DMC!
GOOOSH
GO TO DMC!
AND SO, SCAT METAL WAS DONE AWAY BY ITS OWN REFUSE.
A
A
SATANIC EMPEROR ...
...IS MINE!!!
THAT WAS MY BAD, GUYS. LET'S START ALL OVER.
THAT'S THE SPIRIT. START ALL OVER.
I'M STARTING ALL OVER WITH MY WIFE TOO.
shput
shput
shput
shput
shput
AND BROUGHT THESE MEN CLOSER TO EACH OTHER.
[TRACK 38, THE END]

DMC LEXICON
♥METAL FART

One of many Scat Metal moves. Performed by
containing the entirety of one's metal soul through
the anus and then projecting it at your opponent.
The "Metal Fart" is frequently confused with a
"metallic-smelling fart." It's all in the tempo.

Usage: Your shit smells metallic because of all the beans you eat.
You better let out a Metal Fart or the evil will kill you from inside.

デトロイト・メタル・シティ

Detroit Metal City

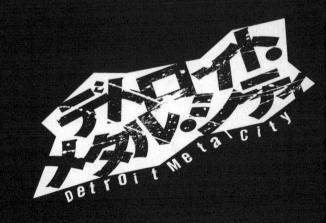

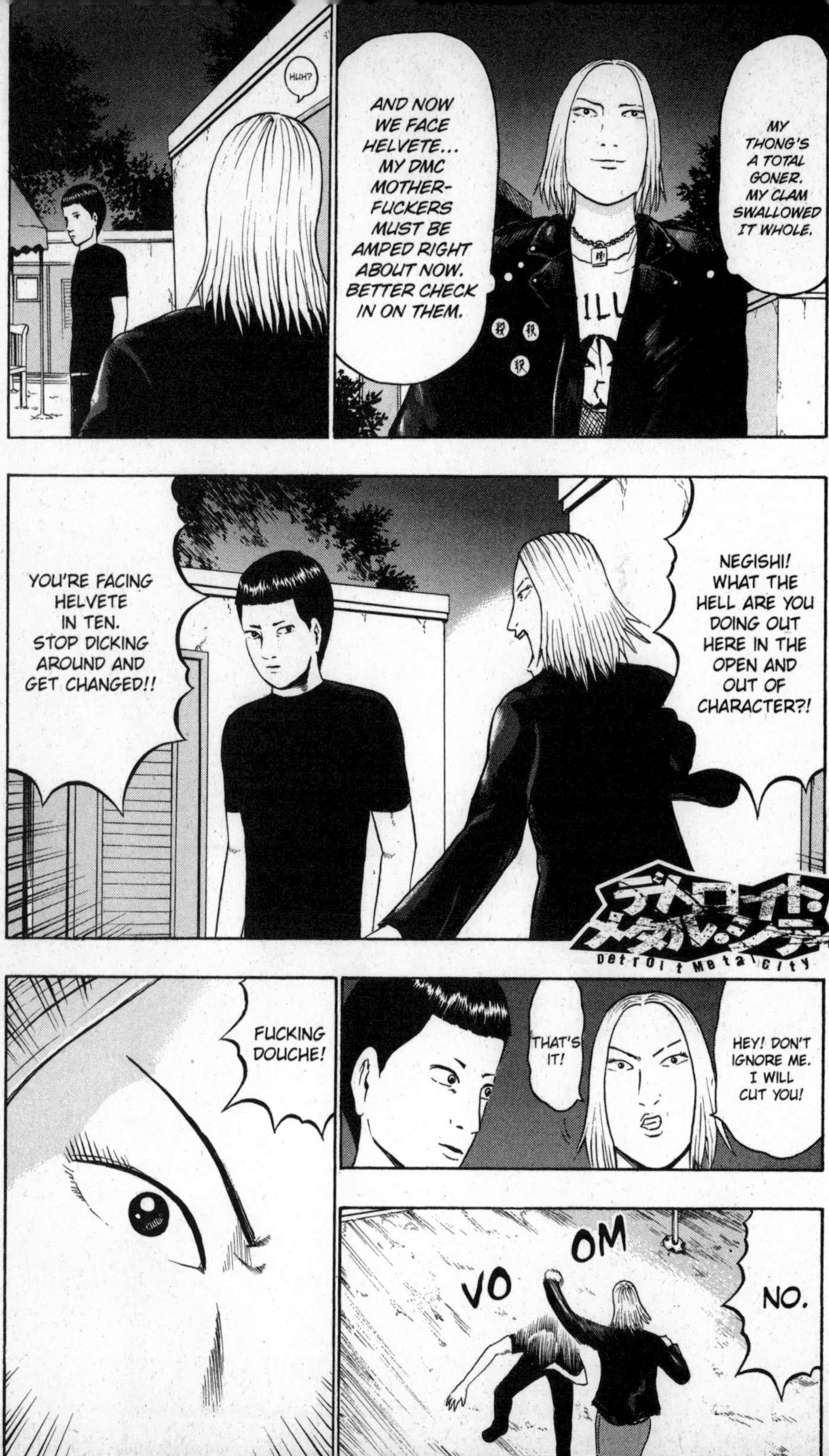
MY THONG'S A TOTAL GONER. MY CLAM SWALLOWED IT WHOLE.
AND NOW WE FACE HELVETE... MY DMC MOTHER-FUCKERS MUST BE AMPED RIGHT ABOUT NOW. BETTER CHECK IN ON THEM.
HUH?
NEGISHI! WHAT THE HELL ARE YOU DOING OUT HERE IN THE OPEN AND OUT OF CHARACTER?!
YOU'RE FACING HELVETE IN TEN. STOP DICKING AROUND AND GET CHANGED!!
HEY! DON'T IGNORE ME. I WILL CUT YOU!
THAT'S IT!
NO.
VO OM
FUCKING DOUCHE!

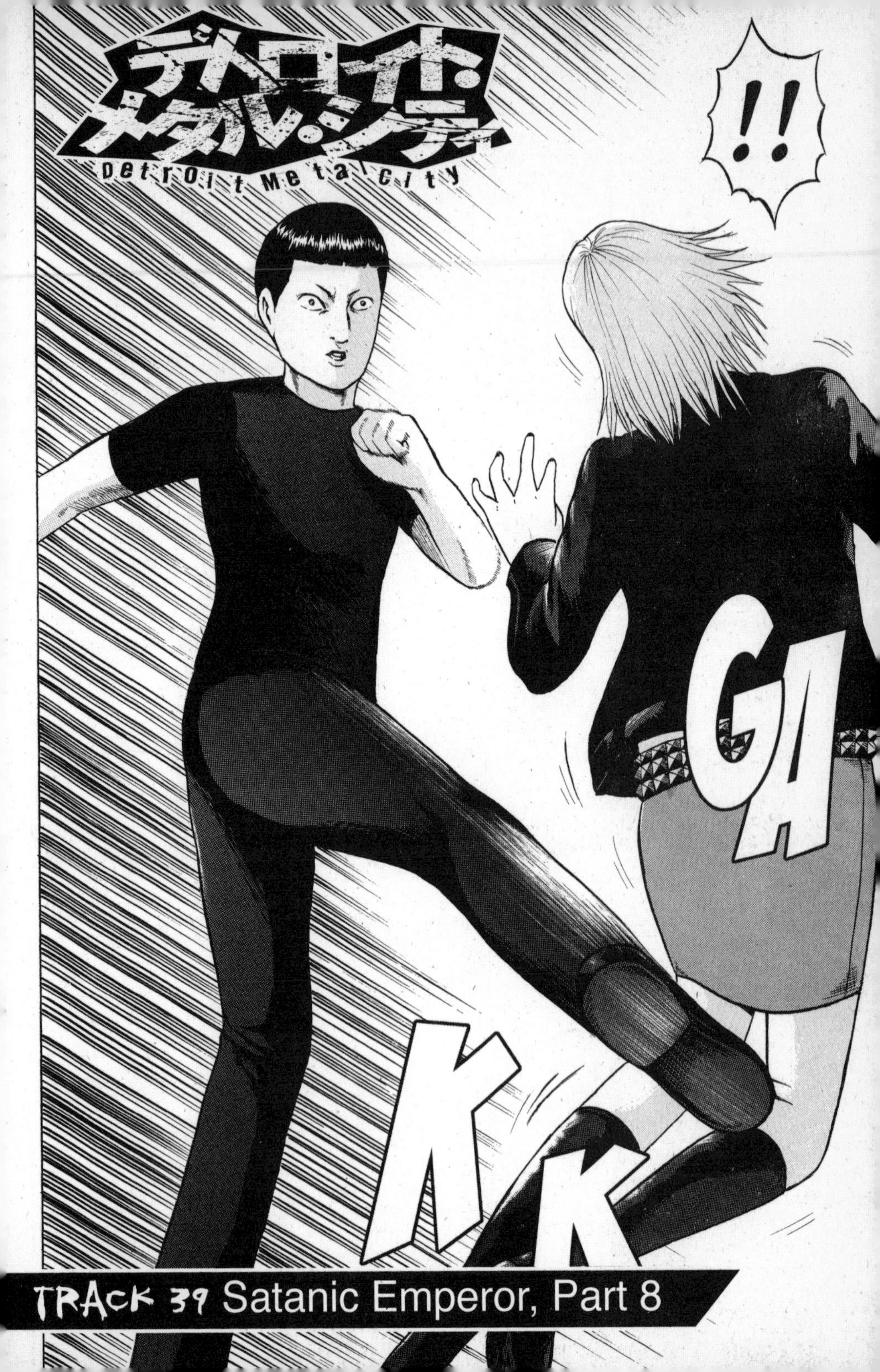
デトロイト・メタル・シティ
Detroit Metal City
!!
GA
KK

TRACK 39 Satanic Emperor, Part 8

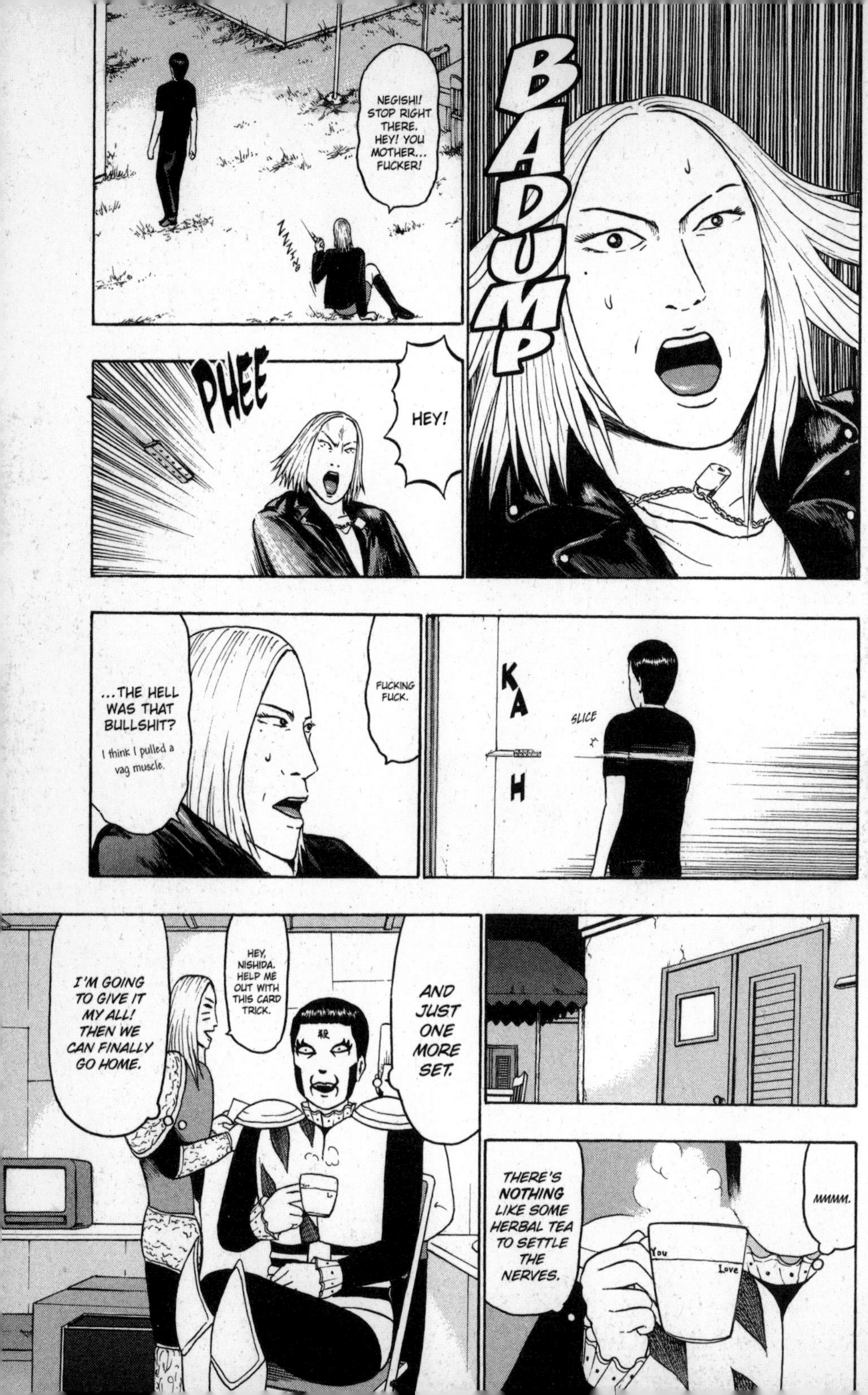
BADUMP
NEGISHI! STOP RIGHT THERE. HEY! YOU MOTHER... FUCKER!
ZZZZZZZ
PHEE
HEY!
KA
H
SLICE
FUCKING FUCK.
...THE HELL WAS THAT BULLSHIT?
I think I pulled a vag muscle.
MMMM.
THERE'S NOTHING LIKE SOME HERBAL TEA TO SETTLE THE NERVES.
You
Love
AND JUST ONE MORE SET.
HEY, NISHIDA. HELP ME OUT WITH THIS CARD TRICK.
I'M GOING TO GIVE IT MY ALL! THEN WE CAN FINALLY GO HOME.

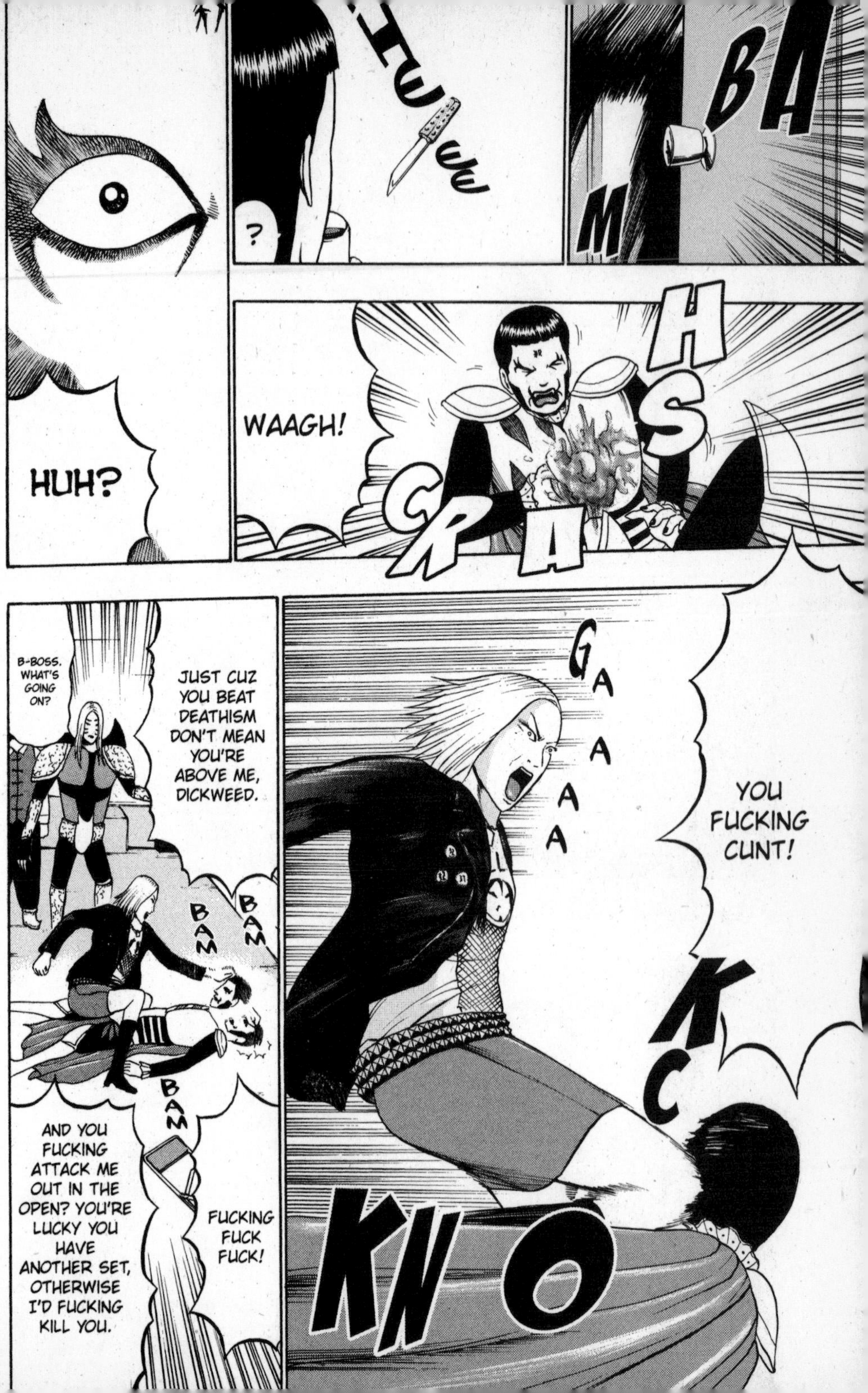
BAM
?
HEEE
WAAGH!
CRASH
HUH?
YOU FUCKING CUNT!
GAAAAA
KNOCK
B-BOSS. WHAT'S GOING ON?
JUST CUZ YOU BEAT DEATHISM DON'T MEAN YOU'RE ABOVE ME, DICKWEED.
BAM
BAM
AND YOU FUCKING ATTACK ME OUT IN THE OPEN? YOU'RE LUCKY YOU HAVE ANOTHER SET, OTHERWISE I'D FUCKING KILL YOU.
FUCKING FUCK FUCK!
BAM

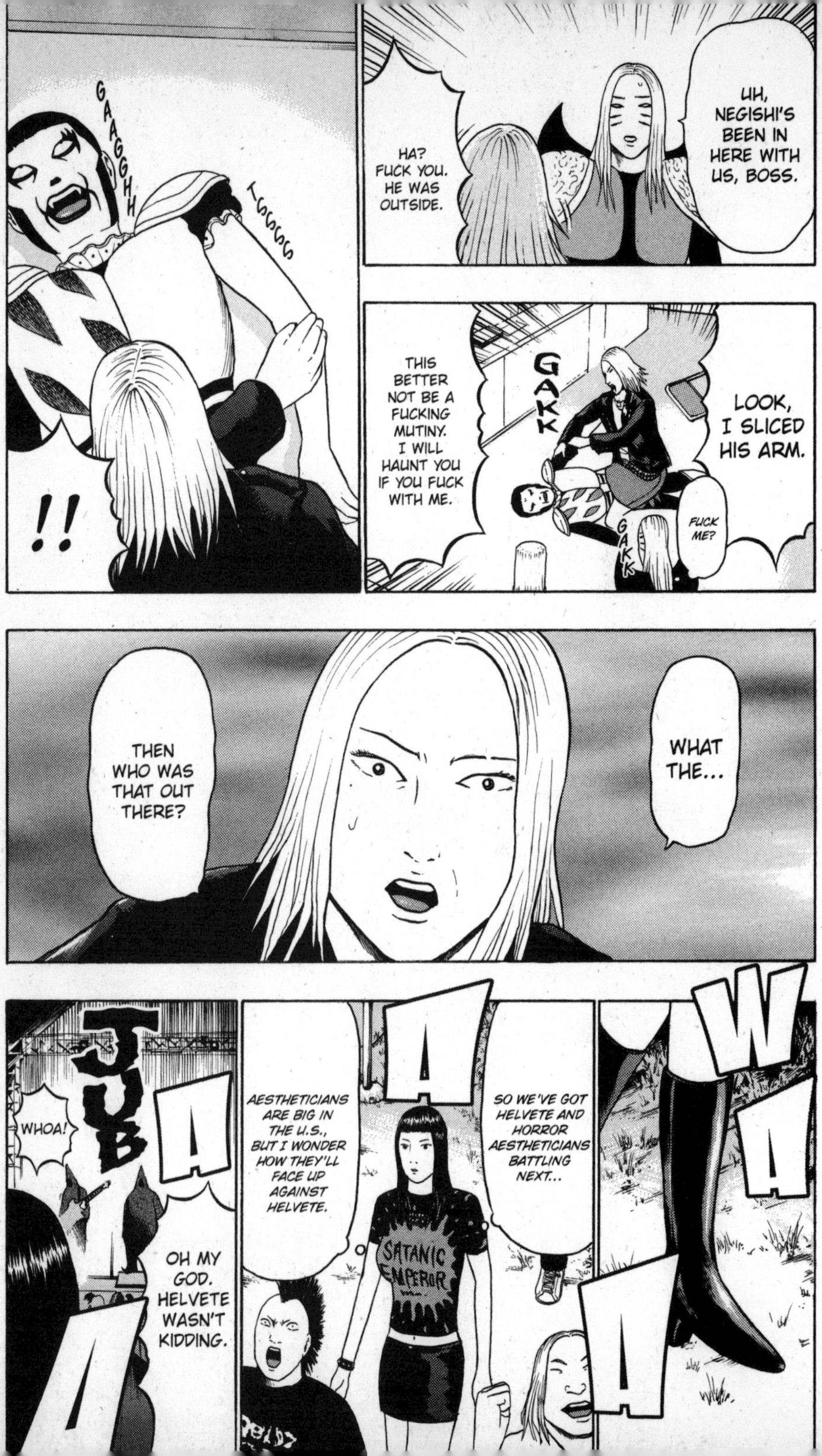
UH, NEGISHI'S BEEN IN HERE WITH US, BOSS.
HA? FUCK YOU. HE WAS OUTSIDE.
LOOK, I SLICED HIS ARM.
GAKK
THIS BETTER NOT BE A FUCKING MUTINY. I WILL HAUNT YOU IF YOU FUCK WITH ME.
FUCK ME?
GAKK
GAAGGHH
!!
WHAT THE...
THEN WHO WAS THAT OUT THERE?
WAAA
SO WE'VE GOT HELVETE AND HORROR AESTHETICIANS BATTLING NEXT...
A
AESTHETICIANS ARE BIG IN THE U.S., BUT I WONDER HOW THEY'LL FACE UP AGAINST HELVETE.
SATANIC EMPEROR
JUBA
A
WHOA!
OH MY GOD. HELVETE WASN'T KIDDING.
A

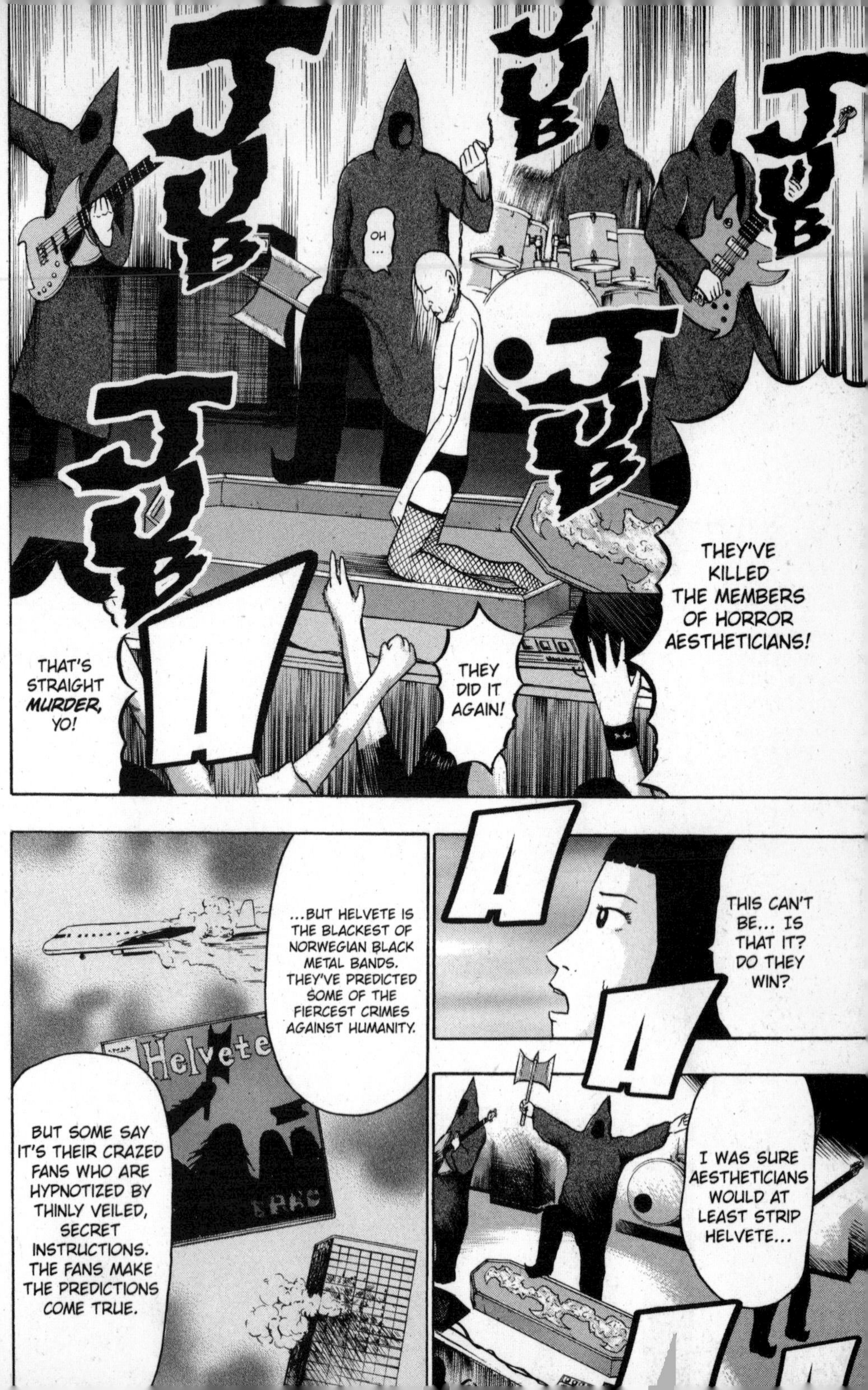
JUB
JUB
OH ...
JUB
JUB
JUB
JUB
THEY'VE KILLED THE MEMBERS OF HORROR AESTHETICIANS!
THEY DID IT AGAIN!
A
THAT'S STRAIGHT *MURDER,* YO!
A
THIS CAN'T BE... IS THAT IT? DO THEY WIN?
...BUT HELVETE IS THE BLACKEST OF NORWEGIAN BLACK METAL BANDS. THEY'VE PREDICTED SOME OF THE FIERCEST CRIMES AGAINST HUMANITY.
Helvete
A
I WAS SURE AESTHETICIANS WOULD AT LEAST STRIP HELVETE...
BUT SOME SAY IT'S THEIR CRAZED FANS WHO ARE HYPNOTIZED BY THINLY VEILED, SECRET INSTRUCTIONS. THE FANS MAKE THE PREDICTIONS COME TRUE.

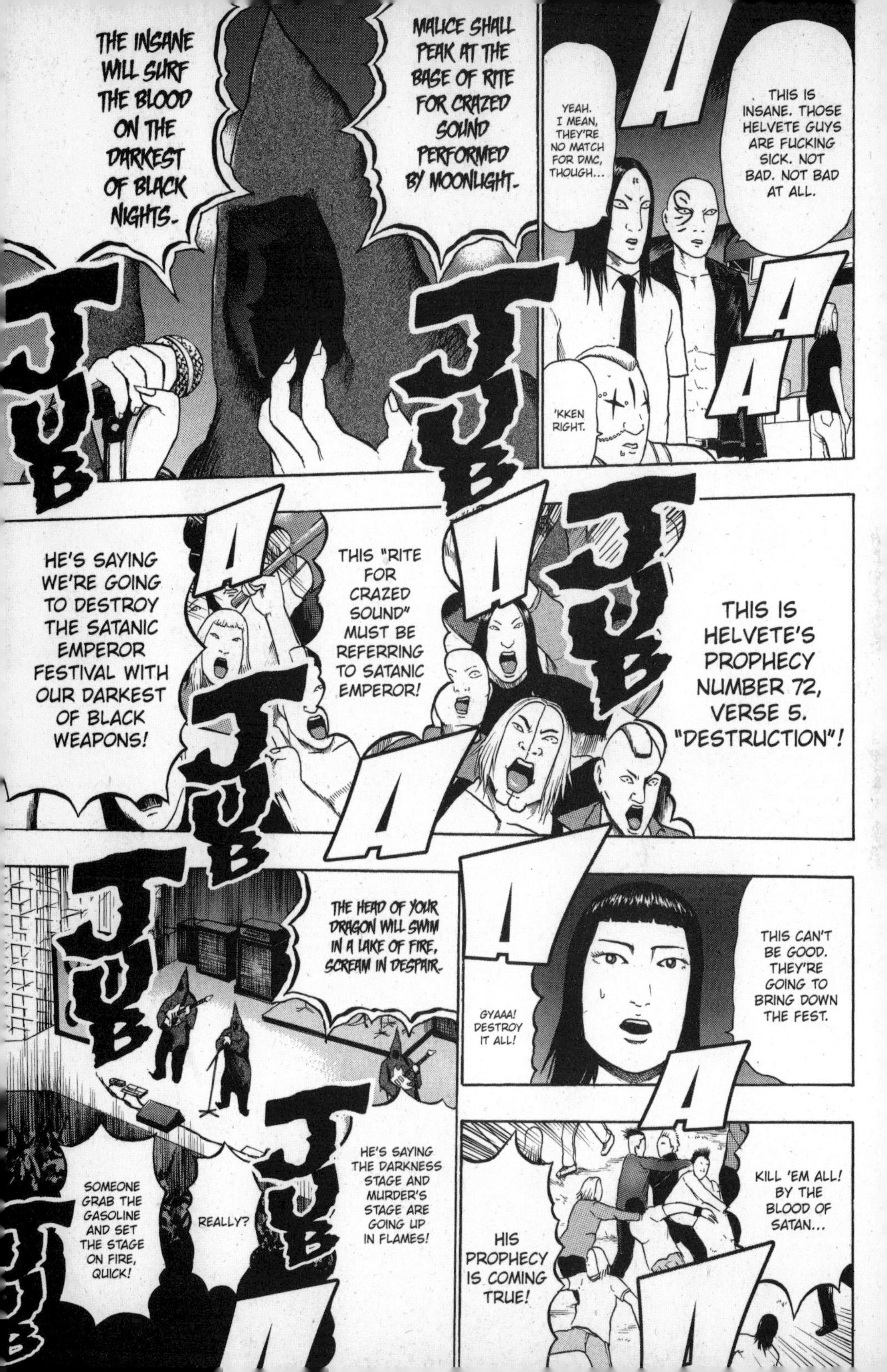
THIS IS INSANE. THOSE HELVETE GUYS ARE FUCKING SICK. NOT BAD. NOT BAD AT ALL.
YEAH. I MEAN, THEY'RE NO MATCH FOR DMC, THOUGH...
'KKEN RIGHT.
A
AAA
MALICE SHALL PEAK AT THE BASE OF RITE FOR CRAZED SOUND PERFORMED BY MOONLIGHT...
THE INSANE WILL SURF THE BLOOD ON THE DARKEST OF BLACK NIGHTS...
JUB
JUB
THIS IS HELVETE'S PROPHECY NUMBER 72, VERSE 5. "DESTRUCTION"!
JUB
A
THIS "RITE FOR CRAZED SOUND" MUST BE REFERRING TO SATANIC EMPEROR!
A
HE'S SAYING WE'RE GOING TO DESTROY THE SATANIC EMPEROR FESTIVAL WITH OUR DARKEST OF BLACK WEAPONS!
JUB
A
A
THIS CAN'T BE GOOD. THEY'RE GOING TO BRING DOWN THE FEST.
GYAAA! DESTROY IT ALL!
THE HEAD OF YOUR DRAGON WILL SWIM IN A LAKE OF FIRE, SCREAM IN DESPAIR...
JUB
A
KILL 'EM ALL! BY THE BLOOD OF SATAN...
HIS PROPHECY IS COMING TRUE!
HE'S SAYING THE DARKNESS STAGE AND MURDER'S STAGE ARE GOING UP IN FLAMES!
REALLY?
JUB
SOMEONE GRAB THE GASOLINE AND SET THE STAGE ON FIRE, QUICK!
JUB

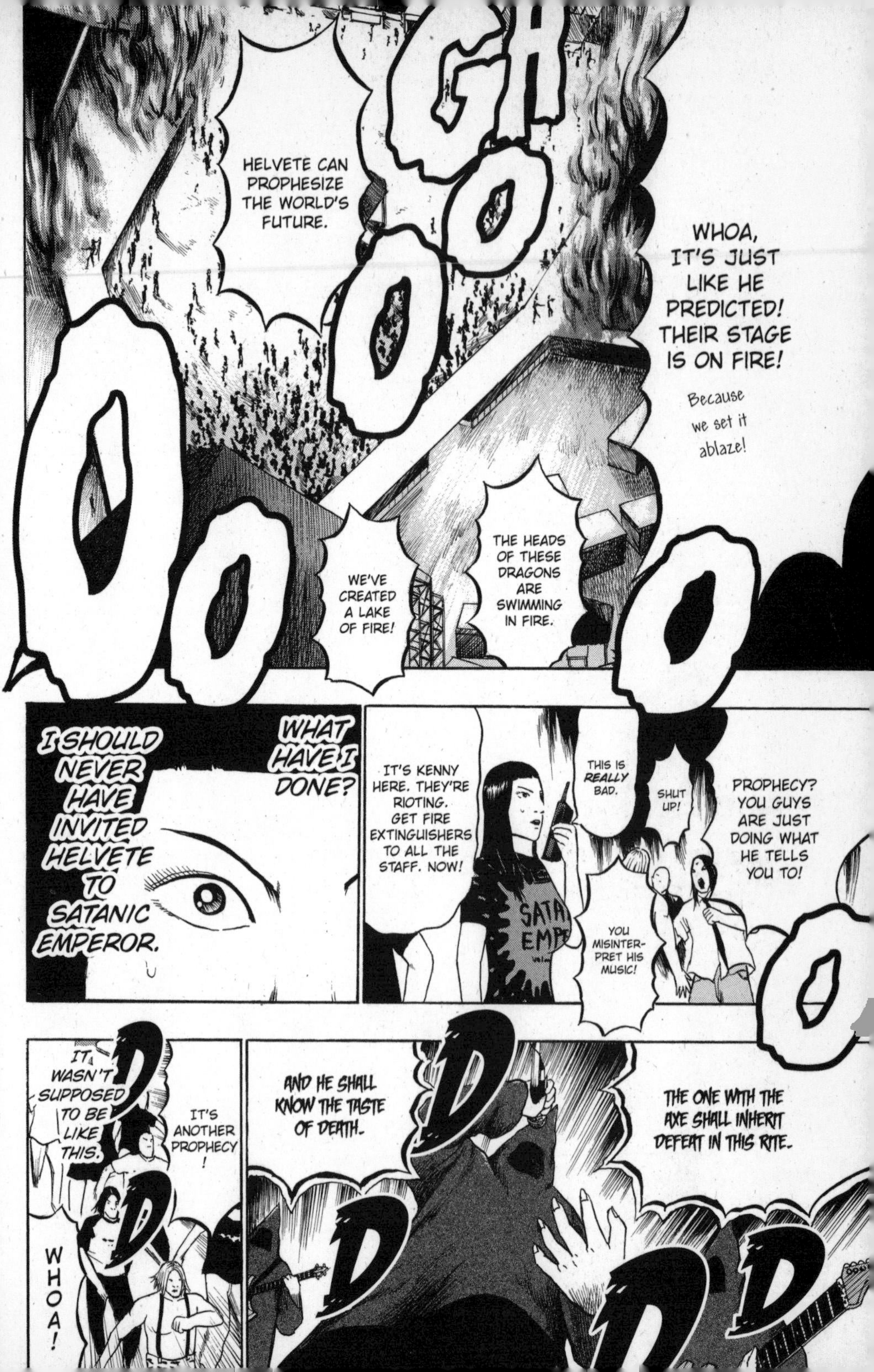
WHOA, IT'S JUST LIKE HE PREDICTED! THEIR STAGE IS ON FIRE!
Because we set it ablaze!
HELVETE CAN PROPHESIZE THE WORLD'S FUTURE.
GHOOOOOOO
THE HEADS OF THESE DRAGONS ARE SWIMMING IN FIRE.
WE'VE CREATED A LAKE OF FIRE!
PROPHECY? YOU GUYS ARE JUST DOING WHAT HE TELLS YOU TO!
SHUT UP!
THIS IS *REALLY* BAD.
YOU MISINTERPRET HIS MUSIC!
IT'S KENNY HERE. THEY'RE RIOTING. GET FIRE EXTINGUISHERS TO ALL THE STAFF. NOW!
WHAT HAVE I DONE?
I SHOULD NEVER HAVE INVITED HELVETE TO SATANIC EMPEROR.
THE ONE WITH THE AXE SHALL INHERIT DEFEAT IN THIS RITE.
AND HE SHALL KNOW THE TASTE OF DEATH.
DDDDD
IT'S ANOTHER PROPHECY!
IT WASN'T SUPPOSED TO BE LIKE THIS.
WHOA!

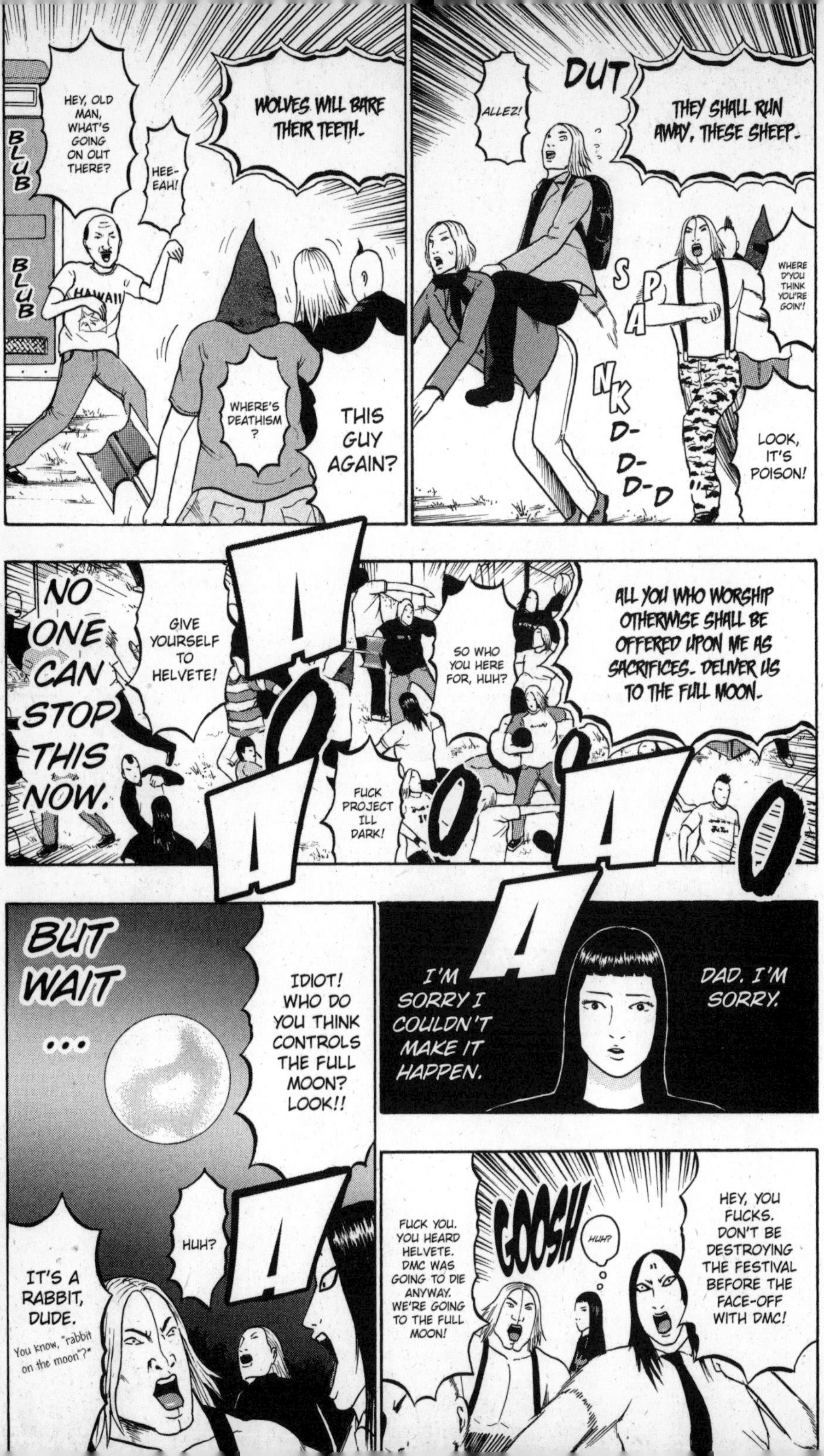
DUT
THEY SHALL RUN AWAY, THESE SHEEP.
ALLEZ!
SPA
WHERE D'YOU THINK YOU'RE GOIN'!
NK
D-D-D-D
LOOK, IT'S POISON!
WOLVES WILL BARE THEIR TEETH.
HEY, OLD MAN, WHAT'S GOING ON OUT THERE?
HEE-EAH!
BLUB
BLUB
WHERE'S DEATHISM?
THIS GUY AGAIN?
ALL YOU WHO WORSHIP OTHERWISE SHALL BE OFFERED UPON ME AS SACRIFICES. DELIVER US TO THE FULL MOON.
SO WHO YOU HERE FOR, HUH?
GIVE YOURSELF TO HELVETE!
NO ONE CAN STOP THIS NOW.
FUCK PROJECT ILL DARK!
DAD. I'M SORRY.
I'M SORRY I COULDN'T MAKE IT HAPPEN.
HEY, YOU FUCKS. DON'T BE DESTROYING THE FESTIVAL BEFORE THE FACE-OFF WITH DMC!
HUH?
GOOSH
FUCK YOU. YOU HEARD HELVETE. DMC WAS GOING TO DIE ANYWAY. WE'RE GOING TO THE FULL MOON!
BUT WAIT...
IDIOT! WHO DO YOU THINK CONTROLS THE FULL MOON? LOOK!!
HUH?
IT'S A RABBIT, DUDE.
You know, "rabbit on the moon"?*

*IN JAPANESE LORE, THERE IS A RABBIT IN THE MOON, COMPARABLE TO AMERICA'S "MAN IN THE MOON."

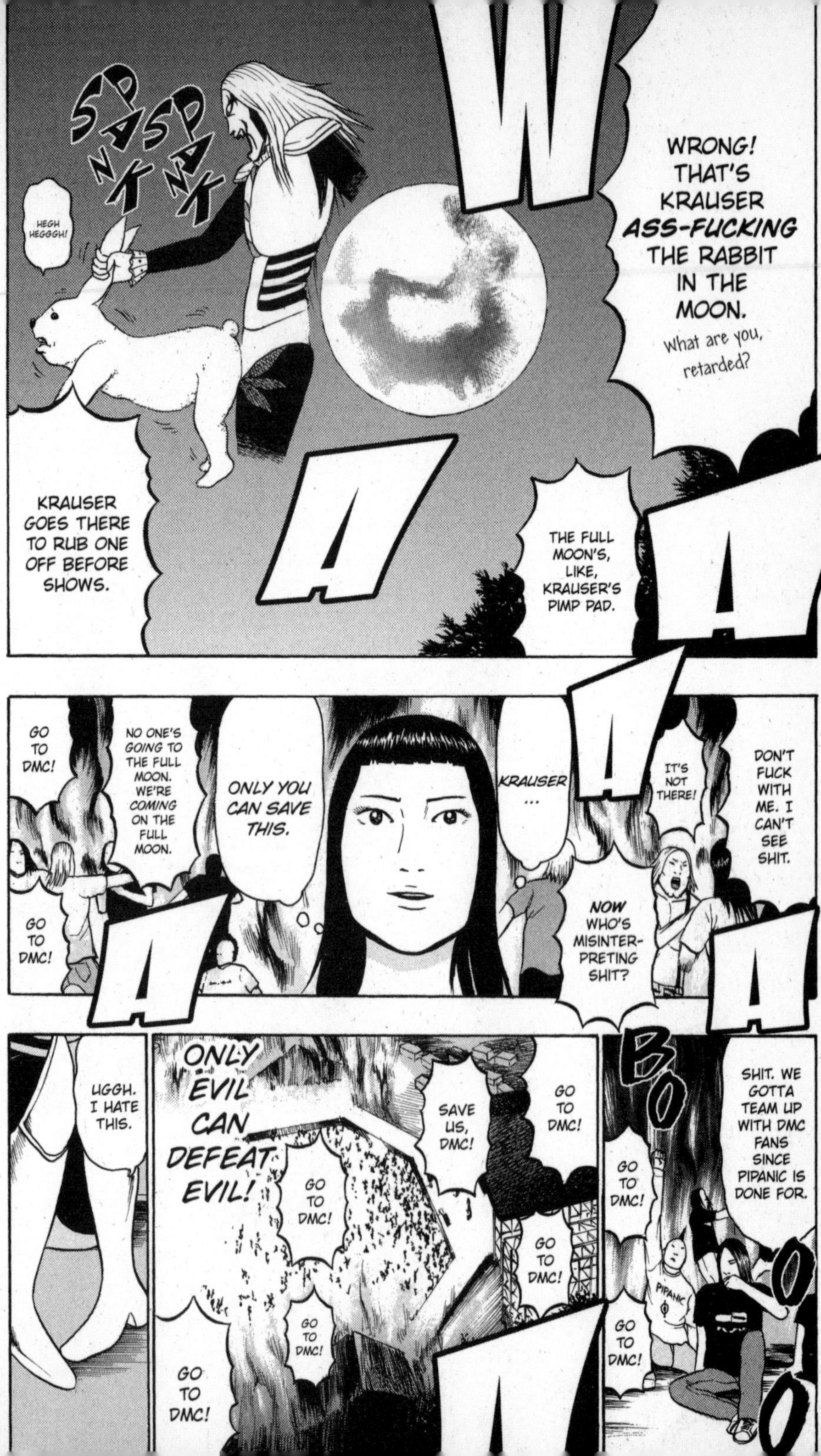
W
WRONG! THAT'S KRAUSER ASS-FUCKING THE RABBIT IN THE MOON.
What are you, retarded?
SPANK SPANK
HEGH HEGGGH!
A
THE FULL MOON'S, LIKE, KRAUSER'S PIMP PAD.
A
KRAUSER GOES THERE TO RUB ONE OFF BEFORE SHOWS.
A
DON'T FUCK WITH ME. I CAN'T SEE SHIT.
IT'S NOT THERE!
NOW WHO'S MISINTERPRETING SHIT?
A
KRAUSER...
ONLY YOU CAN SAVE THIS.
NO ONE'S GOING TO THE FULL MOON. WE'RE COMING ON THE FULL MOON.
GO TO DMC!
GO TO DMC!
A
A
BO
SHIT. WE GOTTA TEAM UP WITH DMC FANS SINCE PIPANIC IS DONE FOR.
GO TO DMC!
PIPANIC
GO TO DMC!
O
O
GO TO DMC!
SAVE US, DMC!
GO TO DMC!
ONLY EVIL CAN DEFEAT EVIL!
GO TO DMC!
GO TO DMC!
GO TO DMC!
UGGH. I HATE THIS.

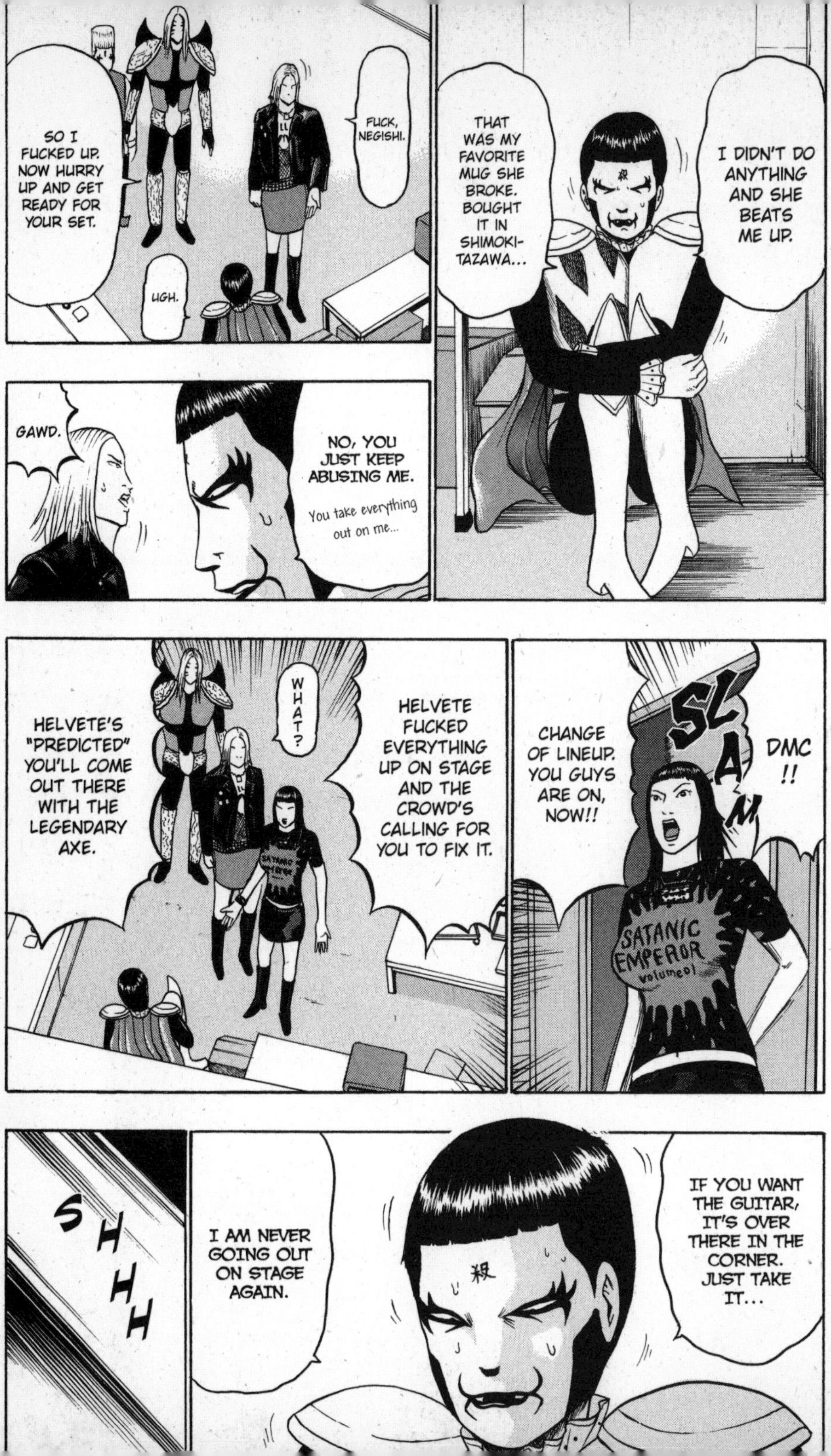
I DIDN'T DO ANYTHING AND SHE BEATS ME UP.
THAT WAS MY FAVORITE MUG SHE BROKE. BOUGHT IT IN SHIMOKI-TAZAWA...
FUCK, NEGISHI.
UGH.
SO I FUCKED UP. NOW HURRY UP AND GET READY FOR YOUR SET.
NO, YOU JUST KEEP ABUSING ME.
You take everything out on me...
GAWD.
DMC!!
SLAM
CHANGE OF LINEUP. YOU GUYS ARE ON, NOW!!
SATANIC EMPEROR volume01
HELVETE FUCKED EVERYTHING UP ON STAGE AND THE CROWD'S CALLING FOR YOU TO FIX IT.
WHAT?
HELVETE'S "PREDICTED" YOU'LL COME OUT THERE WITH THE LEGENDARY AXE.
IF YOU WANT THE GUITAR, IT'S OVER THERE IN THE CORNER. JUST TAKE IT...
I AM NEVER GOING OUT ON STAGE AGAIN.
SHHH

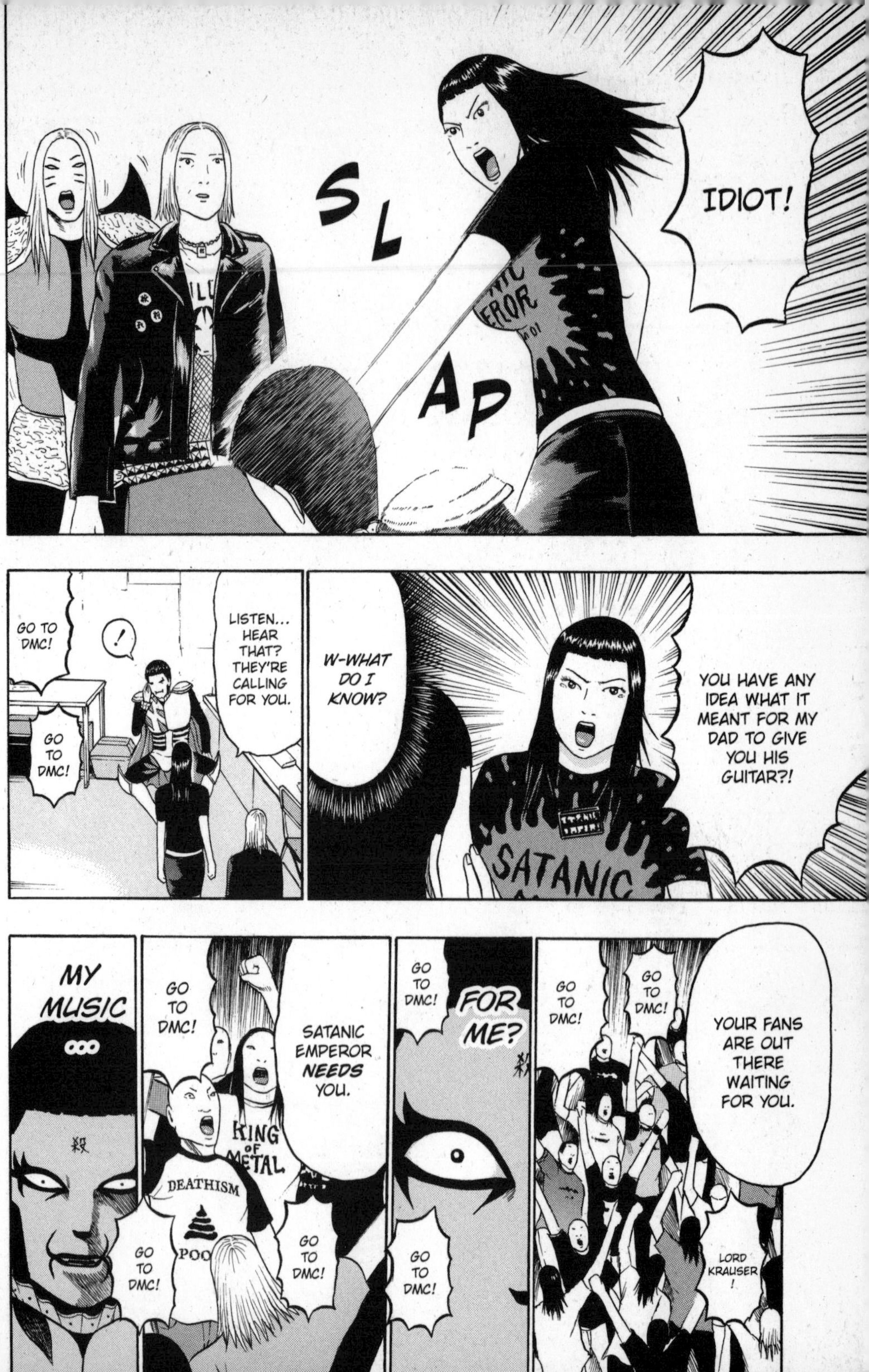
IDIOT!
SLAP
YOU HAVE ANY IDEA WHAT IT MEANT FOR MY DAD TO GIVE YOU HIS GUITAR?!
SATANIC
W-WHAT DO I KNOW?
LISTEN... HEAR THAT? THEY'RE CALLING FOR YOU.
!
GO TO DMC!
GO TO DMC!
YOUR FANS ARE OUT THERE WAITING FOR YOU.
GO TO DMC!
GO TO DMC!
LORD KRAUSER!
FOR ME?
GO TO DMC!
GO TO DMC!
SATANIC EMPEROR NEEDS YOU.
GO TO DMC!
KING OF METAL
DEATHISM
POO
GO TO DMC!
GO TO DMC!
MY MUSIC...

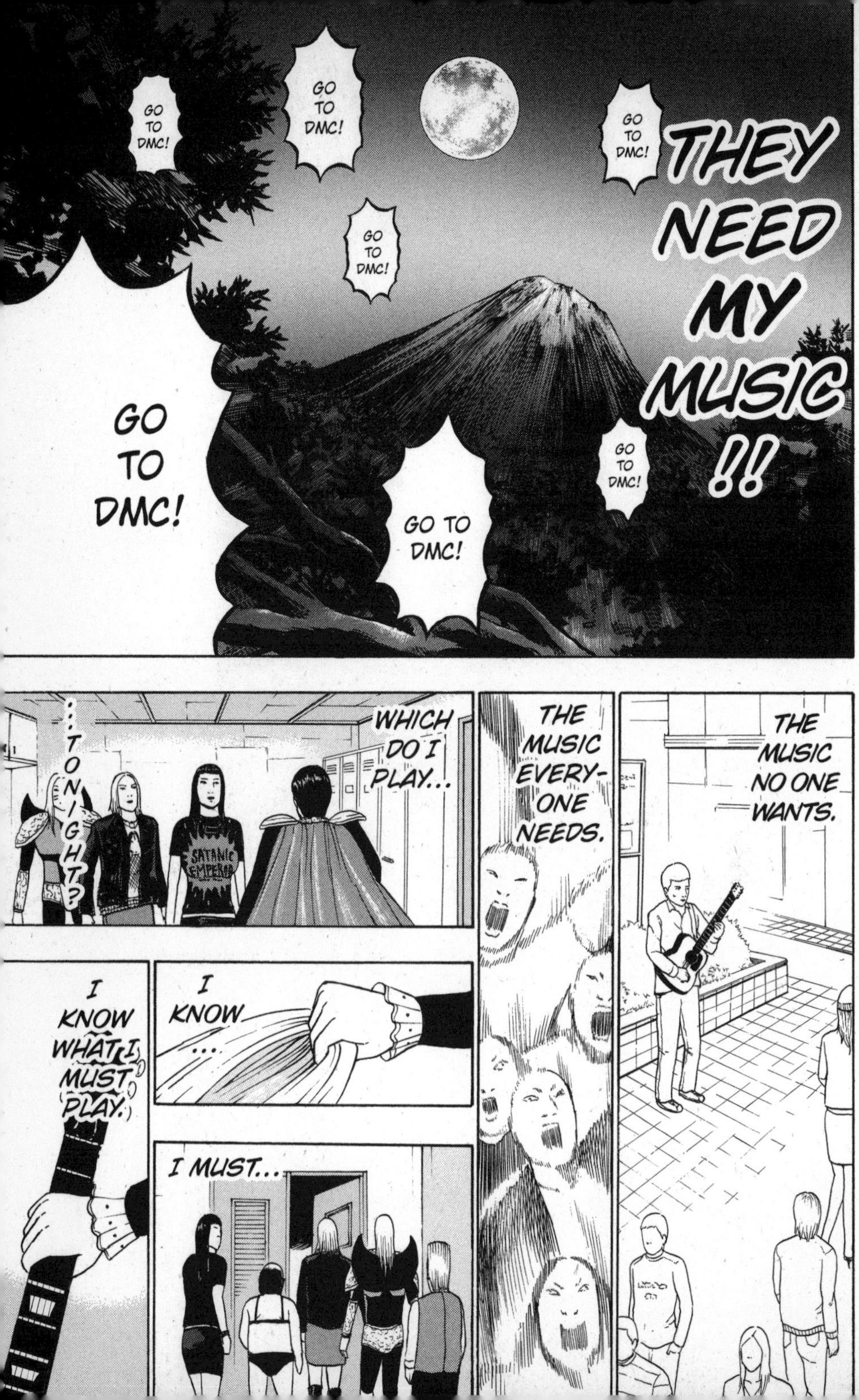
GO TO DMC!
THEY NEED MY MUSIC!!
GO TO DMC!
GO TO DMC!
GO TO DMC!
GO TO DMC!
GO TO DMC!
GO TO DMC!
THE MUSIC NO ONE WANTS.
THE MUSIC EVERYONE NEEDS.
WHICH DO I PLAY...
...TONIGHT?
I KNOW...
I MUST...
I KNOW WHAT I MUST PLAY.

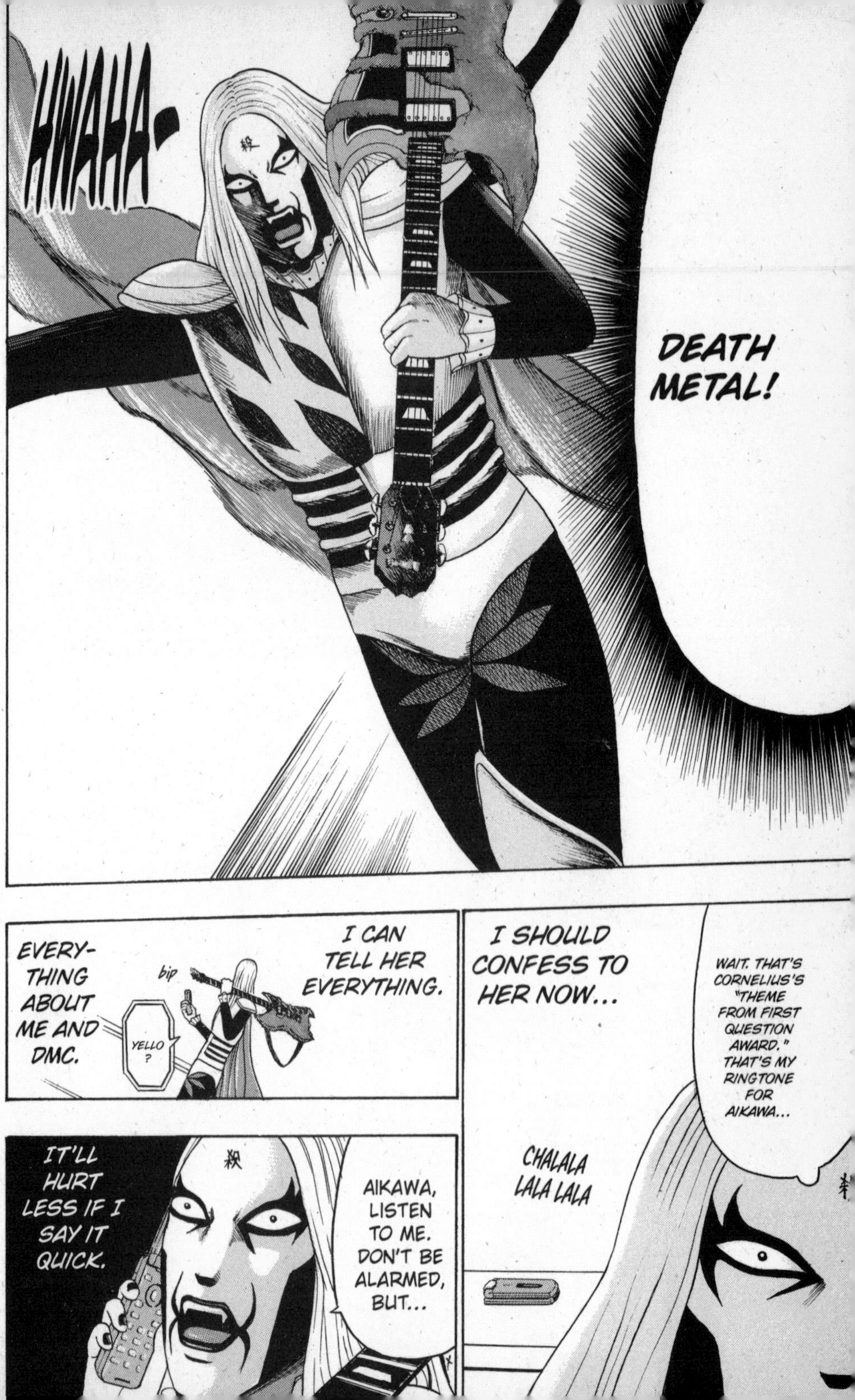
HWAHA-
DEATH METAL!
I SHOULD CONFESS TO HER NOW...
WAIT. THAT'S CORNELIUS'S "THEME FROM FIRST QUESTION AWARD." THAT'S MY RINGTONE FOR AIKAWA...
CHALALA LALA LALA
I CAN TELL HER EVERYTHING.
EVERY-THING ABOUT ME AND DMC.
bip
YELLO?
AIKAWA, LISTEN TO ME. DON'T BE ALARMED, BUT...
IT'LL HURT LESS IF I SAY IT QUICK.

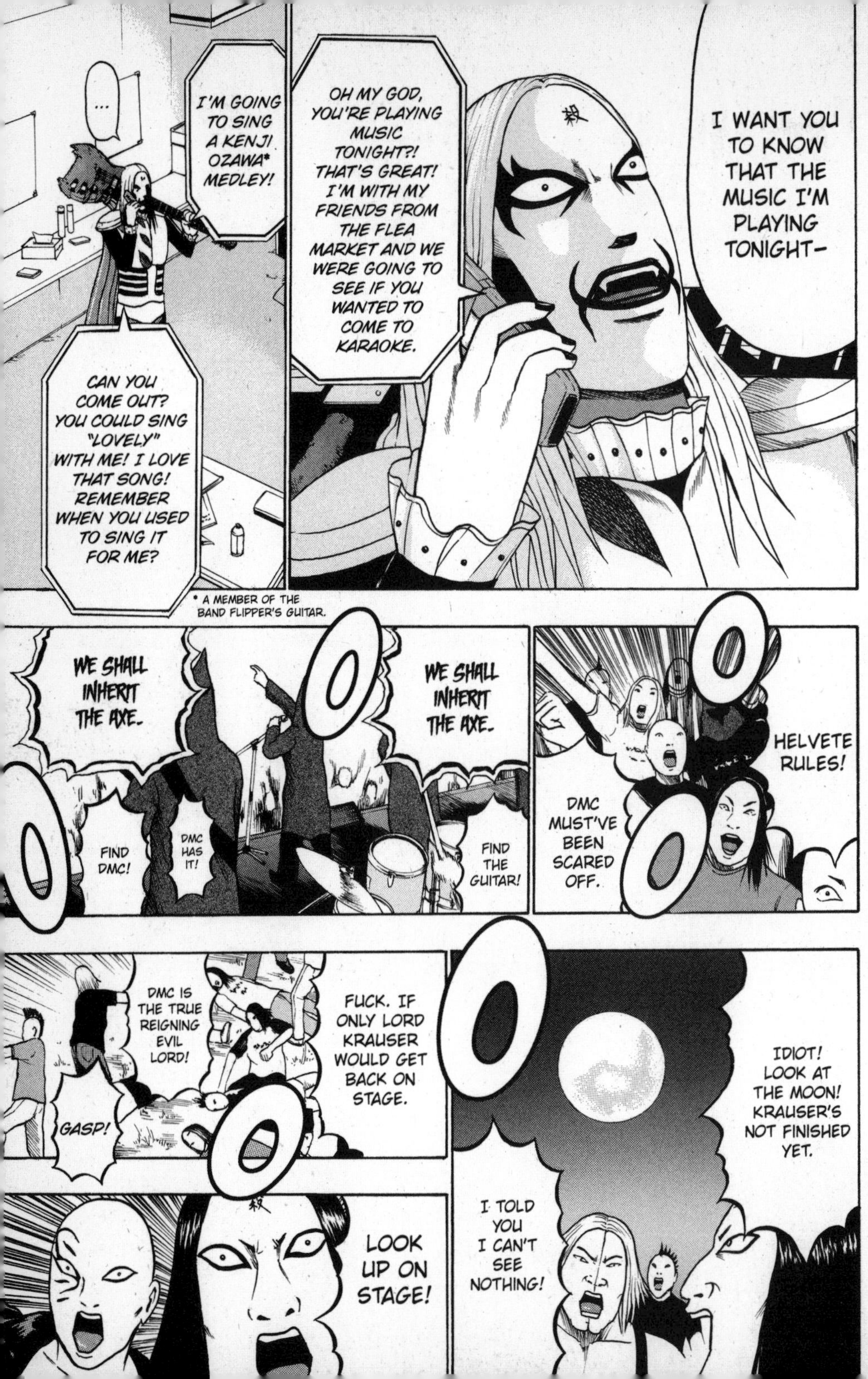
I WANT YOU TO KNOW THAT THE MUSIC I'M PLAYING TONIGHT-
OH MY GOD, YOU'RE PLAYING MUSIC TONIGHT?! THAT'S GREAT! I'M WITH MY FRIENDS FROM THE FLEA MARKET AND WE WERE GOING TO SEE IF YOU WANTED TO COME TO KARAOKE.
I'M GOING TO SING A KENJI OZAWA* MEDLEY!
...
CAN YOU COME OUT? YOU COULD SING "LOVELY" WITH ME! I LOVE THAT SONG! REMEMBER WHEN YOU USED TO SING IT FOR ME?
HELVETE RULES!
DMC MUST'VE BEEN SCARED OFF.
WE SHALL INHERIT THE AXE.
FIND THE GUITAR!
WE SHALL INHERIT THE AXE.
DMC HAS IT!
FIND DMC!
IDIOT! LOOK AT THE MOON! KRAUSER'S NOT FINISHED YET.
I TOLD YOU I CAN'T SEE NOTHING!
FUCK. IF ONLY LORD KRAUSER WOULD GET BACK ON STAGE.
DMC IS THE TRUE REIGNING EVIL LORD!
GASP!
LOOK UP ON STAGE!

* A MEMBER OF THE BAND FLIPPER'S GUITAR.

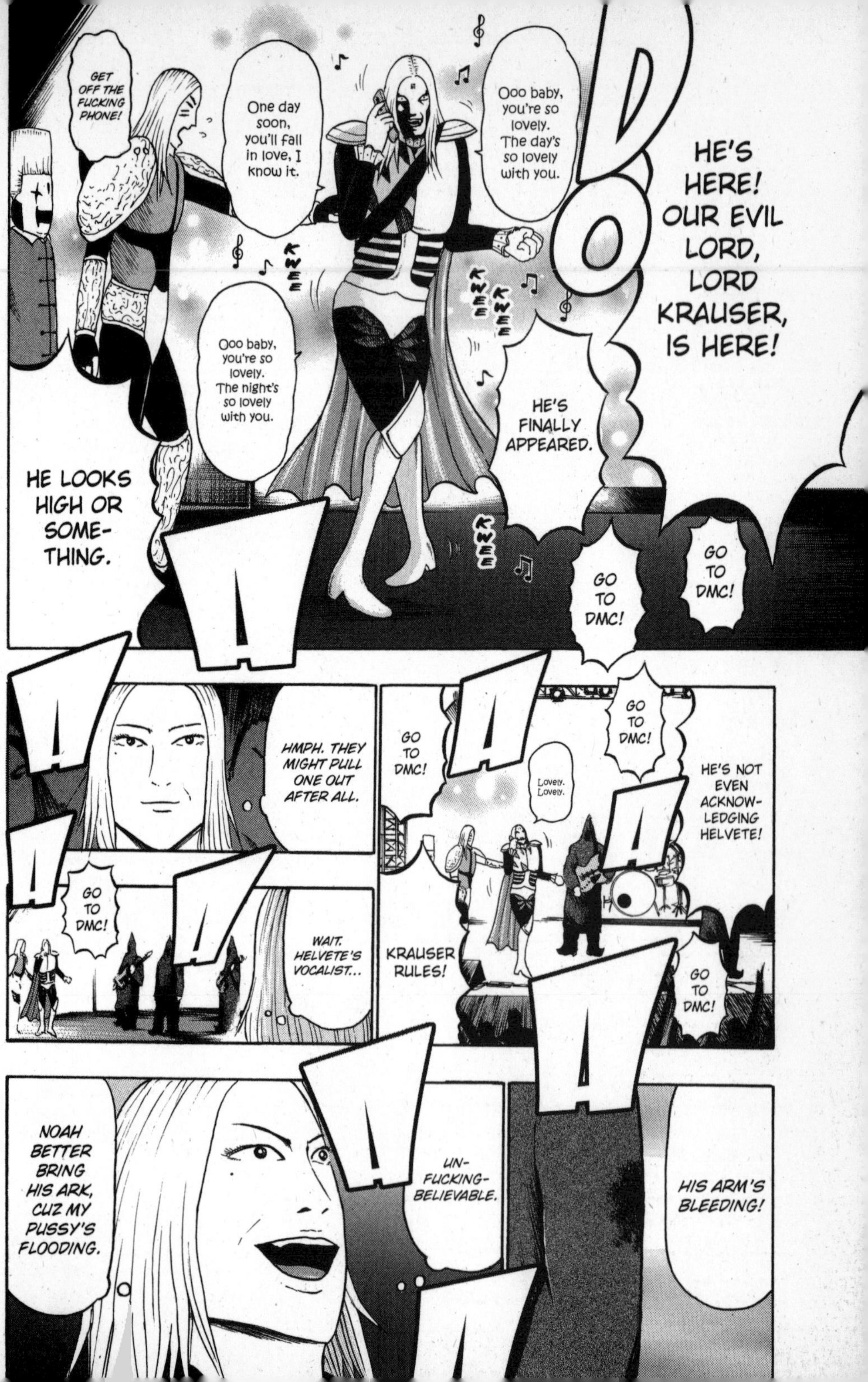
DO
HE'S HERE! OUR EVIL LORD, LORD KRAUSER, IS HERE!
Ooo baby, you're so lovely. The day's so lovely with you.
One day soon, you'll fall in love, I know it.
GET OFF THE FUCKING PHONE!
KWEE
KWEE
KWEE
HE'S FINALLY APPEARED.
Ooo baby, you're so lovely. The night's so lovely with you.
KWEE
GO TO DMC!
GO TO DMC!
HE LOOKS HIGH OR SOME-THING.
GO TO DMC!
HE'S NOT EVEN ACKNOW-LEDGING HELVETE!
GO TO DMC!
Lovely. Lovely.
KRAUSER RULES!
GO TO DMC!
HMPH. THEY MIGHT PULL ONE OUT AFTER ALL.
WAIT. HELVETE'S VOCALIST...
GO TO DMC!
HIS ARM'S BLEEDING!
UN-FUCKING-BELIEVABLE.
NOAH BETTER BRING HIS ARK, CUZ MY PUSSY'S FLOODING.

DMC LEXICON

♥ PROPHECY

A declaration of things to pass, before they occur. These events can vary according to interpretation. Prophecies should not be confused with "Ponzi schemes," in which someone says you'll make lots of money by bringing five of your close friends in on a money-making scheme and then each of them brings five people.

Usage: Son, you're going to go bald one day. I can already see it. (Prophecy of the Father, Verse 3)

デトロイト・メタル・シティ

Detroit Metal City

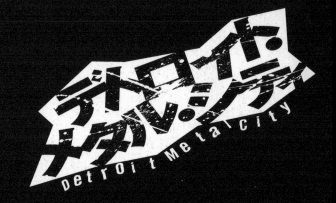

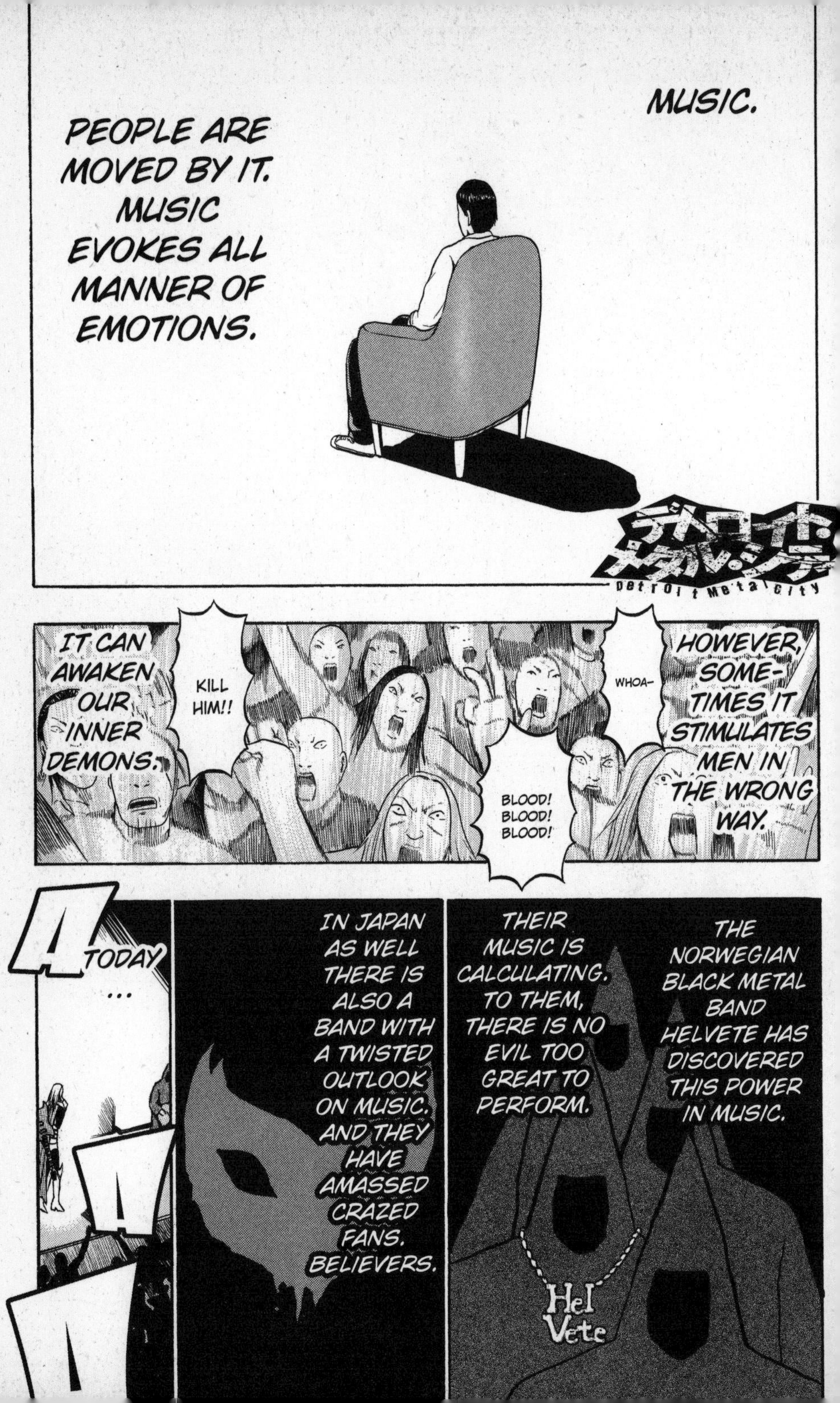
MUSIC.
PEOPLE ARE MOVED BY IT. MUSIC EVOKES ALL MANNER OF EMOTIONS.
Detroit Metal City
HOWEVER, SOME-TIMES IT STIMULATES MEN IN THE WRONG WAY.
WHOA-
BLOOD! BLOOD! BLOOD!
KILL HIM!!
IT CAN AWAKEN OUR INNER DEMONS.
THE NORWEGIAN BLACK METAL BAND HELVETE HAS DISCOVERED THIS POWER IN MUSIC.
THEIR MUSIC IS CALCULATING. TO THEM, THERE IS NO EVIL TOO GREAT TO PERFORM.
Hel Vete
IN JAPAN AS WELL THERE IS ALSO A BAND WITH A TWISTED OUTLOOK ON MUSIC. AND THEY HAVE AMASSED CRAZED FANS. BELIEVERS.
A
TODAY ...
A
A

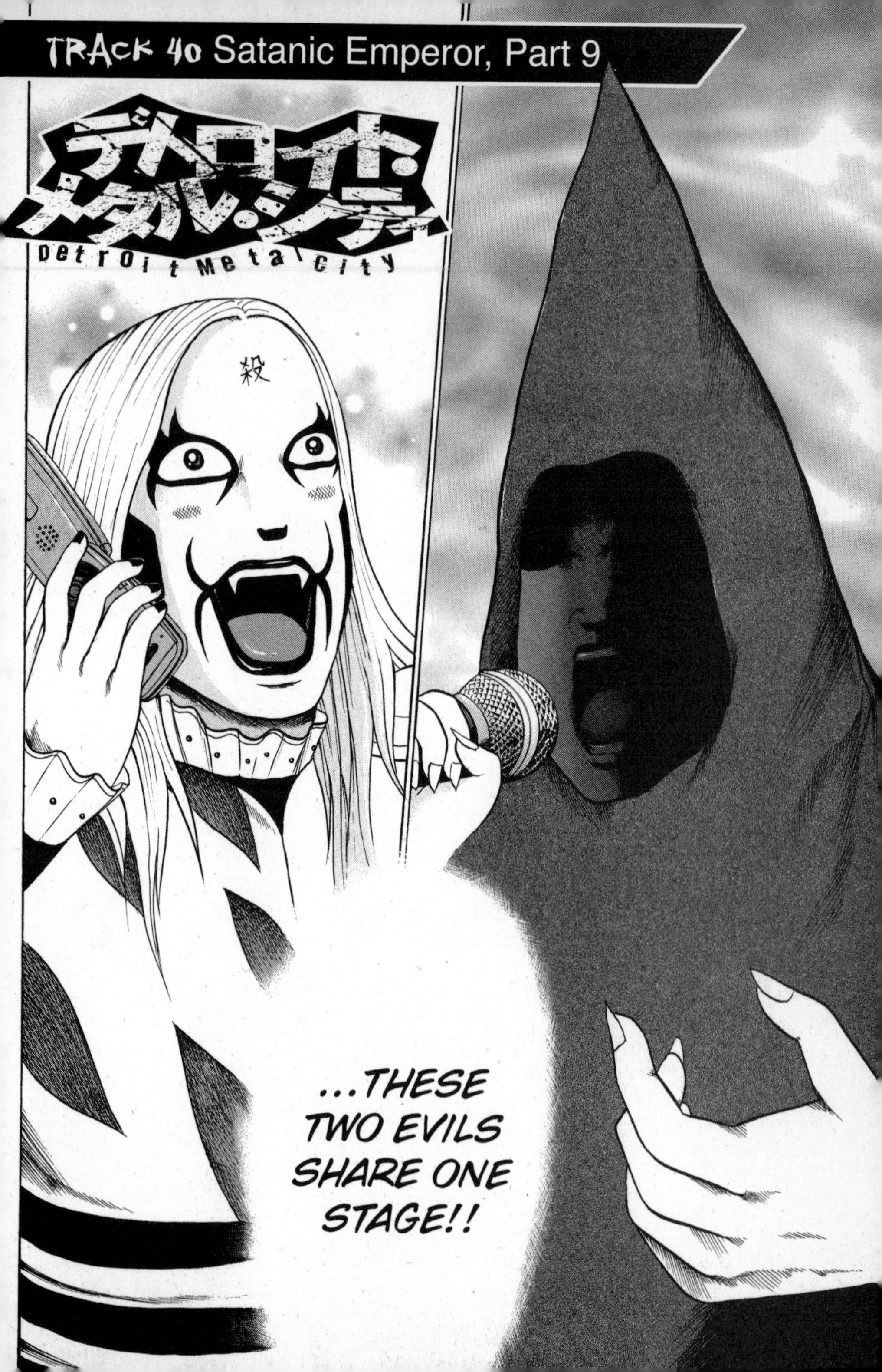
TRACK 40 Satanic Emperor, Part 9
Detroit Metal City
殺
...THESE TWO EVILS SHARE ONE STAGE!!

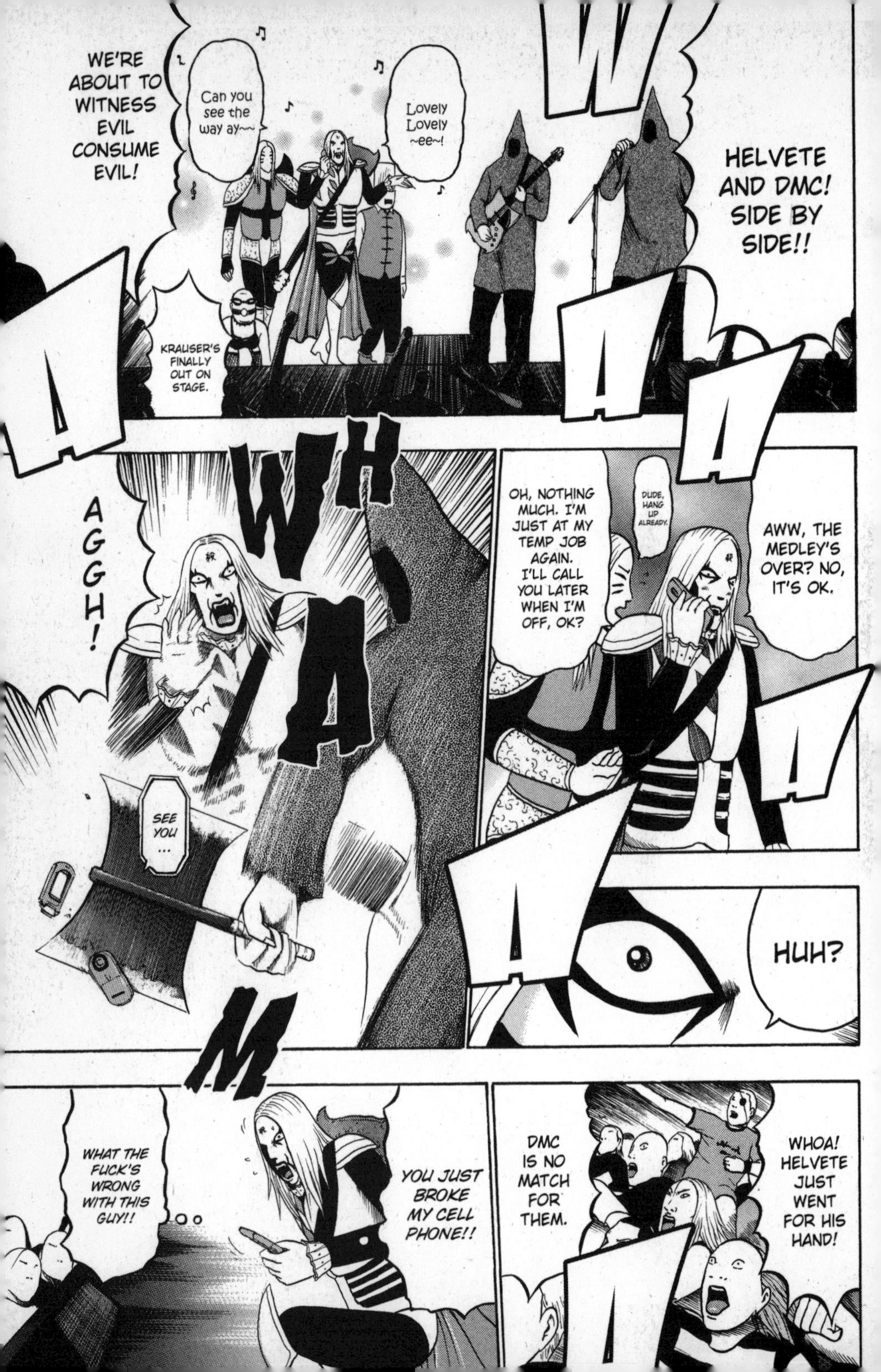
HELVETE AND DMC! SIDE BY SIDE!!
Lovely Lovely ~ee~!
Can you see the way ay~~
WE'RE ABOUT TO WITNESS EVIL CONSUME EVIL!
KRAUSER'S FINALLY OUT ON STAGE.
AWW, THE MEDLEY'S OVER? NO, IT'S OK.
DUDE, HANG UP ALREADY.
OH, NOTHING MUCH. I'M JUST AT MY TEMP JOB AGAIN. I'LL CALL YOU LATER WHEN I'M OFF, OK?
HUH?
AGGH!
WHAM
SEE YOU ...
WHOA! HELVETE JUST WENT FOR HIS HAND!
DMC IS NO MATCH FOR THEM.
YOU JUST BROKE MY CELL PHONE!!
WHAT THE FUCK'S WRONG WITH THIS GUY!!

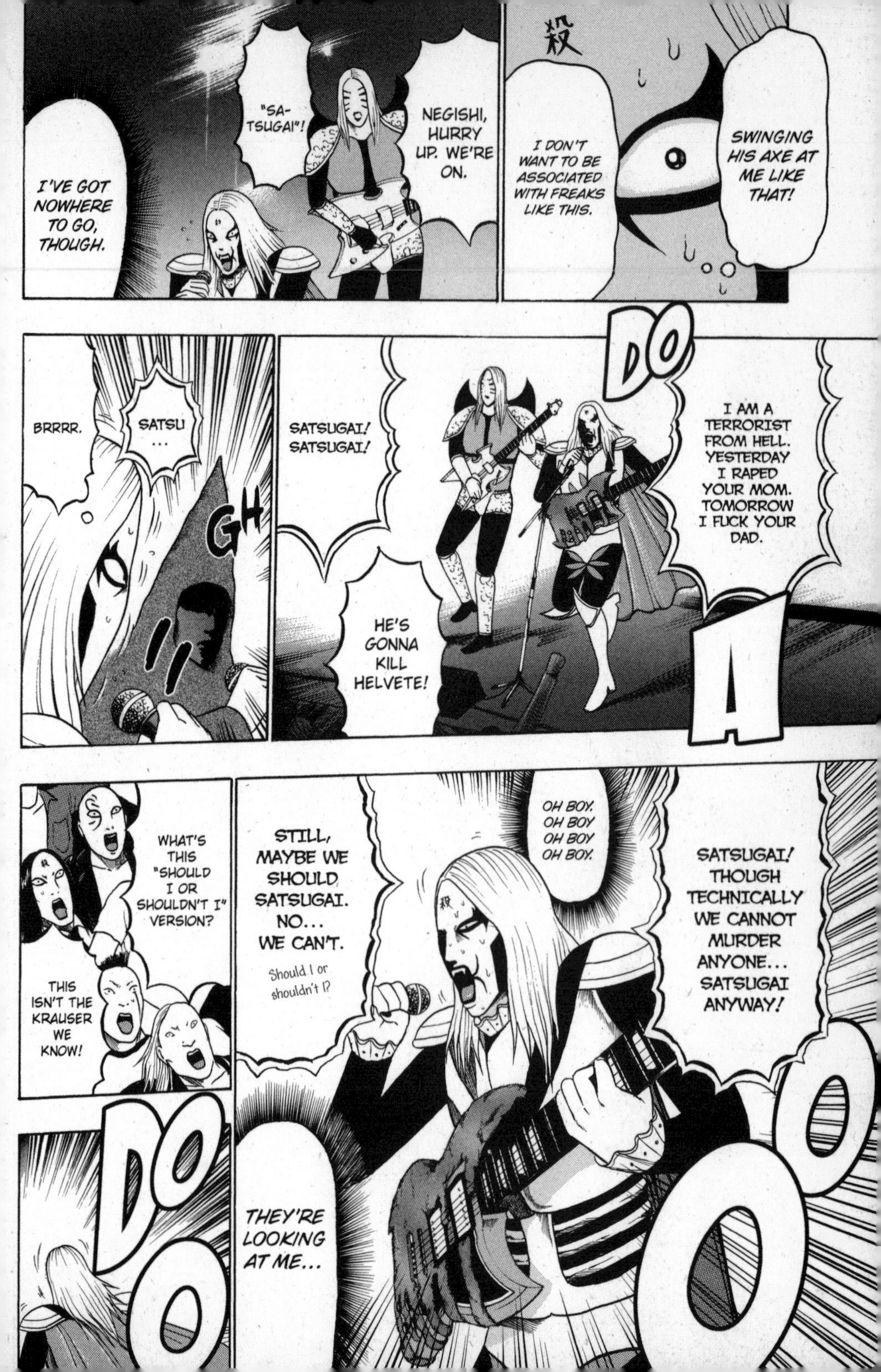
殺
SWINGING HIS AXE AT ME LIKE THAT!
I DON'T WANT TO BE ASSOCIATED WITH FREAKS LIKE THIS.
NEGISHI, HURRY UP. WE'RE ON.
"SA-TSUGAI"!
I'VE GOT NOWHERE TO GO, THOUGH.
DO
I AM A TERRORIST FROM HELL. YESTERDAY I RAPED YOUR MOM. TOMORROW I FUCK YOUR DAD.
SATSUGAI! SATSUGAI!
HE'S GONNA KILL HELVETE!
A
SATSU...
BRRRR.
GH
SATSUGAI! THOUGH TECHNICALLY WE CANNOT MURDER ANYONE... SATSUGAI ANYWAY!
OH BOY. OH BOY OH BOY OH BOY.
STILL, MAYBE WE SHOULD SATSUGAI. NO... WE CAN'T.
Should I or shouldn't I?
OOO
THEY'RE LOOKING AT ME...
WHAT'S THIS "SHOULD I OR SHOULDN'T I" VERSION?
THIS ISN'T THE KRAUSER WE KNOW!
DOO

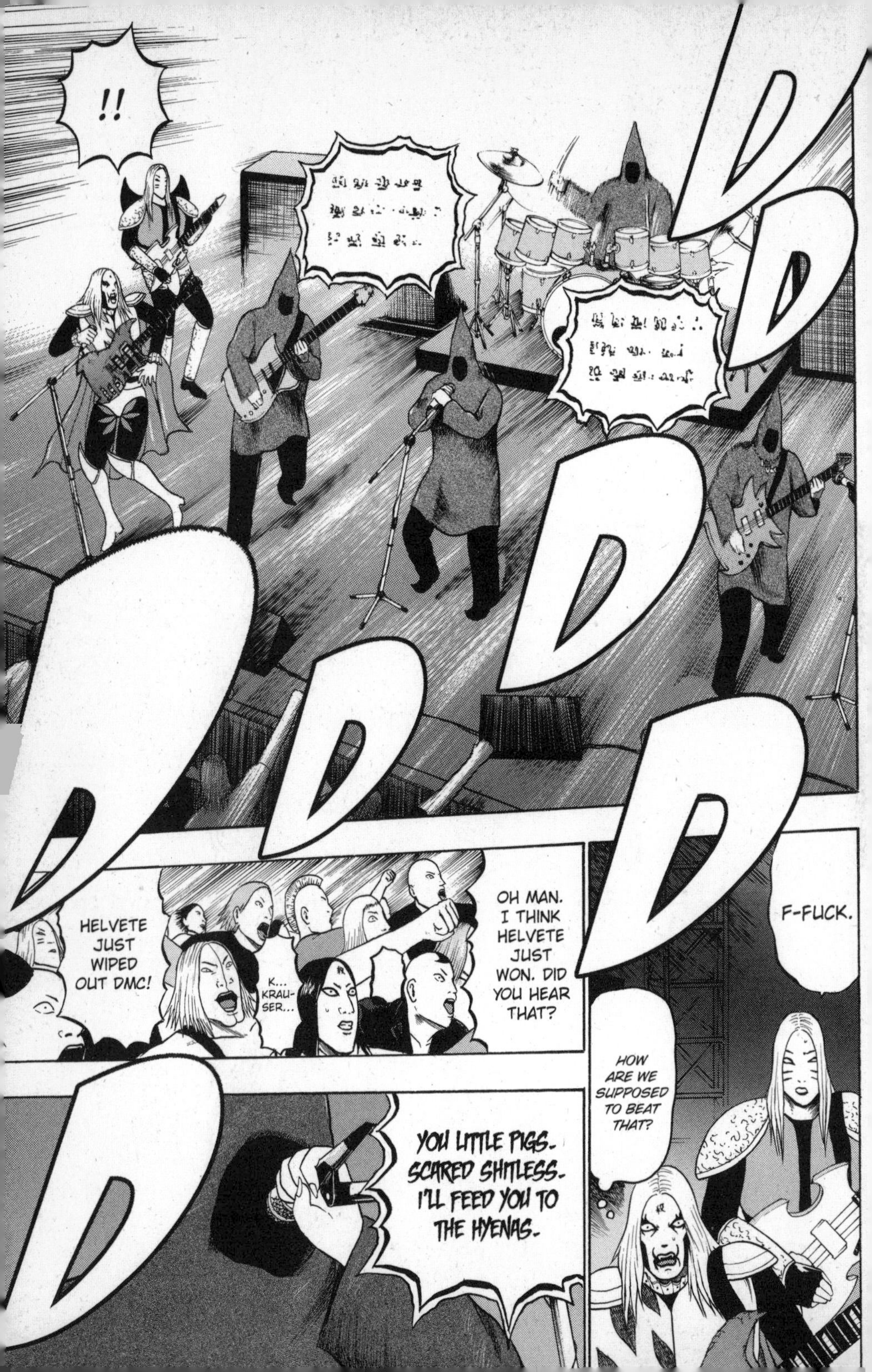
!!
DDDDDDDD
F-FUCK.
OH MAN. I THINK HELVETE JUST WON. DID YOU HEAR THAT?
K... KRAU-SER...
HELVETE JUST WIPED OUT DMC!
HOW ARE WE SUPPOSED TO BEAT THAT?
YOU LITTLE PIGS. SCARED SHITLESS. I'LL FEED YOU TO THE HYENAS.

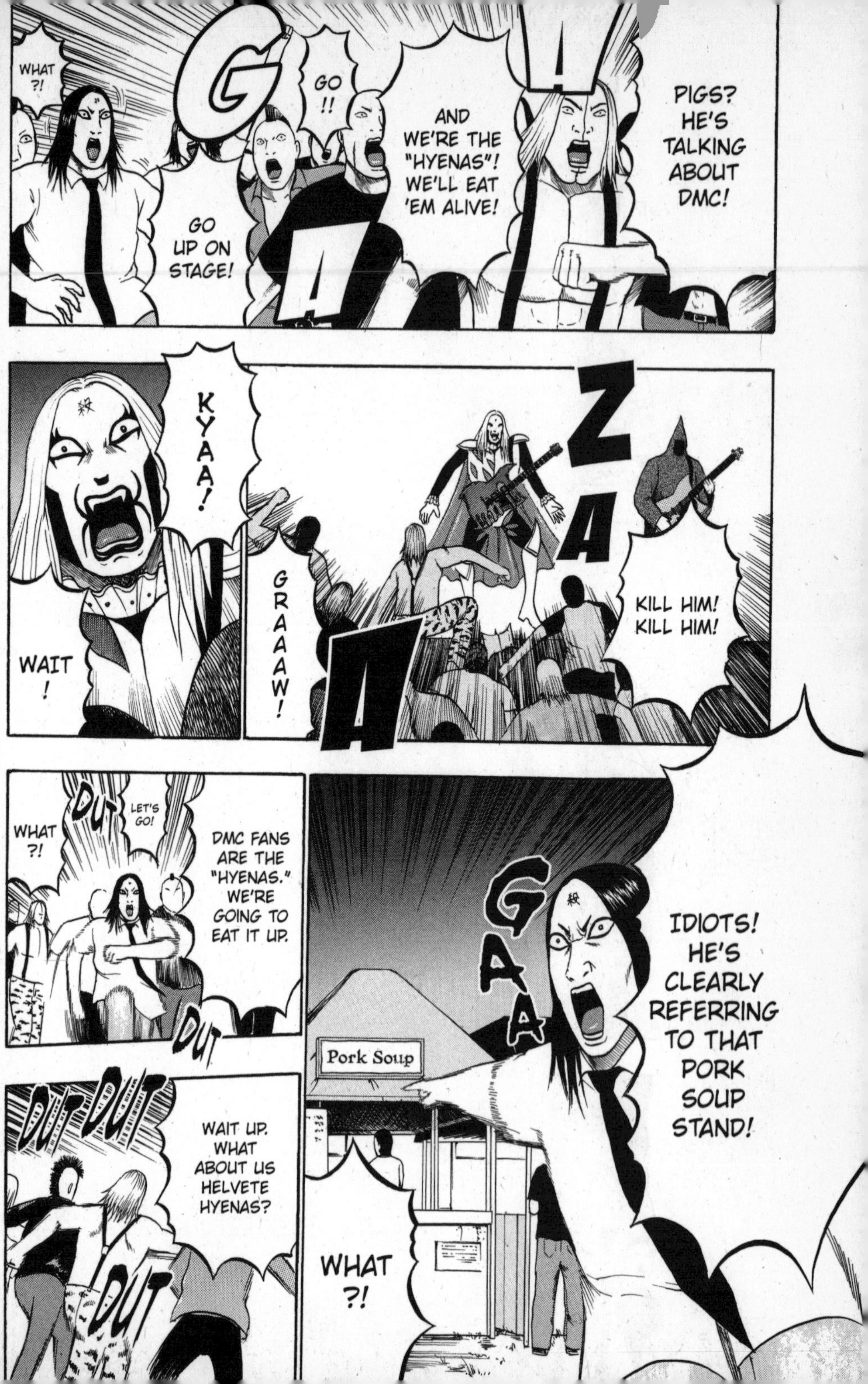
PIGS? HE'S TALKING ABOUT DMC!
GAA
AND WE'RE THE "HYENAS"! WE'LL EAT 'EM ALIVE!
GO !!
GO UP ON STAGE!
WHAT ?!
ZAA
KILL HIM! KILL HIM!
A
GRAAAAW!
KYAA!
WAIT !
GAA
IDIOTS! HE'S CLEARLY REFERRING TO THAT PORK SOUP STAND!
Pork Soup
WHAT ?!
DMC FANS ARE THE "HYENAS." WE'RE GOING TO EAT IT UP.
LET'S GO!
DUT
WHAT ?!
DUT
WAIT UP. WHAT ABOUT US HELVETE HYENAS?
DUT DUT
DUT

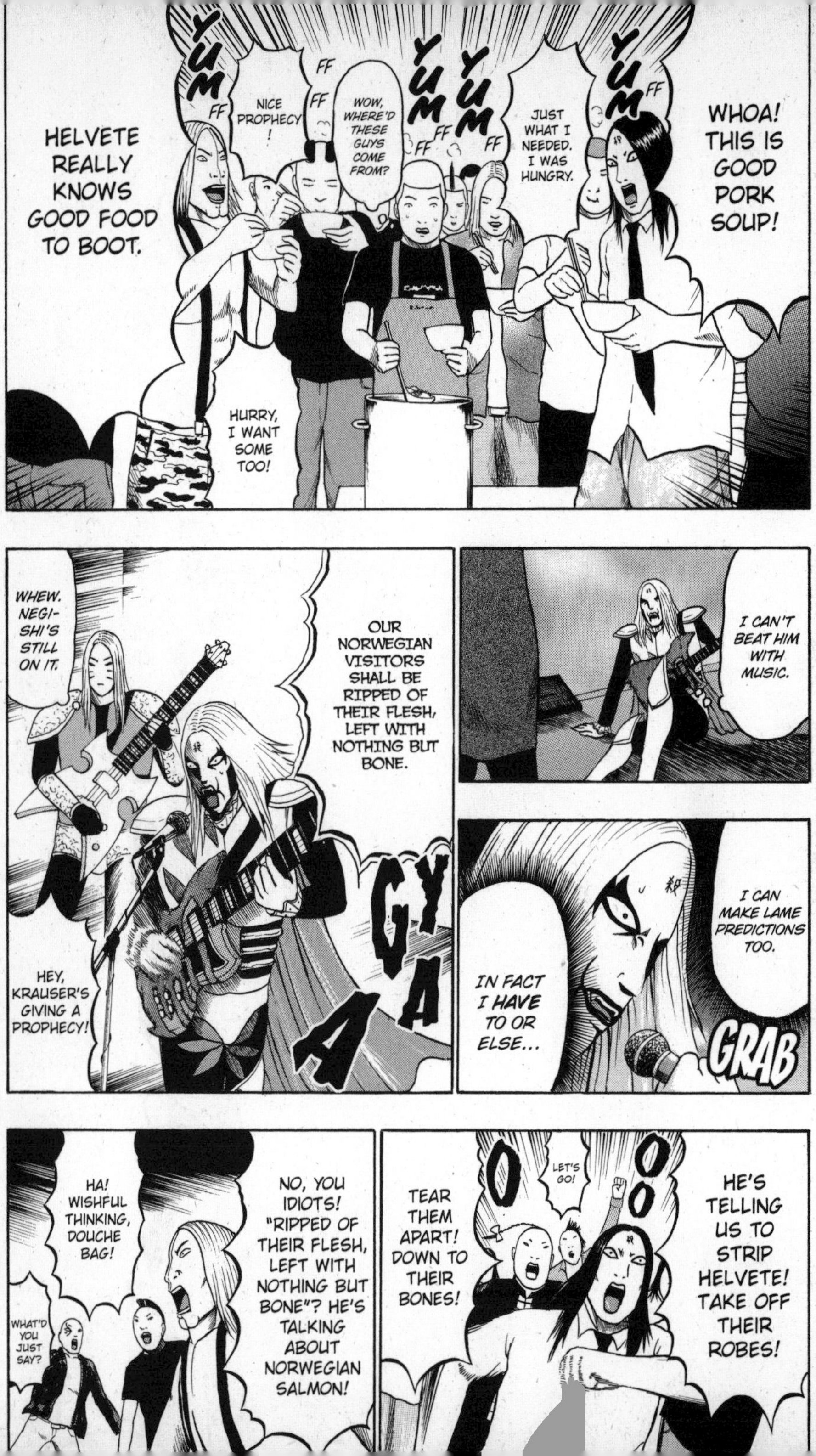
WHOA! THIS IS GOOD PORK SOUP!
YUM
FF
JUST WHAT I NEEDED. I WAS HUNGRY.
YUM
YUM
FF
FF
FF
WOW, WHERE'D THESE GUYS COME FROM?
FF
FF
NICE PROPHECY!
YUM
FF
HELVETE REALLY KNOWS GOOD FOOD TO BOOT.
HURRY, I WANT SOME TOO!
I CAN'T BEAT HIM WITH MUSIC.
I CAN MAKE LAME PREDICTIONS TOO.
IN FACT I HAVE TO OR ELSE...
GRAB
OUR NORWEGIAN VISITORS SHALL BE RIPPED OF THEIR FLESH, LEFT WITH NOTHING BUT BONE.
WHEW. NEGI-SHI'S STILL ON IT.
GYAA
HEY, KRAUSER'S GIVING A PROPHECY!
HE'S TELLING US TO STRIP HELVETE! TAKE OFF THEIR ROBES!
LET'S GO!
TEAR THEM APART! DOWN TO THEIR BONES!
NO, YOU IDIOTS! "RIPPED OF THEIR FLESH, LEFT WITH NOTHING BUT BONE"? HE'S TALKING ABOUT NORWEGIAN SALMON!
HA! WISHFUL THINKING, DOUCHE BAG!
WHAT'D YOU JUST SAY?

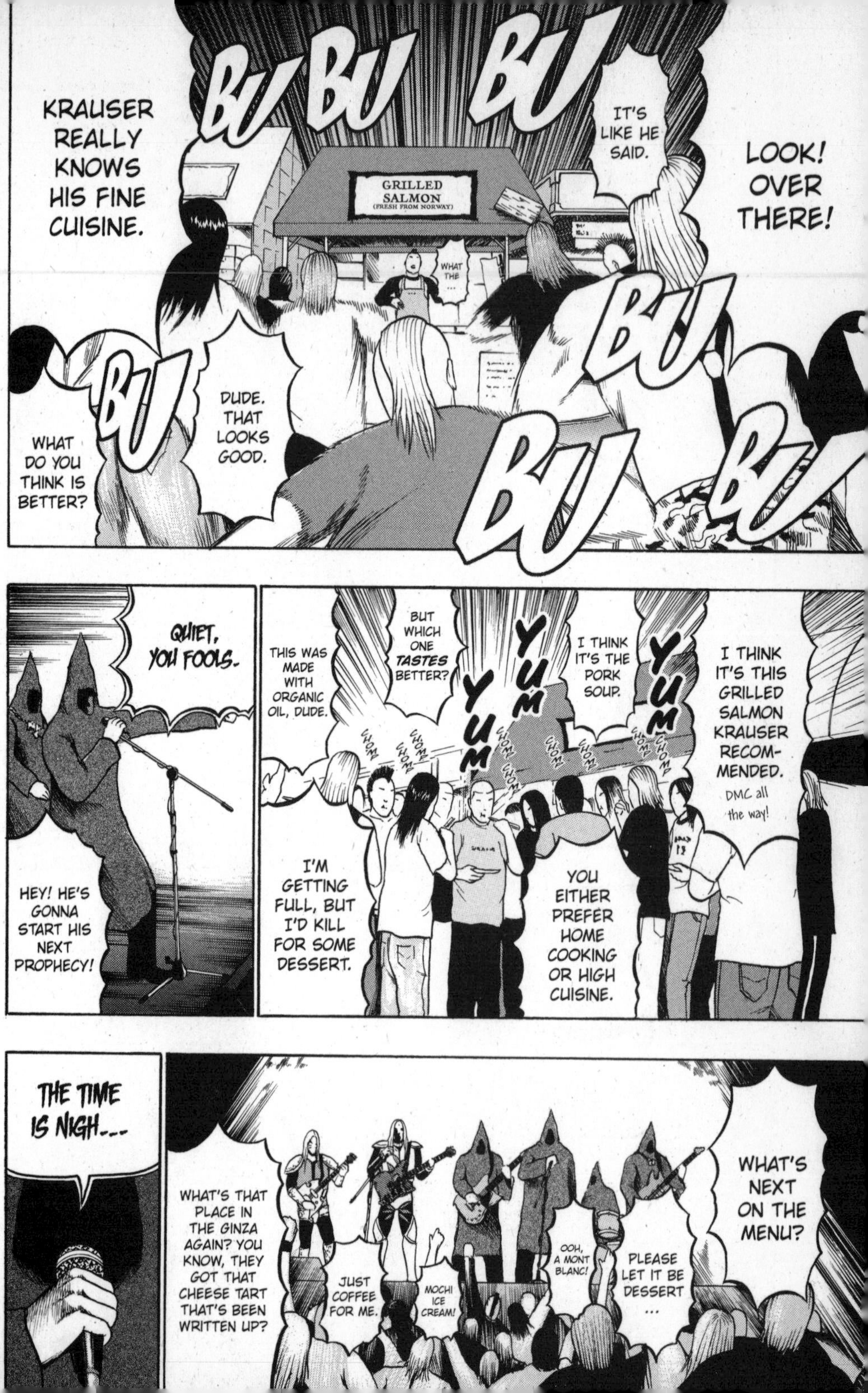
LOOK! OVER THERE!
IT'S LIKE HE SAID.
BU BU BU
GRILLED SALMON (FRESH FROM NORWAY)
WHAT THE ...
KRAUSER REALLY KNOWS HIS FINE CUISINE.
BU BU BU BU
DUDE. THAT LOOKS GOOD.
BU
WHAT DO YOU THINK IS BETTER?
I THINK IT'S THIS GRILLED SALMON KRAUSER RECOMMENDED.
DMC all the way!
YUM YUM
CHOMP CHOMP
I THINK IT'S THE PORK SOUP.
CHOMP CHOMP CHOMP CHOMP
YUM YUM
BUT WHICH ONE *TASTES* BETTER?
THIS WAS MADE WITH ORGANIC OIL, DUDE.
CHOMP CHOMP CHOMP
YOU EITHER PREFER HOME COOKING OR HIGH CUISINE.
I'M GETTING FULL, BUT I'D KILL FOR SOME DESSERT.
QUIET, YOU FOOLS.
HEY! HE'S GONNA START HIS NEXT PROPHECY!
WHAT'S NEXT ON THE MENU?
PLEASE LET IT BE DESSERT ...
OOH, A MONT BLANC!
MOCHI ICE CREAM!
JUST COFFEE FOR ME.
WHAT'S THAT PLACE IN THE GINZA AGAIN? YOU KNOW, THEY GOT THAT CHEESE TART THAT'S BEEN WRITTEN UP?
THE TIME IS NIGH...

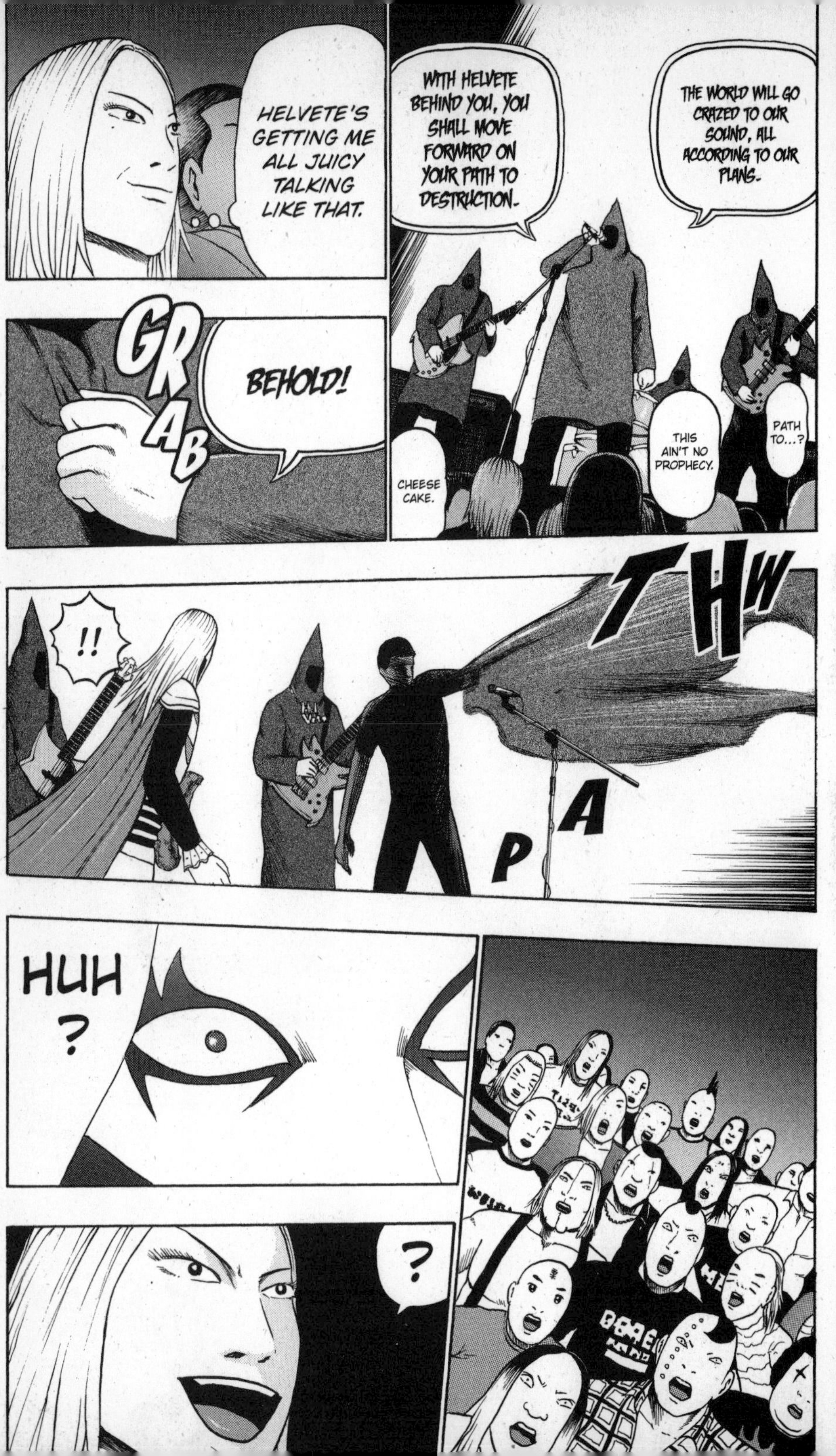
THE WORLD WILL GO CRAZED TO OUR SOUND, ALL ACCORDING TO OUR PLANS.
WITH HELVETE BEHIND YOU, YOU SHALL MOVE FORWARD ON YOUR PATH TO DESTRUCTION.
PATH TO...?
THIS AIN'T NO PROPHECY.
CHEESE CAKE.
HELVETE'S GETTING ME ALL JUICY TALKING LIKE THAT.
BEHOLD!
GRAB
THWAP
!!
HUH?
?

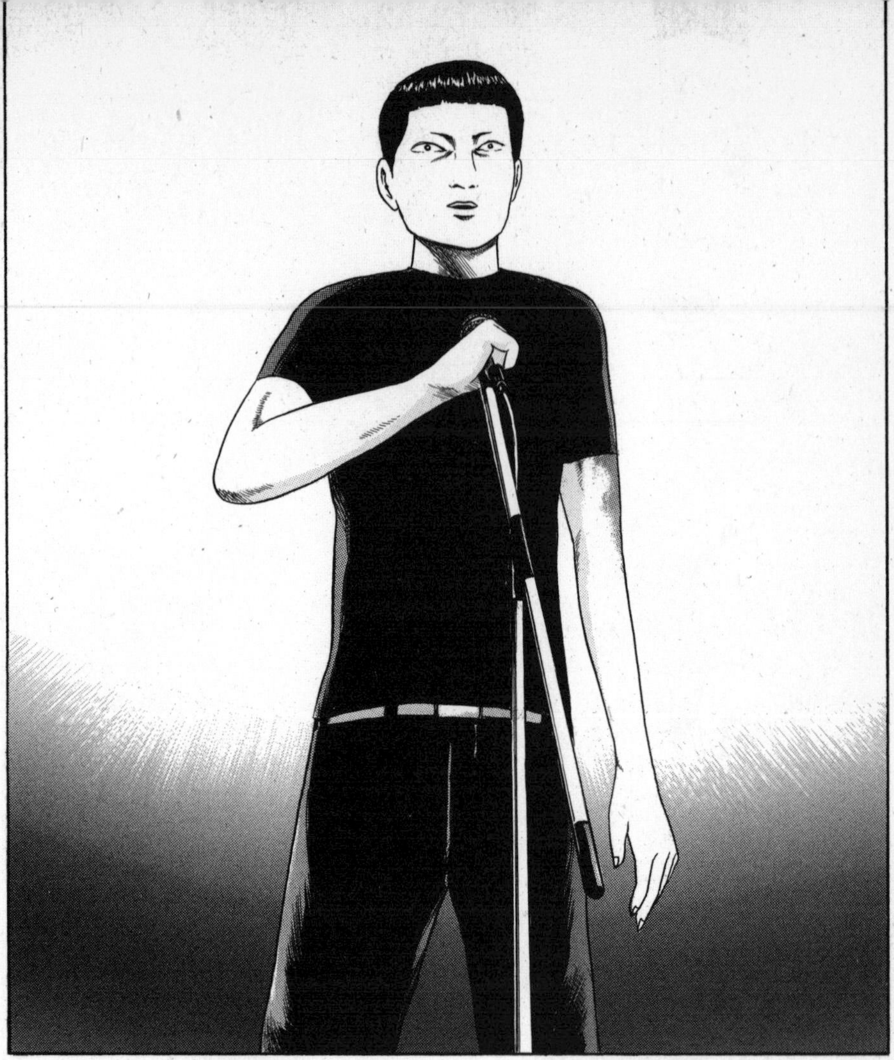

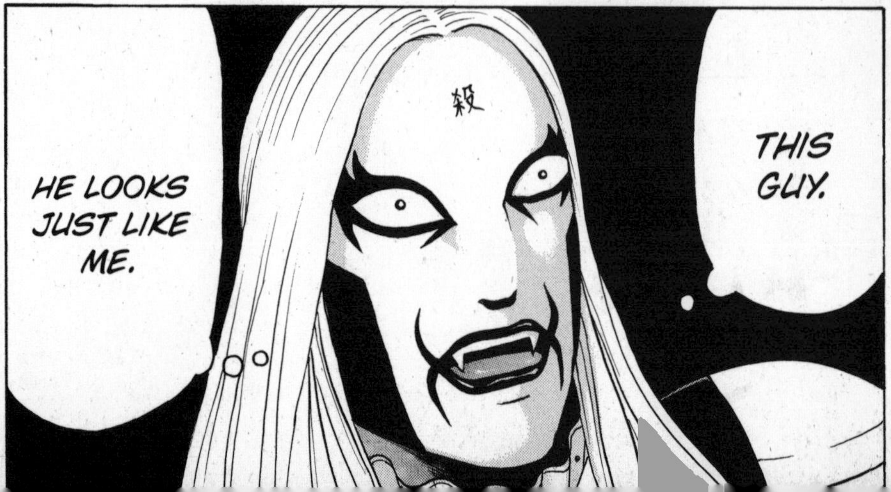
殺
THIS GUY.
HE LOOKS JUST LIKE ME.

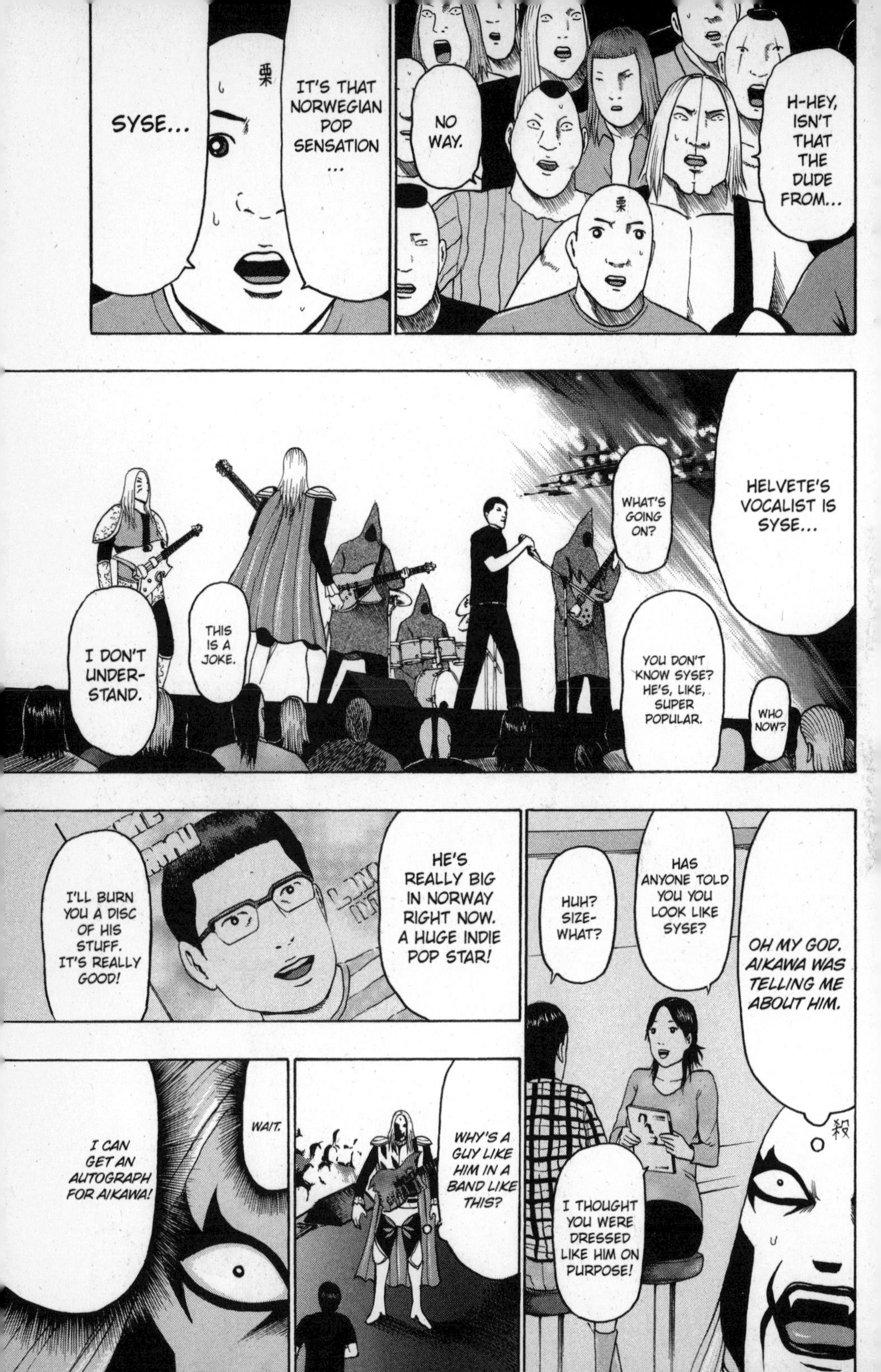
H-HEY, ISN'T THAT THE DUDE FROM...
NO WAY.
IT'S THAT NORWEGIAN POP SENSATION ...
SYSE...
HELVETE'S VOCALIST IS SYSE...
WHAT'S GOING ON?
WHO NOW?
YOU DON'T KNOW SYSE? HE'S, LIKE, SUPER POPULAR.
THIS IS A JOKE.
I DON'T UNDER-STAND.
OH MY GOD. AIKAWA WAS TELLING ME ABOUT HIM.
HAS ANYONE TOLD YOU YOU LOOK LIKE SYSE?
HUH? SIZE-WHAT?
I THOUGHT YOU WERE DRESSED LIKE HIM ON PURPOSE!
HE'S REALLY BIG IN NORWAY RIGHT NOW. A HUGE INDIE POP STAR!
I'LL BURN YOU A DISC OF HIS STUFF. IT'S REALLY GOOD!
WHY'S A GUY LIKE HIM IN A BAND LIKE THIS?
WAIT.
I CAN GET AN AUTOGRAPH FOR AIKAWA!

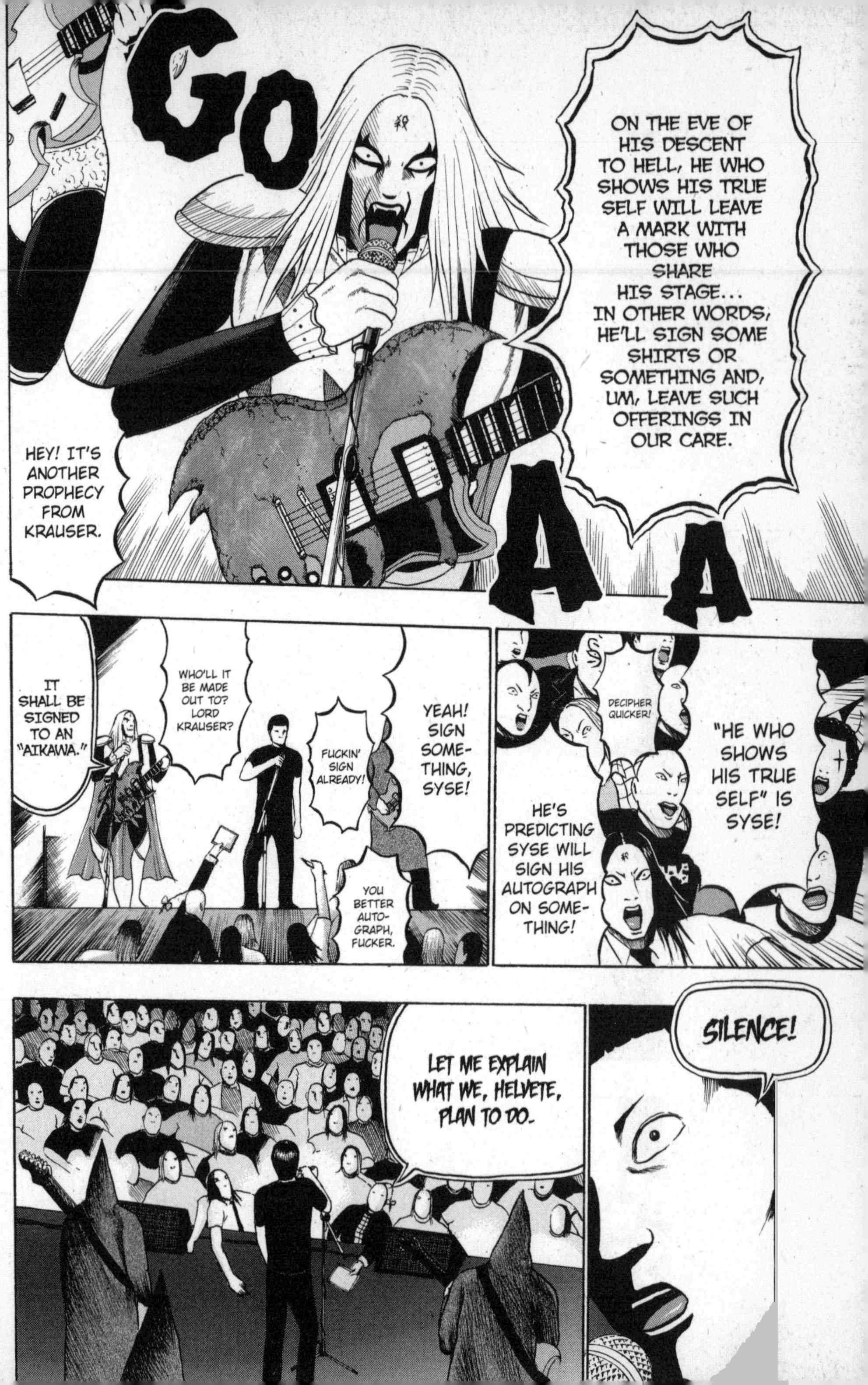
ON THE EVE OF HIS DESCENT TO HELL, HE WHO SHOWS HIS TRUE SELF WILL LEAVE A MARK WITH THOSE WHO SHARE HIS STAGE... IN OTHER WORDS, HE'LL SIGN SOME SHIRTS OR SOMETHING AND, UM, LEAVE SUCH OFFERINGS IN OUR CARE.
GO
A A
HEY! IT'S ANOTHER PROPHECY FROM KRAUSER.
"HE WHO SHOWS HIS TRUE SELF" IS SYSE!
DECIPHER QUICKER!
HE'S PREDICTING SYSE WILL SIGN HIS AUTOGRAPH ON SOMETHING!
YEAH! SIGN SOMETHING, SYSE!
WHO'LL IT BE MADE OUT TO? LORD KRAUSER?
FUCKIN' SIGN ALREADY!
IT SHALL BE SIGNED TO AN "AIKAWA."
YOU BETTER AUTOGRAPH, FUCKER.
SILENCE!
LET ME EXPLAIN WHAT WE, HELVETE, PLAN TO DO.

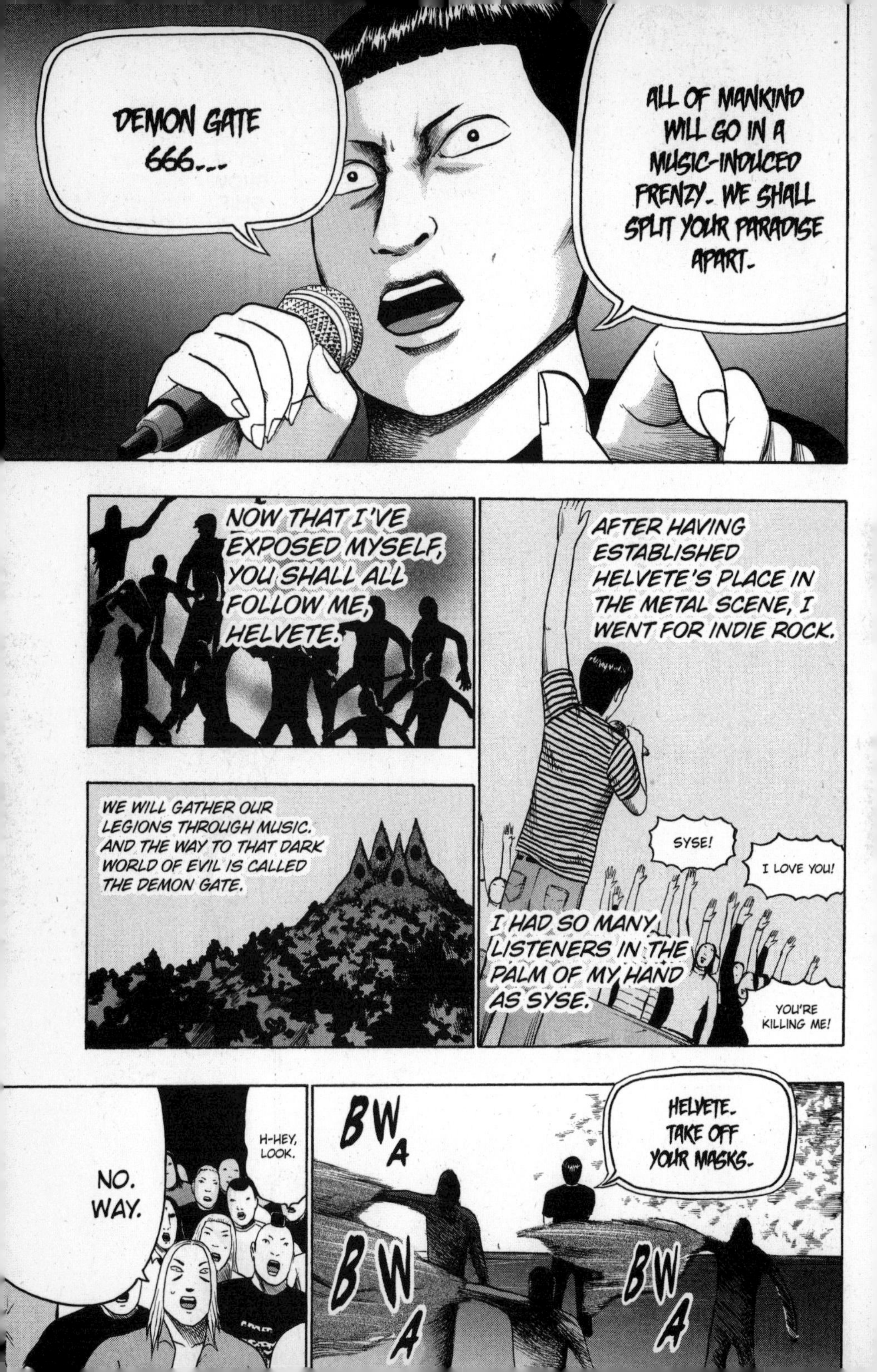
ALL OF MANKIND WILL GO IN A MUSIC-INDUCED FRENZY. WE SHALL SPLIT YOUR PARADISE APART.
DEMON GATE 666...
AFTER HAVING ESTABLISHED HELVETE'S PLACE IN THE METAL SCENE, I WENT FOR INDIE ROCK.
SYSE!
I LOVE YOU!
I HAD SO MANY LISTENERS IN THE PALM OF MY HAND AS SYSE.
YOU'RE KILLING ME!
NOW THAT I'VE EXPOSED MYSELF, YOU SHALL ALL FOLLOW ME, HELVETE.
WE WILL GATHER OUR LEGIONS THROUGH MUSIC. AND THE WAY TO THAT DARK WORLD OF EVIL IS CALLED THE DEMON GATE.
HELVETE. TAKE OFF YOUR MASKS.
BWA
BWA
BWA
H-HEY, LOOK.
NO. WAY.

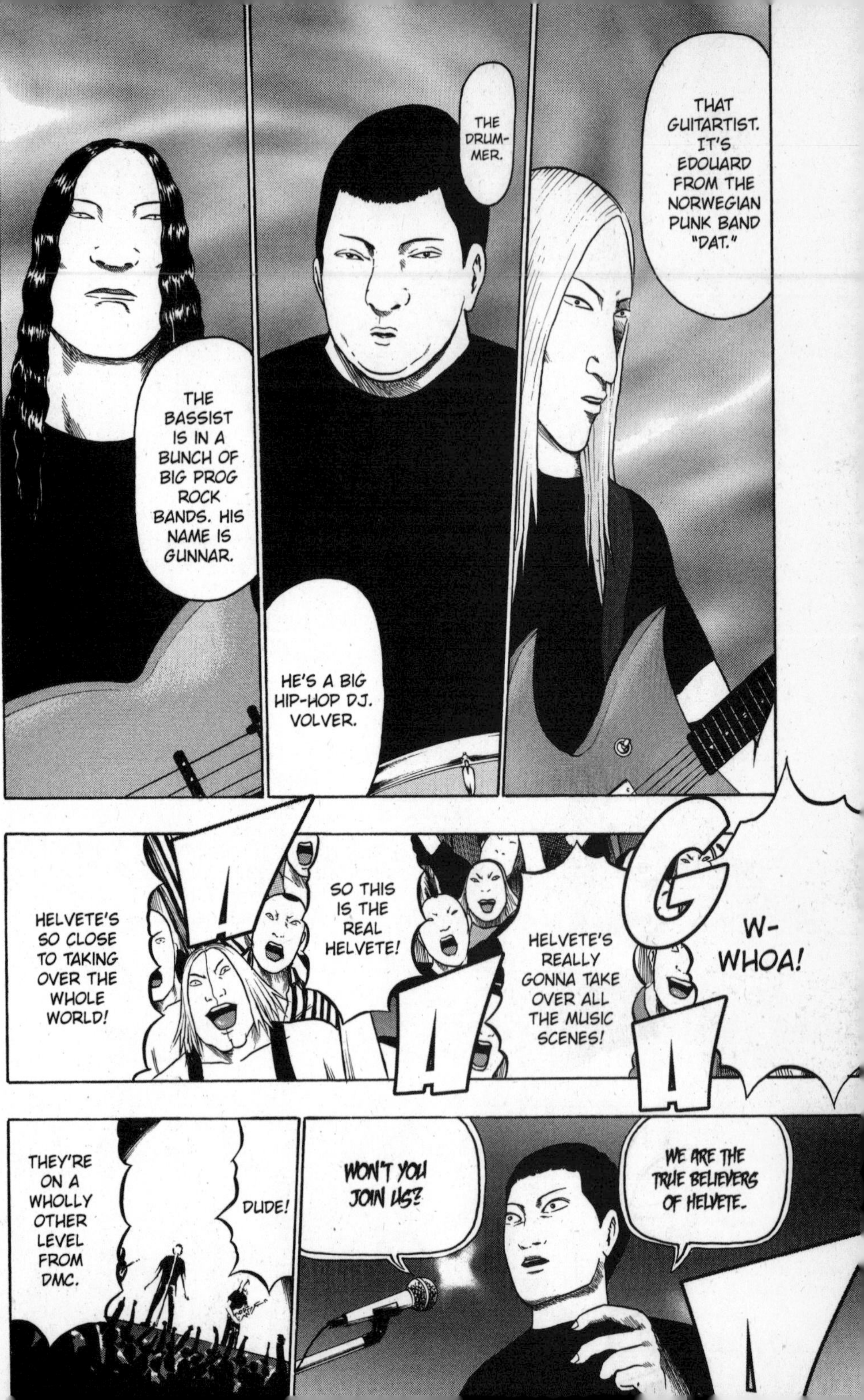
THAT GUITARIST. IT'S EDOUARD FROM THE NORWEGIAN PUNK BAND "DAT."
THE DRUMMER.
HE'S A BIG HIP-HOP DJ. VOLVER.
THE BASSIST IS IN A BUNCH OF BIG PROG ROCK BANDS. HIS NAME IS GUNNAR.
W-WHOA!
GAAA
HELVETE'S REALLY GONNA TAKE OVER ALL THE MUSIC SCENES!
SO THIS IS THE REAL HELVETE!
HELVETE'S SO CLOSE TO TAKING OVER THE WHOLE WORLD!
WE ARE THE TRUE BELIEVERS OF HELVETE.
WON'T YOU JOIN US?
DUDE!
THEY'RE ON A WHOLLY OTHER LEVEL FROM DMC.

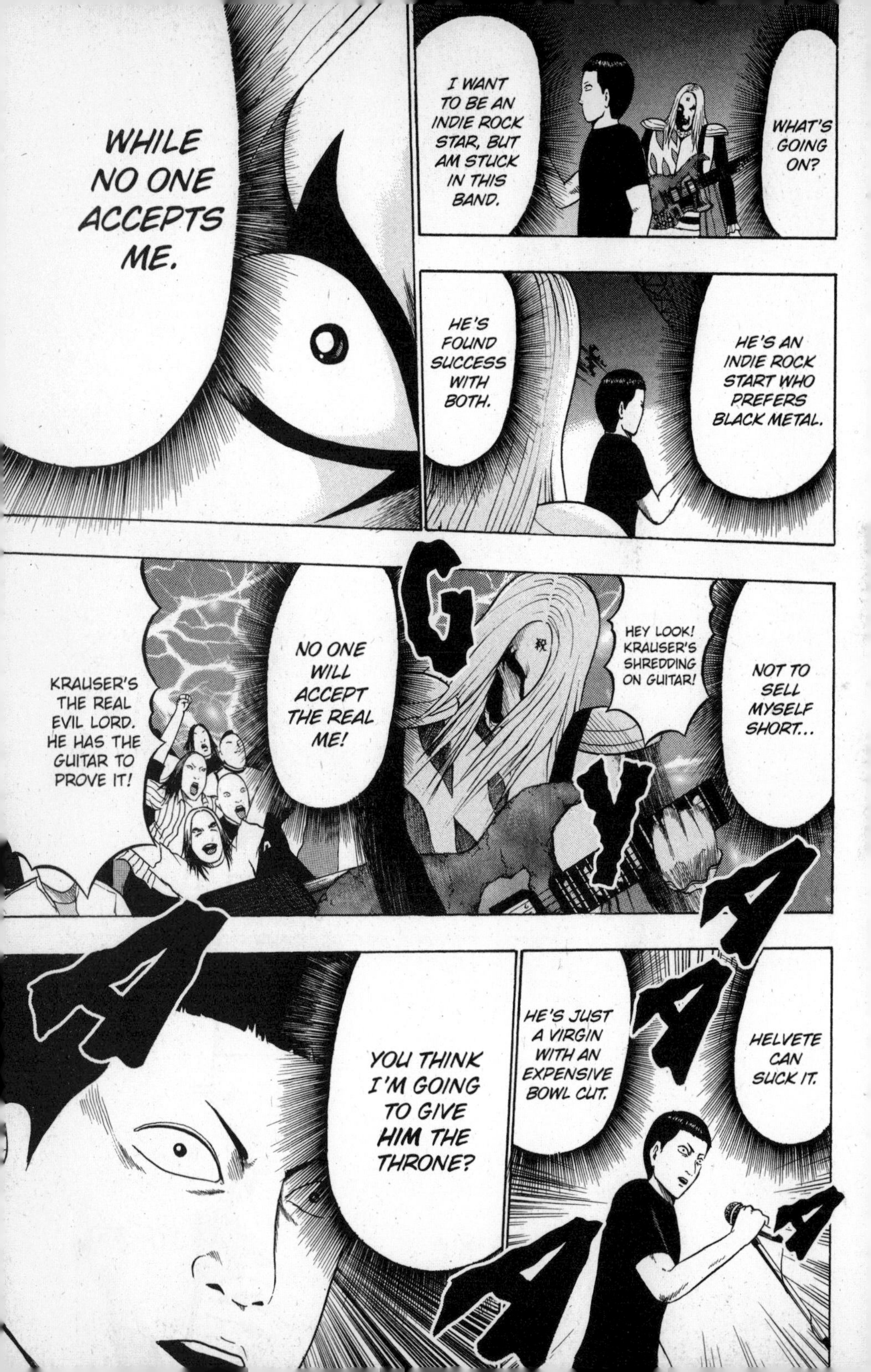
WHAT'S GOING ON?
I WANT TO BE AN INDIE ROCK STAR, BUT AM STUCK IN THIS BAND.
HE'S AN INDIE ROCK START WHO PREFERS BLACK METAL.
HE'S FOUND SUCCESS WITH BOTH.
WHILE NO ONE ACCEPTS ME.
GYAAAAA
NOT TO SELL MYSELF SHORT...
HEY LOOK! KRAUSER'S SHREDDING ON GUITAR!
NO ONE WILL ACCEPT THE REAL ME!
KRAUSER'S THE REAL EVIL LORD. HE HAS THE GUITAR TO PROVE IT!
HELVETE CAN SUCK IT.
HE'S JUST A VIRGIN WITH AN EXPENSIVE BOWL CUT.
YOU THINK I'M GOING TO GIVE HIM THE THRONE?

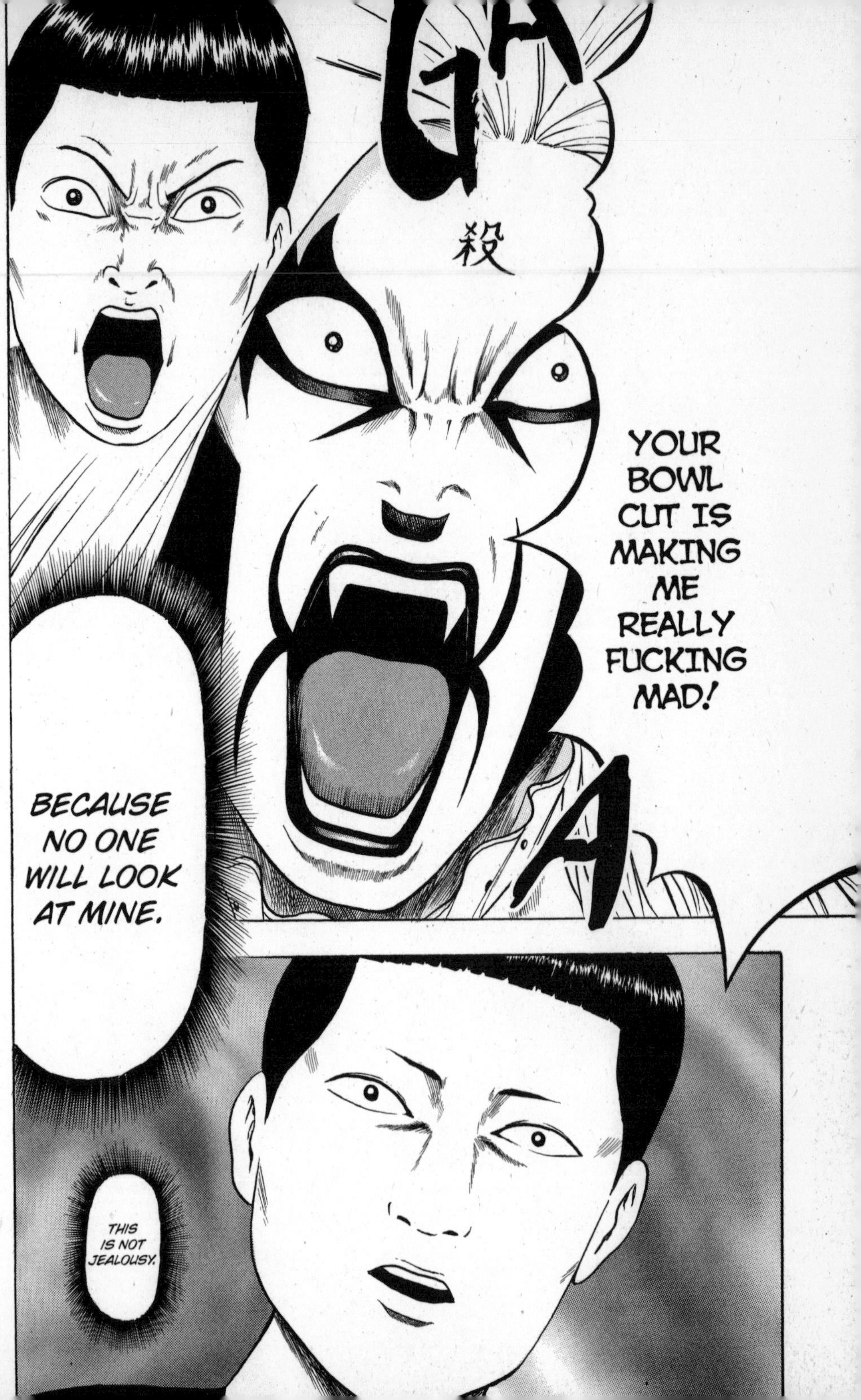
殺
A
YOUR BOWL CUT IS MAKING ME REALLY FUCKING MAD!
BECAUSE NO ONE WILL LOOK AT MINE.
THIS IS NOT JEALOUSY.

DMC LEXICON
PORK SOUP

Made by stewing weak, enfeebled pigs with gobo, carrot,
potato, onion, etc. in a broth of miso. Every region, even every
family, has a different recipe. For example, in the red light
district the dish calls for female pigs, known as hookers, and
the person eating them out, known as a john, has to sit in the
soup, known as a hot tub, with them.

Usage: Ewwwwww. That's not sweat. It's "pork soup"!

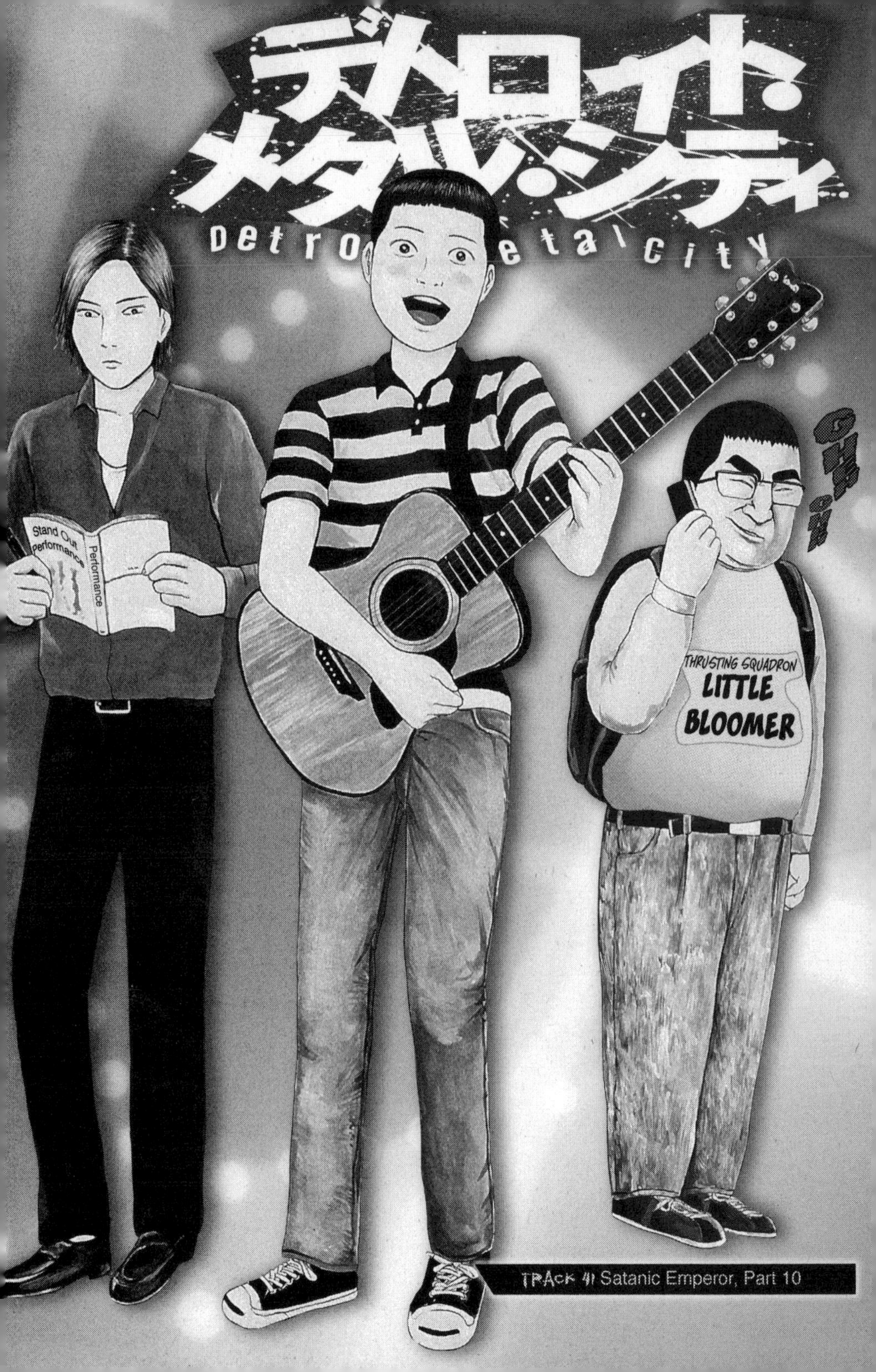
デトロイト・メタル・シティ
Detro etal city
Stand Out Performance
Performance
THRUSTING SQUADRON
LITTLE BLOOMER
TRACK 41 Satanic Emperor, Part 10

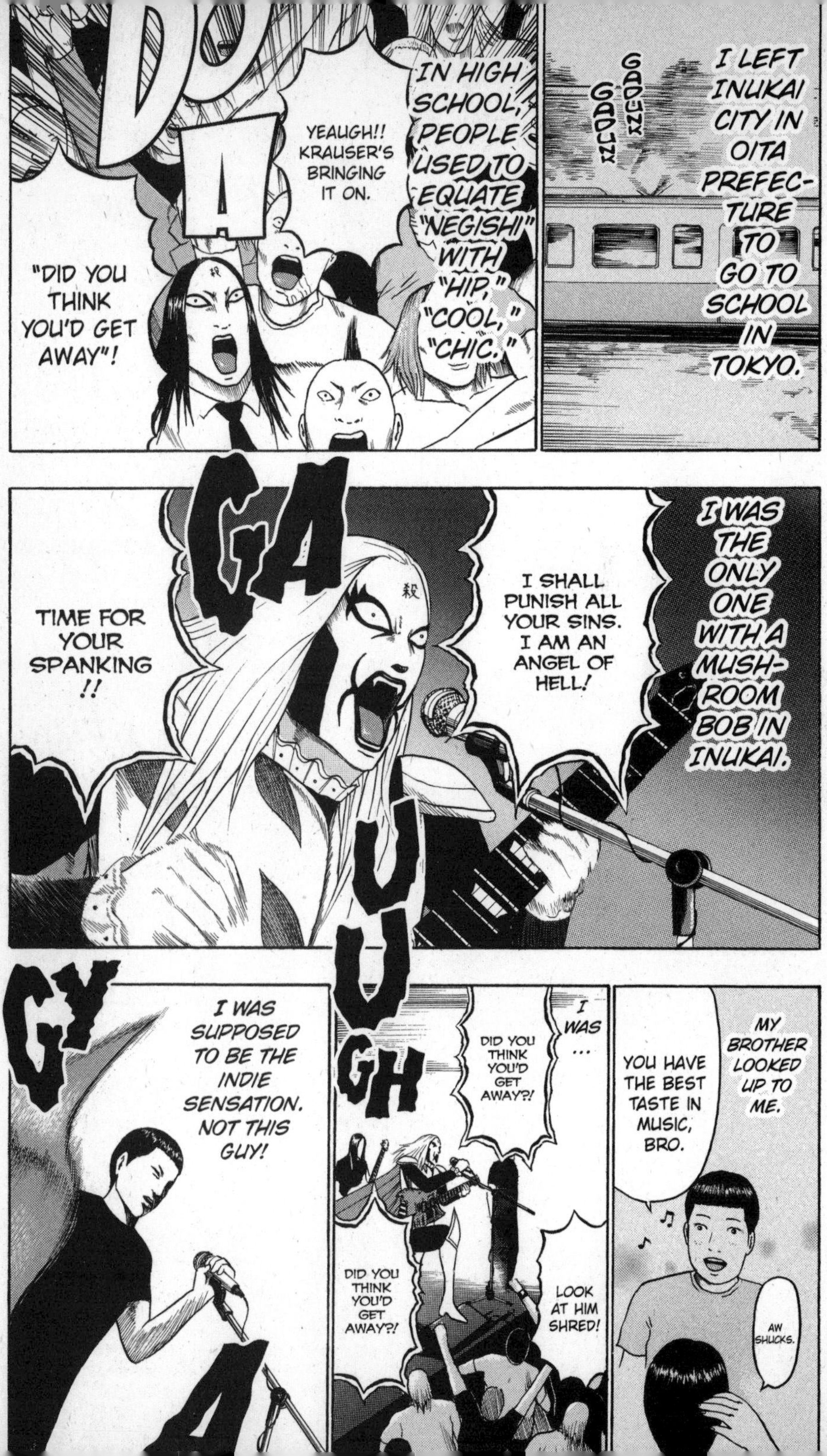
I LEFT INUKAI CITY IN OITA PREFECTURE TO GO TO SCHOOL IN TOKYO.
GADUNK
GADUNK
IN HIGH SCHOOL, PEOPLE USED TO EQUATE "NEGISHI" WITH "HIP," "COOL," "CHIC."
DO
A
YEAUGH!! KRAUSER'S BRINGING IT ON.
"DID YOU THINK YOU'D GET AWAY"!
I WAS THE ONLY ONE WITH A MUSH-ROOM BOB IN INUKAI.
I SHALL PUNISH ALL YOUR SINS. I AM AN ANGEL OF HELL!
GA
TIME FOR YOUR SPANKING!!
MY BROTHER LOOKED UP TO ME.
YOU HAVE THE BEST TASTE IN MUSIC, BRO.
AW SHUCKS.
I WAS ...
DID YOU THINK YOU'D GET AWAY?!
LOOK AT HIM SHRED!
DID YOU THINK YOU'D GET AWAY?!
U
U
GH
I WAS SUPPOSED TO BE THE INDIE SENSATION. NOT THIS GUY!
GY
A

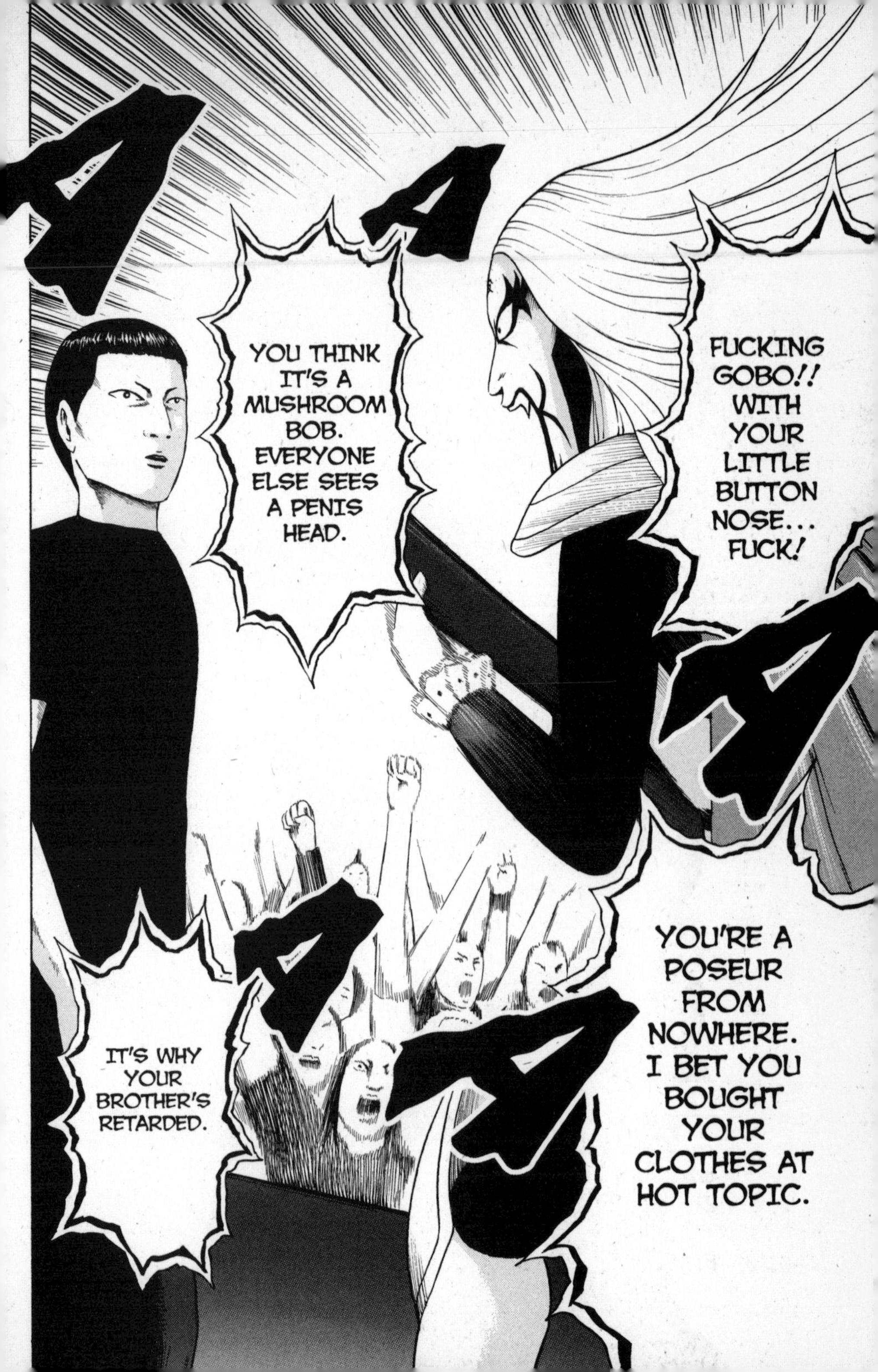
FUCKING GOBO!! WITH YOUR LITTLE BUTTON NOSE... FUCK!
YOU THINK IT'S A MUSHROOM BOB. EVERYONE ELSE SEES A PENIS HEAD.
YOU'RE A POSEUR FROM NOWHERE. I BET YOU BOUGHT YOUR CLOTHES AT HOT TOPIC.
IT'S WHY YOUR BROTHER'S RETARDED.

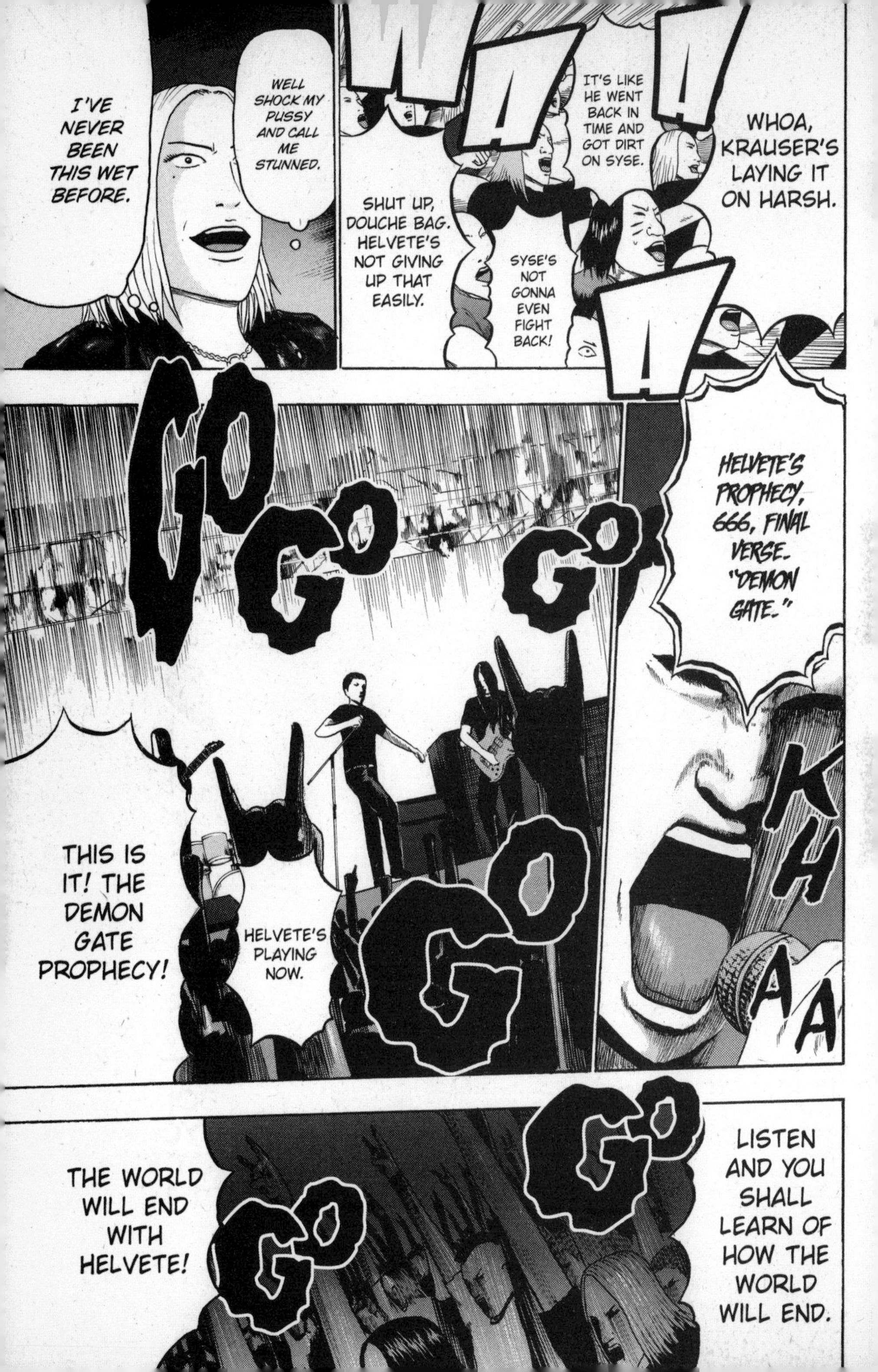
WAAAA
WHOA, KRAUSER'S LAYING IT ON HARSH.
IT'S LIKE HE WENT BACK IN TIME AND GOT DIRT ON SYSE.
SYSE'S NOT GONNA EVEN FIGHT BACK!
SHUT UP, DOUCHE BAG. HELVETE'S NOT GIVING UP THAT EASILY.
WELL SHOCK MY PUSSY AND CALL ME STUNNED.
I'VE NEVER BEEN THIS WET BEFORE.
HELVETE'S PROPHECY, 666, FINAL VERSE. "DEMON GATE."
KHAAA
GO GO GO GO
HELVETE'S PLAYING NOW.
THIS IS IT! THE DEMON GATE PROPHECY!
LISTEN AND YOU SHALL LEARN OF HOW THE WORLD WILL END.
GO GO
THE WORLD WILL END WITH HELVETE!

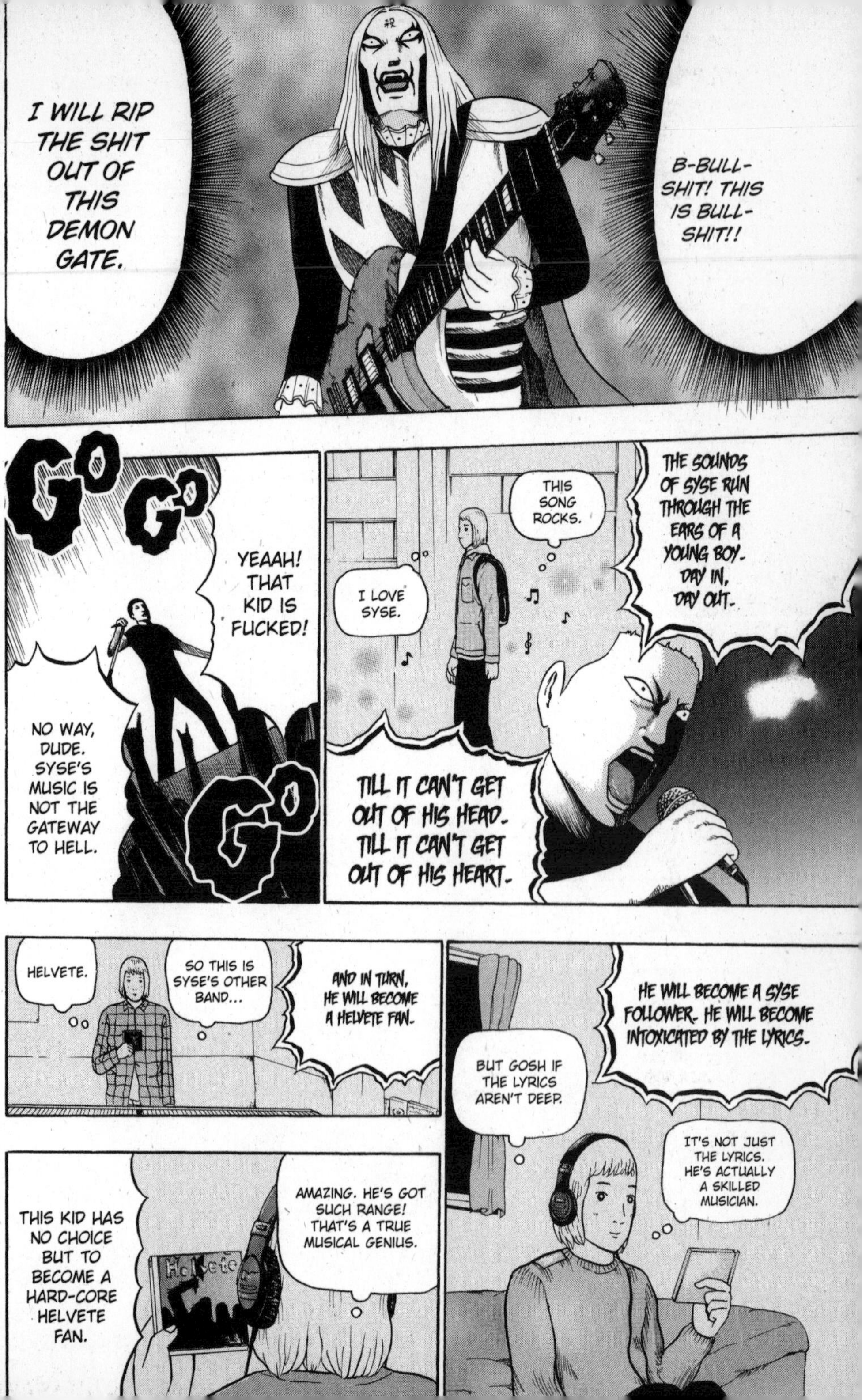
B-BULL-SHIT! THIS IS BULL-SHIT!!
I WILL RIP THE SHIT OUT OF THIS DEMON GATE.
THE SOUNDS OF SYSE RUN THROUGH THE EARS OF A YOUNG BOY. DAY IN, DAY OUT.
THIS SONG ROCKS.
I LOVE SYSE.
TILL IT CAN'T GET OUT OF HIS HEAD. TILL IT CAN'T GET OUT OF HIS HEART.
GO GO
YEAAH! THAT KID IS FUCKED!
NO WAY, DUDE. SYSE'S MUSIC IS NOT THE GATEWAY TO HELL.
GO
HE WILL BECOME A SYSE FOLLOWER. HE WILL BECOME INTOXICATED BY THE LYRICS.
BUT GOSH IF THE LYRICS AREN'T DEEP.
IT'S NOT JUST THE LYRICS. HE'S ACTUALLY A SKILLED MUSICIAN.
AND IN TURN, HE WILL BECOME A HELVETE FAN.
SO THIS IS SYSE'S OTHER BAND...
HELVETE.
AMAZING. HE'S GOT SUCH RANGE! THAT'S A TRUE MUSICAL GENIUS.
THIS KID HAS NO CHOICE BUT TO BECOME A HARD-CORE HELVETE FAN.

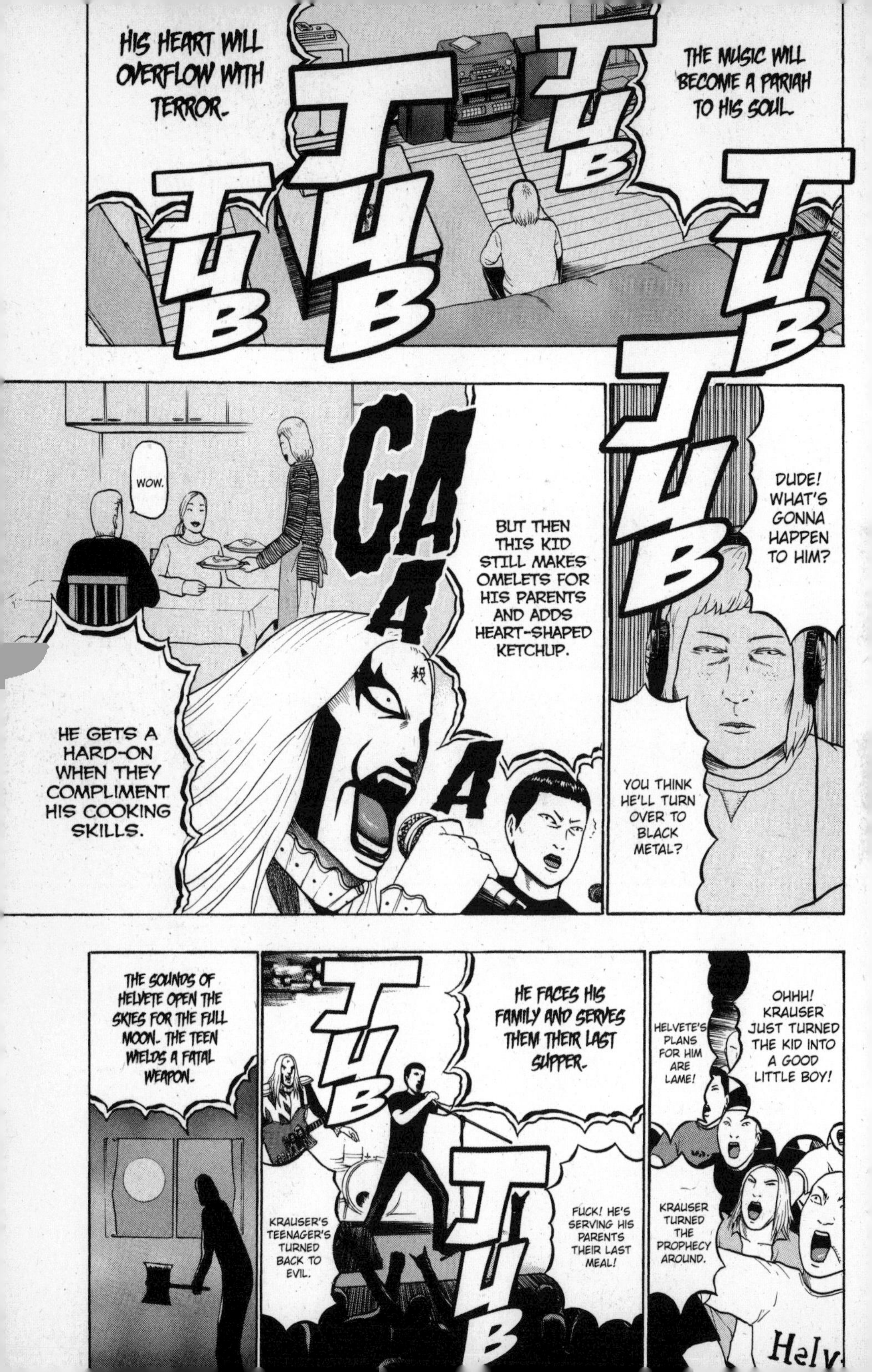
THE MUSIC WILL BECOME A PARIAH TO HIS SOUL.
HIS HEART WILL OVERFLOW WITH TERROR.
TUB
TUB
TUB
TUB
TUB
DUDE! WHAT'S GONNA HAPPEN TO HIM?
YOU THINK HE'LL TURN OVER TO BLACK METAL?
GA
A
A
BUT THEN THIS KID STILL MAKES OMELETS FOR HIS PARENTS AND ADDS HEART-SHAPED KETCHUP.
WOW.
HE GETS A HARD-ON WHEN THEY COMPLIMENT HIS COOKING SKILLS.
OHHH! KRAUSER JUST TURNED THE KID INTO A GOOD LITTLE BOY!
HELVETE'S PLANS FOR HIM ARE LAME!
KRAUSER TURNED THE PROPHECY AROUND.
Helv
HE FACES HIS FAMILY AND SERVES THEM THEIR LAST SUPPER.
TUB
TUB
FUCK! HE'S SERVING HIS PARENTS THEIR LAST MEAL!
KRAUSER'S TEENAGER'S TURNED BACK TO EVIL.
THE SOUNDS OF HELVETE OPEN THE SKIES FOR THE FULL MOON. THE TEEN WIELDS A FATAL WEAPON.

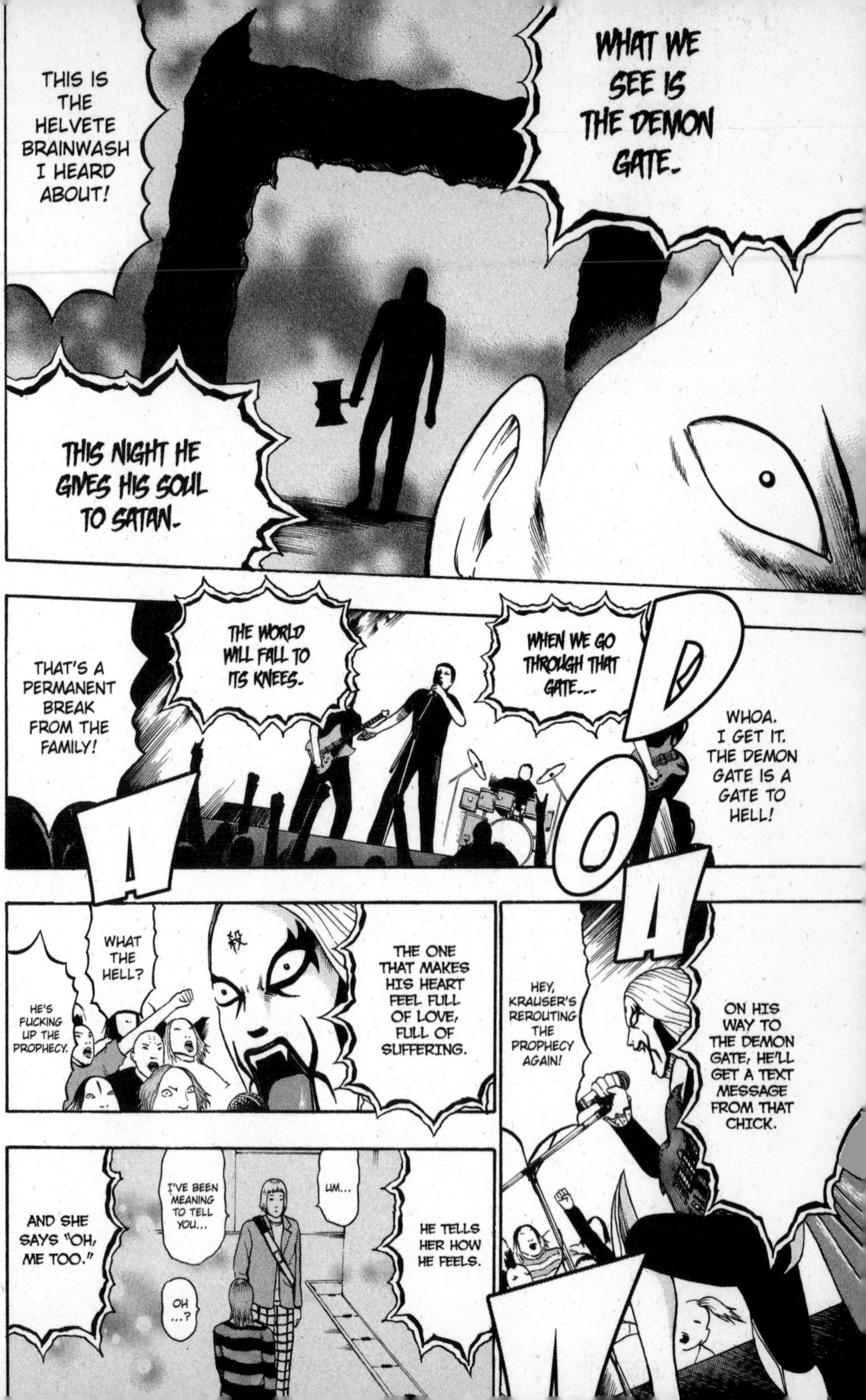
WHAT WE SEE IS THE DEMON GATE.
THIS IS THE HELVETE BRAINWASH I HEARD ABOUT!
THIS NIGHT HE GIVES HIS SOUL TO SATAN.
DOA
WHEN WE GO THROUGH THAT GATE...
THE WORLD WILL FALL TO ITS KNEES.
WHOA. I GET IT. THE DEMON GATE IS A GATE TO HELL!
THAT'S A PERMANENT BREAK FROM THE FAMILY!
A
ON HIS WAY TO THE DEMON GATE, HE'LL GET A TEXT MESSAGE FROM THAT CHICK.
HEY, KRAUSER'S REROUTING THE PROPHECY AGAIN!
THE ONE THAT MAKES HIS HEART FEEL FULL OF LOVE, FULL OF SUFFERING.
WHAT THE HELL?
HE'S FUCKING UP THE PROPHECY.
HE TELLS HER HOW HE FEELS.
UM...
I'VE BEEN MEANING TO TELL YOU...
OH ...?
AND SHE SAYS "OH, ME TOO."

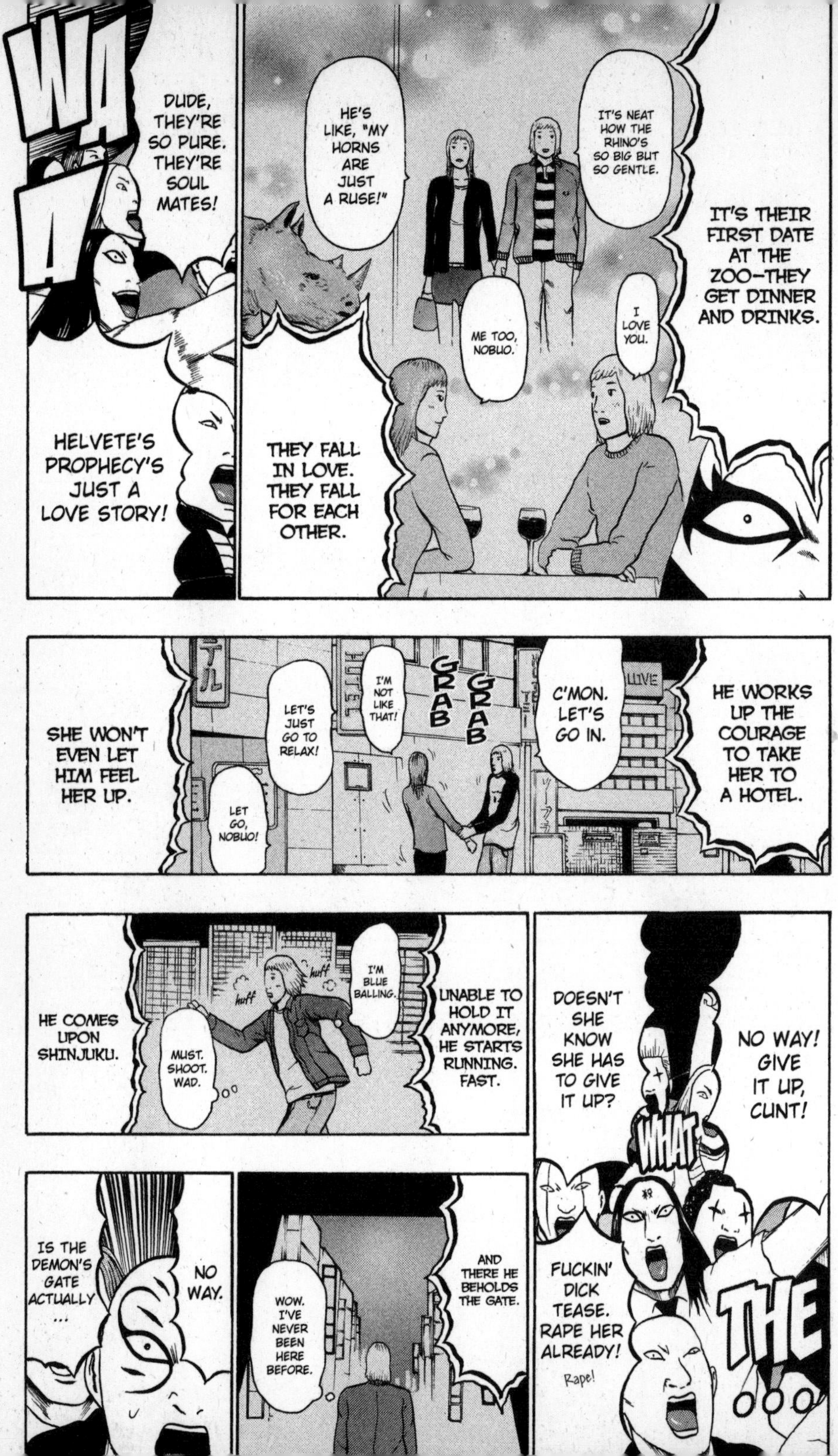
IT'S THEIR FIRST DATE AT THE ZOO—THEY GET DINNER AND DRINKS.
IT'S NEAT HOW THE RHINO'S SO BIG BUT SO GENTLE.
HE'S LIKE, "MY HORNS ARE JUST A RUSE!"
I LOVE YOU.
ME TOO, NOBUO.
THEY FALL IN LOVE. THEY FALL FOR EACH OTHER.
WA
A
DUDE, THEY'RE SO PURE. THEY'RE SOUL MATES!
HELVETE'S PROPHECY'S JUST A LOVE STORY!
HE WORKS UP THE COURAGE TO TAKE HER TO A HOTEL.
C'MON. LET'S GO IN.
GRAB GRAB
I'M NOT LIKE THAT!
LET'S JUST GO TO RELAX!
LET GO, NOBUO!
SHE WON'T EVEN LET HIM FEEL HER UP.
NO WAY! GIVE IT UP, CUNT!
DOESN'T SHE KNOW SHE HAS TO GIVE IT UP?
WHAT
THE
FUCKIN' DICK TEASE. RAPE HER ALREADY!
Rape!
UNABLE TO HOLD IT ANYMORE, HE STARTS RUNNING. FAST.
I'M BLUE BALLING.
huff
huff
MUST. SHOOT. WAD.
HE COMES UPON SHINJUKU.
AND THERE HE BEHOLDS THE GATE.
WOW. I'VE NEVER BEEN HERE BEFORE.
NO WAY.
IS THE DEMON'S GATE ACTUALLY ...

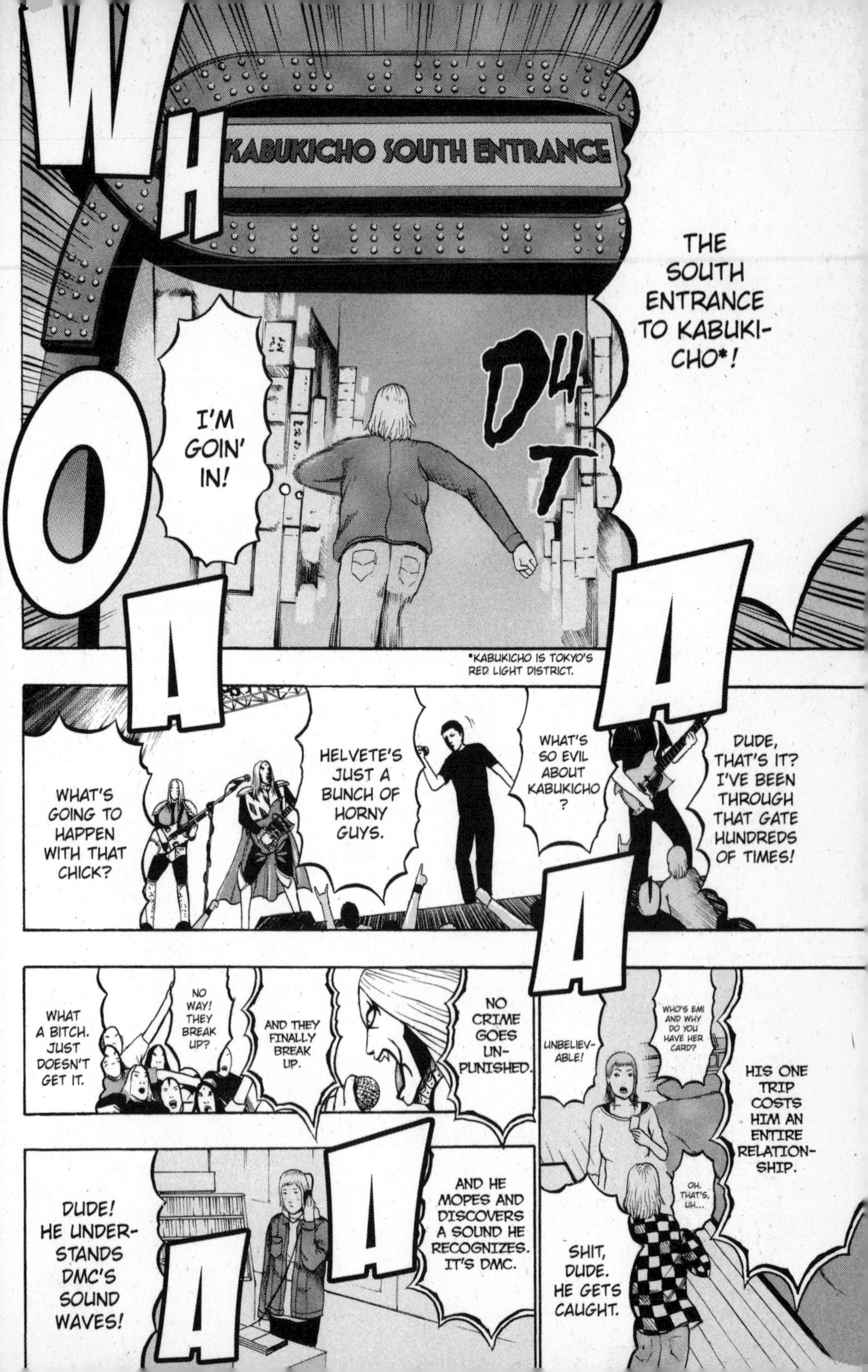
KABUKICHO SOUTH ENTRANCE
THE SOUTH ENTRANCE TO KABUKI-CHO*!
I'M GOIN' IN!
DUT
WHOAAAAAA
*KABUKICHO IS TOKYO'S RED LIGHT DISTRICT.
DUDE, THAT'S IT? I'VE BEEN THROUGH THAT GATE HUNDREDS OF TIMES!
WHAT'S SO EVIL ABOUT KABUKICHO?
HELVETE'S JUST A BUNCH OF HORNY GUYS.
WHAT'S GOING TO HAPPEN WITH THAT CHICK?
HIS ONE TRIP COSTS HIM AN ENTIRE RELATIONSHIP.
WHO'S EMI AND WHY DO YOU HAVE HER CARD?
UNBELIEVABLE!
OH. THAT'S, UH...
SHIT, DUDE. HE GETS CAUGHT.
NO CRIME GOES UNPUNISHED.
AND THEY FINALLY BREAK UP.
NO WAY! THEY BREAK UP?
WHAT A BITCH. JUST DOESN'T GET IT.
AND HE MOPES AND DISCOVERS A SOUND HE RECOGNIZES. IT'S DMC.
DUDE! HE UNDERSTANDS DMC'S SOUND WAVES!

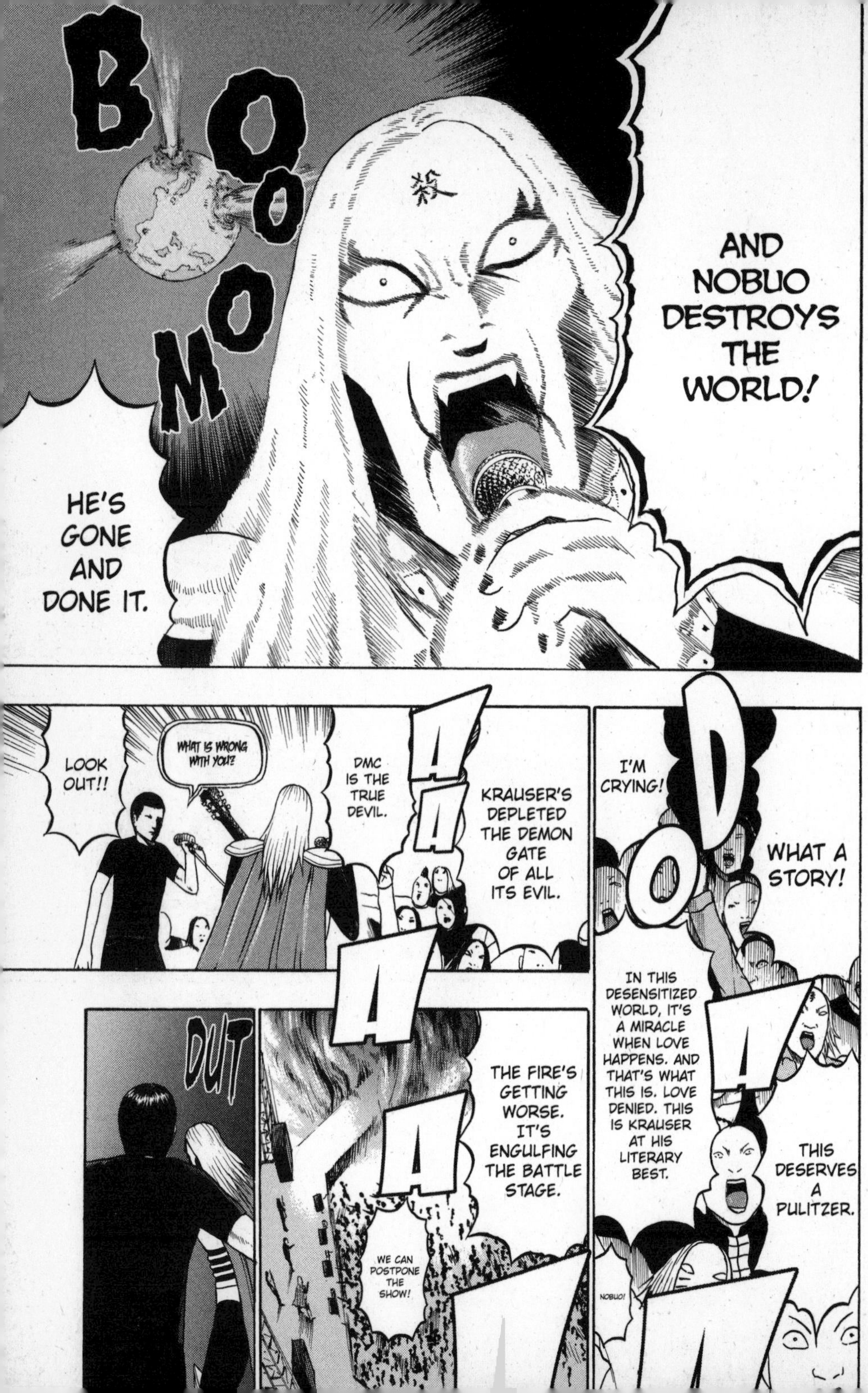
AND NOBUO DESTROYS THE WORLD!
BOOOOM
HE'S GONE AND DONE IT.
I'M CRYING!
WHAT A STORY!
DO
KRAUSER'S DEPLETED THE DEMON GATE OF ALL ITS EVIL.
AA
DMC IS THE TRUE DEVIL.
WHAT IS WRONG WITH YOU?
LOOK OUT!!
A
IN THIS DESENSITIZED WORLD, IT'S A MIRACLE WHEN LOVE HAPPENS. AND THAT'S WHAT THIS IS. LOVE DENIED. THIS IS KRAUSER AT HIS LITERARY BEST.
THIS DESERVES A PULITZER.
NOBUO!
A
THE FIRE'S GETTING WORSE. IT'S ENGULFING THE BATTLE STAGE.
A
WE CAN POSTPONE THE SHOW!
A
DUT

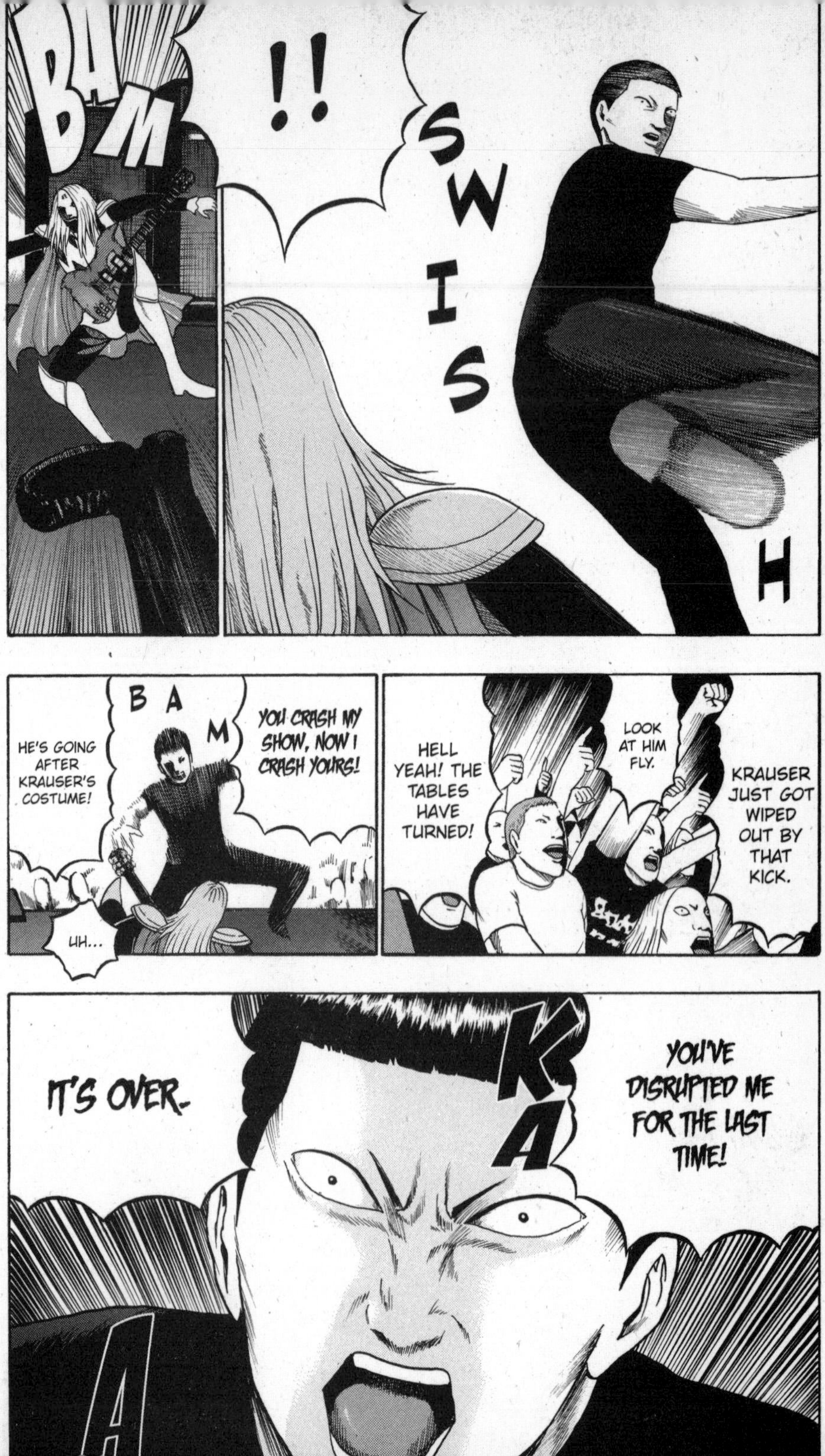
!!
SWISH
BAM
KRAUSER JUST GOT WIPED OUT BY THAT KICK.
LOOK AT HIM FLY.
HELL YEAH! THE TABLES HAVE TURNED!
BAM
YOU CRASH MY SHOW, NOW I CRASH YOURS!
HE'S GOING AFTER KRAUSER'S COSTUME!
UH...
YOU'VE DISRUPTED ME FOR THE LAST TIME!
KA
IT'S OVER-
A

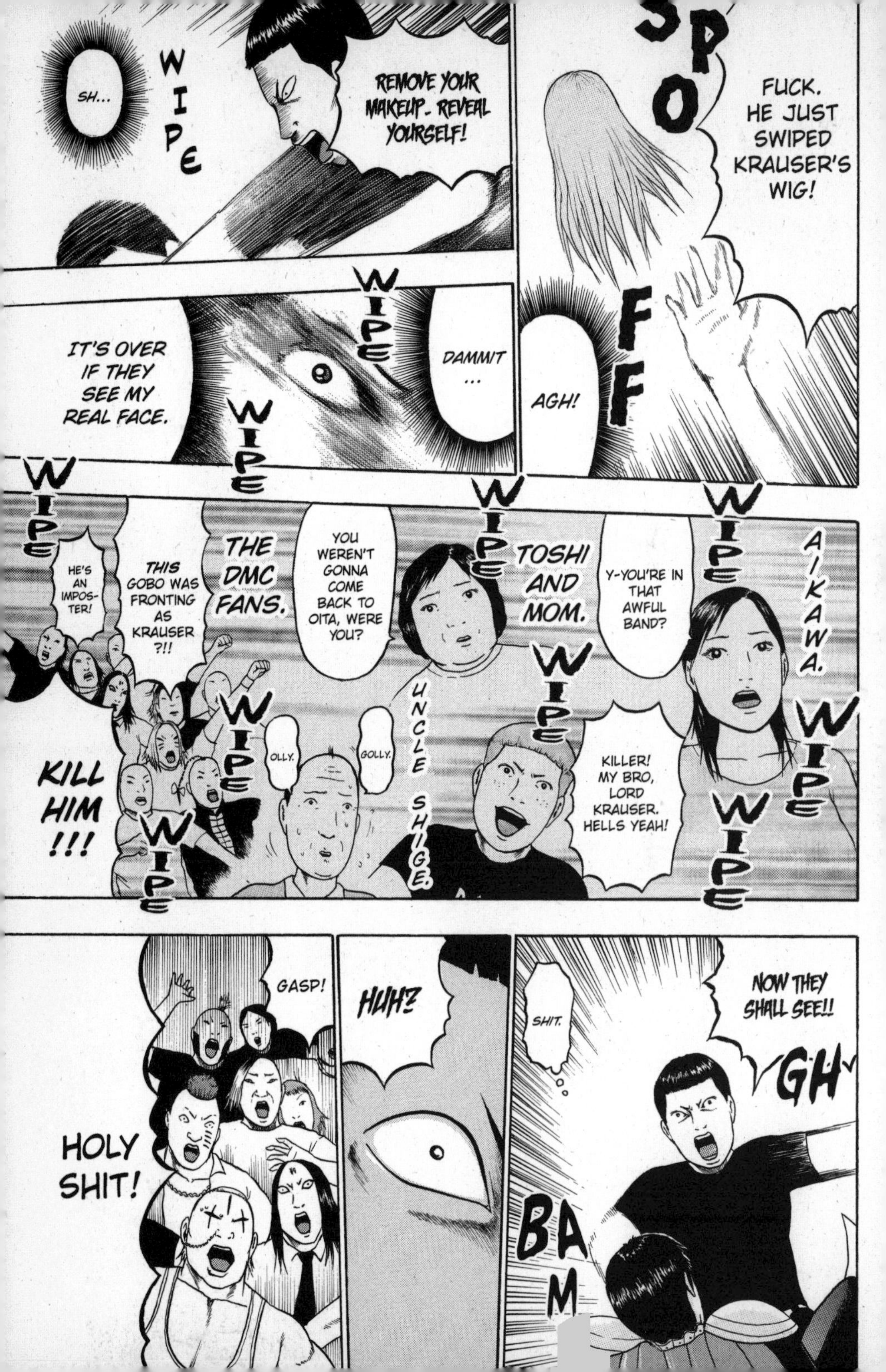
SPOFF
FUCK. HE JUST SWIPED KRAUSER'S WIG!
AGH!
REMOVE YOUR MAKEUP- REVEAL YOURSELF!
WIPE
SH...
WIPE
DAMMIT ...
IT'S OVER IF THEY SEE MY REAL FACE.
WIPE
AIKAWA.
WIPE
Y-YOU'RE IN THAT AWFUL BAND?
TOSHI AND MOM.
WIPE
YOU WEREN'T GONNA COME BACK TO OITA, WERE YOU?
WIPE
THE DMC FANS.
THIS GOBO WAS FRONTING AS KRAUSER ?!!
HE'S AN IMPOS-TER!
WIPE
WIPE
KILLER! MY BRO, LORD KRAUSER. HELLS YEAH!
WIPE
WIPE
UNCLE SHIGE.
GOLLY.
OLLY.
WIPE
KILL HIM !!!
WIPE
NOW THEY SHALL SEE!!
GH
SHIT.
BAM
HUH?
GASP!
HOLY SHIT!

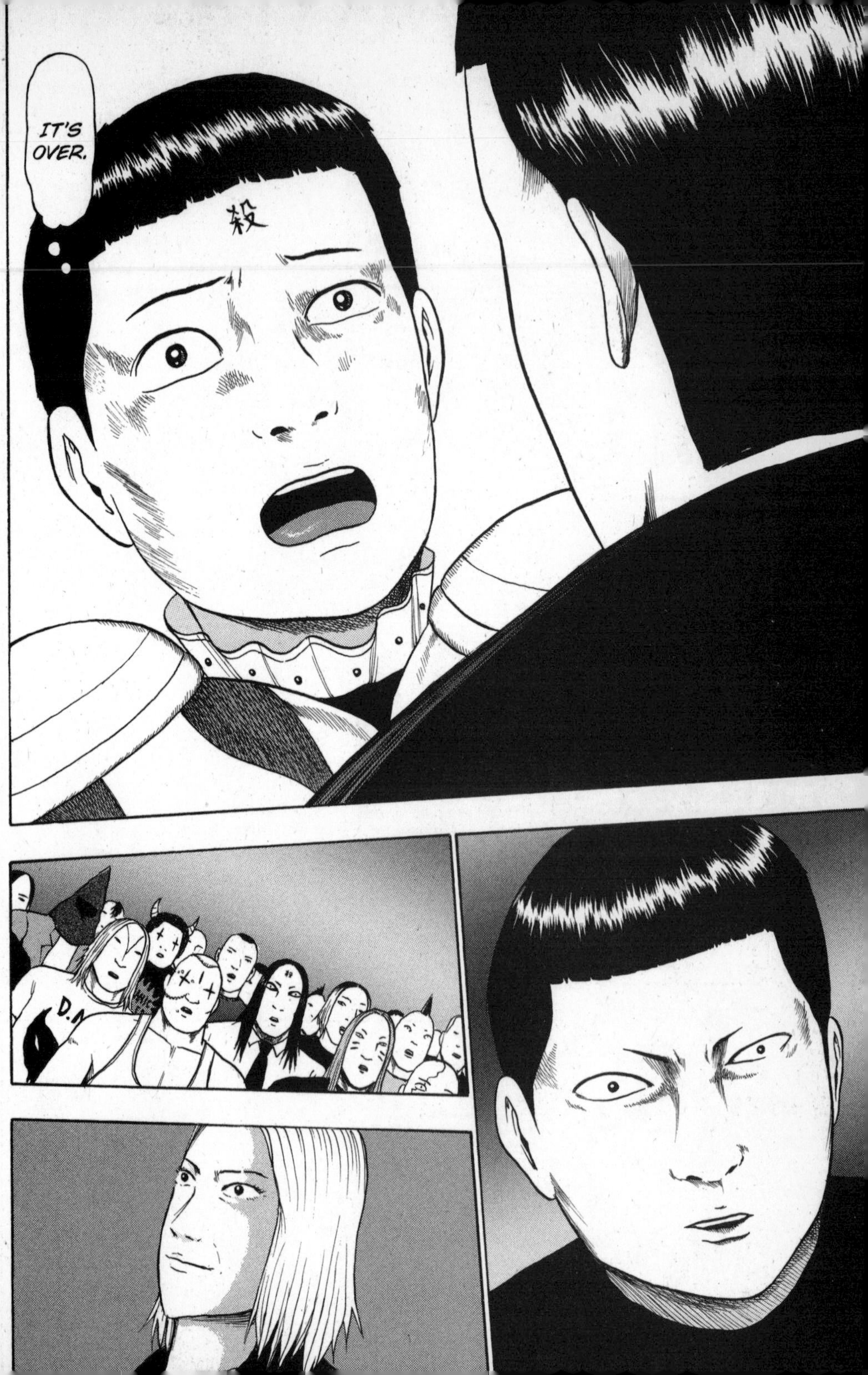
IT'S OVER.
殺

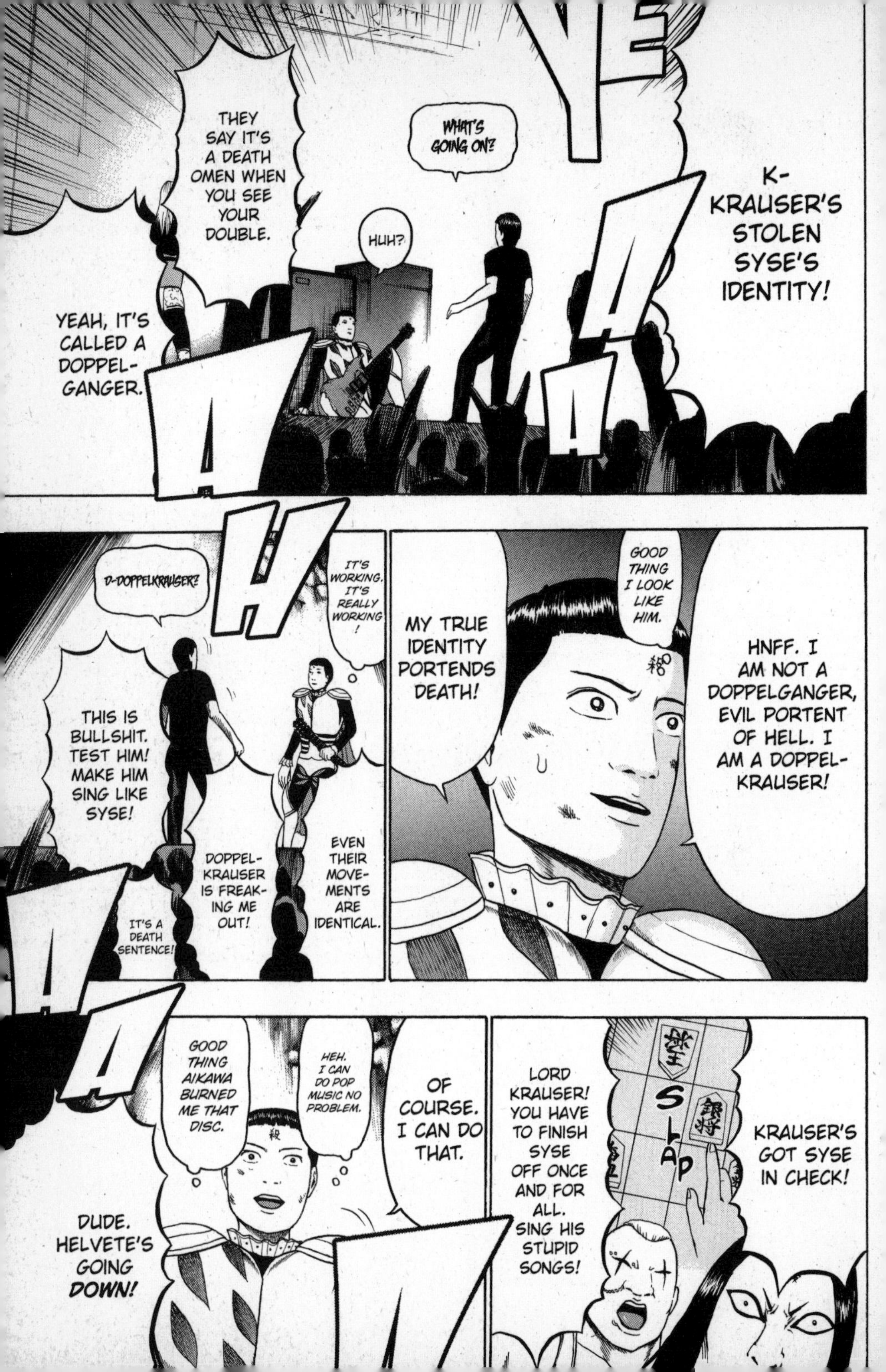
YEAAAAHAA
K-KRAUSER'S STOLEN SYSE'S IDENTITY!
WHAT'S GOING ON?
HUH?
THEY SAY IT'S A DEATH OMEN WHEN YOU SEE YOUR DOUBLE.
YEAH, IT'S CALLED A DOPPEL-GANGER.
GOOD THING I LOOK LIKE HIM.
HNFF. I AM NOT A DOPPELGANGER, EVIL PORTENT OF HELL. I AM A DOPPEL-KRAUSER!
MY TRUE IDENTITY PORTENDS DEATH!
IT'S WORKING. IT'S REALLY WORKING!
D-DOPPELKRAUSER?
THIS IS BULLSHIT. TEST HIM! MAKE HIM SING LIKE SYSE!
EVEN THEIR MOVEMENTS ARE IDENTICAL.
DOPPEL-KRAUSER IS FREAKING ME OUT!
IT'S A DEATH SENTENCE!
KRAUSER'S GOT SYSE IN CHECK!
SLAP
LORD KRAUSER! YOU HAVE TO FINISH SYSE OFF ONCE AND FOR ALL. SING HIS STUPID SONGS!
OF COURSE. I CAN DO THAT.
HEH. I CAN DO POP MUSIC NO PROBLEM.
GOOD THING AIKAWA BURNED ME THAT DISC.
DUDE. HELVETE'S GOING DOWN!

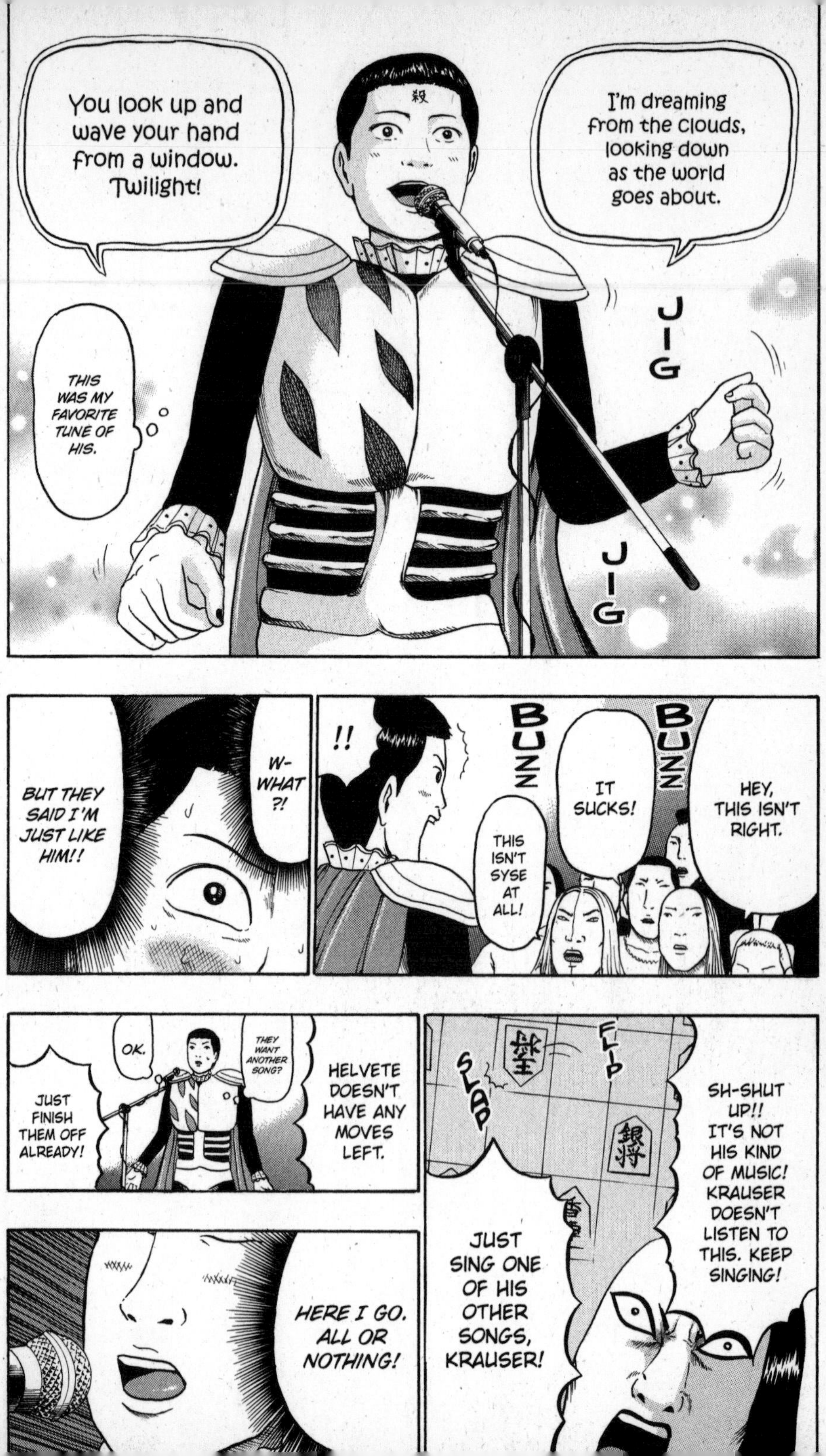
I'm dreaming from the clouds, looking down as the world goes about.
You look up and wave your hand from a window. Twilight!
JIG
JIG
THIS WAS MY FAVORITE TUNE OF HIS.
HEY, THIS ISN'T RIGHT.
BUZZ
BUZZ
IT SUCKS!
THIS ISN'T SYSE AT ALL!
!!
W-WHAT?!
BUT THEY SAID I'M JUST LIKE HIM!!
FLIP
SLAP
SH-SHUT UP!! IT'S NOT HIS KIND OF MUSIC! KRAUSER DOESN'T LISTEN TO THIS. KEEP SINGING!
JUST SING ONE OF HIS OTHER SONGS, KRAUSER!
HELVETE DOESN'T HAVE ANY MOVES LEFT.
THEY WANT ANOTHER SONG?
OK.
JUST FINISH THEM OFF ALREADY!
HERE I GO. ALL OR NOTHING!

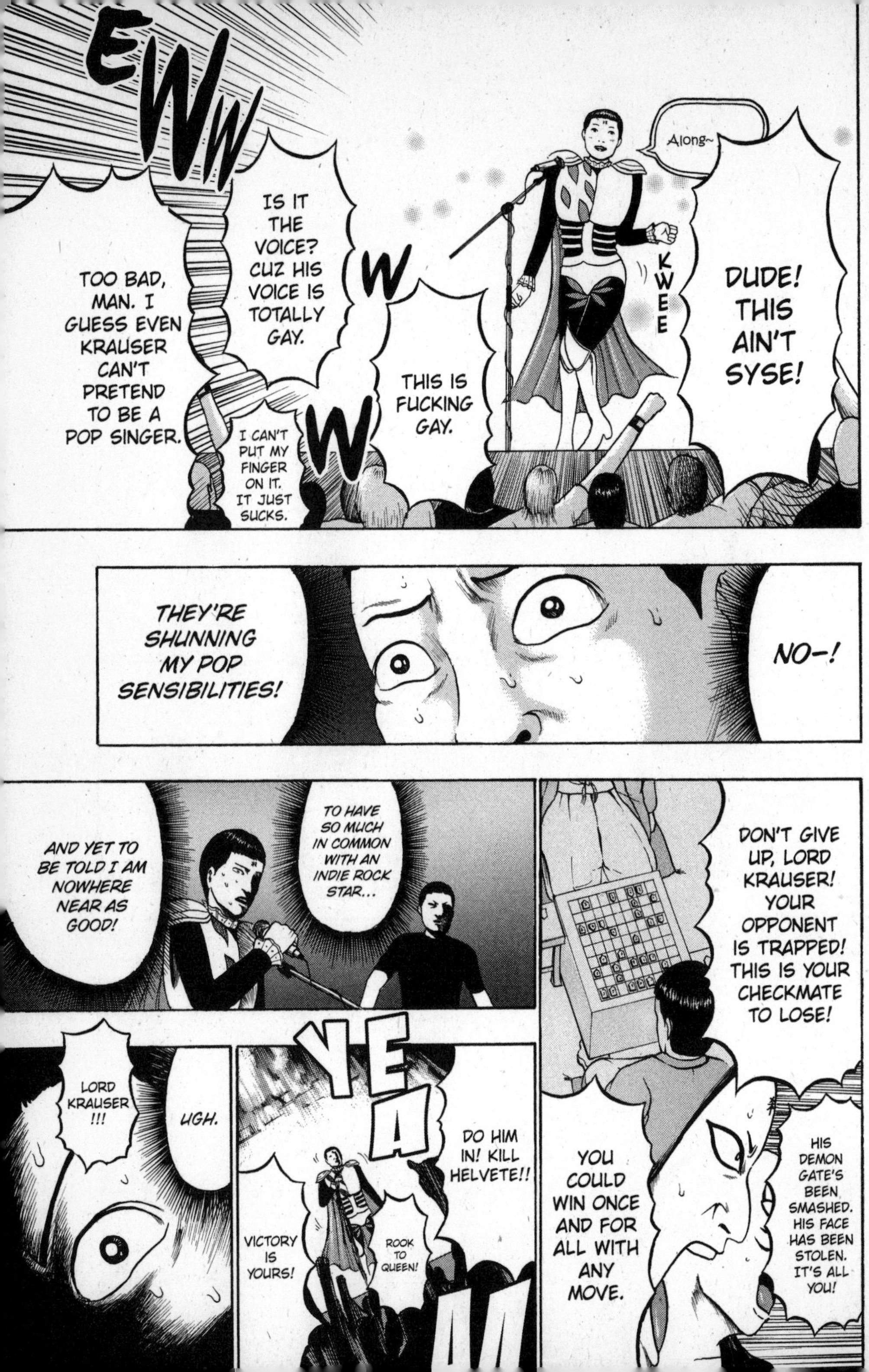
Along~
DUDE! THIS AIN'T SYSE!
KWEE
IS IT THE VOICE? CUZ HIS VOICE IS TOTALLY GAY.
W
THIS IS FUCKING GAY.
W
I CAN'T PUT MY FINGER ON IT. IT JUST SUCKS.
EWW
TOO BAD, MAN. I GUESS EVEN KRAUSER CAN'T PRETEND TO BE A POP SINGER.
NO-!
THEY'RE SHUNNING MY POP SENSIBILITIES!
DON'T GIVE UP, LORD KRAUSER! YOUR OPPONENT IS TRAPPED! THIS IS YOUR CHECKMATE TO LOSE!
HIS DEMON GATE'S BEEN SMASHED. HIS FACE HAS BEEN STOLEN. IT'S ALL YOU!
YOU COULD WIN ONCE AND FOR ALL WITH ANY MOVE.
TO HAVE SO MUCH IN COMMON WITH AN INDIE ROCK STAR...
AND YET TO BE TOLD I AM NOWHERE NEAR AS GOOD!
YEA
DO HIM IN! KILL HELVETE!!
ROOK TO QUEEN!
VICTORY IS YOURS!
UGH.
LORD KRAUSER !!!

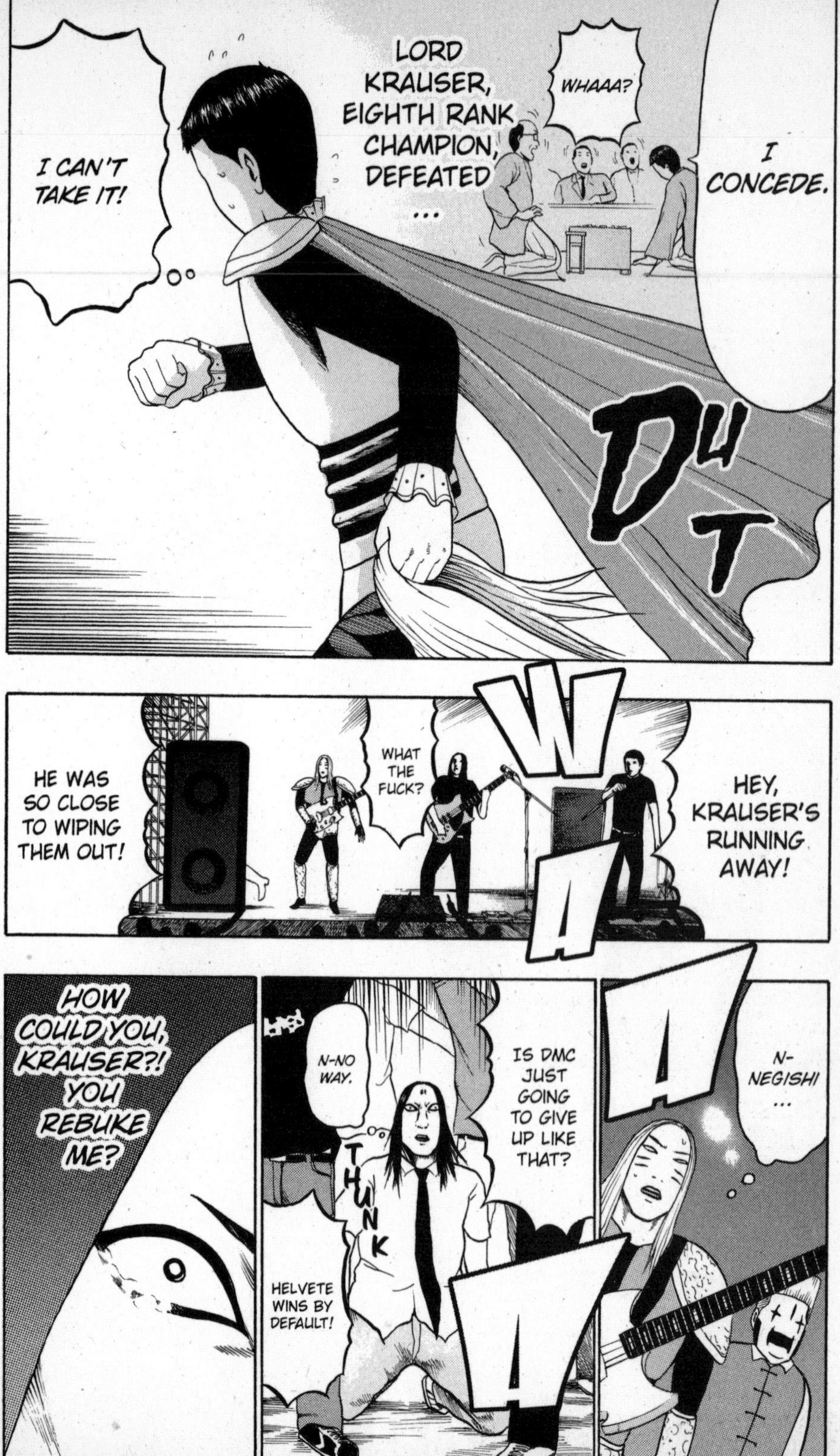
I CONCEDE.
WHAAA?
LORD KRAUSER, EIGHTH RANK CHAMPION, DEFEATED...
I CAN'T TAKE IT!
DUT
HEY, KRAUSER'S RUNNING AWAY!
WAAAA
WHAT THE FUCK?
HE WAS SO CLOSE TO WIPING THEM OUT!
N-NEGISHI...
IS DMC JUST GOING TO GIVE UP LIKE THAT?
N-NO WAY.
THUNK
HELVETE WINS BY DEFAULT!
HOW COULD YOU, KRAUSER?! YOU REBUKE ME?

DMC LEXICON

 ## DOPPELGANGER SYNDROME

When you see someone identical to yourself. Rumored to be a deathly omen to those who come across them, doppelgangers are widely feared. Doppelkrauser syndrome is when the look-alike actually kills you on sight. Conversely, if someone claims to have seen your "identical twin" at a brothel, you can tell them they are suffering from "doped up idiot" syndrome.

Usage: I hope I never run into Brad Pitt. You know, cuz he's my doppelganger.

デトロイト・メタル・シティ

Detroit Metal City

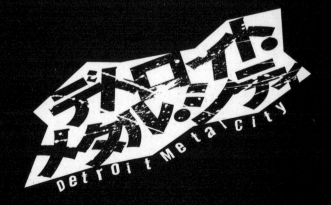

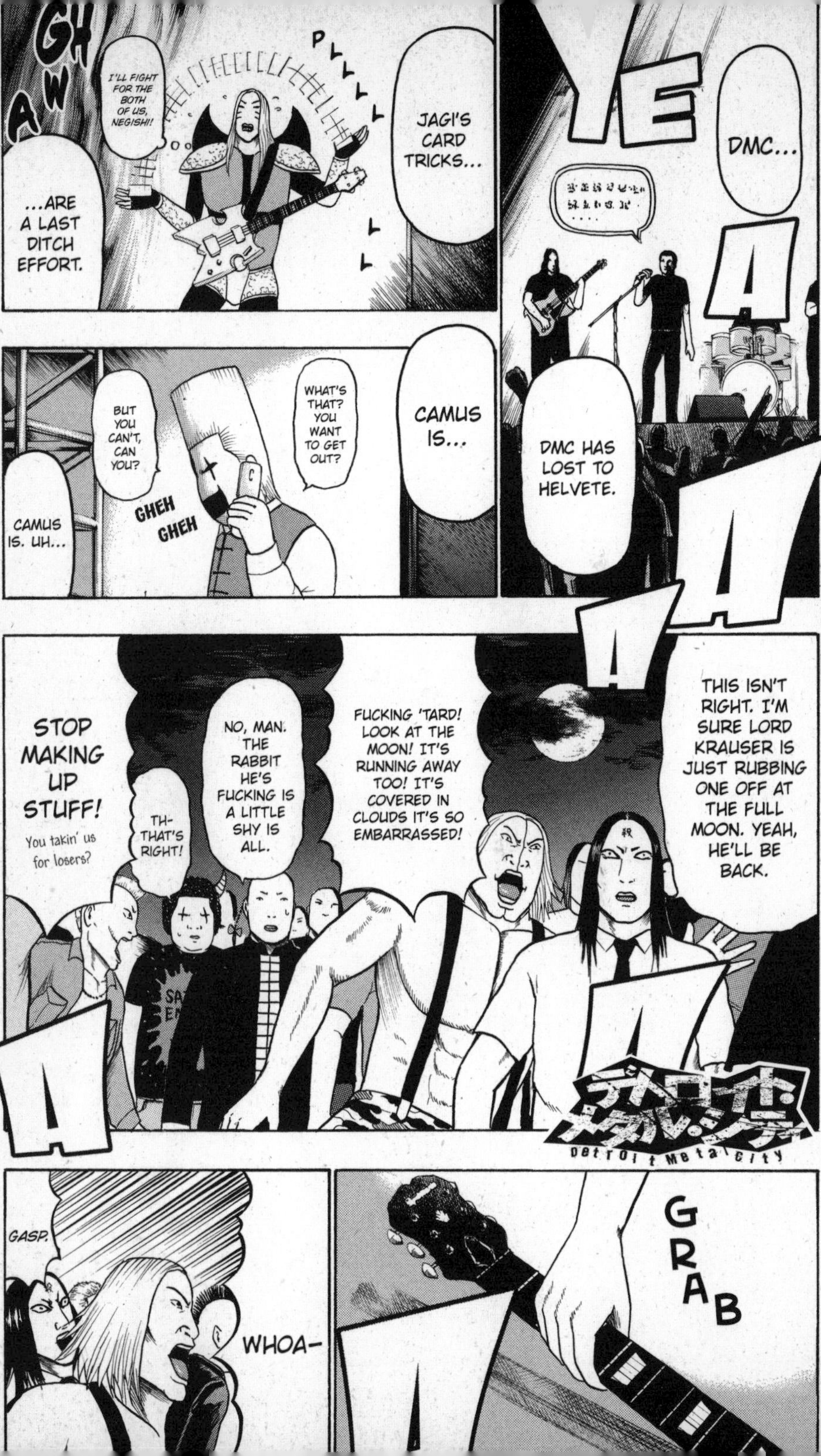
DMC...
DMC HAS LOST TO HELVETE.
JAGI'S CARD TRICKS...
...ARE A LAST DITCH EFFORT.
I'LL FIGHT FOR THE BOTH OF US, NEGISHI!
CAMUS IS...
WHAT'S THAT? YOU WANT TO GET OUT?
BUT YOU CAN'T, CAN YOU?
GHEH GHEH
CAMUS IS. UH...
THIS ISN'T RIGHT. I'M SURE LORD KRAUSER IS JUST RUBBING ONE OFF AT THE FULL MOON. YEAH, HE'LL BE BACK.
FUCKING 'TARD! LOOK AT THE MOON! IT'S RUNNING AWAY TOO! IT'S COVERED IN CLOUDS IT'S SO EMBARRASSED!
NO, MAN. THE RABBIT HE'S FUCKING IS A LITTLE SHY IS ALL.
TH-THAT'S RIGHT!
STOP MAKING UP STUFF!
You takin' us for losers?
Detroit Metal City
GRAB
GASP.
WHOA-

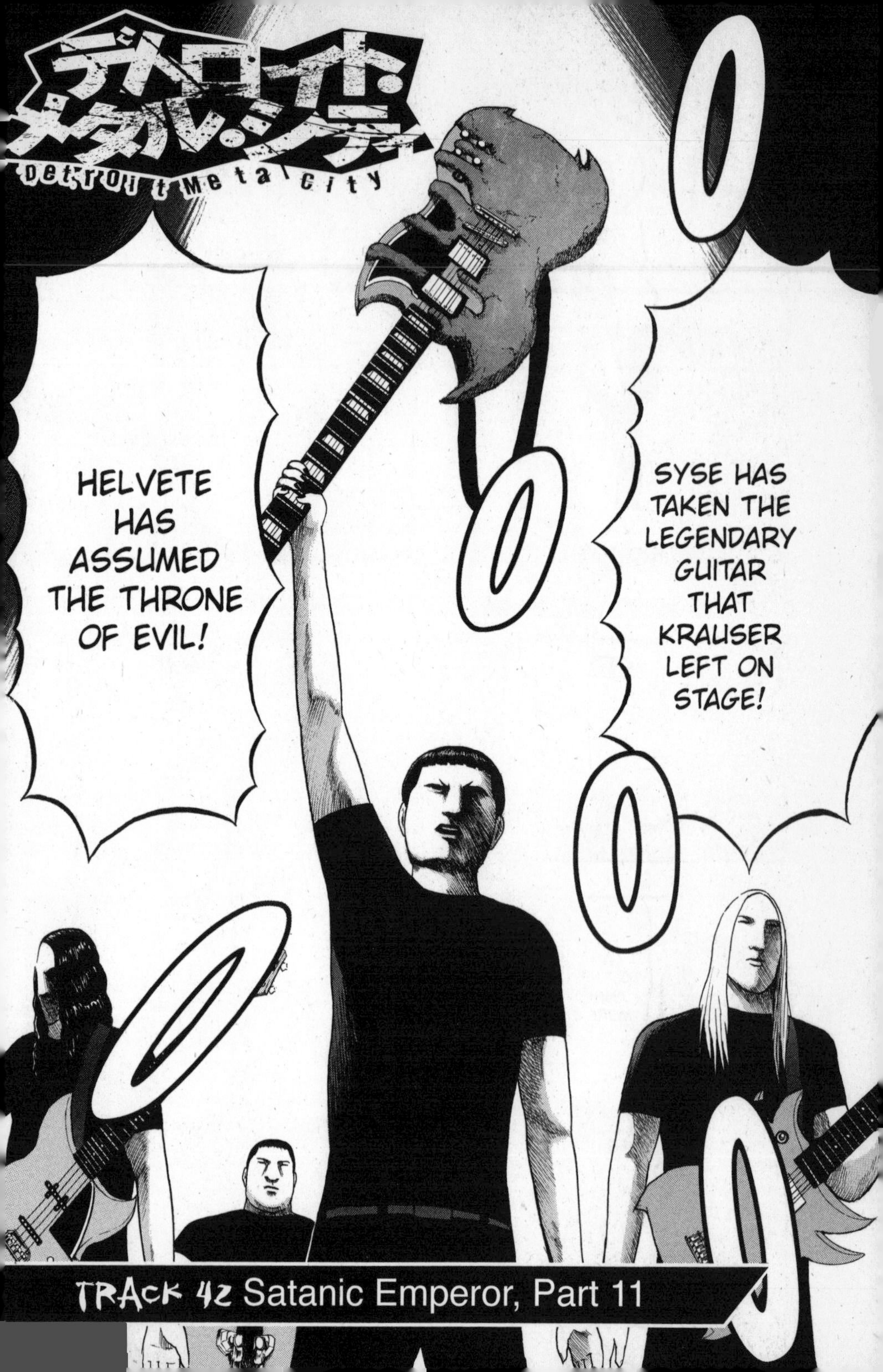
Detroit Metal City
SYSE HAS TAKEN THE LEGENDARY GUITAR THAT KRAUSER LEFT ON STAGE!
HELVETE HAS ASSUMED THE THRONE OF EVIL!
TRACK 42 Satanic Emperor, Part 11

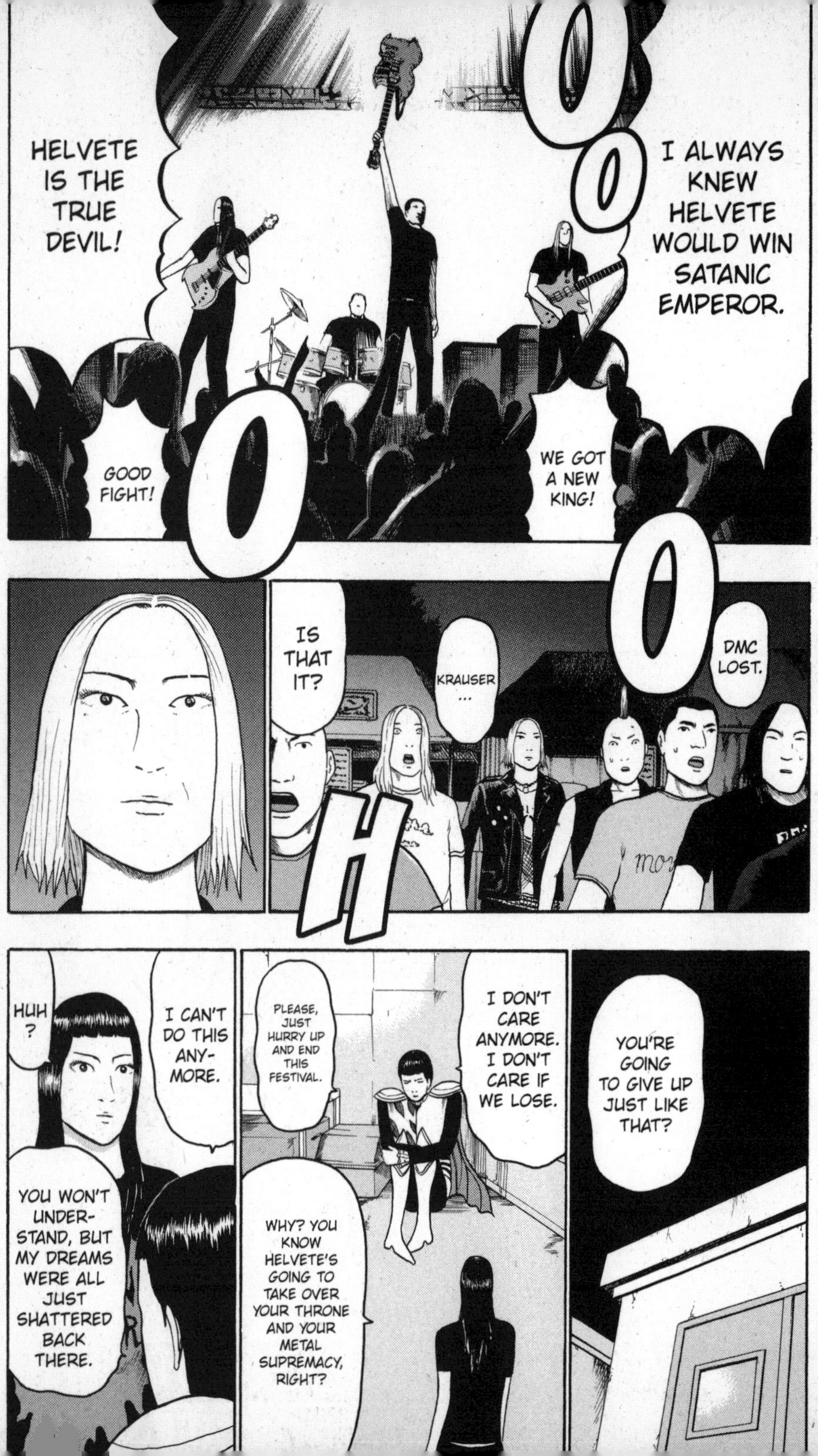
I ALWAYS KNEW HELVETE WOULD WIN SATANIC EMPEROR.
HELVETE IS THE TRUE DEVIL!
OOOOOH
WE GOT A NEW KING!
GOOD FIGHT!
DMC LOST.
KRAUSER...
IS THAT IT?
YOU'RE GOING TO GIVE UP JUST LIKE THAT?
I DON'T CARE ANYMORE. I DON'T CARE IF WE LOSE.
PLEASE, JUST HURRY UP AND END THIS FESTIVAL.
WHY? YOU KNOW HELVETE'S GOING TO TAKE OVER YOUR THRONE AND YOUR METAL SUPREMACY, RIGHT?
I CAN'T DO THIS ANY-MORE.
HUH?
YOU WON'T UNDER-STAND, BUT MY DREAMS WERE ALL JUST SHATTERED BACK THERE.

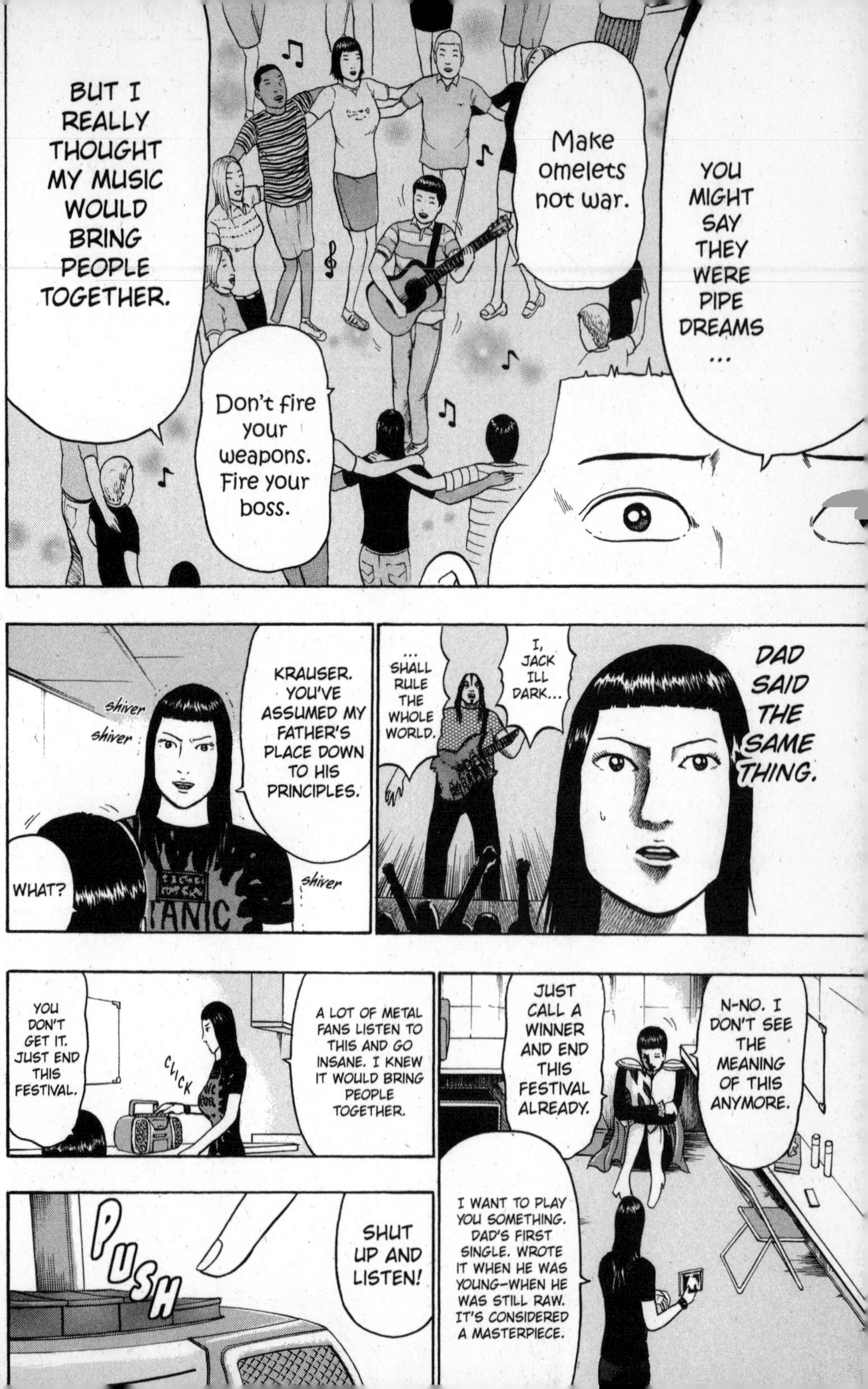
YOU MIGHT SAY THEY WERE PIPE DREAMS...
Make omelets not war.
BUT I REALLY THOUGHT MY MUSIC WOULD BRING PEOPLE TOGETHER.
Don't fire your weapons. Fire your boss.
DAD SAID THE SAME THING.
I, JACK ILL DARK...
...SHALL RULE THE WHOLE WORLD.
KRAUSER. YOU'VE ASSUMED MY FATHER'S PLACE DOWN TO HIS PRINCIPLES.
shiver
shiver
WHAT?
shiver
N-NO. I DON'T SEE THE MEANING OF THIS ANYMORE.
JUST CALL A WINNER AND END THIS FESTIVAL ALREADY.
I WANT TO PLAY YOU SOMETHING. DAD'S FIRST SINGLE. WROTE IT WHEN HE WAS YOUNG—WHEN HE WAS STILL RAW. IT'S CONSIDERED A MASTERPIECE.
A LOT OF METAL FANS LISTEN TO THIS AND GO INSANE. I KNEW IT WOULD BRING PEOPLE TOGETHER.
CLICK
YOU DON'T GET IT. JUST END THIS FESTIVAL.
SHUT UP AND LISTEN!
PUSH

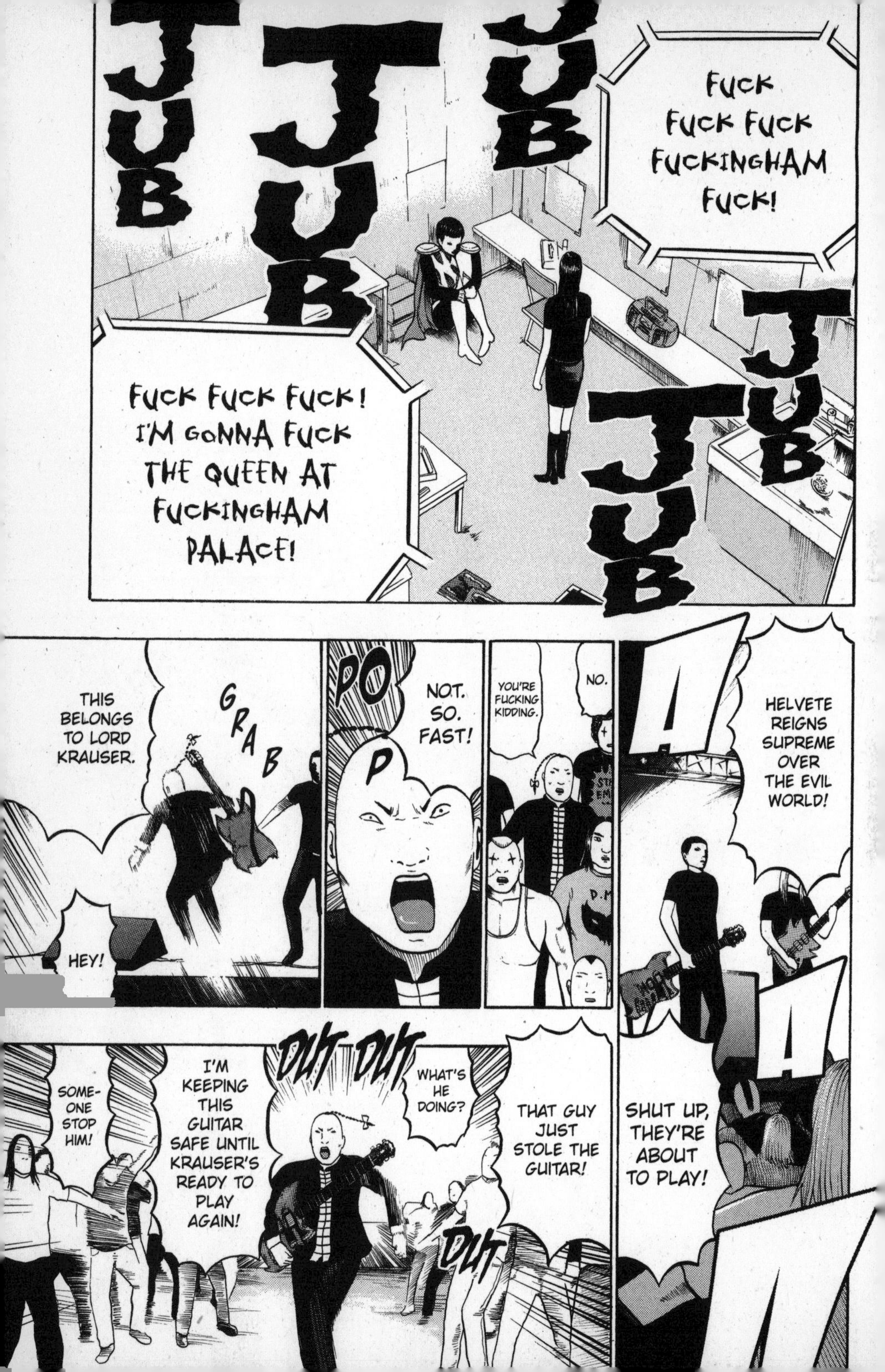
JUB
FUCK FUCK FUCK FUCKINGHAM FUCK!
JUB
JUB
FUCK FUCK FUCK! I'M GONNA FUCK THE QUEEN AT FUCKINGHAM PALACE!
JUB
JUB
A
HELVETE REIGNS SUPREME OVER THE EVIL WORLD!
A
SHUT UP, THEY'RE ABOUT TO PLAY!
NO.
YOU'RE FUCKING KIDDING.
NOT. SO. FAST!
POP
THIS BELONGS TO LORD KRAUSER.
GRAB
HEY!
THAT GUY JUST STOLE THE GUITAR!
WHAT'S HE DOING?
DUT DUT
I'M KEEPING THIS GUITAR SAFE UNTIL KRAUSER'S READY TO PLAY AGAIN!
SOME-ONE STOP HIM!
DUT

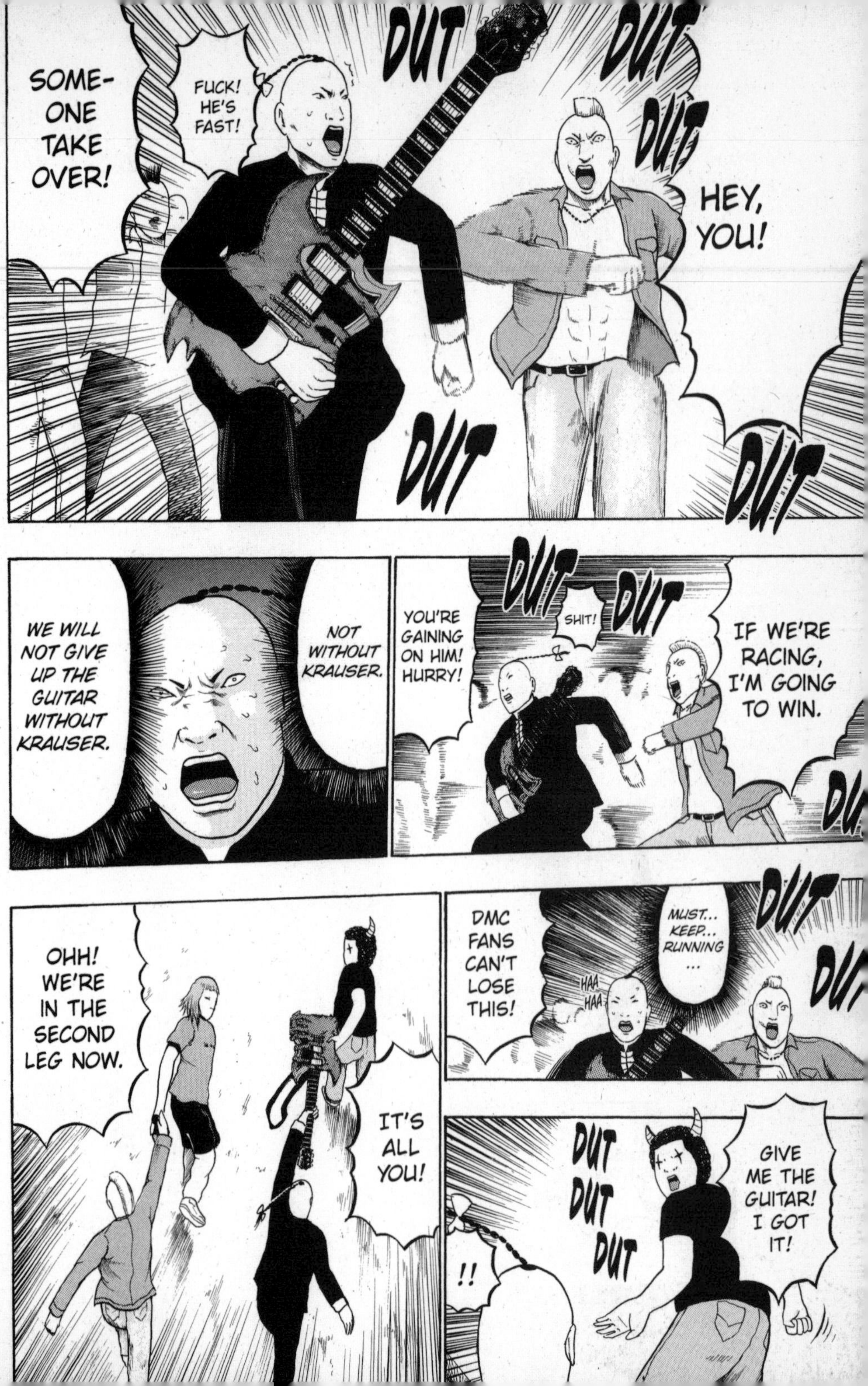
DUT
DUT
DUT
HEY, YOU!
FUCK! HE'S FAST!
SOME-ONE TAKE OVER!
DUT
DUT
DUT
DUT
IF WE'RE RACING, I'M GOING TO WIN.
SHIT!
YOU'RE GAINING ON HIM! HURRY!
NOT WITHOUT KRAUSER.
WE WILL NOT GIVE UP THE GUITAR WITHOUT KRAUSER.
DUT
MUST... KEEP... RUNNING...
HAA HAA
DMC FANS CAN'T LOSE THIS!
GIVE ME THE GUITAR! I GOT IT!
DUT DUT DUT
!!
OHH! WE'RE IN THE SECOND LEG NOW.
IT'S ALL YOU!

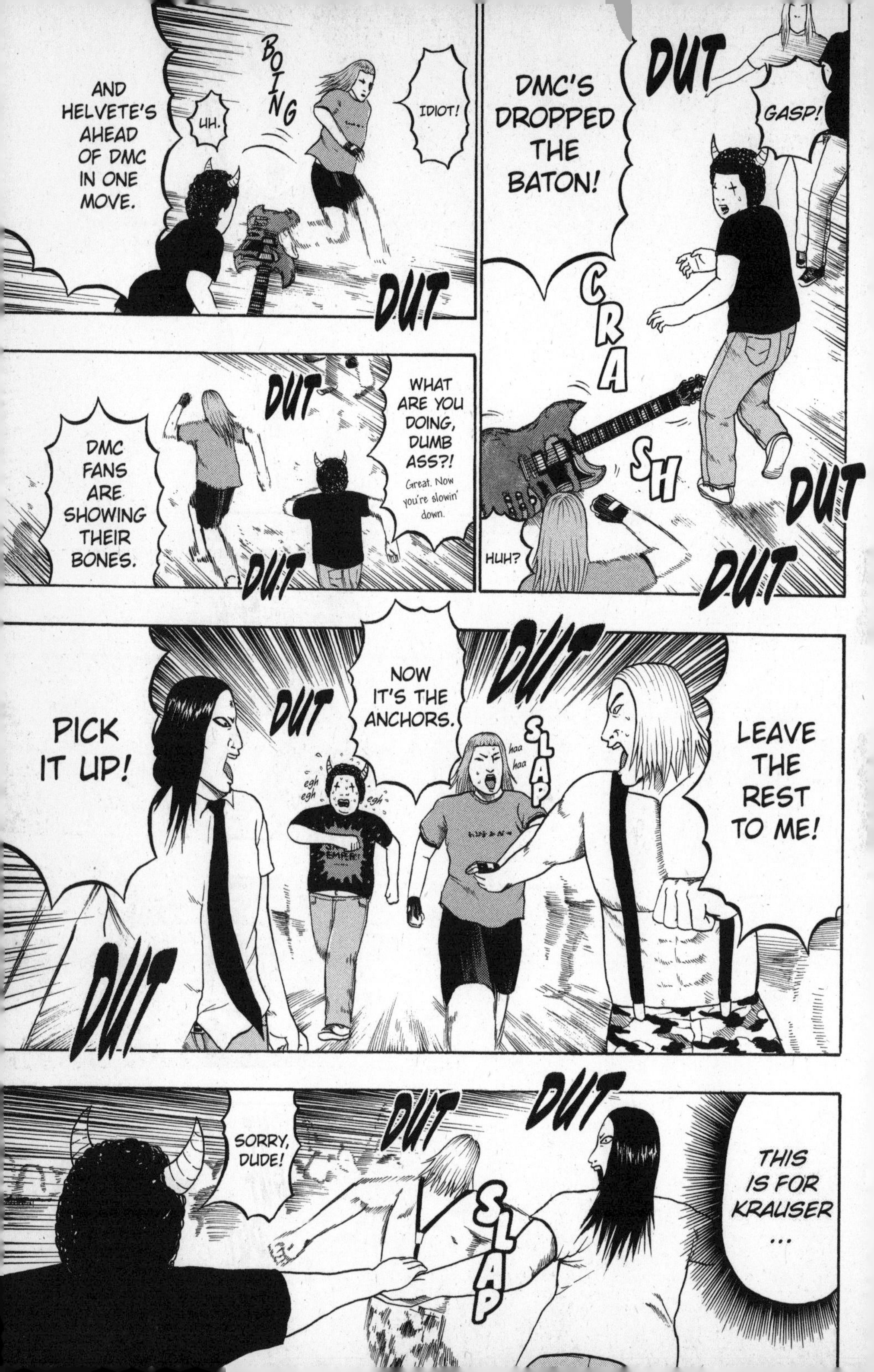
DUT
DMC'S DROPPED THE BATON!
GASP!
CRASH
DUT
DUT
HUH?
AND HELVETE'S AHEAD OF DMC IN ONE MOVE.
IDIOT!
BOING
UH.
DUT
WHAT ARE YOU DOING, DUMB ASS?!
Great. Now you're slowin' down.
DUT
DMC FANS ARE SHOWING THEIR BONES.
DUT
LEAVE THE REST TO ME!
DUT
SLAP
haa haa
NOW IT'S THE ANCHORS.
egh egh
egh
DUT
PICK IT UP!
DUT
THIS IS FOR KRAUSER ...
DUT
SLAP
DUT
SORRY, DUDE!

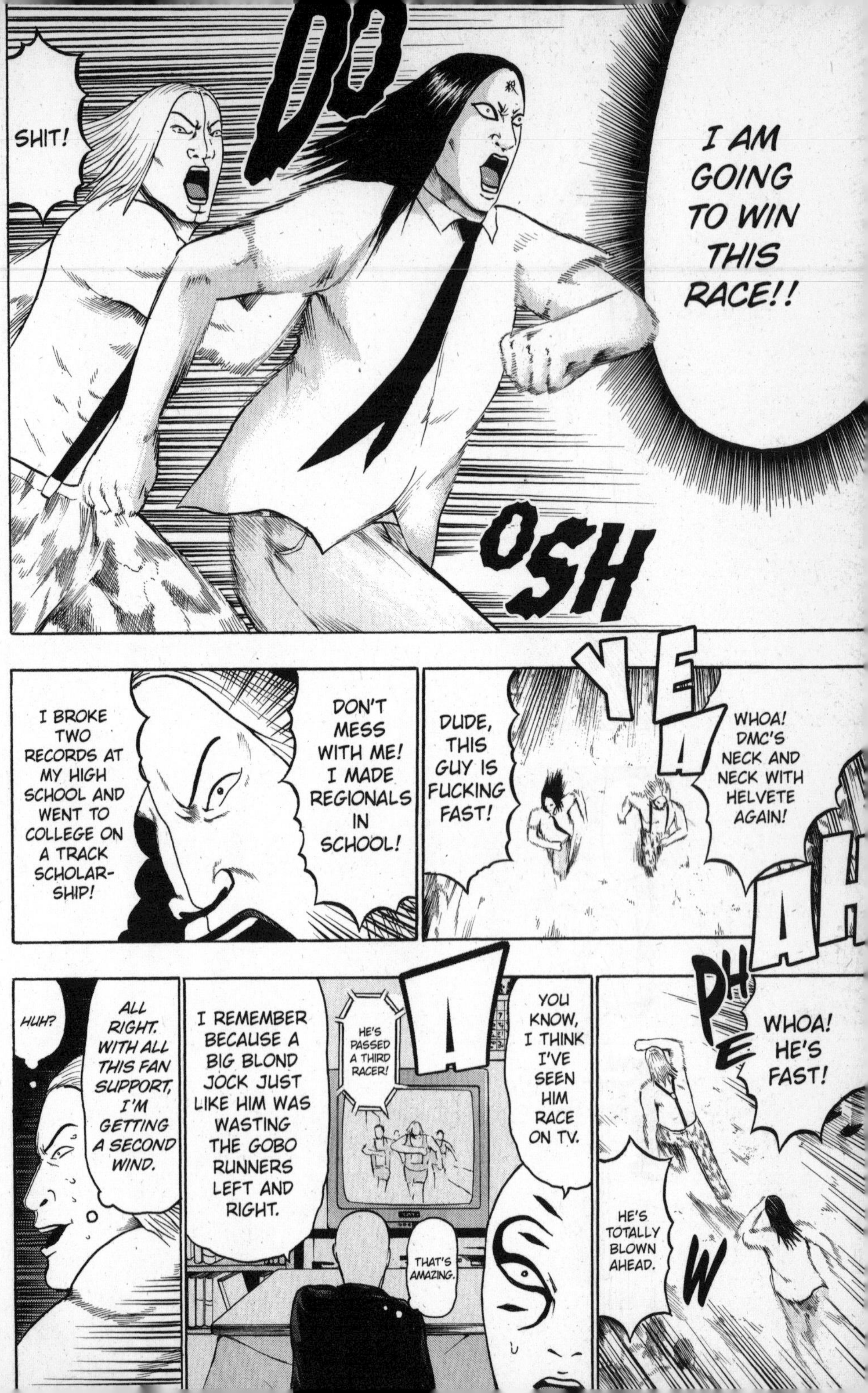
DO
I AM GOING TO WIN THIS RACE!!
SHIT!
OSH
YEAH
WHOA! DMC'S NECK AND NECK WITH HELVETE AGAIN!
DUDE, THIS GUY IS FUCKING FAST!
DON'T MESS WITH ME! I MADE REGIONALS IN SCHOOL!
I BROKE TWO RECORDS AT MY HIGH SCHOOL AND WENT TO COLLEGE ON A TRACK SCHOLAR-SHIP!
PHEW
WHOA! HE'S FAST!
HE'S TOTALLY BLOWN AHEAD.
YOU KNOW, I THINK I'VE SEEN HIM RACE ON TV.
A
HE'S PASSED A THIRD RACER!
THAT'S AMAZING.
I REMEMBER BECAUSE A BIG BLOND JOCK JUST LIKE HIM WAS WASTING THE GOBO RUNNERS LEFT AND RIGHT.
ALL RIGHT. WITH ALL THIS FAN SUPPORT, I'M GETTING A SECOND WIND.
HUH?

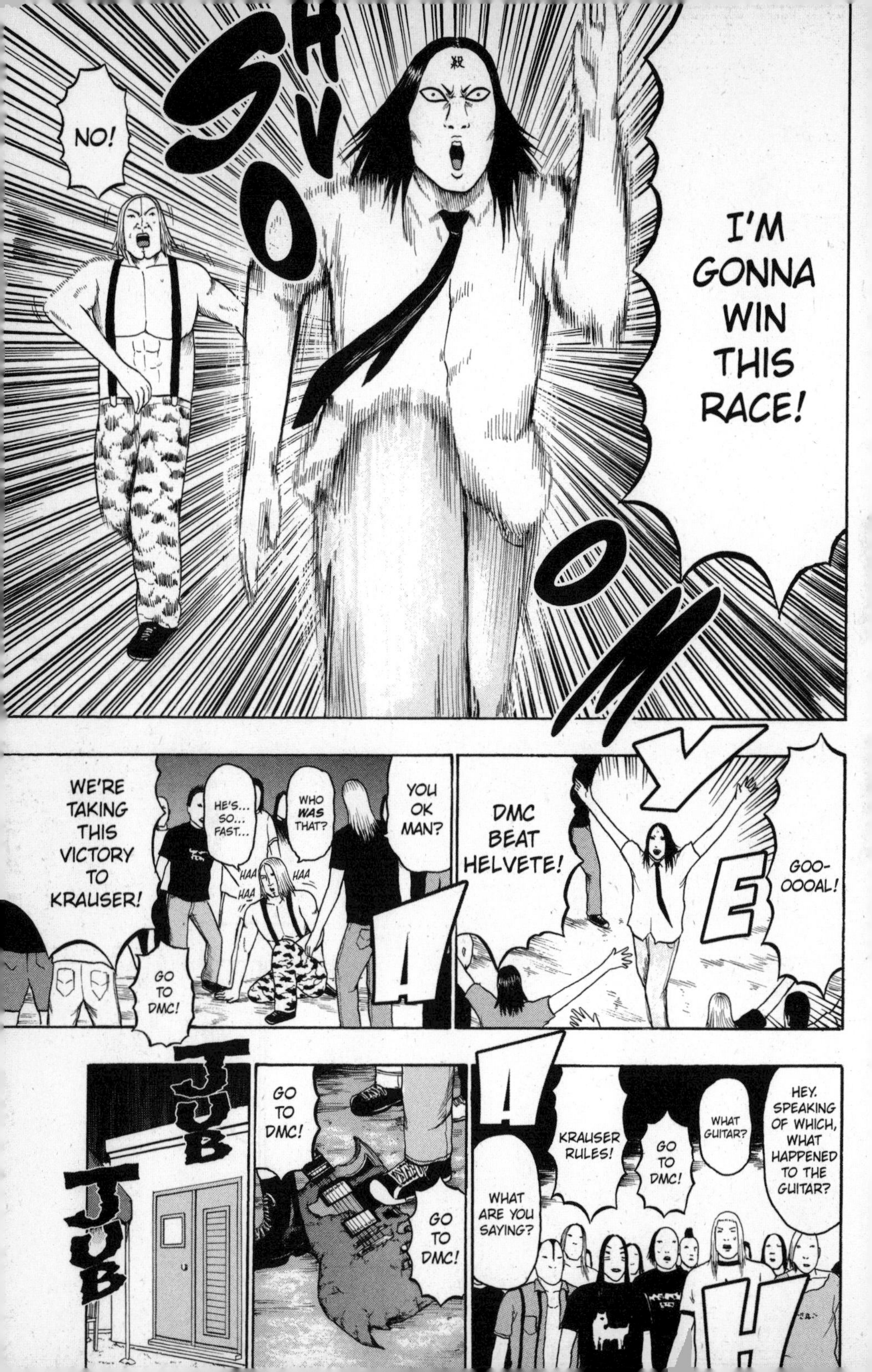

SHVOOM
I'M GONNA WIN THIS RACE!
NO!
YEAAH!
GOO-OOOAL!
DMC BEAT HELVETE!
YOU OK MAN?
WHO WAS THAT?
HE'S... SO... FAST...
HAA HAA HAA
WE'RE TAKING THIS VICTORY TO KRAUSER!
GO TO DMC!
HEY. SPEAKING OF WHICH, WHAT HAPPENED TO THE GUITAR?
WHAT GUITAR?
GO TO DMC!
KRAUSER RULES!
WHAT ARE YOU SAYING?
GO TO DMC!
GO TO DMC!
JUB
JUB

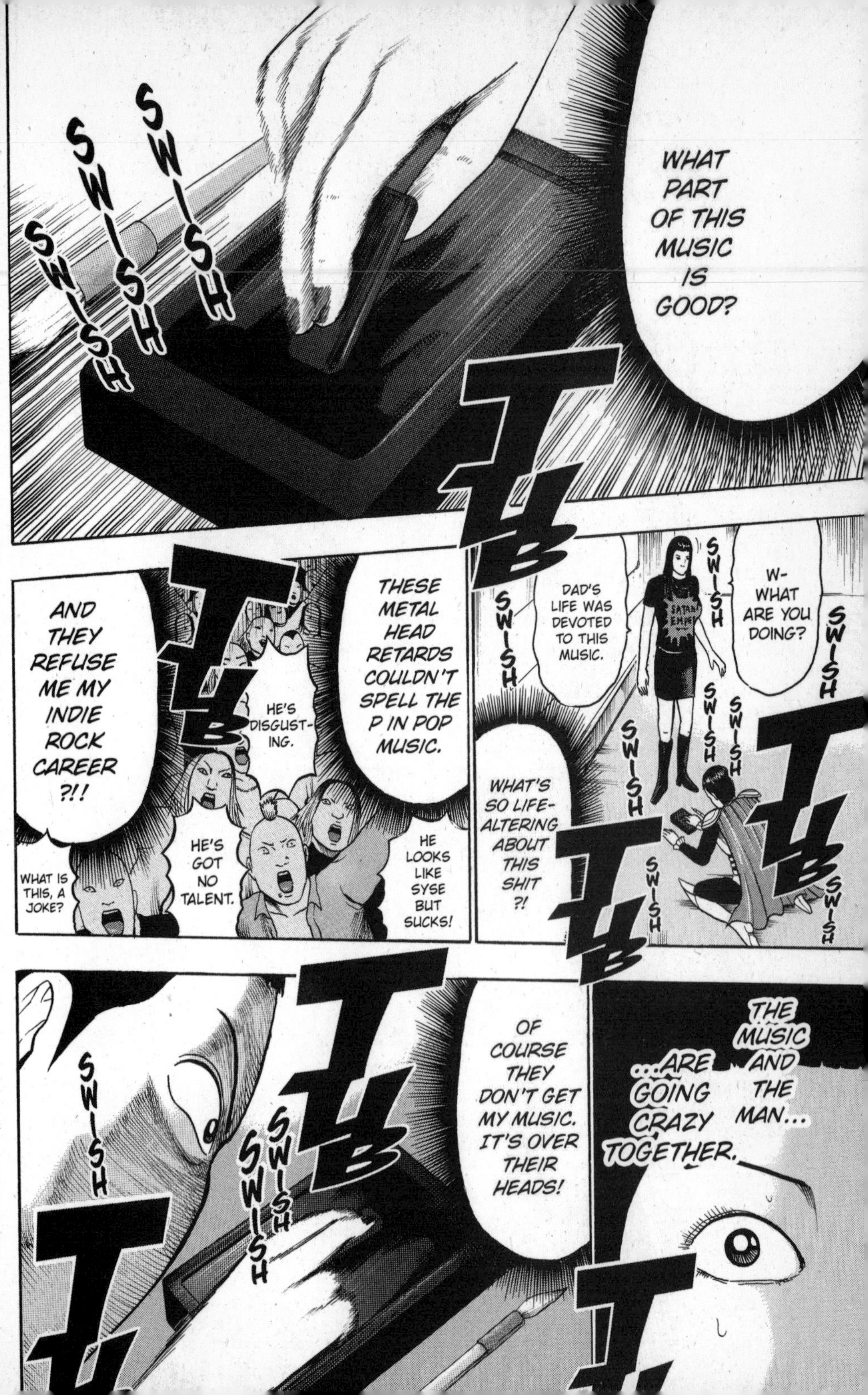
WHAT PART OF THIS MUSIC IS GOOD?
SWISH SWISH SWISH
W- WHAT ARE YOU DOING?
DAD'S LIFE WAS DEVOTED TO THIS MUSIC.
WHAT'S SO LIFE-ALTERING ABOUT THIS SHIT ?!
SWISH SWISH SWISH SWISH SWISH SWISH SWISH SWISH
THESE METAL HEAD RETARDS COULDN'T SPELL THE P IN POP MUSIC.
AND THEY REFUSE ME MY INDIE ROCK CAREER ?!!
HE'S DISGUSTING.
HE LOOKS LIKE SYSE BUT SUCKS!
HE'S GOT NO TALENT.
WHAT IS THIS, A JOKE?
THE MUSIC AND THE MAN...
...ARE GOING CRAZY TOGETHER.
OF COURSE THEY DON'T GET MY MUSIC. IT'S OVER THEIR HEADS!
SWISH SWISH SWISH

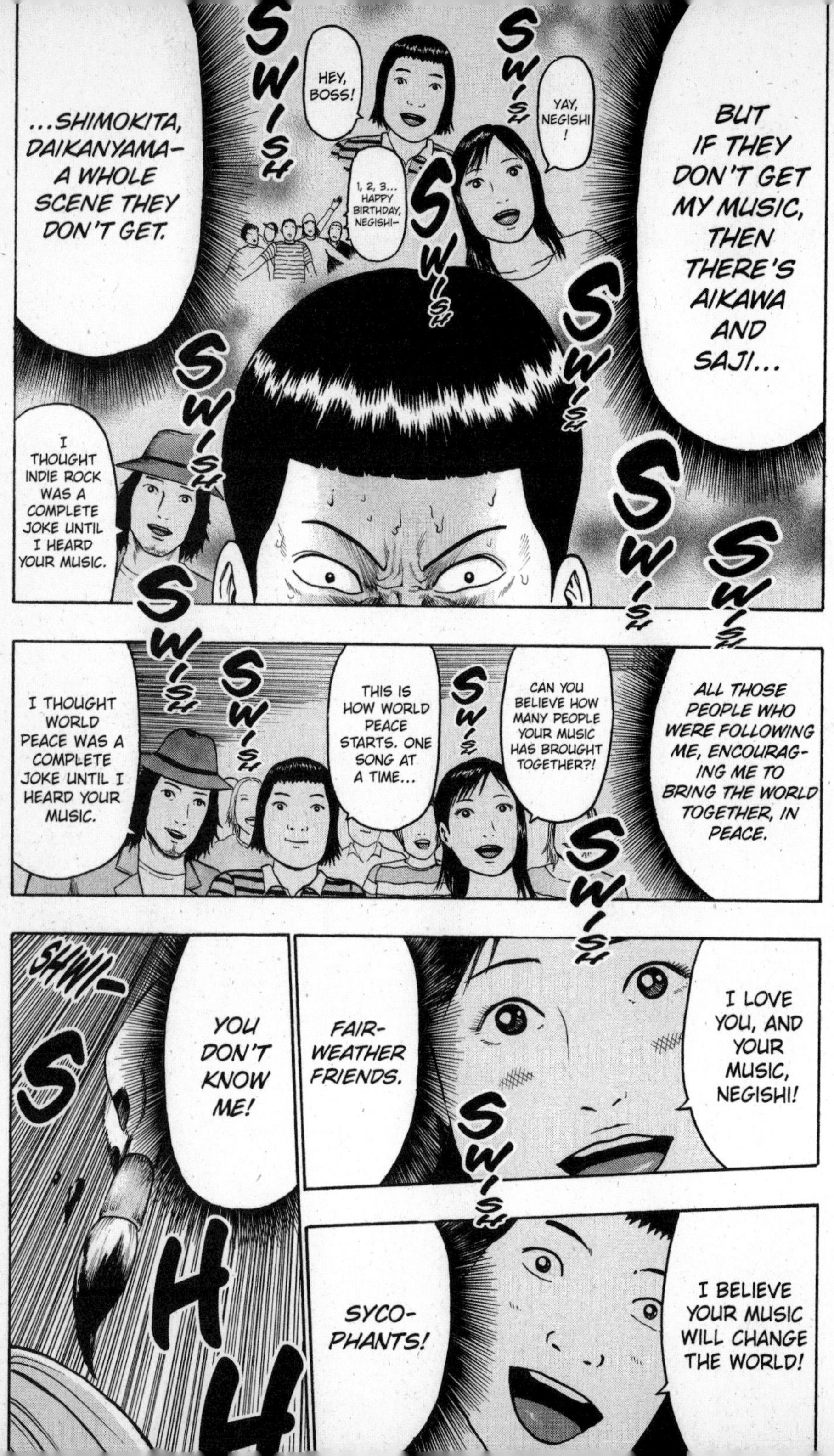
BUT IF THEY DON'T GET MY MUSIC, THEN THERE'S AIKAWA AND SAJI...
SWISH
YAY, NEGISHI!
SWISH
HEY, BOSS!
1, 2, 3... HAPPY BIRTHDAY, NEGISHI—
SWISH
...SHIMOKITA, DAIKANYAMA— A WHOLE SCENE THEY DON'T GET.
SWISH
SWISH
SWISH
SWISH
I THOUGHT INDIE ROCK WAS A COMPLETE JOKE UNTIL I HEARD YOUR MUSIC.
SWISH
ALL THOSE PEOPLE WHO WERE FOLLOWING ME, ENCOURAG-ING ME TO BRING THE WORLD TOGETHER, IN PEACE.
CAN YOU BELIEVE HOW MANY PEOPLE YOUR MUSIC HAS BROUGHT TOGETHER?!
SWISH
THIS IS HOW WORLD PEACE STARTS. ONE SONG AT A TIME...
SWISH
I THOUGHT WORLD PEACE WAS A COMPLETE JOKE UNTIL I HEARD YOUR MUSIC.
SWISH
I LOVE YOU, AND YOUR MUSIC, NEGISHI!
SWISH
FAIR-WEATHER FRIENDS.
I BELIEVE YOUR MUSIC WILL CHANGE THE WORLD!
SYCO-PHANTS!
YOU DON'T KNOW ME!
SHWI-
SHH

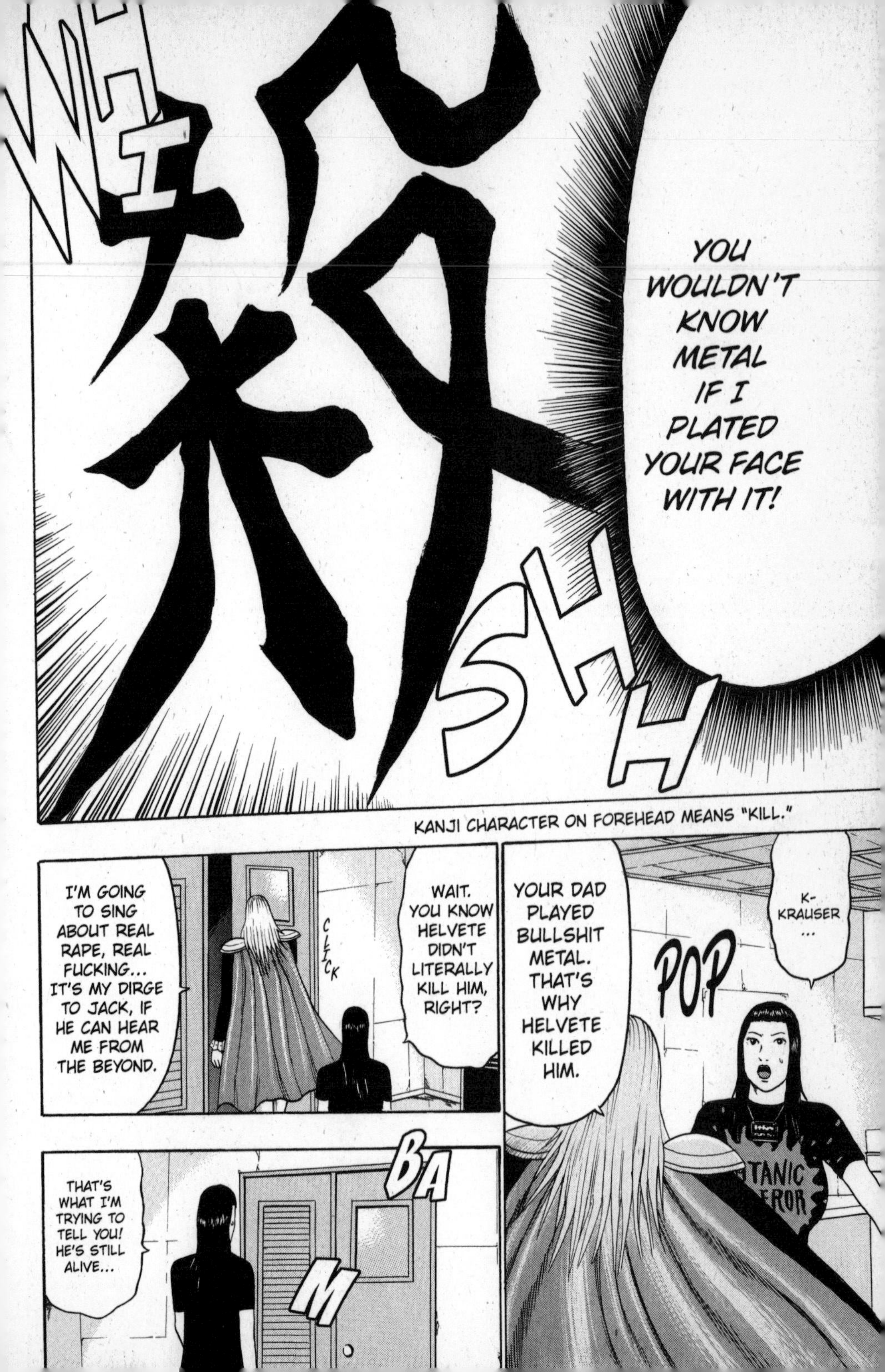
WHI
YOU WOULDN'T KNOW METAL IF I PLATED YOUR FACE WITH IT!
SHH
KANJI CHARACTER ON FOREHEAD MEANS "KILL."
K-KRAUSER...
POP
YOUR DAD PLAYED BULLSHIT METAL. THAT'S WHY HELVETE KILLED HIM.
WAIT. YOU KNOW HELVETE DIDN'T LITERALLY KILL HIM, RIGHT?
CLICK
I'M GOING TO SING ABOUT REAL RAPE, REAL FUCKING... IT'S MY DIRGE TO JACK, IF HE CAN HEAR ME FROM THE BEYOND.
BAM
THAT'S WHAT I'M TRYING TO TELL YOU! HE'S STILL ALIVE...

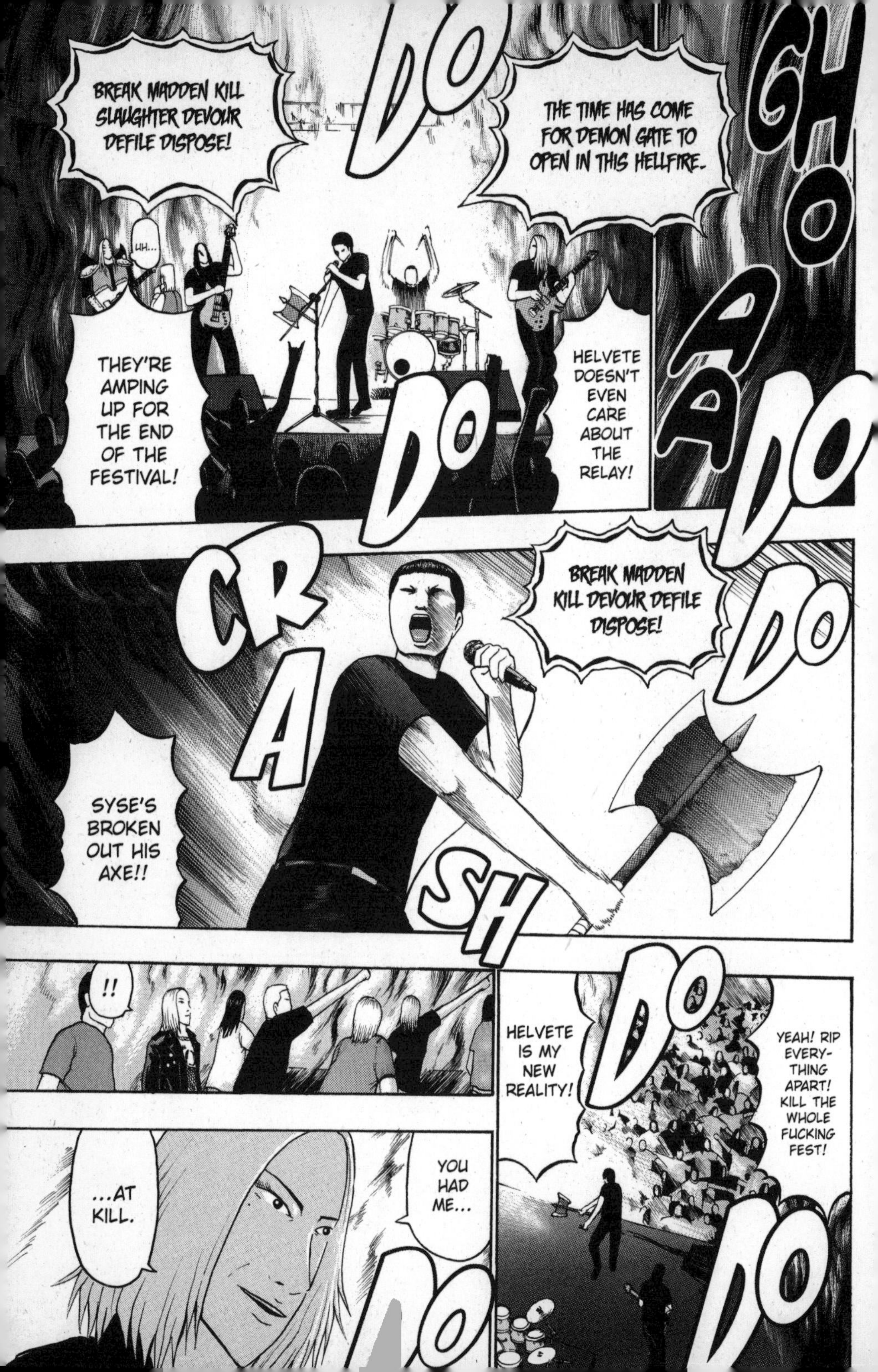
GHOOAA
THE TIME HAS COME FOR DEMON GATE TO OPEN IN THIS HELLFIRE.
DO
BREAK MADDEN KILL SLAUGHTER DEVOUR DEFILE DISPOSE!
DO
HELVETE DOESN'T EVEN CARE ABOUT THE RELAY!
UH...
THEY'RE AMPING UP FOR THE END OF THE FESTIVAL!
DO DO
BREAK MADDEN KILL DEVOUR DEFILE DISPOSE!
CRASH
SYSE'S BROKEN OUT HIS AXE!!
YEAH! RIP EVERYTHING APART! KILL THE WHOLE FUCKING FEST!
DODO
HELVETE IS MY NEW REALITY!
!!
DO
YOU HAD ME...
...AT KILL.
DO

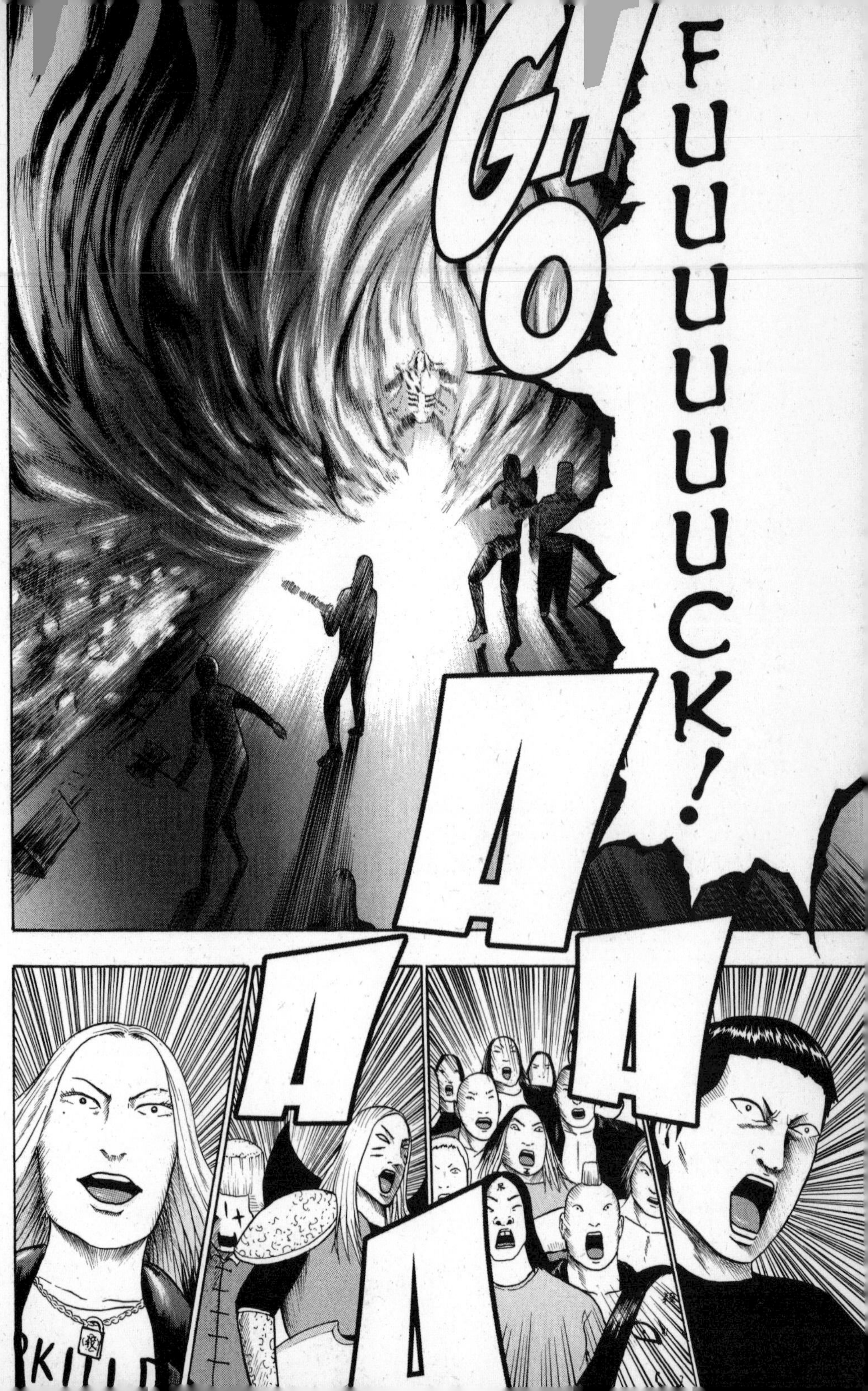
GHO
FUUUUUUCK!
AAAAA

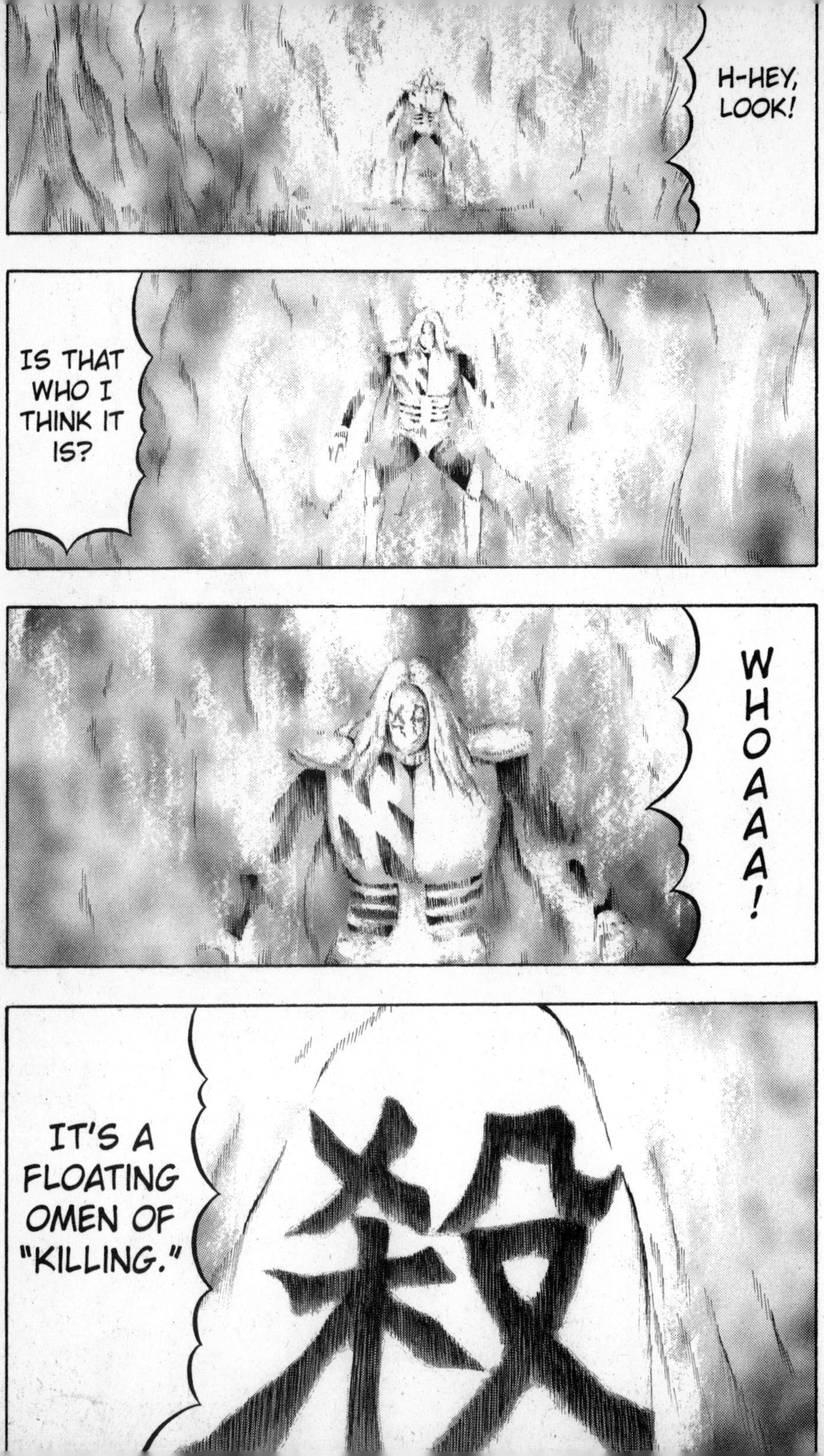
H-HEY, LOOK!
IS THAT WHO I THINK IT IS?
WHOAAAA!
IT'S A FLOATING OMEN OF "KILLING."
殺

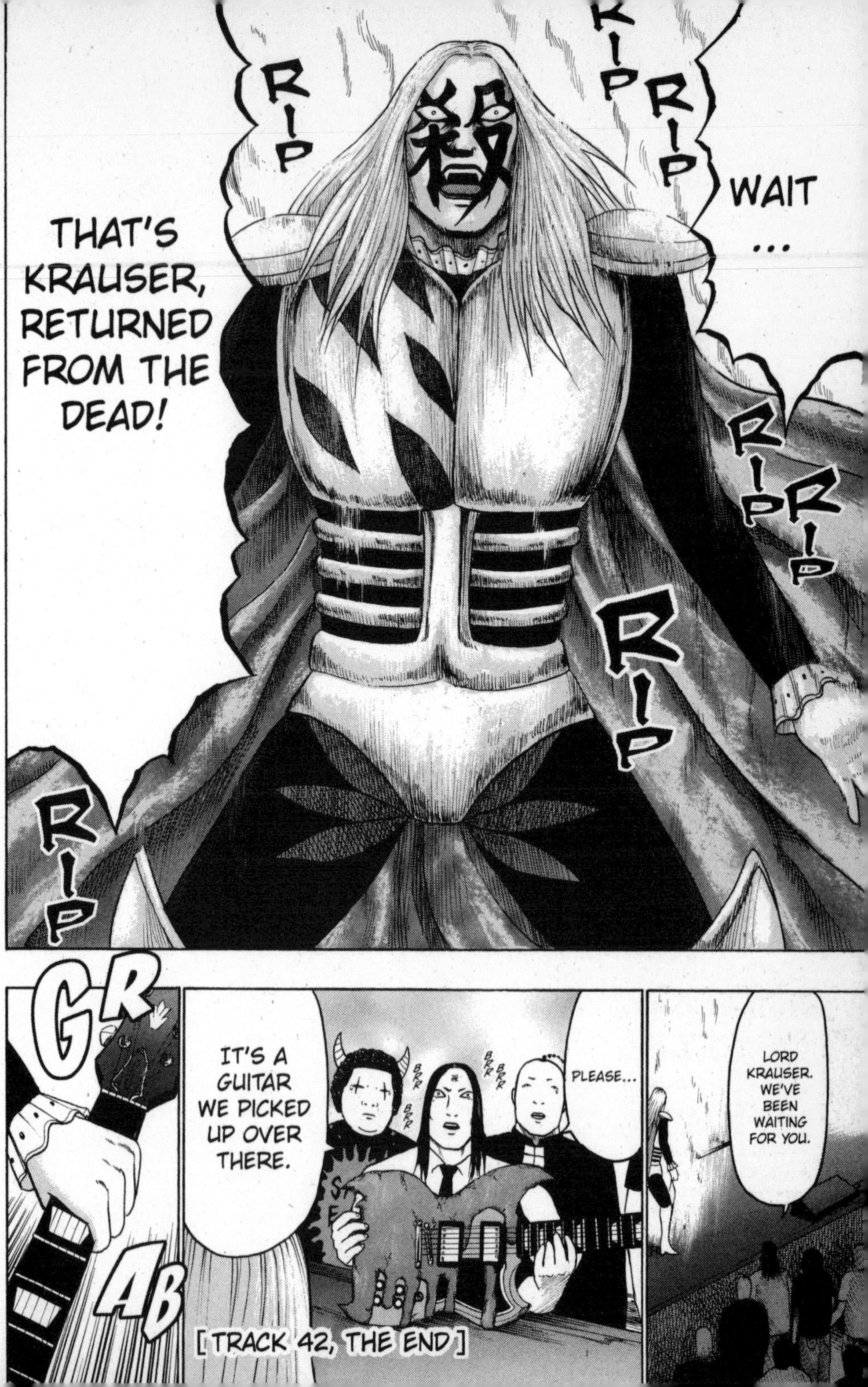
RIP RIP
RIP
WAIT ...
RIP
THAT'S KRAUSER, RETURNED FROM THE DEAD!
RIP RIP
RIP
RIP
RIP
LORD KRAUSER. WE'VE BEEN WAITING FOR YOU.
PLEASE...
BRR BRR BRR
IT'S A GUITAR WE PICKED UP OVER THERE.
GR
AB
[TRACK 42, THE END]

DMC LEXICON

♡ RELAY

A competitive race wherein several people run toward a finish line, usually in group sets of four. It can involve an obstacle course, but the baton pass is always the turning point. It goes without saying that relays (which sound an awful lot like "threeways") sometimes require refreshments and a little extra endurance (especially if you're going at it all night), but nothing excites people like group sets (which sounds an awful lot like an orgy).

Usage: "Last night's relay was something else, eh? You lapped everyone!"
"H-how d-did you know about that?!"

デトロイト・メタル・シティ

Detroit Metal City

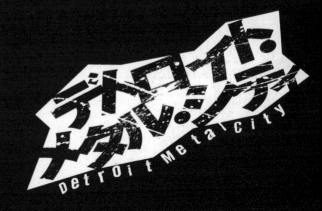

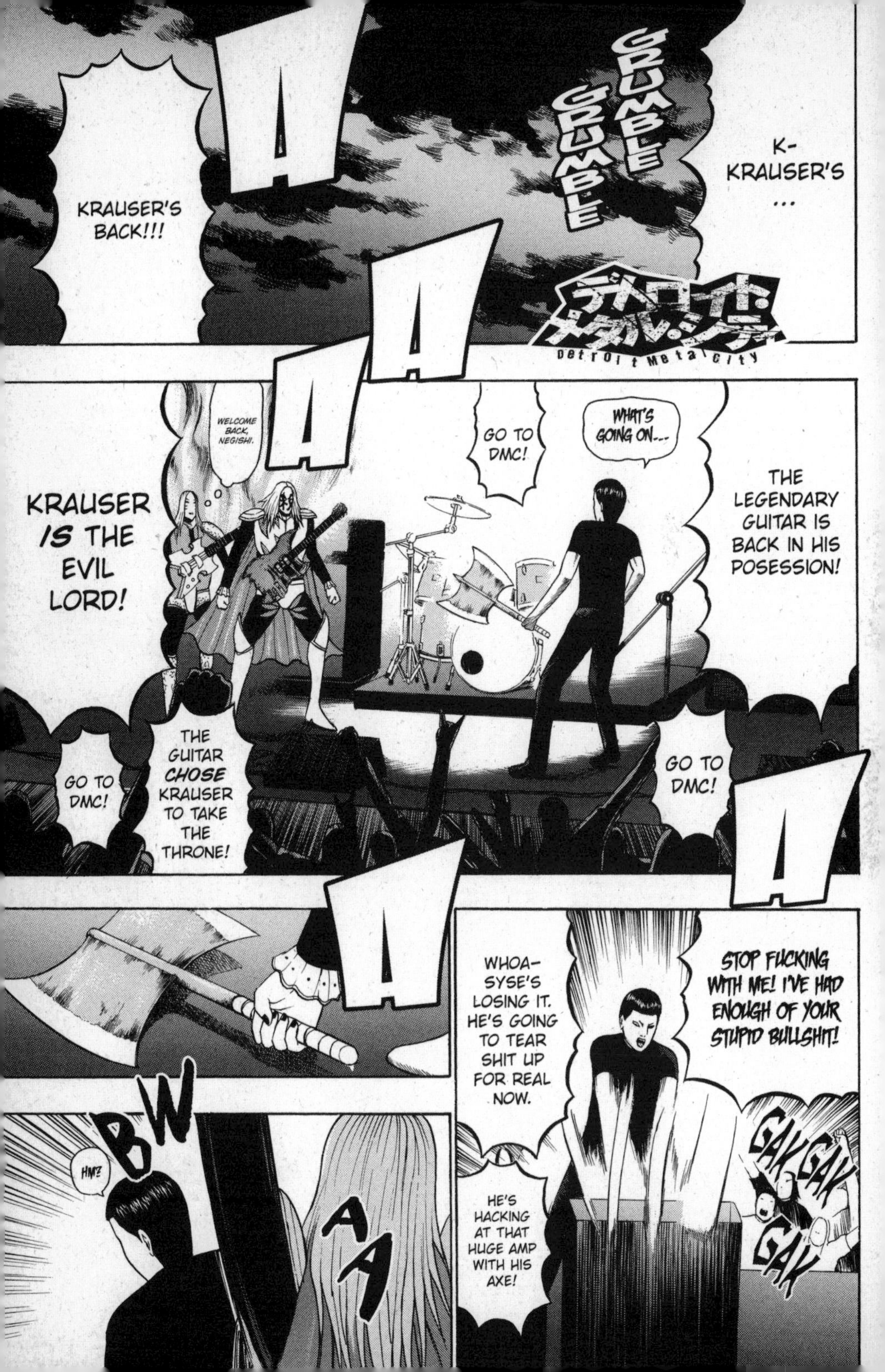
K-KRAUSER'S ...
GRUMBLE
GRUMBLE
A
A
A
KRAUSER'S BACK!!!
Detroit Metal City
THE LEGENDARY GUITAR IS BACK IN HIS POSESSION!
WHAT'S GOING ON...
GO TO DMC!
WELCOME BACK, NEGISHI.
A
KRAUSER *IS* THE EVIL LORD!
GO TO DMC!
A
THE GUITAR *CHOSE* KRAUSER TO TAKE THE THRONE!
GO TO DMC!
STOP FUCKING WITH ME! I'VE HAD ENOUGH OF YOUR STUPID BULLSHIT!
WHOA-SYSE'S LOSING IT. HE'S GOING TO TEAR SHIT UP FOR REAL NOW.
GAK GAK
GAK
HE'S HACKING AT THAT HUGE AMP WITH HIS AXE!
A
BW
AA
HM?

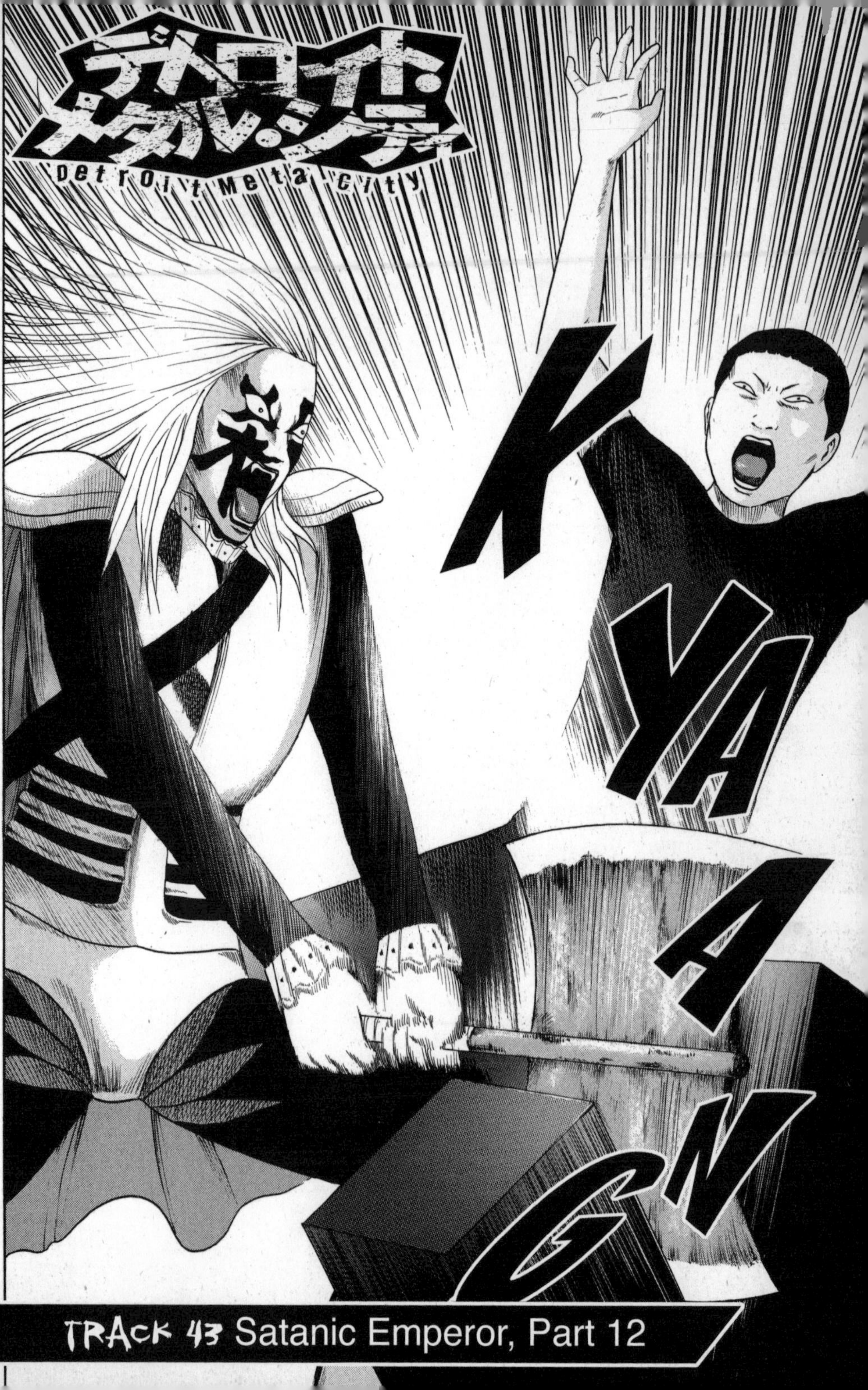
Detroit Metal City
KYAANG

TRACK 43 Satanic Emperor, Part 12

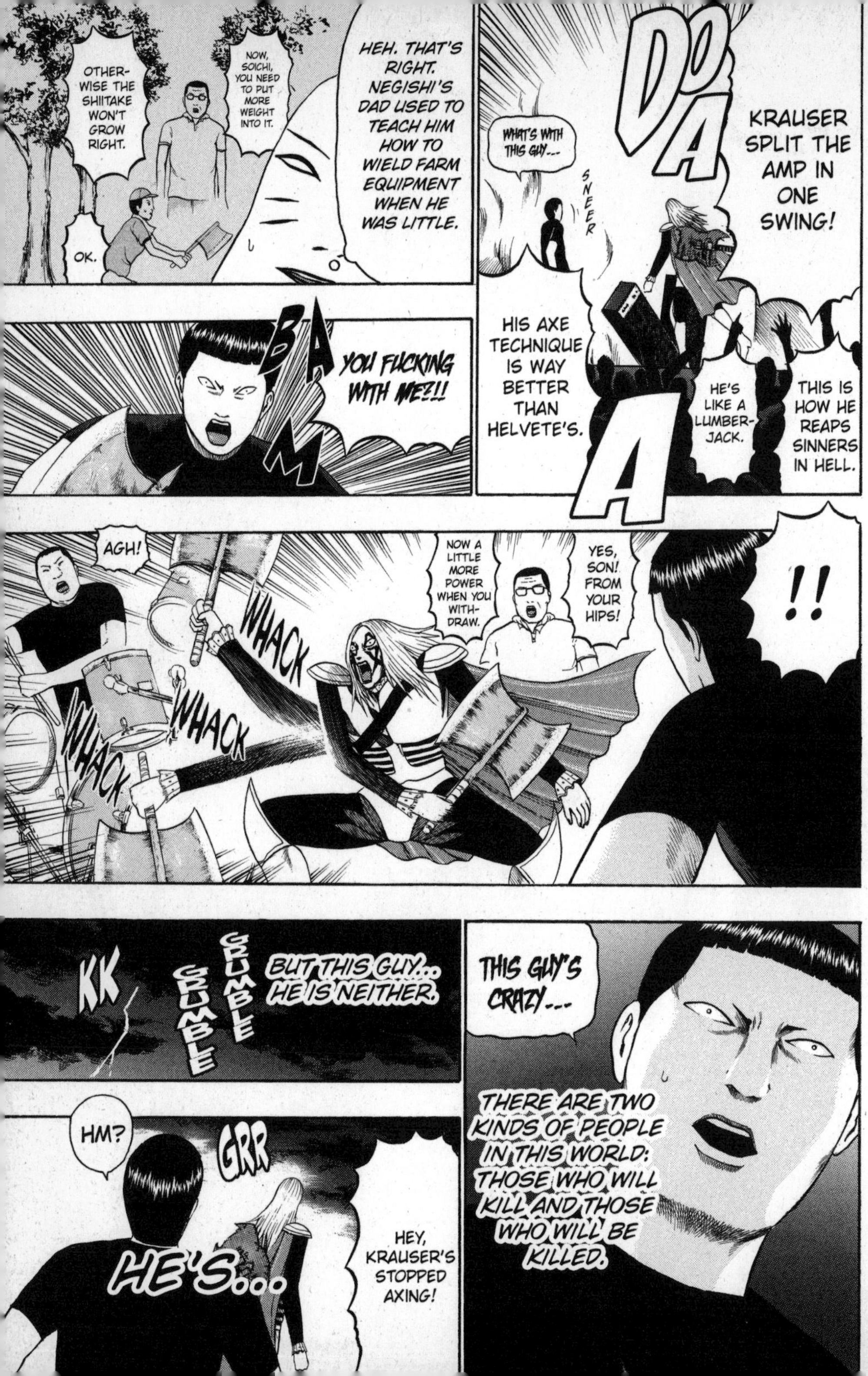
DOA
KRAUSER SPLIT THE AMP IN ONE SWING!
WHAT'S WITH THIS GUY...
SNEER
THIS IS HOW HE REAPS SINNERS IN HELL.
HE'S LIKE A LUMBERJACK.
HIS AXE TECHNIQUE IS WAY BETTER THAN HELVETE'S.
A
HEH. THAT'S RIGHT. NEGISHI'S DAD USED TO TEACH HIM HOW TO WIELD FARM EQUIPMENT WHEN HE WAS LITTLE.
NOW, SOICHI, YOU NEED TO PUT MORE WEIGHT INTO IT.
OTHERWISE THE SHIITAKE WON'T GROW RIGHT.
OK.
YOU FUCKING WITH ME?!!
BAM
!!
YES, SON! FROM YOUR HIPS!
NOW A LITTLE MORE POWER WHEN YOU WITHDRAW.
WHACK
AGH!
WHACK
WHACK
THIS GUY'S CRAZY...
THERE ARE TWO KINDS OF PEOPLE IN THIS WORLD: THOSE WHO WILL KILL AND THOSE WHO WILL BE KILLED.
BUT THIS GUY... HE IS NEITHER.
GRUMBLE
GRUMBLE
KK
GRR
HM?
HEY, KRAUSER'S STOPPED AXING!
HE'S...

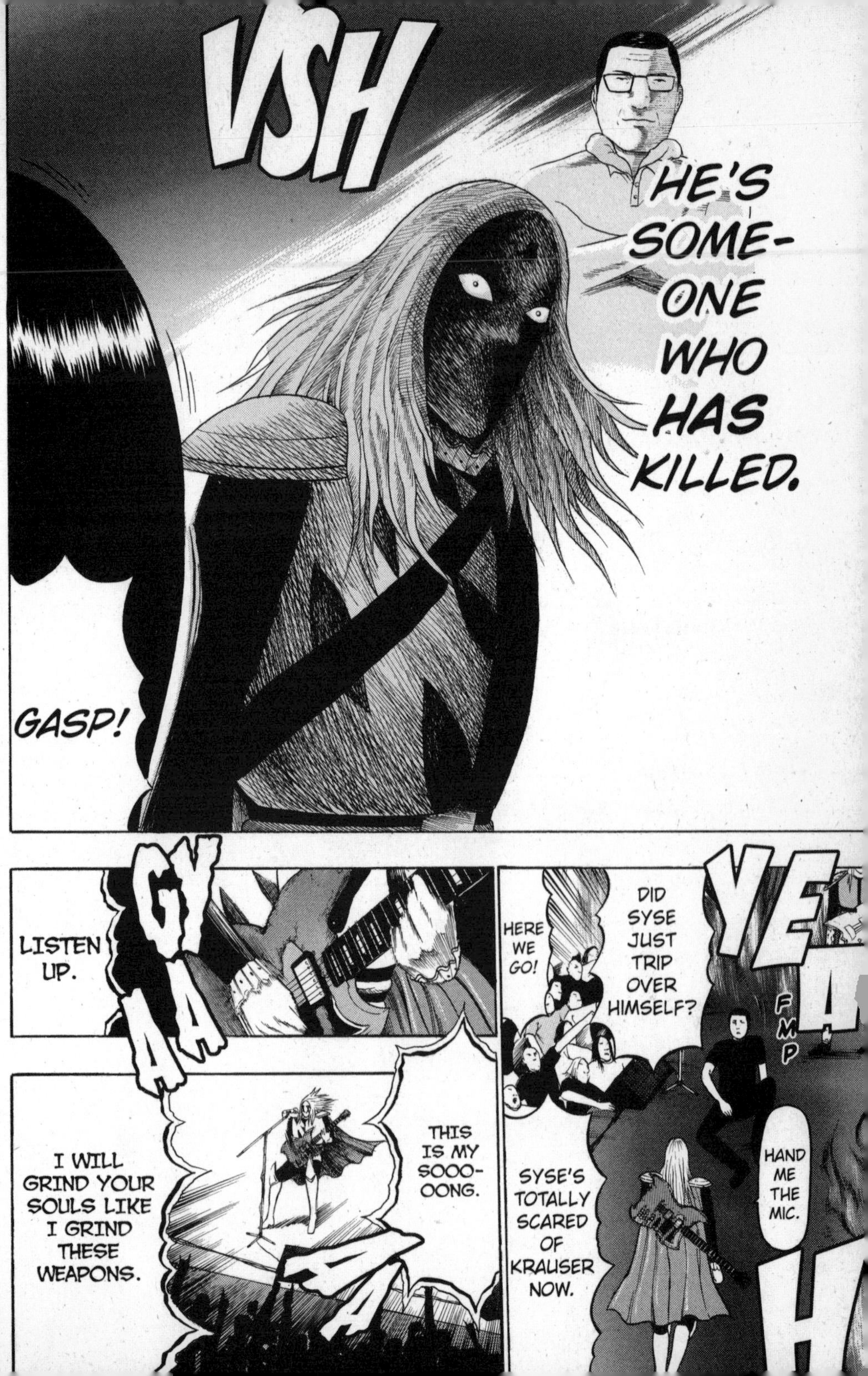
VSH
HE'S SOME-ONE WHO HAS KILLED.
GASP!
DID SYSE JUST TRIP OVER HIMSELF?
HERE WE GO!
FMP
HAND ME THE MIC.
SYSE'S TOTALLY SCARED OF KRAUSER NOW.
GYAAA
LISTEN UP.
THIS IS MY SOOO-OONG.
I WILL GRIND YOUR SOULS LIKE I GRIND THESE WEAPONS.

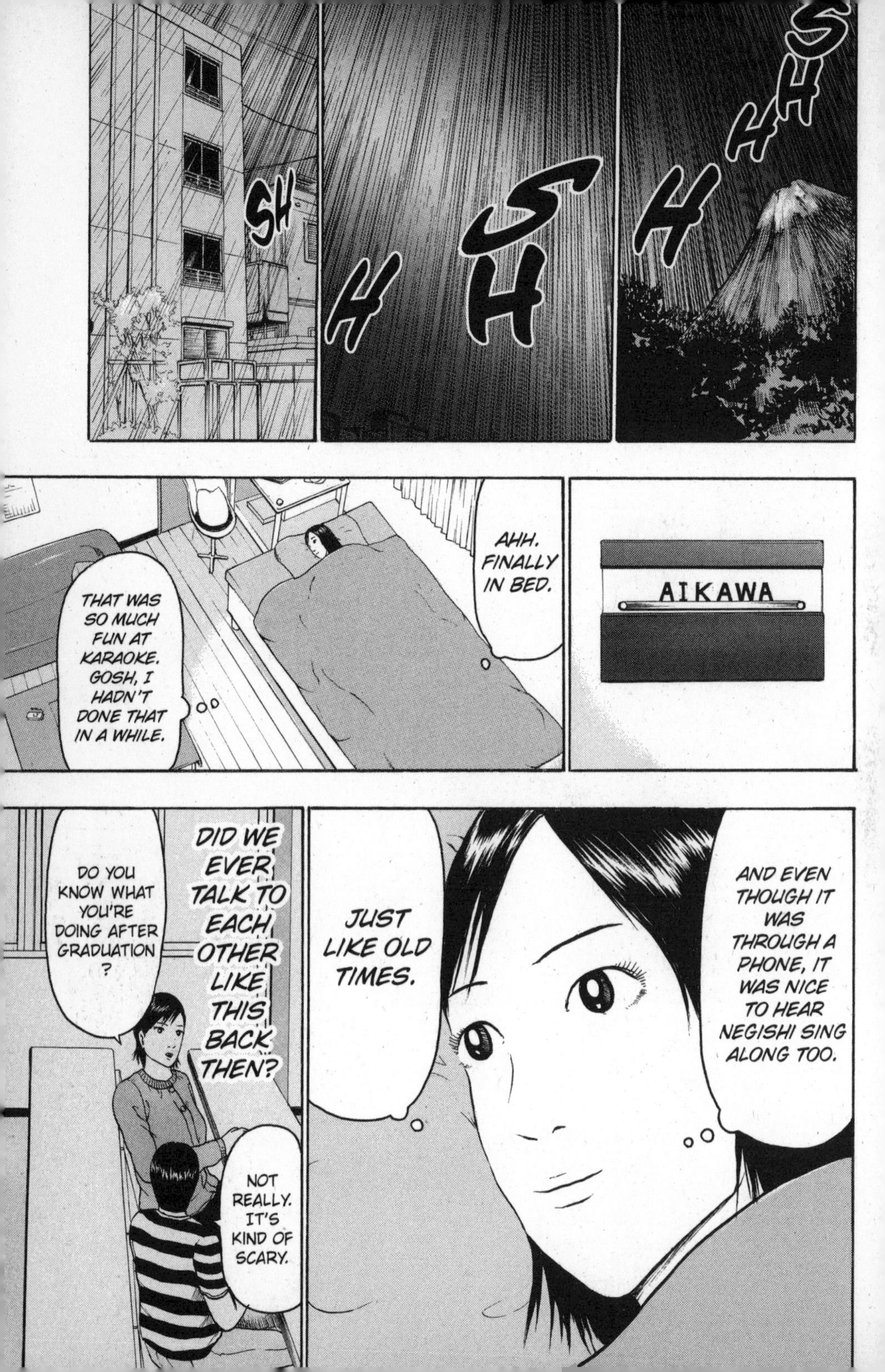
SHHSHHHHS
AIKAWA
AHH. FINALLY IN BED.
THAT WAS SO MUCH FUN AT KARAOKE. GOSH, I HADN'T DONE THAT IN A WHILE.
AND EVEN THOUGH IT WAS THROUGH A PHONE, IT WAS NICE TO HEAR NEGISHI SING ALONG TOO.
JUST LIKE OLD TIMES.
DID WE EVER TALK TO EACH OTHER LIKE THIS BACK THEN?
DO YOU KNOW WHAT YOU'RE DOING AFTER GRADUATION?
NOT REALLY. IT'S KIND OF SCARY.

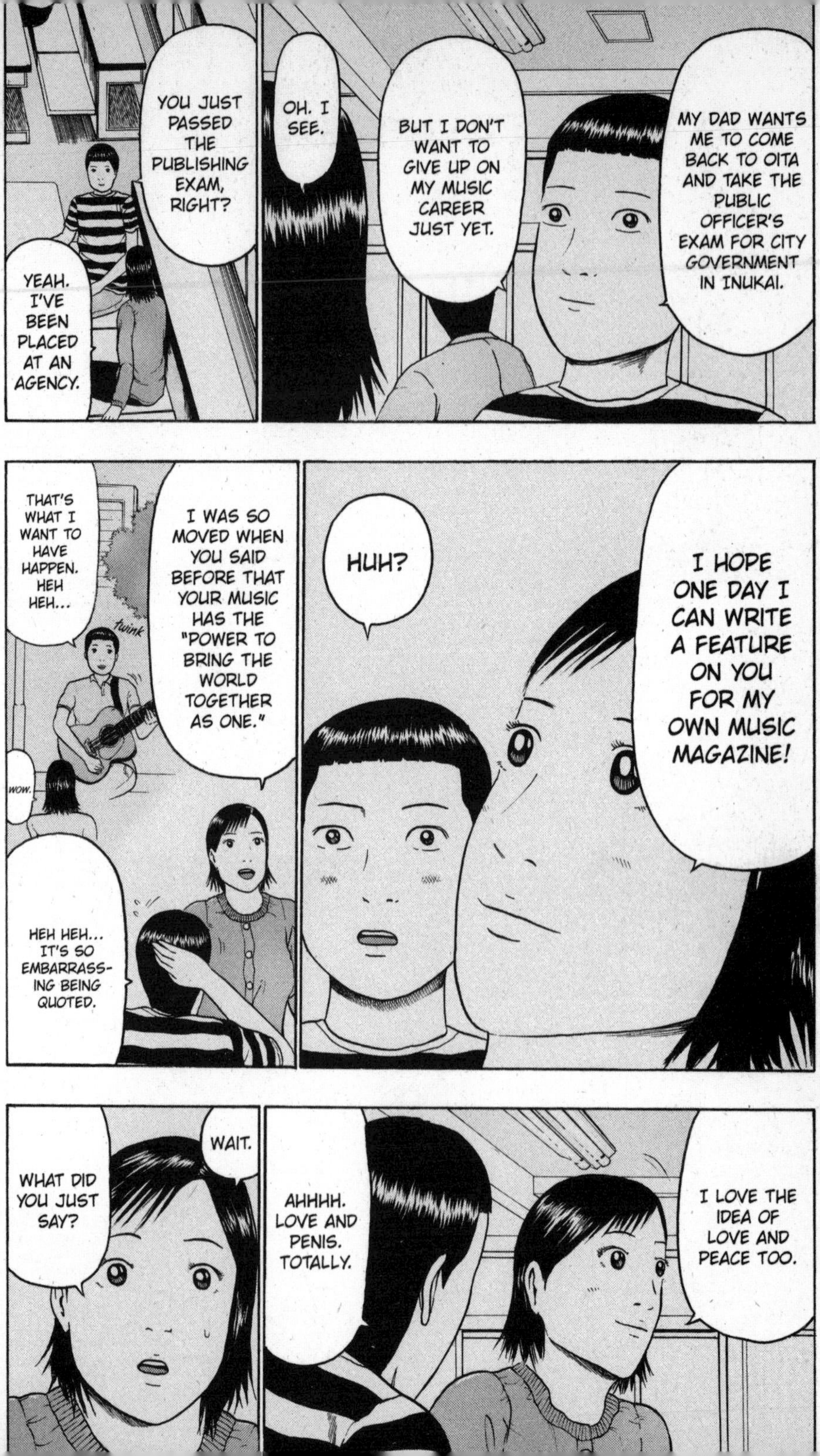
MY DAD WANTS ME TO COME BACK TO OITA AND TAKE THE PUBLIC OFFICER'S EXAM FOR CITY GOVERNMENT IN INUKAI.
BUT I DON'T WANT TO GIVE UP ON MY MUSIC CAREER JUST YET.
OH. I SEE.
YOU JUST PASSED THE PUBLISHING EXAM, RIGHT?
YEAH. I'VE BEEN PLACED AT AN AGENCY.
I HOPE ONE DAY I CAN WRITE A FEATURE ON YOU FOR MY OWN MUSIC MAGAZINE!
HUH?
I WAS SO MOVED WHEN YOU SAID BEFORE THAT YOUR MUSIC HAS THE "POWER TO BRING THE WORLD TOGETHER AS ONE."
THAT'S WHAT I WANT TO HAVE HAPPEN. HEH HEH...
twink
WOW.
HEH HEH... IT'S SO EMBARRASS-ING BEING QUOTED.
I LOVE THE IDEA OF LOVE AND PEACE TOO.
AHHHH. LOVE AND PENIS. TOTALLY.
WAIT.
WHAT DID YOU JUST SAY?

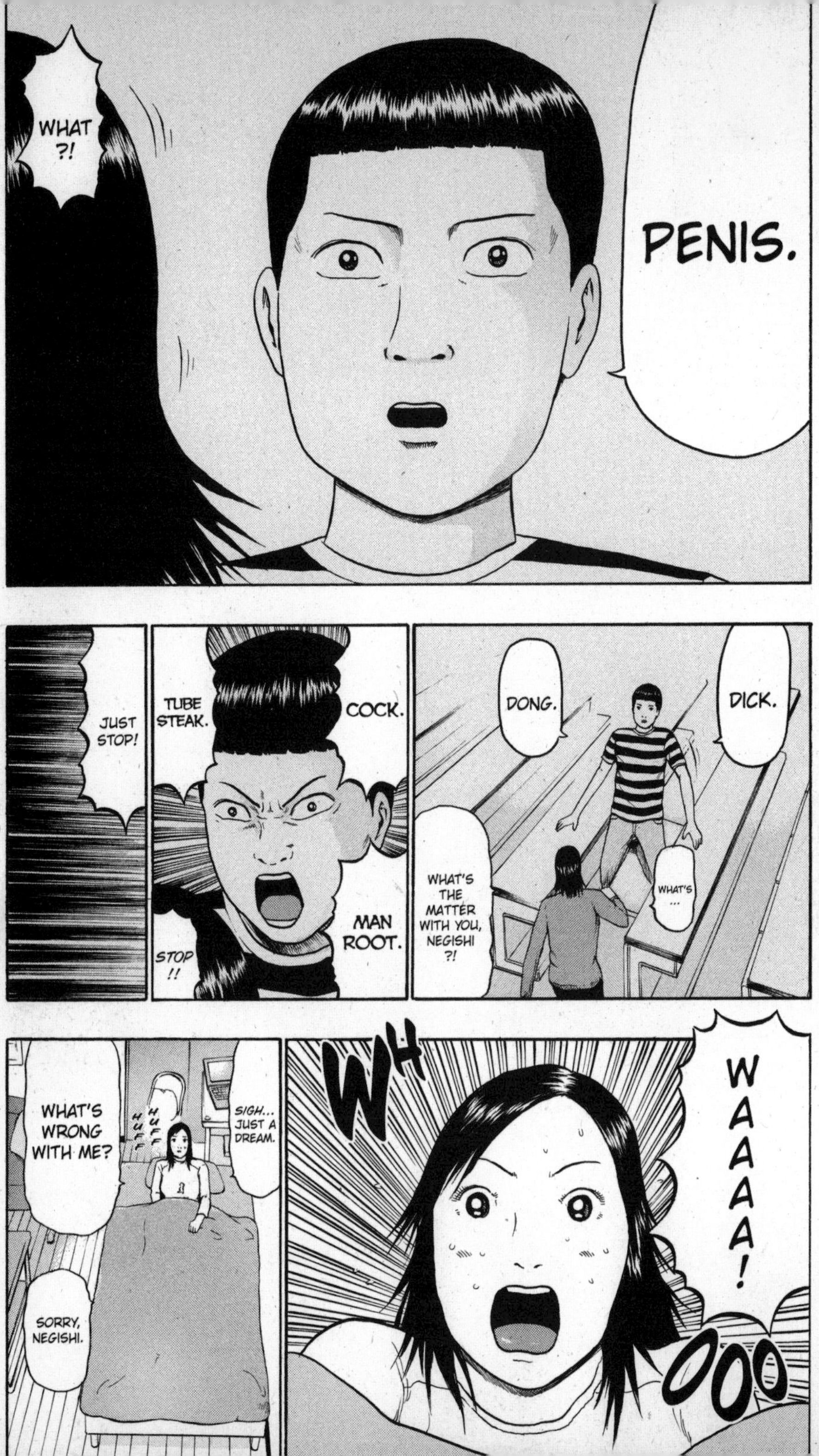
PENIS.
WHAT ?!
DICK.
DONG.
WHAT'S ...
WHAT'S THE MATTER WITH YOU, NEGISHI ?!
COCK.
TUBE STEAK.
MAN ROOT.
STOP !!
JUST STOP!
WAAAAA!
WH
OOO
SIGH... JUST A DREAM.
HUFF HUFF
WHAT'S WRONG WITH ME?
SORRY, NEGISHI.

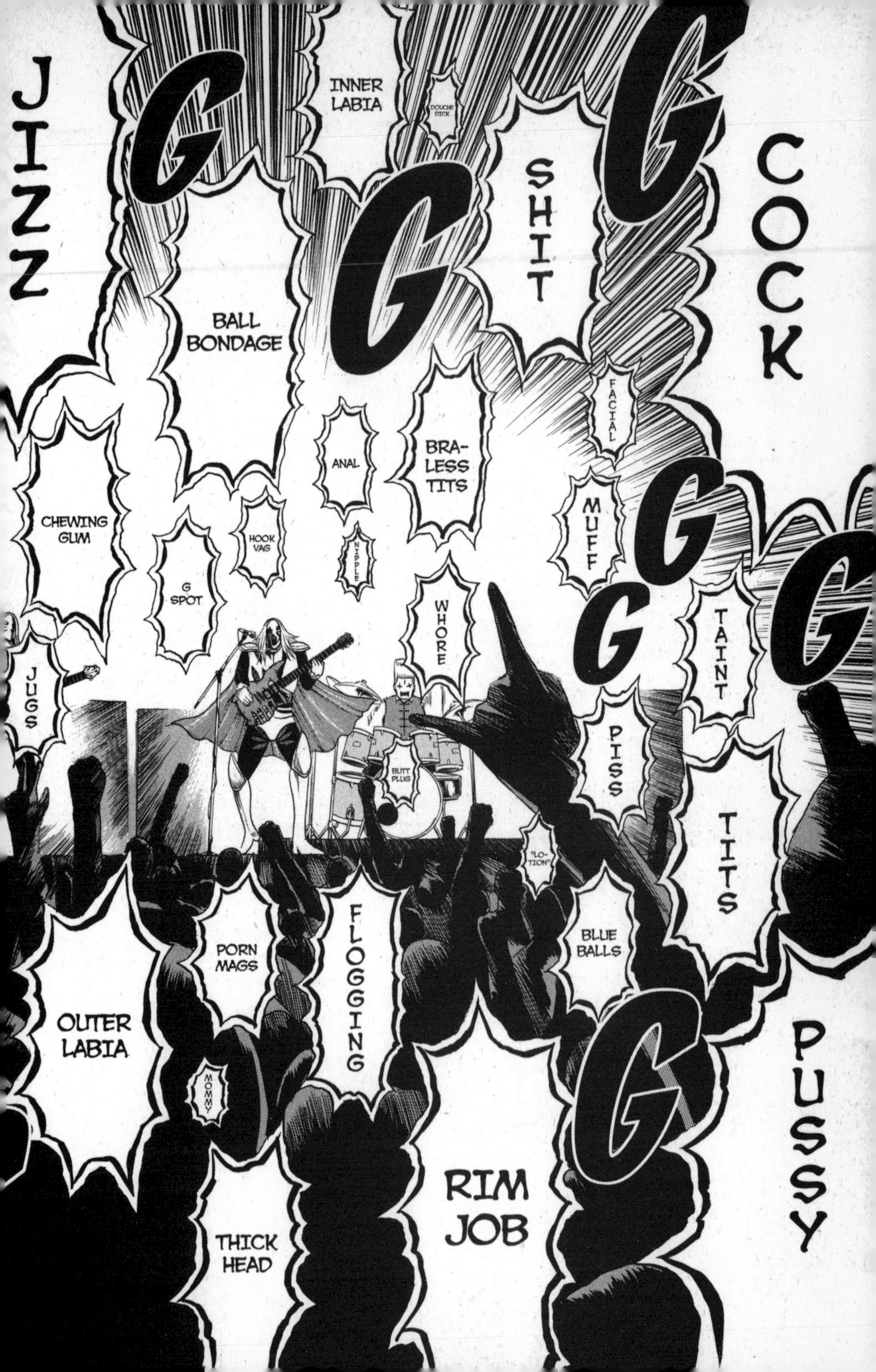
G
G
G
G
G
G
G
G
COCK
SHIT
DOUCHE DICK
INNER LABIA
JIZZ
BALL BONDAGE
FACIAL
BRA-LESS TITS
ANAL
MUFF
NIPPLE
HOOK VAG
CHEWING GUM
G SPOT
TAINT
WHORE
JUGS
PISS
BUTT PLUG
TITS
"LO-TION"
BLUE BALLS
FLOGGING
PORN MAGS
OUTER LABIA
MOMMY
PUSSY
RIM JOB
THICK HEAD

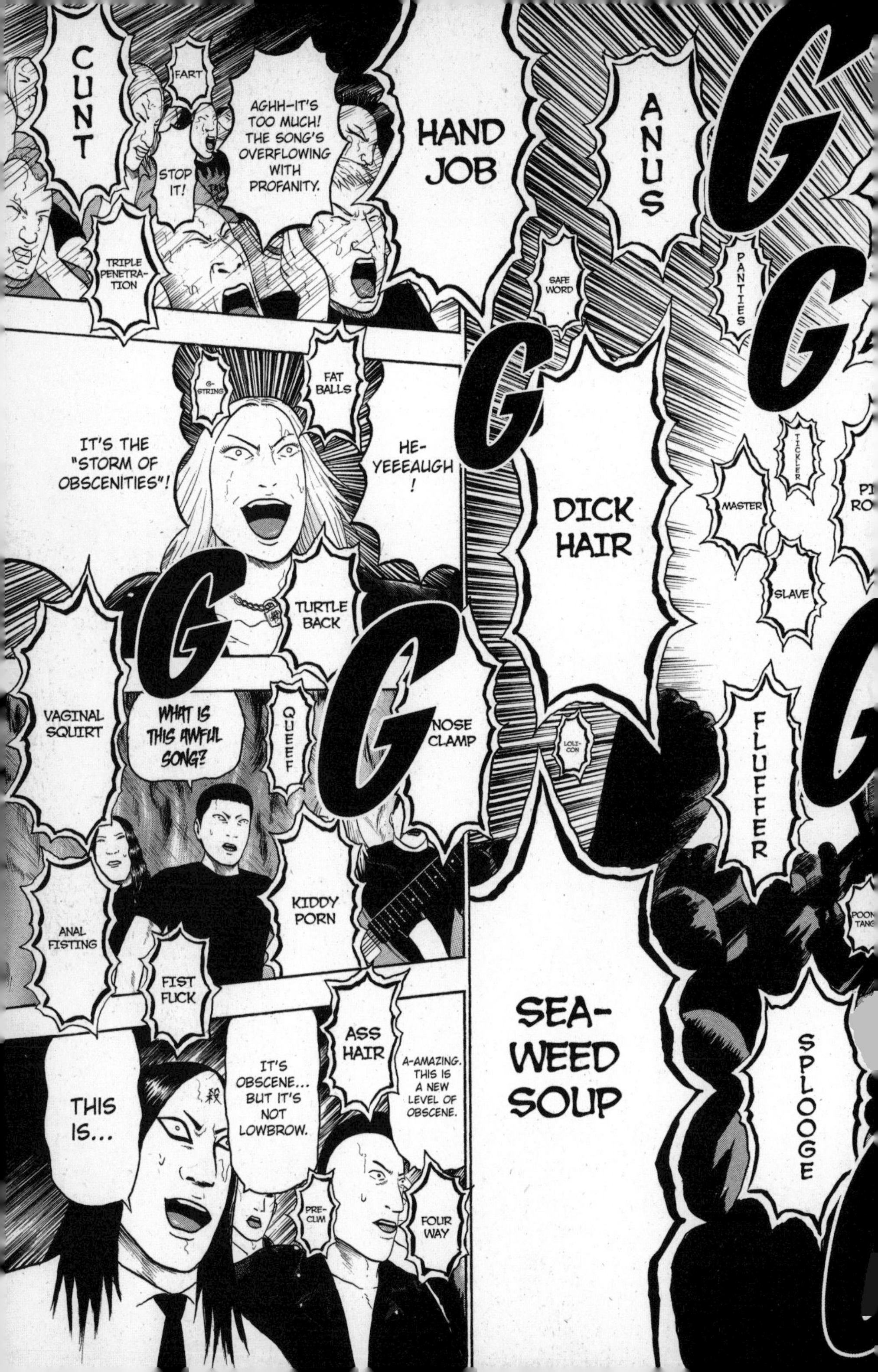
G
G
G
ANUS
PANTIES
SAFE WORD
G
G
DICK HAIR
TICKLER
MASTER
SLAVE
G
LOLI-CON
FLUFFER
POON TANG
SEA-WEED SOUP
SPLOOGE
HAND JOB
AGHH—IT'S TOO MUCH! THE SONG'S OVERFLOWING WITH PROFANITY.
FART
STOP IT!
CUNT
TRIPLE PENETRATION
FAT BALLS
G-STRING
HE-YEEEAUGH!
IT'S THE "STORM OF OBSCENITIES"!
TURTLE BACK
G
G
NOSE CLAMP
QUEEF
WHAT IS THIS AWFUL SONG?
VAGINAL SQUIRT
KIDDY PORN
FIST FUCK
ANAL FISTING
A-AMAZING. THIS IS A NEW LEVEL OF OBSCENE.
ASS HAIR
IT'S OBSCENE... BUT IT'S NOT LOWBROW.
THIS IS...
FOUR WAY
PRE-CUM

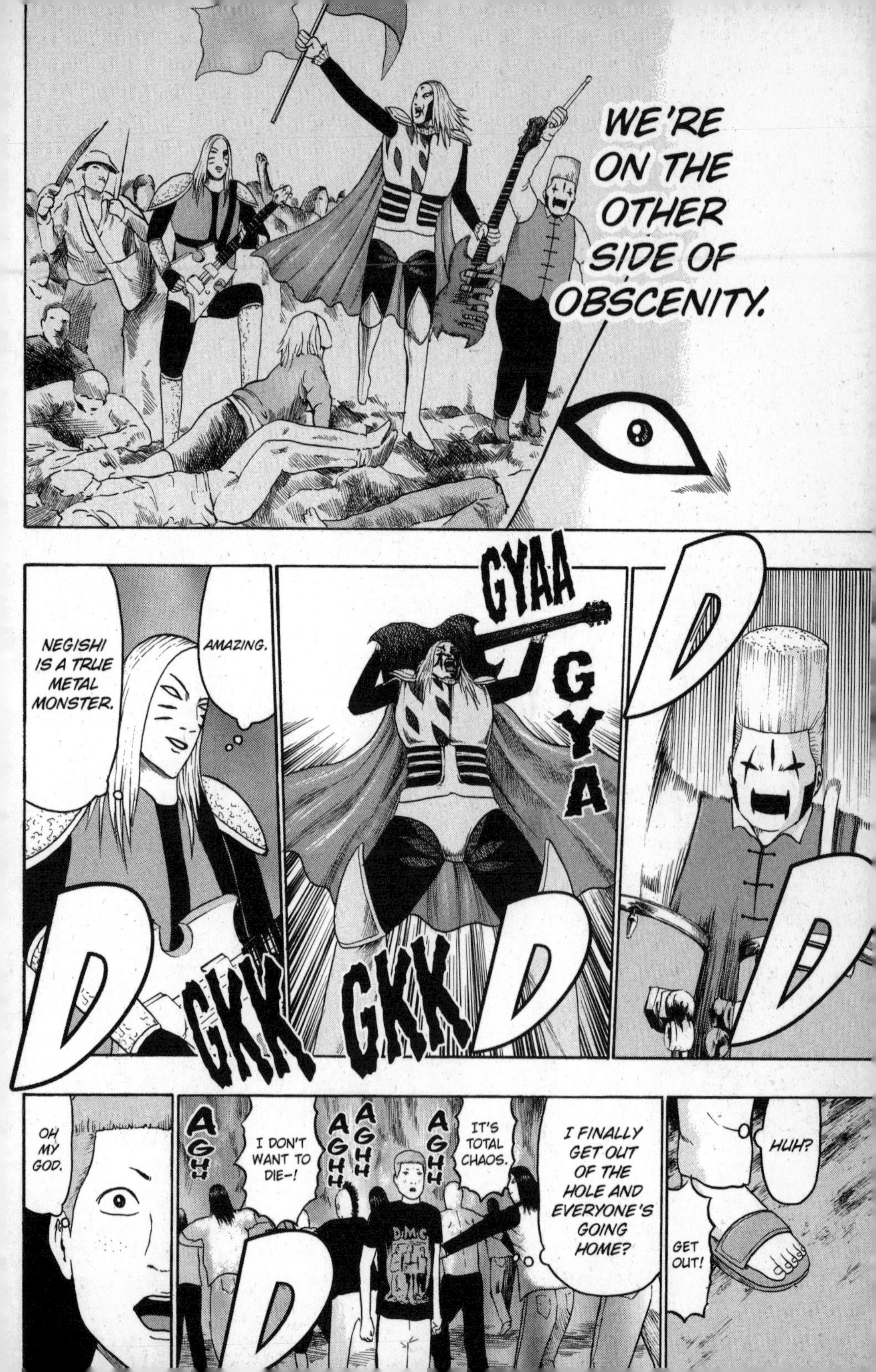
WE'RE ON THE OTHER SIDE OF OBSCENITY.
D
D
D
D
GYAA
GGYA
GKK
D
AMAZING.
NEGISHI IS A TRUE METAL MONSTER.
D
GKK
HUH?
GET OUT!
I FINALLY GET OUT OF THE HOLE AND EVERYONE'S GOING HOME?
IT'S TOTAL CHAOS.
AGHH
AGHH
AGHH
I DON'T WANT TO DIE–!
AGHH
DMC
OH MY GOD.
D

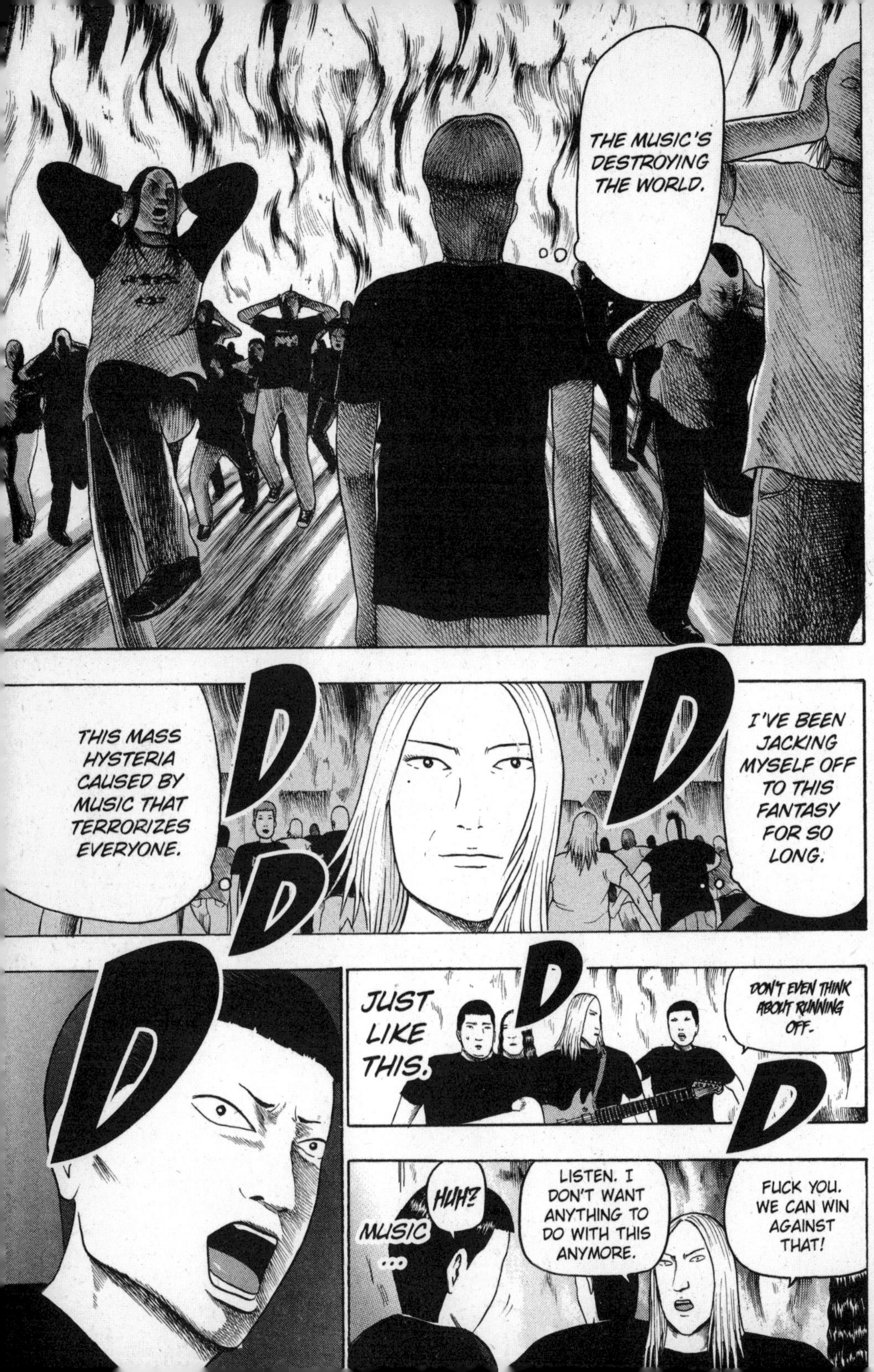
THE MUSIC'S DESTROYING THE WORLD.
D
I'VE BEEN JACKING MYSELF OFF TO THIS FANTASY FOR SO LONG.
D
THIS MASS HYSTERIA CAUSED BY MUSIC THAT TERRORIZES EVERYONE.
D
DON'T EVEN THINK ABOUT RUNNING OFF.
D
JUST LIKE THIS.
D
FUCK YOU. WE CAN WIN AGAINST THAT!
LISTEN. I DON'T WANT ANYTHING TO DO WITH THIS ANYMORE.
HUH?
MUSIC...
D

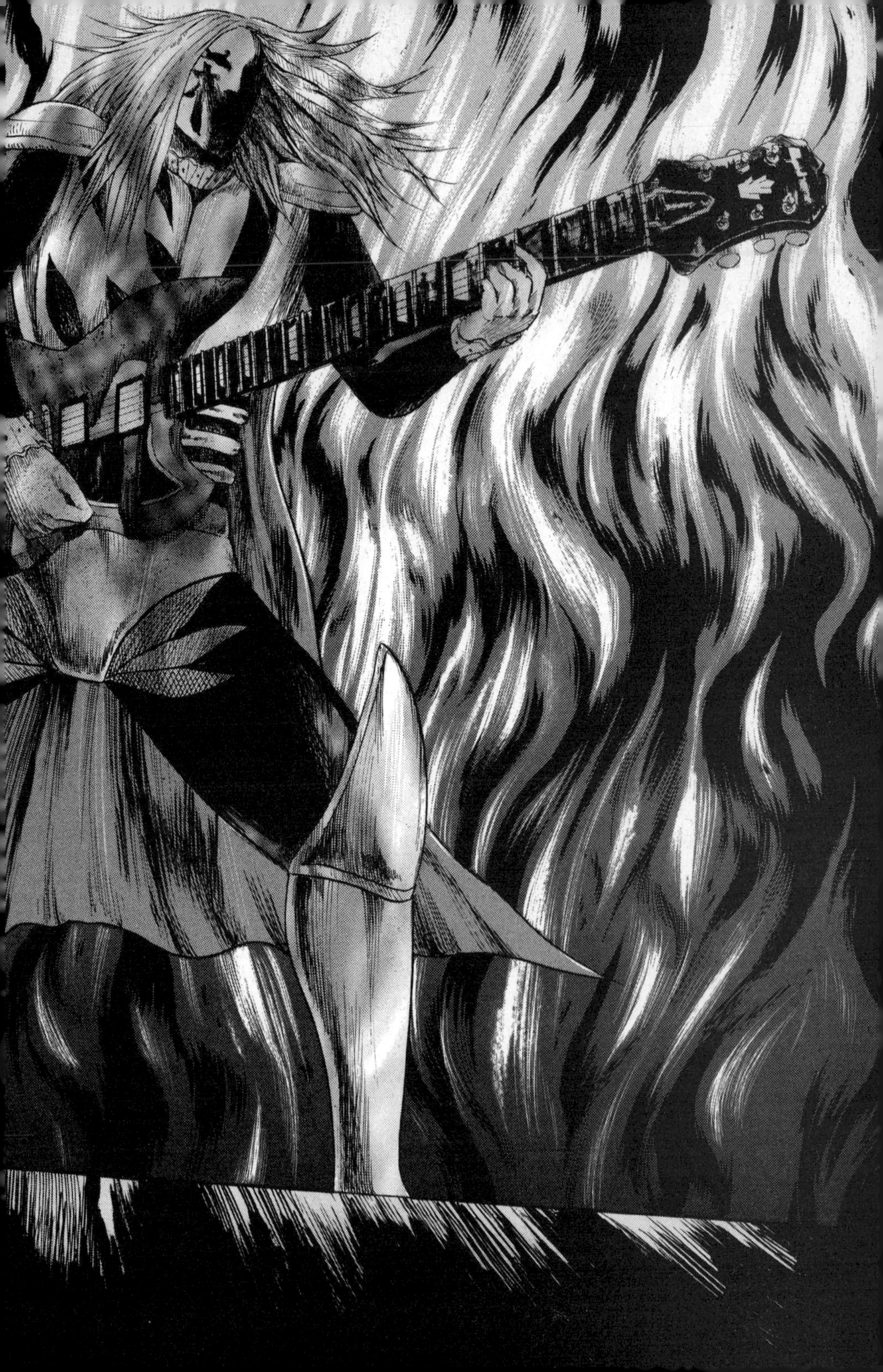

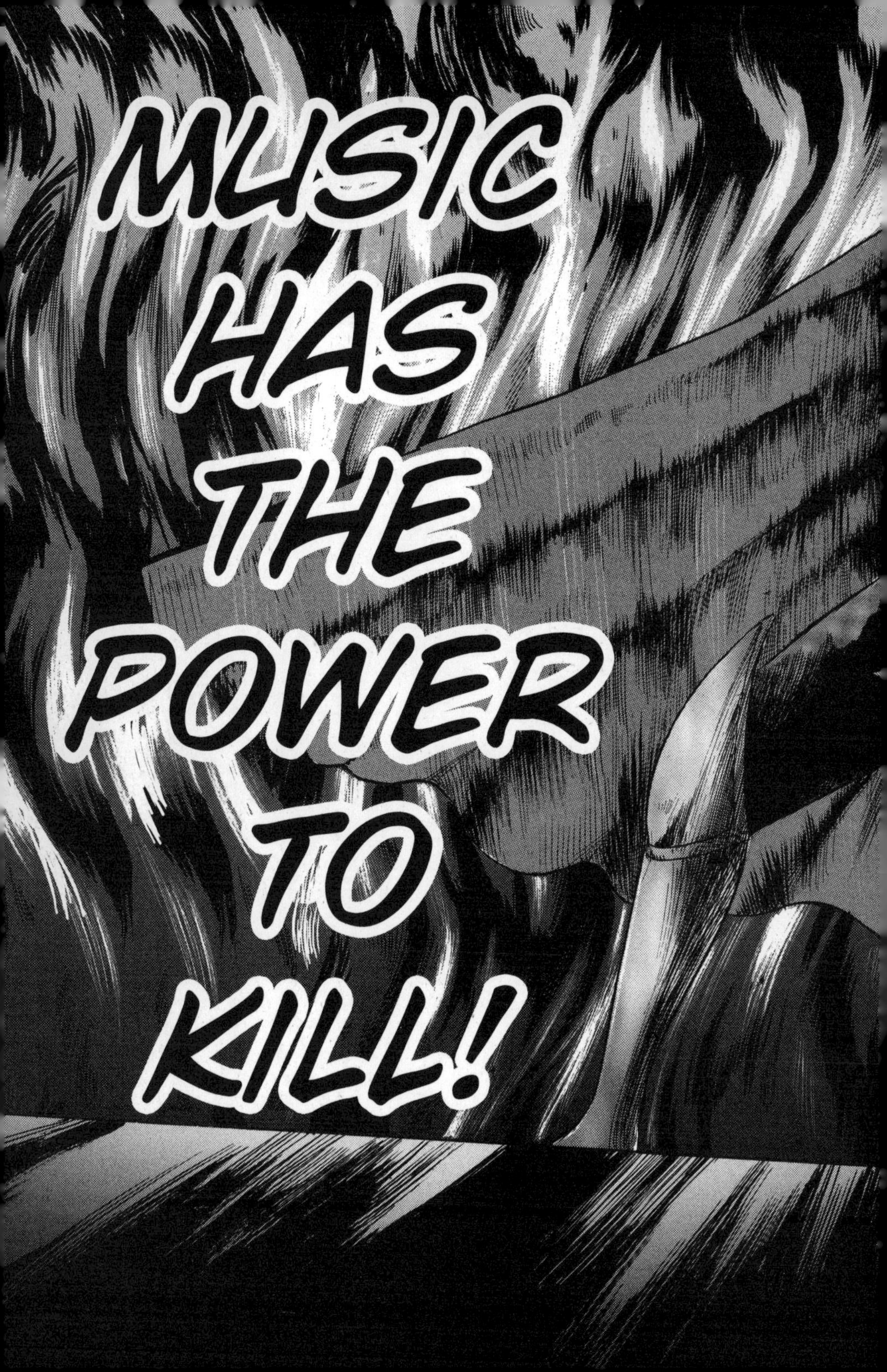
MUSIC HAS THE POWER TO KILL!

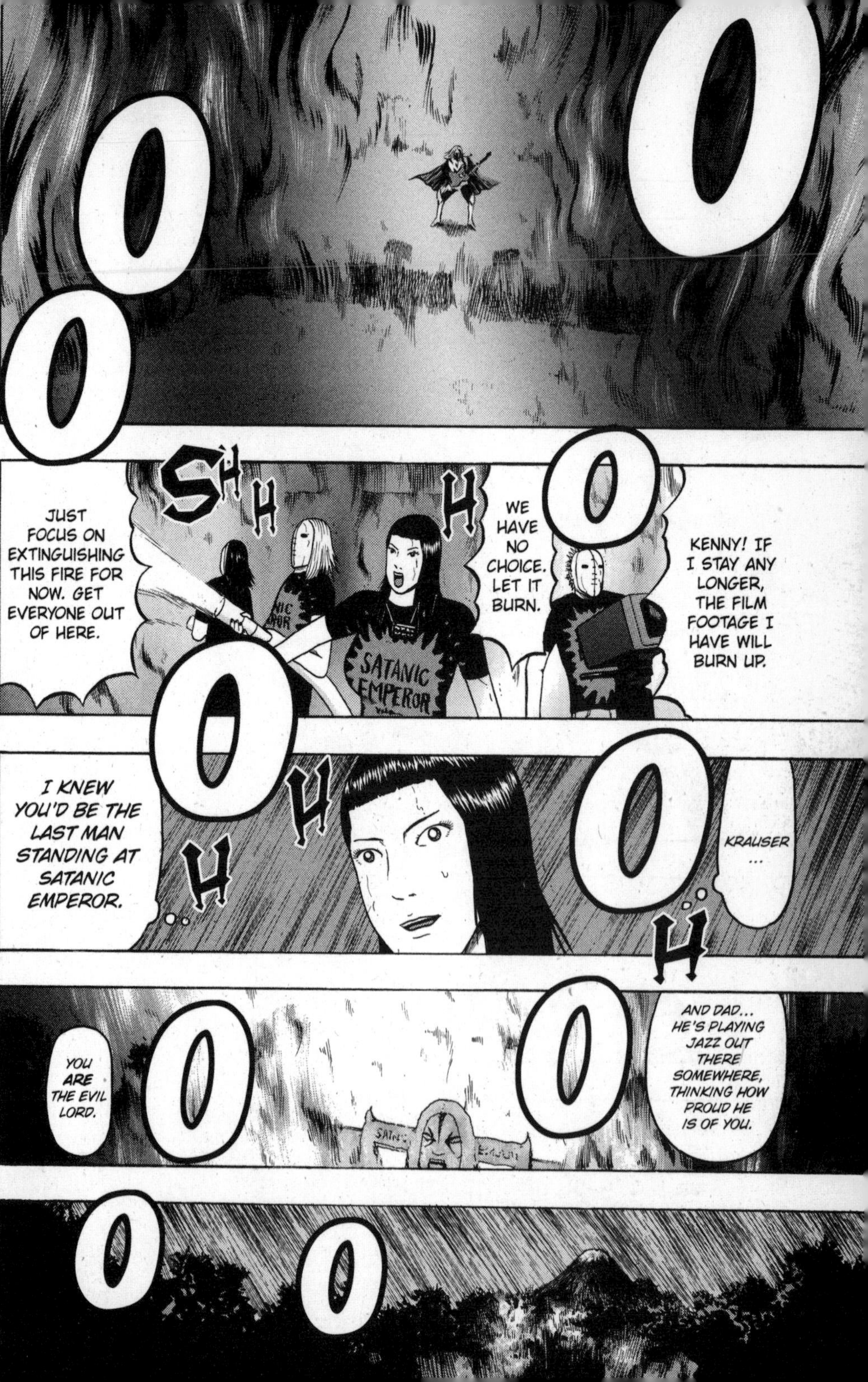
OOOO
SHHH
KENNY! IF I STAY ANY LONGER, THE FILM FOOTAGE I HAVE WILL BURN UP.
WE HAVE NO CHOICE. LET IT BURN.
JUST FOCUS ON EXTINGUISHING THIS FIRE FOR NOW. GET EVERYONE OUT OF HERE.
SATANIC EMPEROR
OOOO
HHH
KRAUSER...
I KNEW YOU'D BE THE LAST MAN STANDING AT SATANIC EMPEROR.
OOO
AND DAD... HE'S PLAYING JAZZ OUT THERE SOMEWHERE, THINKING HOW PROUD HE IS OF YOU.
YOU ARE THE EVIL LORD.
OO

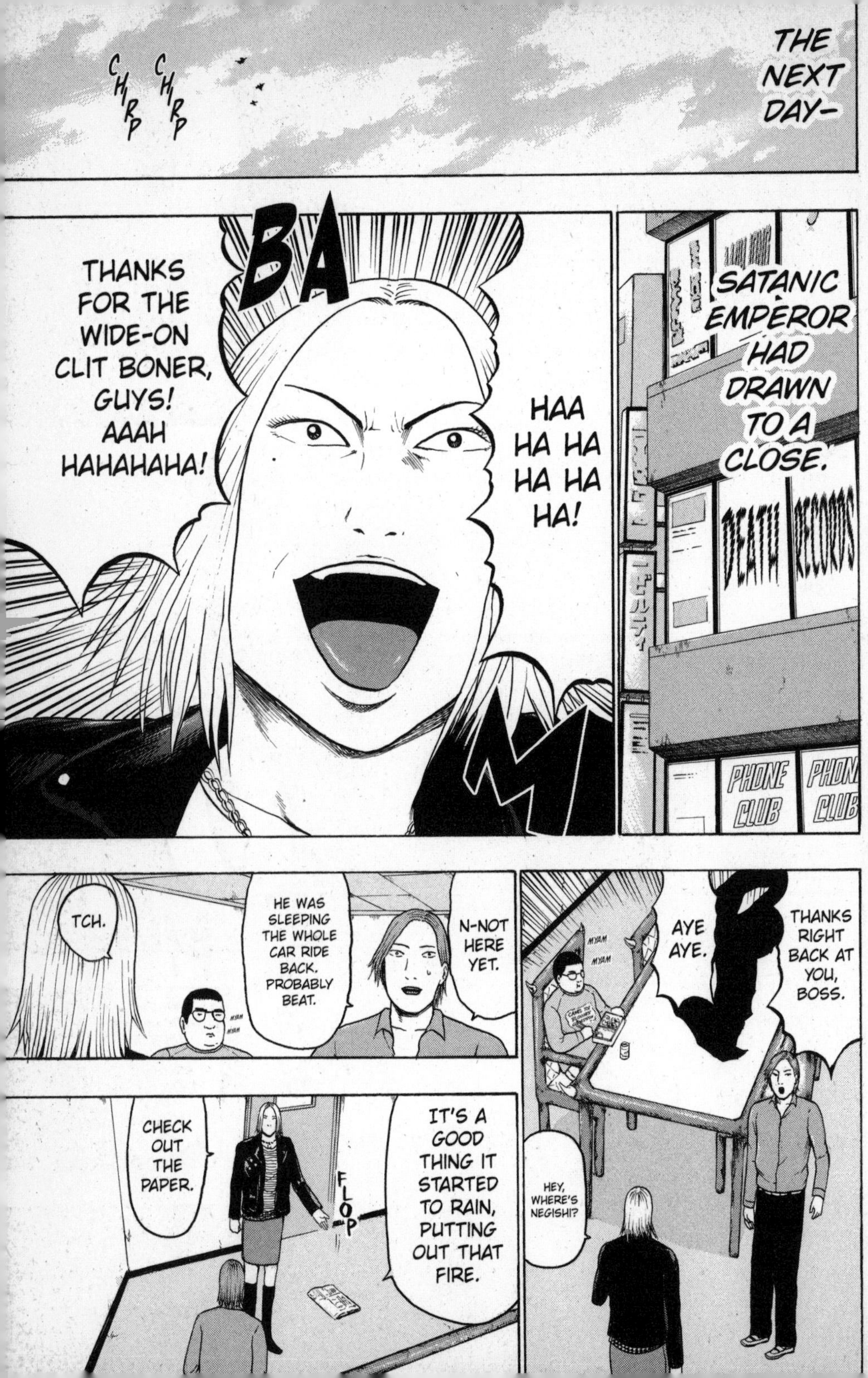
THE NEXT DAY—
CHIRP CHIRP
SATANIC EMPEROR HAD DRAWN TO A CLOSE.
DEATH RECORDS
PHONE CLUB
BA
M
HAA HA HA HA HA HA!
THANKS FOR THE WIDE-ON CLIT BONER, GUYS! AAAH HAHAHAHA!
THANKS RIGHT BACK AT YOU, BOSS.
AYE AYE.
B
MYAM MYAM
HEY, WHERE'S NEGISHI!?
N-NOT HERE YET.
HE WAS SLEEPING THE WHOLE CAR RIDE BACK. PROBABLY BEAT.
MYAM MYAM
TCH.
IT'S A GOOD THING IT STARTED TO RAIN, PUTTING OUT THAT FIRE.
FLOP
CHECK OUT THE PAPER.

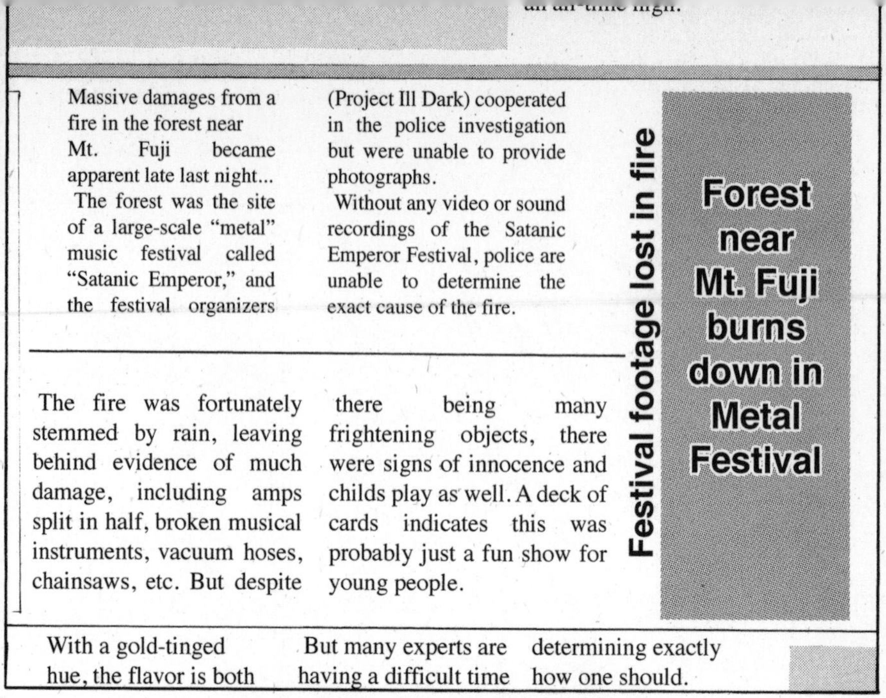
an all-time high.

Forest near Mt. Fuji burns down in Metal Festival

Festival footage lost in fire

Massive damages from a fire in the forest near Mt. Fuji became apparent late last night... The forest was the site of a large-scale "metal" music festival called "Satanic Emperor," and the festival organizers (Project Ill Dark) cooperated in the police investigation but were unable to provide photographs. Without any video or sound recordings of the Satanic Emperor Festival, police are unable to determine the exact cause of the fire.

The fire was fortunately stemmed by rain, leaving behind evidence of much damage, including amps split in half, broken musical instruments, vacuum hoses, chainsaws, etc. But despite there being many frightening objects, there were signs of innocence and childs play as well. A deck of cards indicates this was probably just a fun show for young people.

With a gold-tinged hue, the flavor is both But many experts are having a difficult time determining exactly how one should.

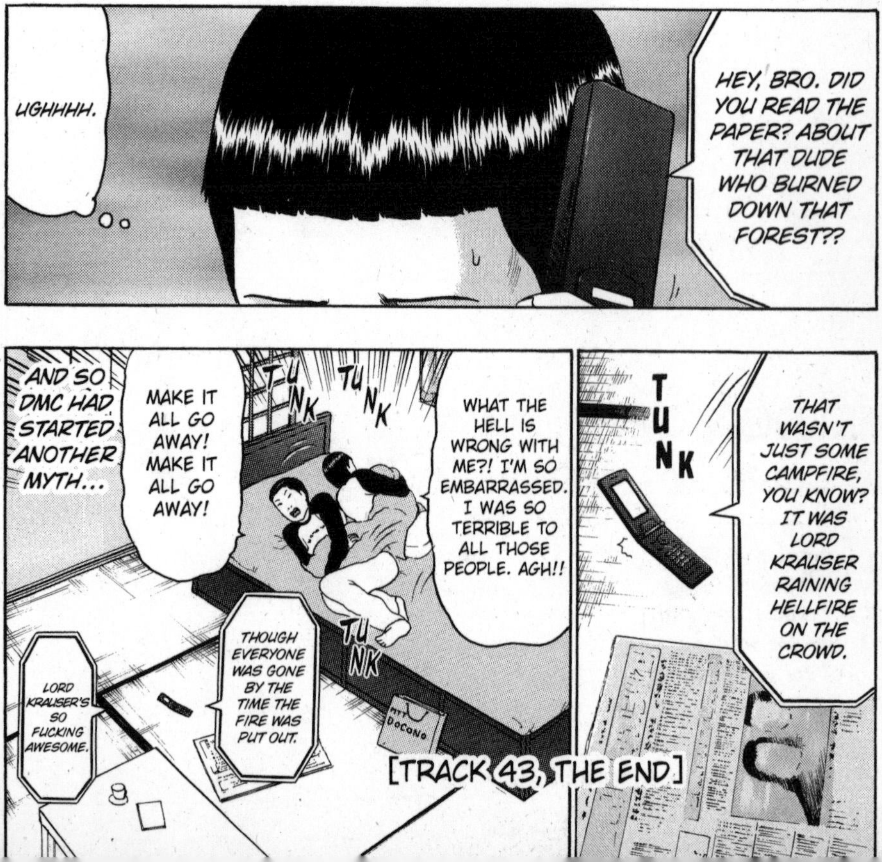
HEY, BRO. DID YOU READ THE PAPER? ABOUT THAT DUDE WHO BURNED DOWN THAT FOREST??
UGHHHH.
THAT WASN'T JUST SOME CAMPFIRE, YOU KNOW? IT WAS LORD KRAUSER RAINING HELLFIRE ON THE CROWD.
TUNK
WHAT THE HELL IS WRONG WITH ME?! I'M SO EMBARRASSED. I WAS SO TERRIBLE TO ALL THOSE PEOPLE. AGH!!
TUNK
TUNK
MAKE IT ALL GO AWAY! MAKE IT ALL GO AWAY!
AND SO DMC HAD STARTED ANOTHER MYTH...
TUNK
THOUGH EVERYONE WAS GONE BY THE TIME THE FIRE WAS PUT OUT.
LORD KRAUSER'S SO FUCKING AWESOME.
DOCONO
[TRACK 43, THE END]

DMC LEXICON

"LOVE AND PENIS"

Exactly what it sounds like, but in the '60s, it was also a catch phrase used by anti-war hippies in America who were frustrated with the endless Vietnam War. The phrase struck a psychological chord with the people. Still, it basically meant "let's have sex."

Usage: Love and penis for the sake of our children! Especially for you fine ladies...

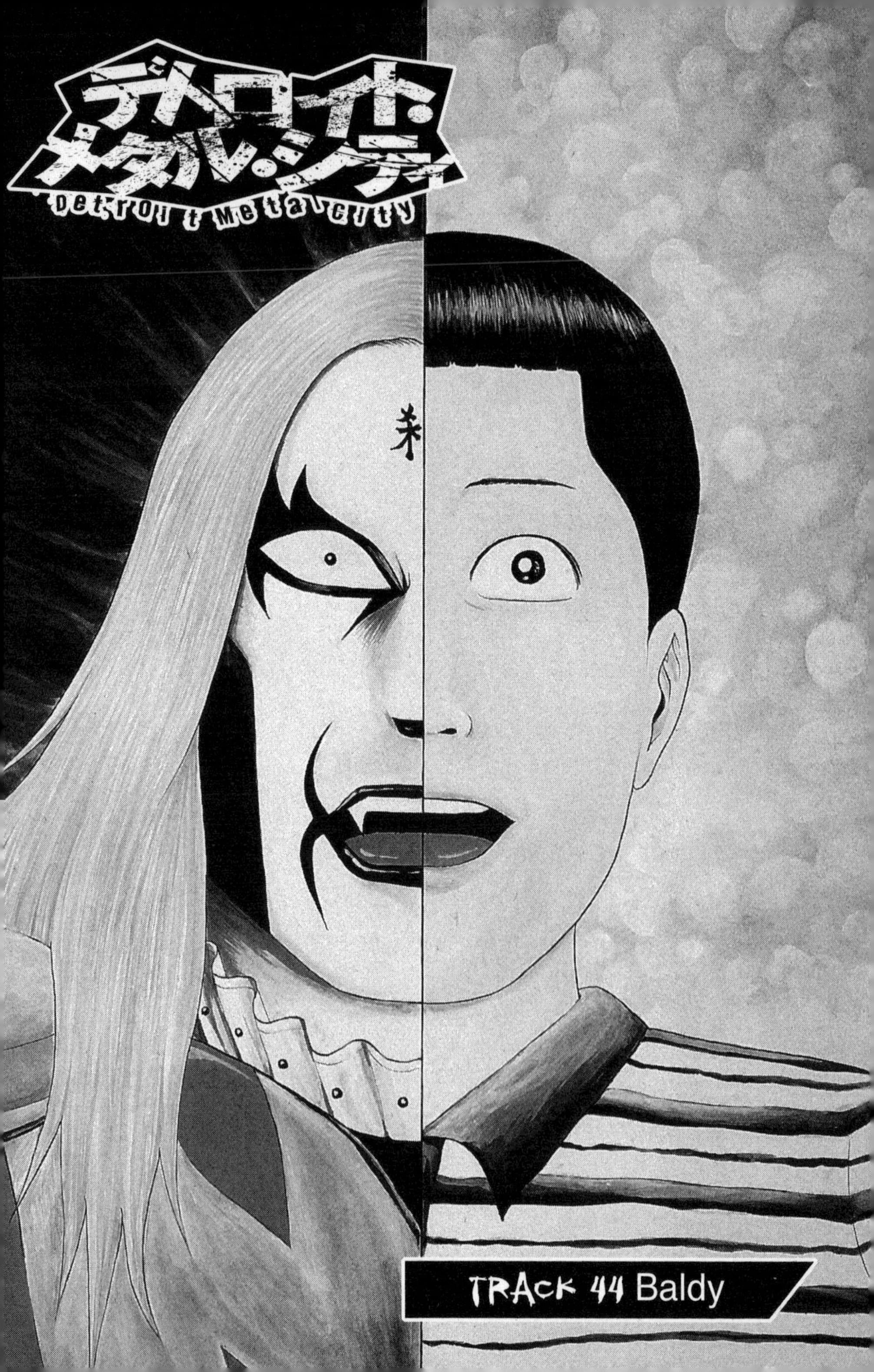
デトロイト・メタル・シティ
Detroit Metal City
TRACK 44 Baldy

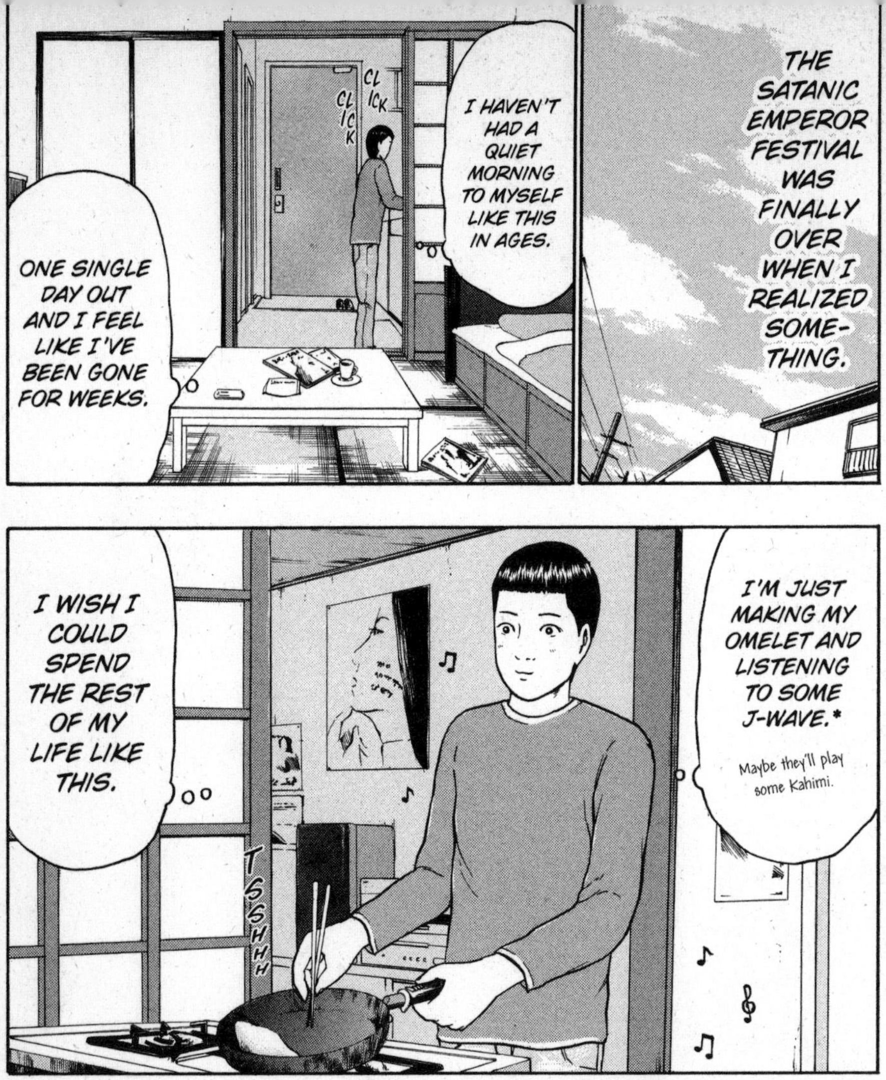
THE SATANIC EMPEROR FESTIVAL WAS FINALLY OVER WHEN I REALIZED SOME-THING.
I HAVEN'T HAD A QUIET MORNING TO MYSELF LIKE THIS IN AGES.
CLICK CLICK
ONE SINGLE DAY OUT AND I FEEL LIKE I'VE BEEN GONE FOR WEEKS.
I'M JUST MAKING MY OMELET AND LISTENING TO SOME J-WAVE.*
Maybe they'll play some Kahimi.
TSSHHH
I WISH I COULD SPEND THE REST OF MY LIFE LIKE THIS.
...

*J-WAVE: A POPULAR RADIO STATION BASED OUT OF TOKYO.

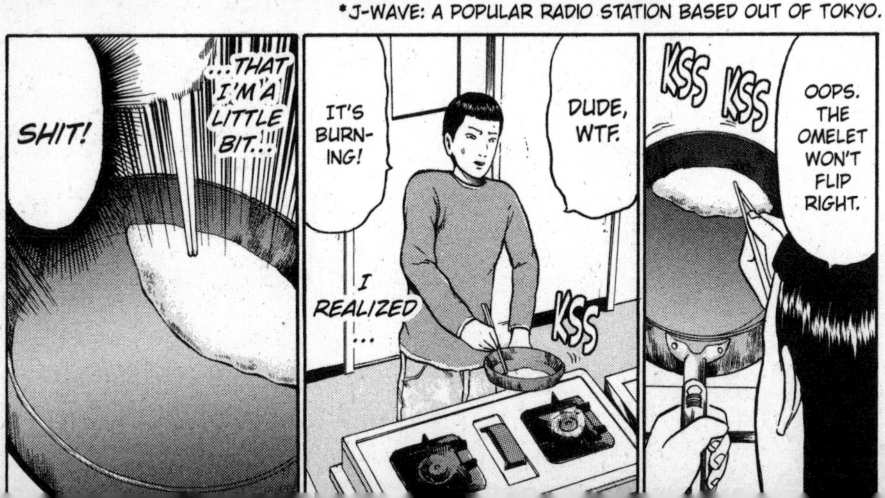
KSS KSS
OOPS. THE OMELET WON'T FLIP RIGHT.
DUDE, WTF.
IT'S BURN-ING!
I REALIZED ...
KSS
...THAT I'M A LITTLE BIT...
SHIT!

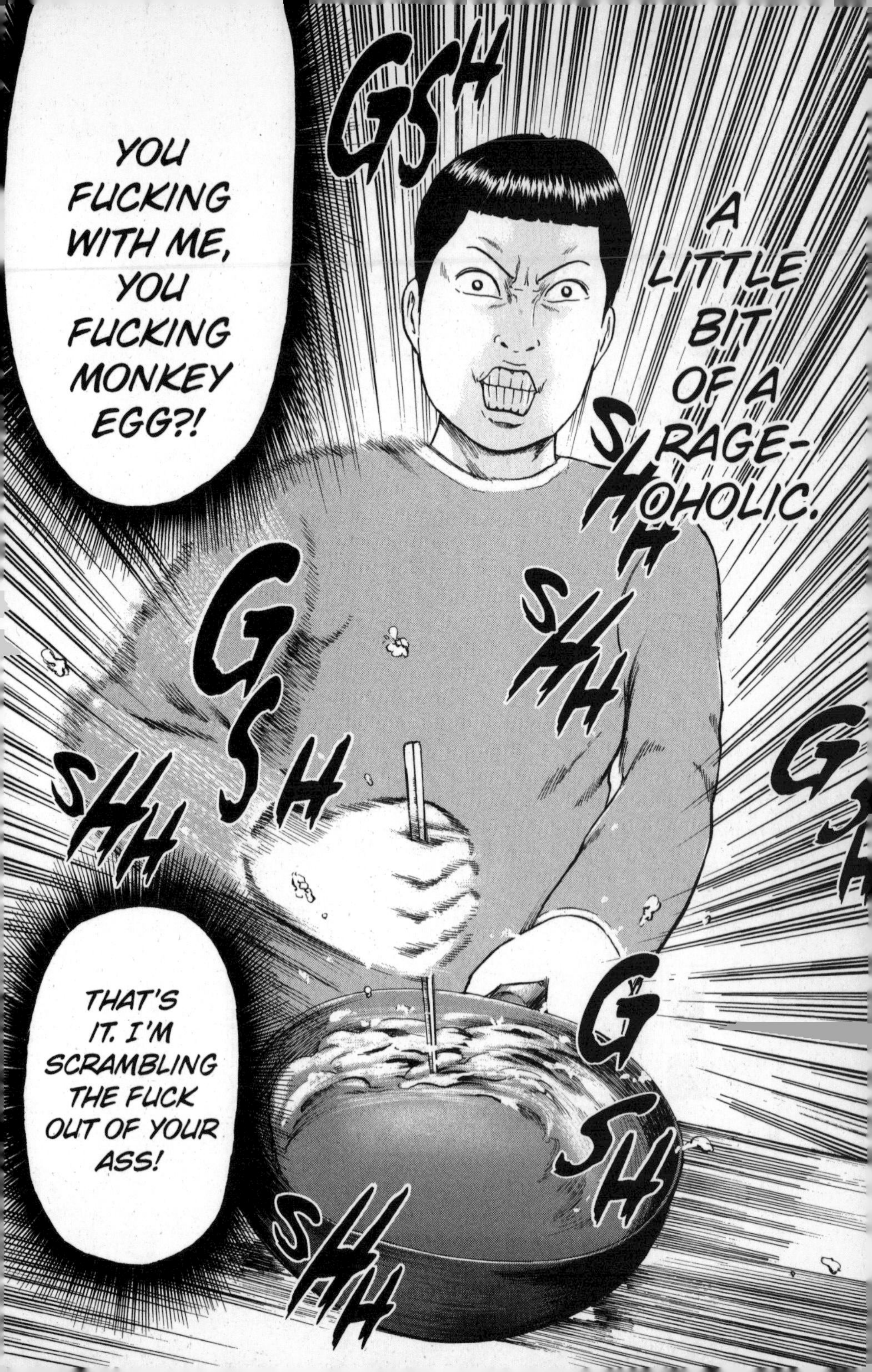
A LITTLE BIT OF A RAGE-OHOLIC.
GSH
YOU FUCKING WITH ME, YOU FUCKING MONKEY EGG?!
SHH
SHH
GSH
SHH
GSH
SHH
THAT'S IT. I'M SCRAMBLING THE FUCK OUT OF YOUR ASS!

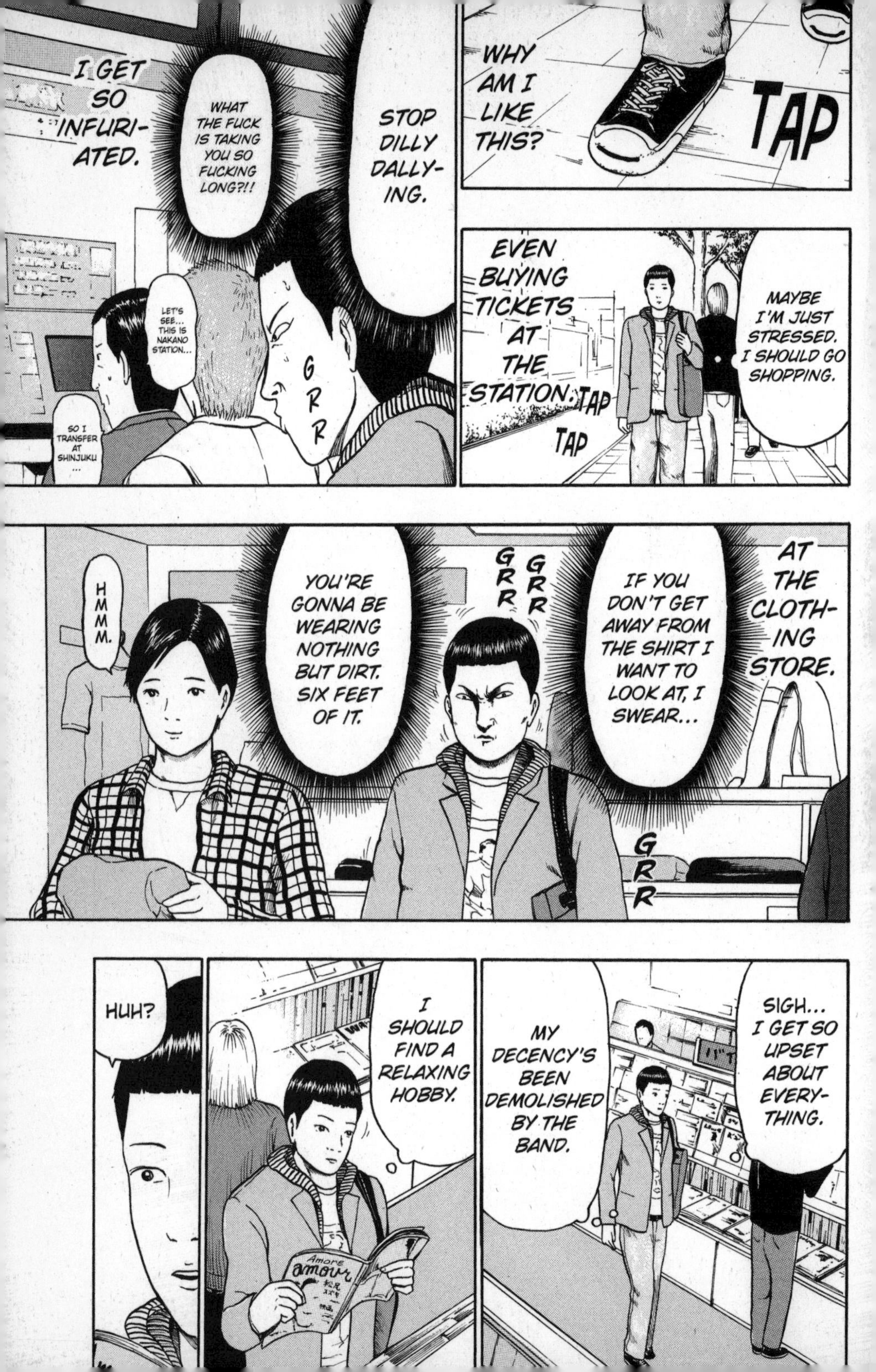
TAP
WHY AM I LIKE THIS?
MAYBE I'M JUST STRESSED. I SHOULD GO SHOPPING.
EVEN BUYING TICKETS AT THE STATION.
TAP TAP
STOP DILLY DALLYING.
WHAT THE FUCK IS TAKING YOU SO FUCKING LONG?!!
I GET SO INFURIATED.
GRR
LET'S SEE... THIS IS NAKANO STATION...
SO I TRANSFER AT SHINJUKU...
AT THE CLOTHING STORE.
IF YOU DON'T GET AWAY FROM THE SHIRT I WANT TO LOOK AT, I SWEAR...
GRR GRR
YOU'RE GONNA BE WEARING NOTHING BUT DIRT. SIX FEET OF IT.
HMMM.
GRR
SIGH... I GET SO UPSET ABOUT EVERYTHING.
MY DECENCY'S BEEN DEMOLISHED BY THE BAND.
I SHOULD FIND A RELAXING HOBBY.
Amore amour
HUH?

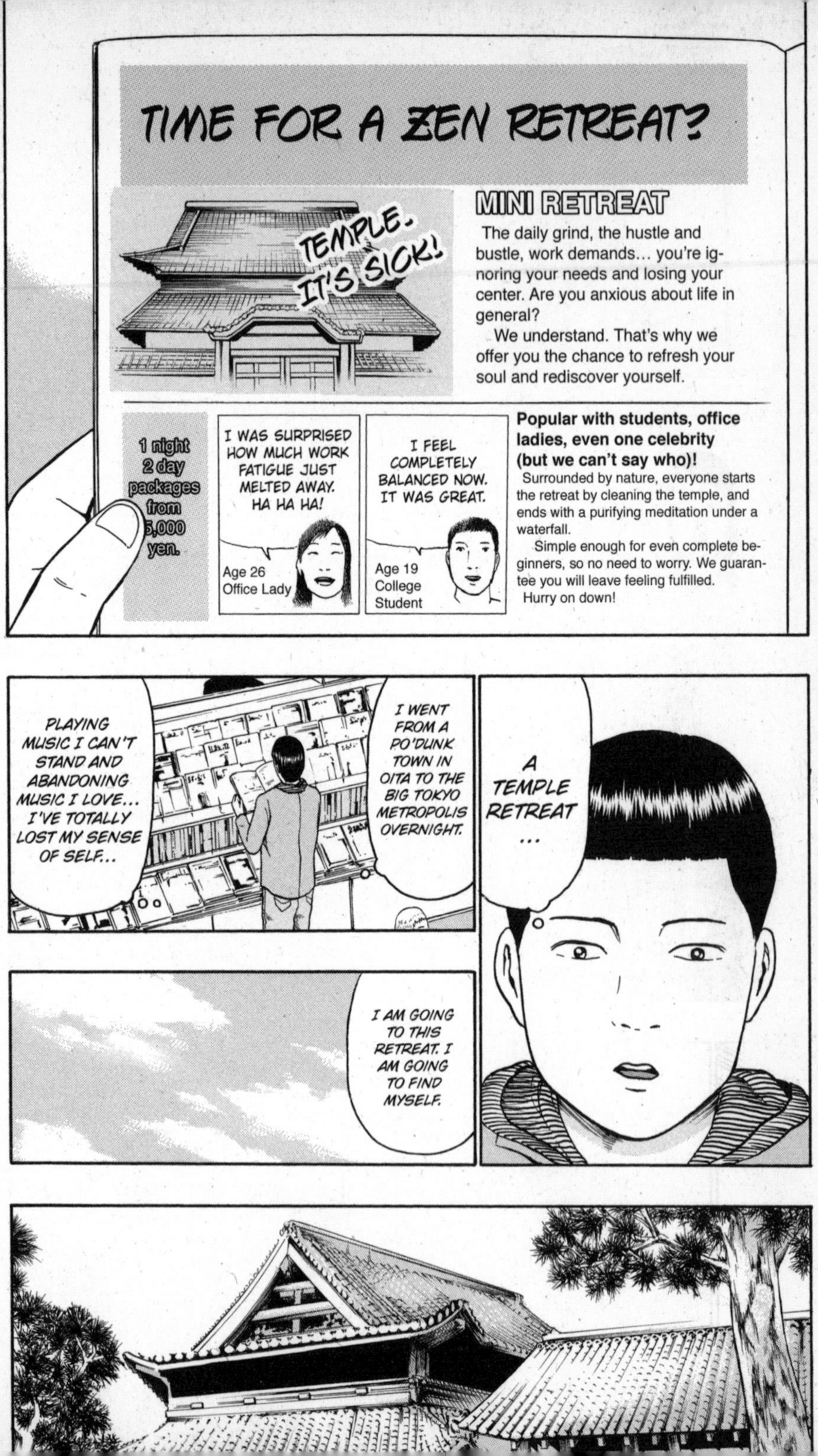
TIME FOR A ZEN RETREAT?
TEMPLE. IT'S SICK!
MINI RETREAT
The daily grind, the hustle and bustle, work demands… you're ignoring your needs and losing your center. Are you anxious about life in general?
We understand. That's why we offer you the chance to refresh your soul and rediscover yourself.
1 night 2 day packages from 5,000 yen.
I WAS SURPRISED HOW MUCH WORK FATIGUE JUST MELTED AWAY. HA HA HA!
Age 26 Office Lady
I FEEL COMPLETELY BALANCED NOW. IT WAS GREAT.
Age 19 College Student
Popular with students, office ladies, even one celebrity (but we can't say who)!
Surrounded by nature, everyone starts the retreat by cleaning the temple, and ends with a purifying meditation under a waterfall.
Simple enough for even complete beginners, so no need to worry. We guarantee you will leave feeling fulfilled.
Hurry on down!
A TEMPLE RETREAT …
I WENT FROM A PO'DUNK TOWN IN OITA TO THE BIG TOKYO METROPOLIS OVERNIGHT.
PLAYING MUSIC I CAN'T STAND AND ABANDONING MUSIC I LOVE… I'VE TOTALLY LOST MY SENSE OF SELF…
I AM GOING TO THIS RETREAT. I AM GOING TO FIND MYSELF.

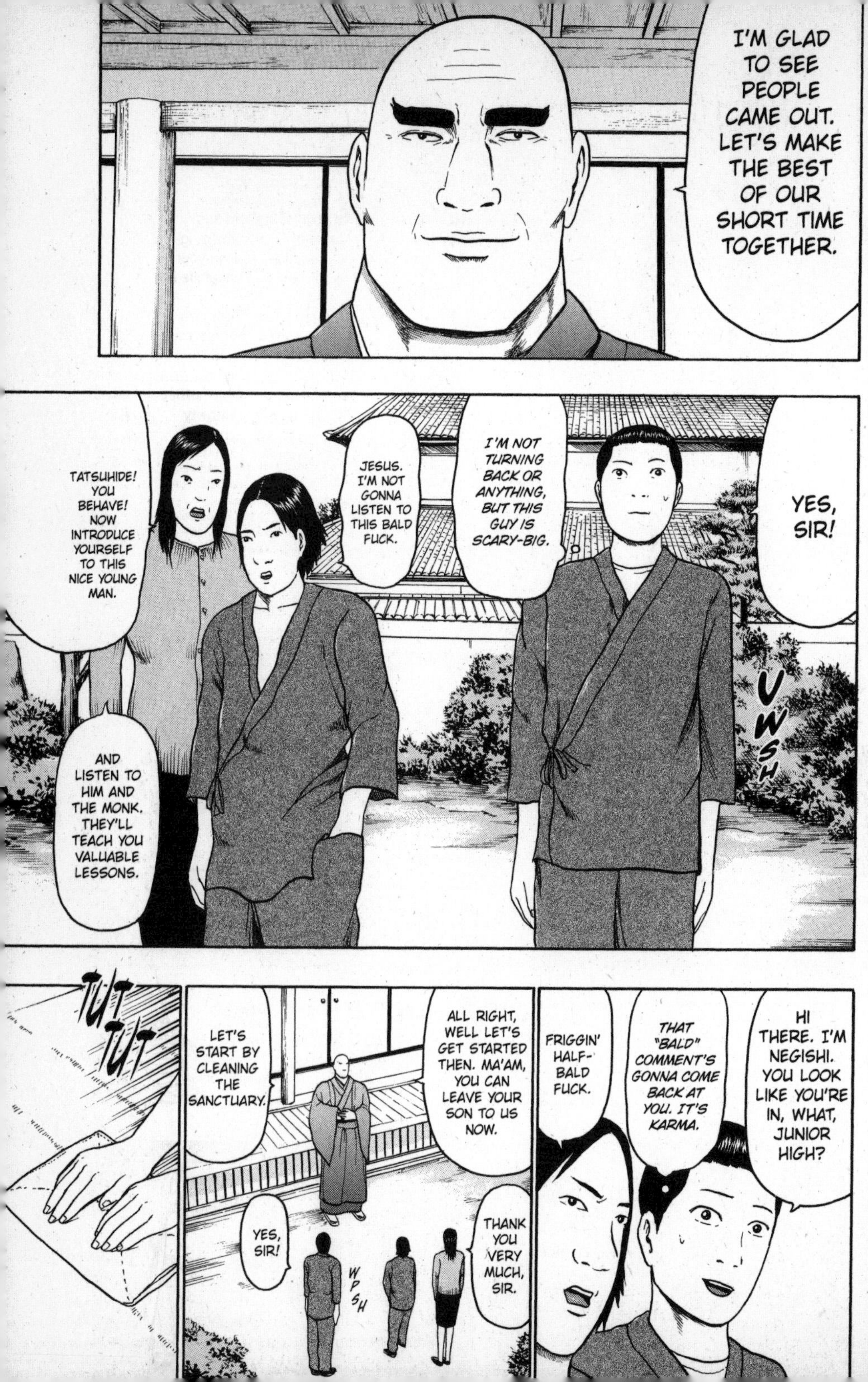
I'M GLAD TO SEE PEOPLE CAME OUT. LET'S MAKE THE BEST OF OUR SHORT TIME TOGETHER.
YES, SIR!
I'M NOT TURNING BACK OR ANYTHING, BUT THIS GUY IS SCARY-BIG.
JESUS. I'M NOT GONNA LISTEN TO THIS BALD FUCK.
TATSUHIDE! YOU BEHAVE! NOW INTRODUCE YOURSELF TO THIS NICE YOUNG MAN.
UWSH
AND LISTEN TO HIM AND THE MONK. THEY'LL TEACH YOU VALUABLE LESSONS.
HI THERE. I'M NEGISHI. YOU LOOK LIKE YOU'RE IN, WHAT, JUNIOR HIGH?
THAT "BALD" COMMENT'S GONNA COME BACK AT YOU. IT'S KARMA.
FRIGGIN' HALF-BALD FUCK.
ALL RIGHT, WELL LET'S GET STARTED THEN. MA'AM, YOU CAN LEAVE YOUR SON TO US NOW.
LET'S START BY CLEANING THE SANCTUARY.
THANK YOU VERY MUCH, SIR.
YES, SIR!
WPSH
TUT TUT

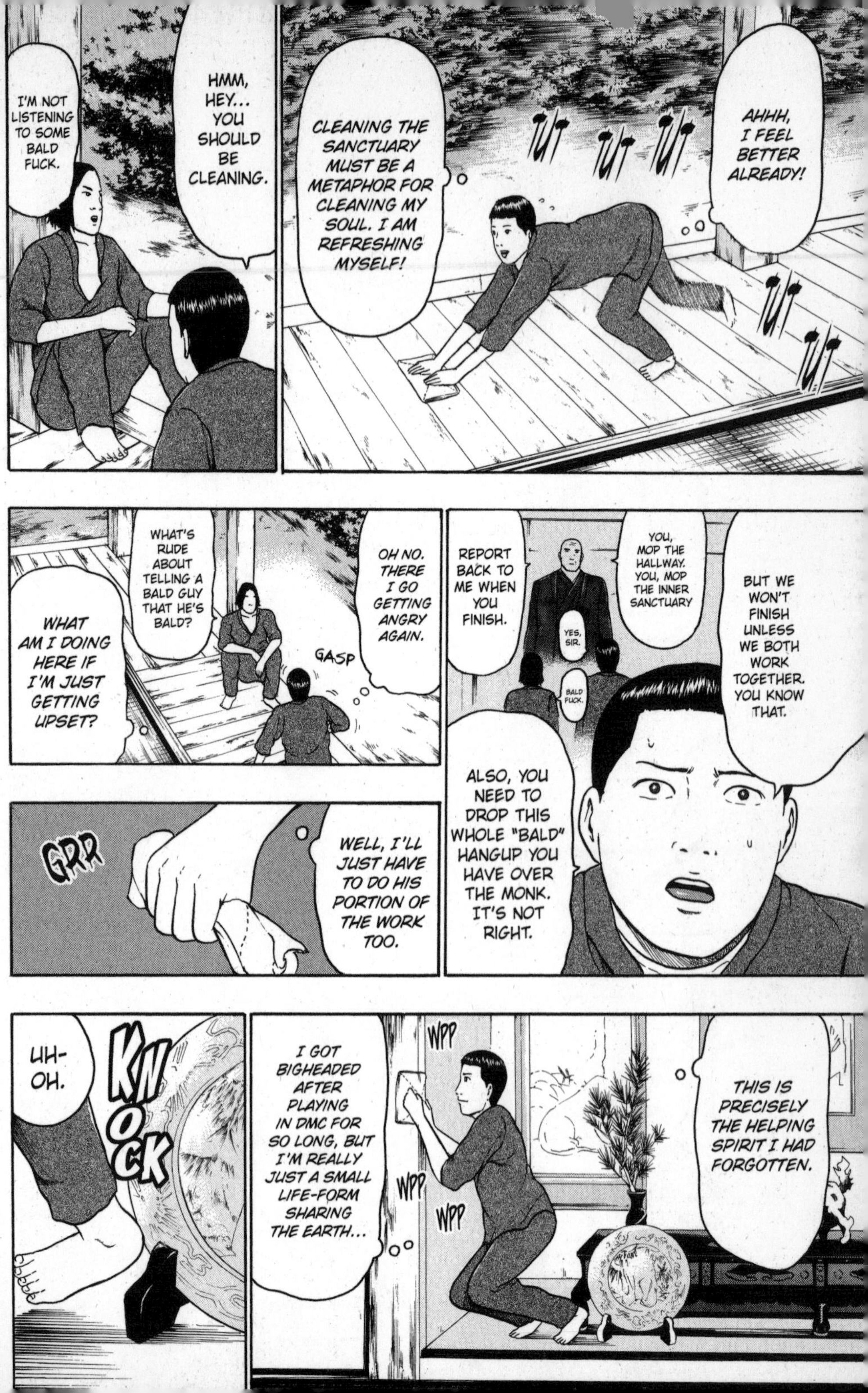
AHHH, I FEEL BETTER ALREADY!
TUT TUT TUT
TUT TUT
CLEANING THE SANCTUARY MUST BE A METAPHOR FOR CLEANING MY SOUL. I AM REFRESHING MYSELF!
HMM, HEY... YOU SHOULD BE CLEANING.
I'M NOT LISTENING TO SOME BALD FUCK.
YOU, MOP THE HALLWAY. YOU, MOP THE INNER SANCTUARY
REPORT BACK TO ME WHEN YOU FINISH.
YES, SIR.
BALD FUCK.
BUT WE WON'T FINISH UNLESS WE BOTH WORK TOGETHER. YOU KNOW THAT.
ALSO, YOU NEED TO DROP THIS WHOLE "BALD" HANGUP YOU HAVE OVER THE MONK. IT'S NOT RIGHT.
OH NO. THERE I GO GETTING ANGRY AGAIN.
GASP
WHAT'S RUDE ABOUT TELLING A BALD GUY THAT HE'S BALD?
WHAT AM I DOING HERE IF I'M JUST GETTING UPSET?
WELL, I'LL JUST HAVE TO DO HIS PORTION OF THE WORK TOO.
GRR
THIS IS PRECISELY THE HELPING SPIRIT I HAD FORGOTTEN.
WPP
WPP
WPP
I GOT BIGHEADED AFTER PLAYING IN DMC FOR SO LONG, BUT I'M REALLY JUST A SMALL LIFE-FORM SHARING THE EARTH...
KNOCK
UH-OH.

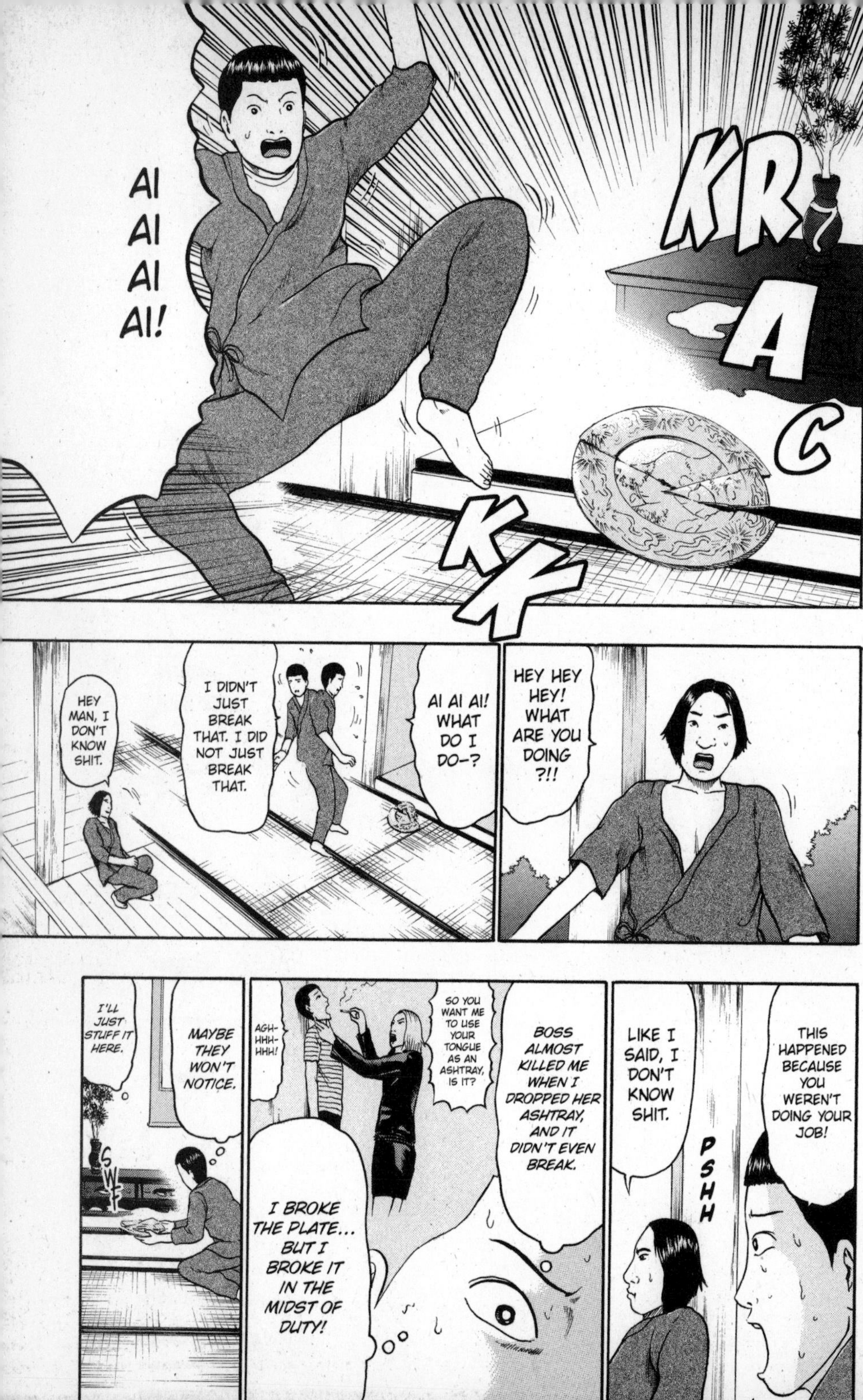
KRACKK
AI AI AI AI!
HEY HEY HEY! WHAT ARE YOU DOING?!!
AI AI AI! WHAT DO I DO--?
I DIDN'T JUST BREAK THAT. I DID NOT JUST BREAK THAT.
HEY MAN, I DON'T KNOW SHIT.
THIS HAPPENED BECAUSE YOU WEREN'T DOING YOUR JOB!
LIKE I SAID, I DON'T KNOW SHIT.
PSHH
BOSS ALMOST KILLED ME WHEN I DROPPED HER ASHTRAY, AND IT DIDN'T EVEN BREAK.
SO YOU WANT ME TO USE YOUR TONGUE AS AN ASHTRAY, IS IT?
AGH-HHH-HHH!
I BROKE THE PLATE... BUT I BROKE IT IN THE MIDST OF DUTY!
MAYBE THEY WON'T NOTICE.
I'LL JUST STUFF IT HERE.
SWF

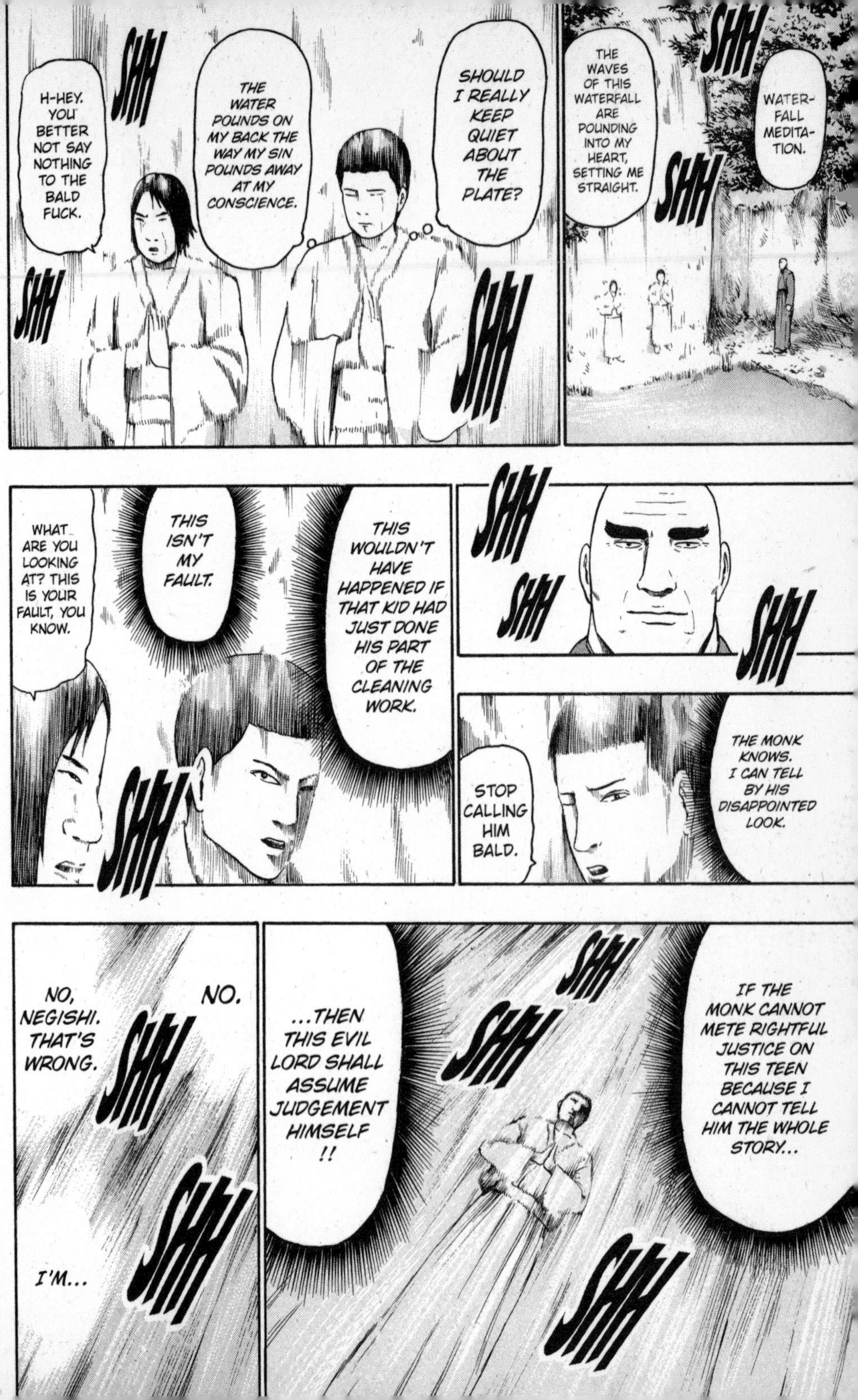
WATERFALL MEDITATION.
SHH
SHH
THE WAVES OF THIS WATERFALL ARE POUNDING INTO MY HEART, SETTING ME STRAIGHT.
SHOULD I REALLY KEEP QUIET ABOUT THE PLATE?
SHH
THE WATER POUNDS ON MY BACK THE WAY MY SIN POUNDS AWAY AT MY CONSCIENCE.
SHH
H-HEY. YOU BETTER NOT SAY NOTHING TO THE BALD FUCK.
SHH
SHH
SHH
SHH
THE MONK KNOWS. I CAN TELL BY HIS DISAPPOINTED LOOK.
STOP CALLING HIM BALD.
THIS WOULDN'T HAVE HAPPENED IF THAT KID HAD JUST DONE HIS PART OF THE CLEANING WORK.
THIS ISN'T MY FAULT.
SHH
WHAT ARE YOU LOOKING AT? THIS IS YOUR FAULT, YOU KNOW.
IF THE MONK CANNOT METE RIGHTFUL JUSTICE ON THIS TEEN BECAUSE I CANNOT TELL HIM THE WHOLE STORY...
SHH
SHH
SHH
...THEN THIS EVIL LORD SHALL ASSUME JUDGEMENT HIMSELF !!
NO.
NO, NEGISHI. THAT'S WRONG.
SHH
SHH
I'M...

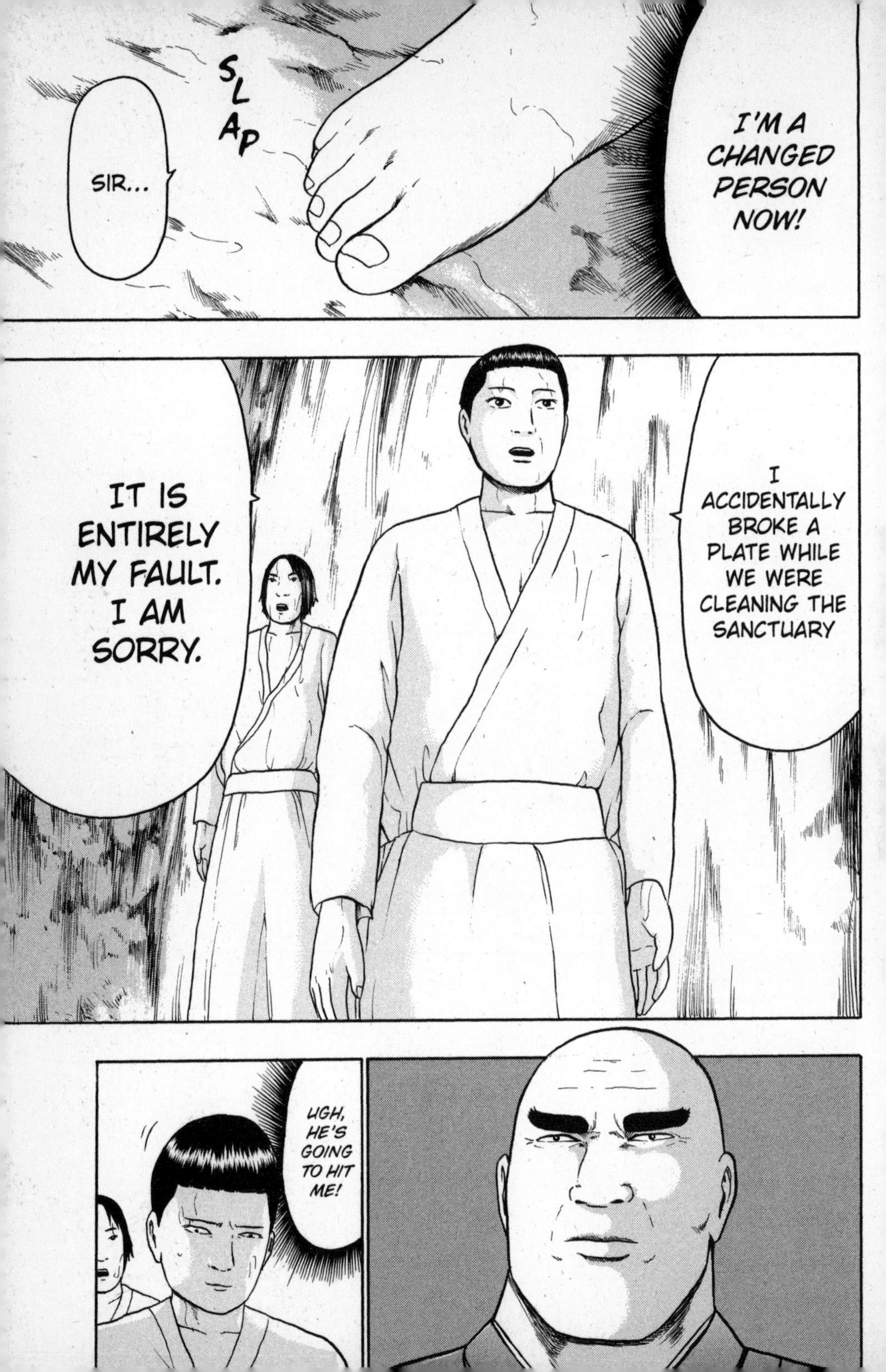
I'M A CHANGED PERSON NOW!
SLAP
SIR...
I ACCIDENTALLY BROKE A PLATE WHILE WE WERE CLEANING THE SANCTUARY
IT IS ENTIRELY MY FAULT. I AM SORRY.
UGH, HE'S GOING TO HIT ME!

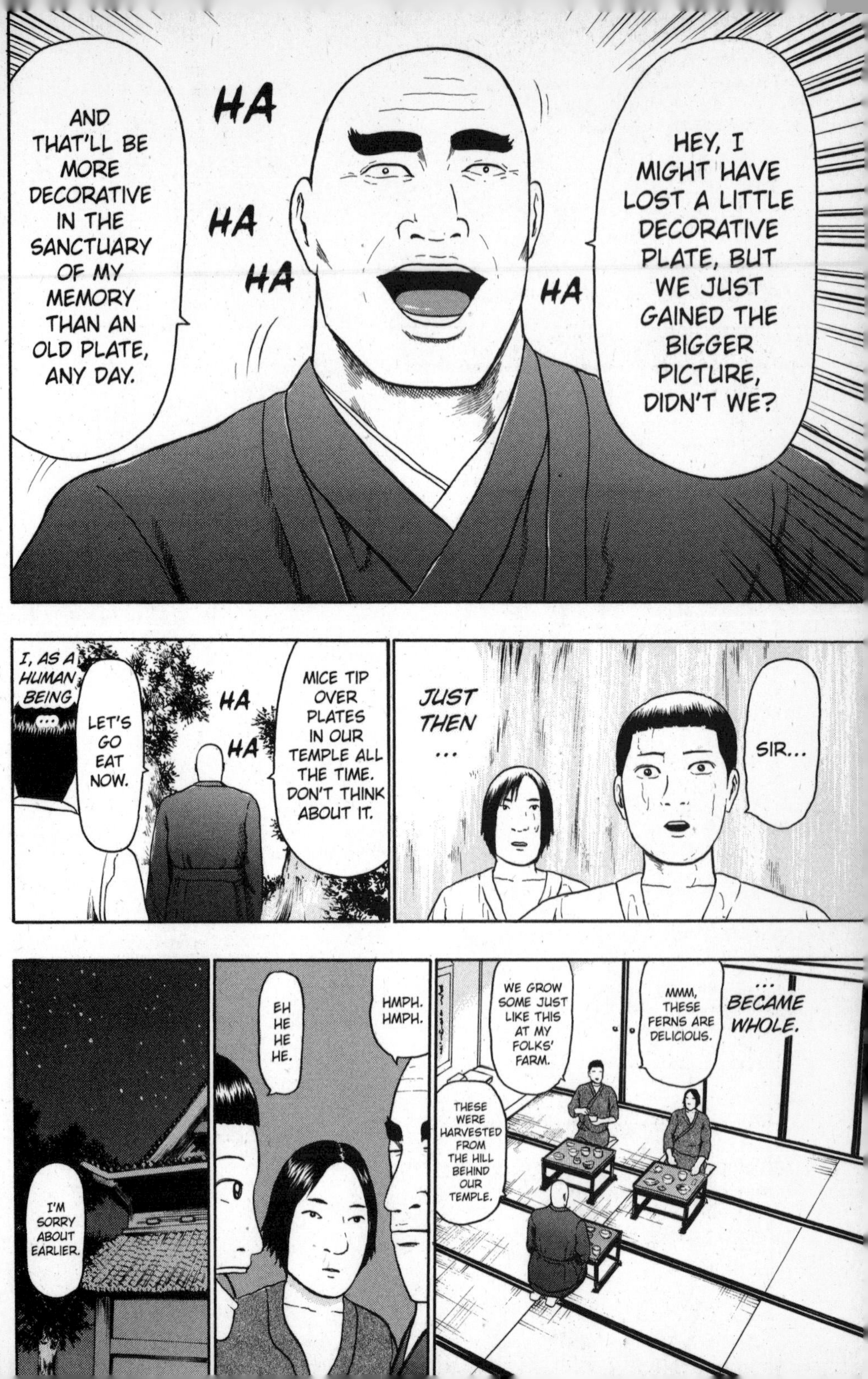
HEY, I MIGHT HAVE LOST A LITTLE DECORATIVE PLATE, BUT WE JUST GAINED THE BIGGER PICTURE, DIDN'T WE?
HA
HA
HA
HA
AND THAT'LL BE MORE DECORATIVE IN THE SANCTUARY OF MY MEMORY THAN AN OLD PLATE, ANY DAY.
SIR...
JUST THEN ...
MICE TIP OVER PLATES IN OUR TEMPLE ALL THE TIME. DON'T THINK ABOUT IT.
HA
HA
LET'S GO EAT NOW.
...
I, AS A HUMAN BEING
... BECAME WHOLE.
MMM, THESE FERNS ARE DELICIOUS.
WE GROW SOME JUST LIKE THIS AT MY FOLKS' FARM.
THESE WERE HARVESTED FROM THE HILL BEHIND OUR TEMPLE.
HMPH. HMPH.
EH HE HE HE.
I'M SORRY ABOUT EARLIER.

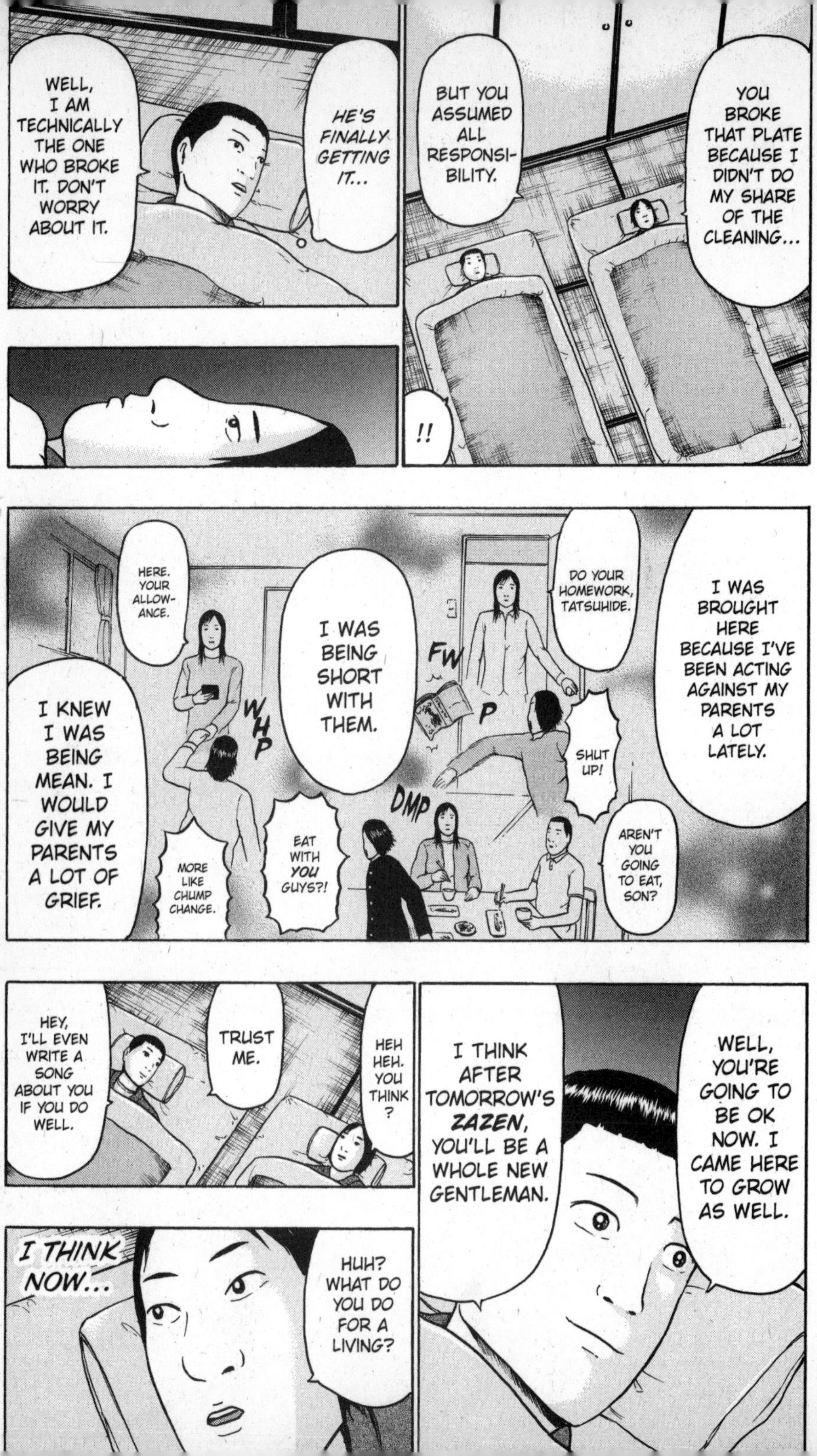
YOU BROKE THAT PLATE BECAUSE I DIDN'T DO MY SHARE OF THE CLEANING...
BUT YOU ASSUMED ALL RESPONSI-BILITY.
HE'S FINALLY GETTING IT...
WELL, I AM TECHNICALLY THE ONE WHO BROKE IT. DON'T WORRY ABOUT IT.
!!
I WAS BROUGHT HERE BECAUSE I'VE BEEN ACTING AGAINST MY PARENTS A LOT LATELY.
DO YOUR HOMEWORK, TATSUHIDE.
SHUT UP!
FW
P
I WAS BEING SHORT WITH THEM.
HERE. YOUR ALLOW-ANCE.
WHP
MORE LIKE CHUMP CHANGE.
AREN'T YOU GOING TO EAT, SON?
DMP
EAT WITH *YOU* GUYS?!
I KNEW I WAS BEING MEAN. I WOULD GIVE MY PARENTS A LOT OF GRIEF.
WELL, YOU'RE GOING TO BE OK NOW. I CAME HERE TO GROW AS WELL.
I THINK AFTER TOMORROW'S ***ZAZEN***, YOU'LL BE A WHOLE NEW GENTLEMAN.
HEH HEH. YOU THINK?
TRUST ME.
HEY, I'LL EVEN WRITE A SONG ABOUT YOU IF YOU DO WELL.
HUH? WHAT DO YOU DO FOR A LIVING?
I THINK NOW...

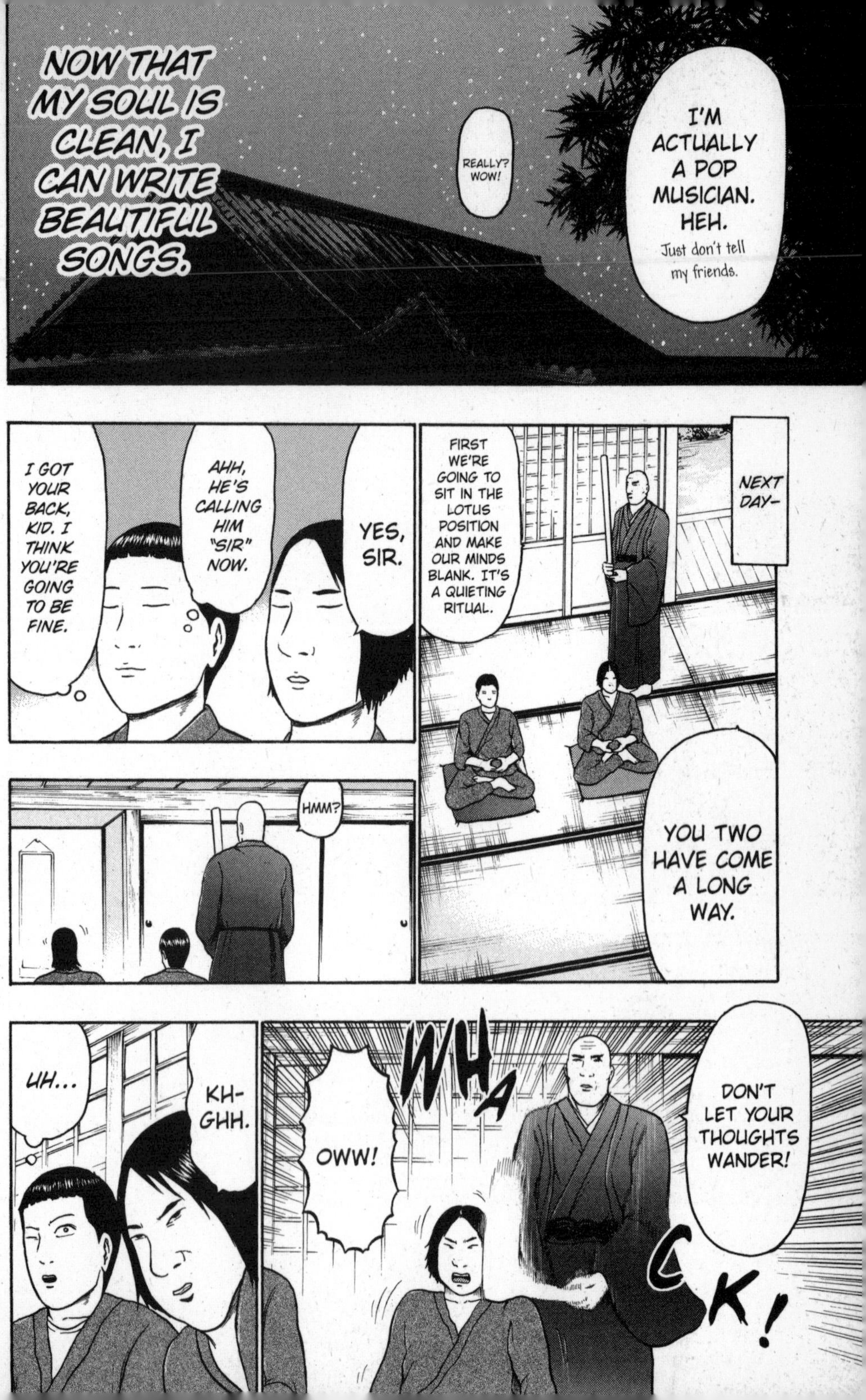

I'M ACTUALLY A POP MUSICIAN. HEH.
Just don't tell my friends.
REALLY? WOW!
NOW THAT MY SOUL IS CLEAN, I CAN WRITE BEAUTIFUL SONGS.
NEXT DAY—
FIRST WE'RE GOING TO SIT IN THE LOTUS POSITION AND MAKE OUR MINDS BLANK. IT'S A QUIETING RITUAL.
YOU TWO HAVE COME A LONG WAY.
YES, SIR.
AHH, HE'S CALLING HIM "SIR" NOW.
I GOT YOUR BACK, KID. I THINK YOU'RE GOING TO BE FINE.
HMM?
DON'T LET YOUR THOUGHTS WANDER!
WHACK!
OWW!
KH-GHH.
UH...

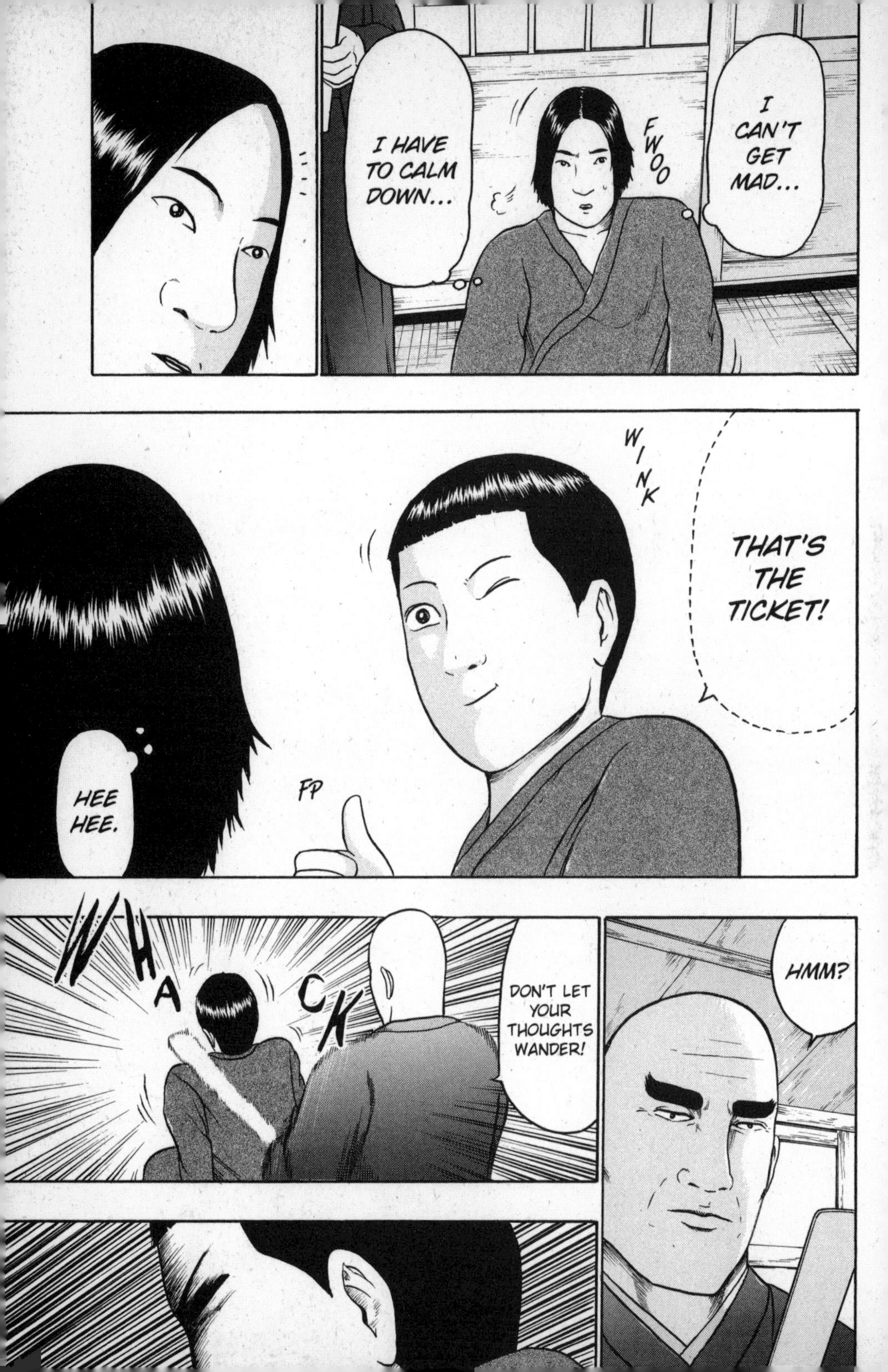
I CAN'T GET MAD...
FWOO
I HAVE TO CALM DOWN...
WINK
THAT'S THE TICKET!
FP
HEE HEE.
HMM?
DON'T LET YOUR THOUGHTS WANDER!
WHACK

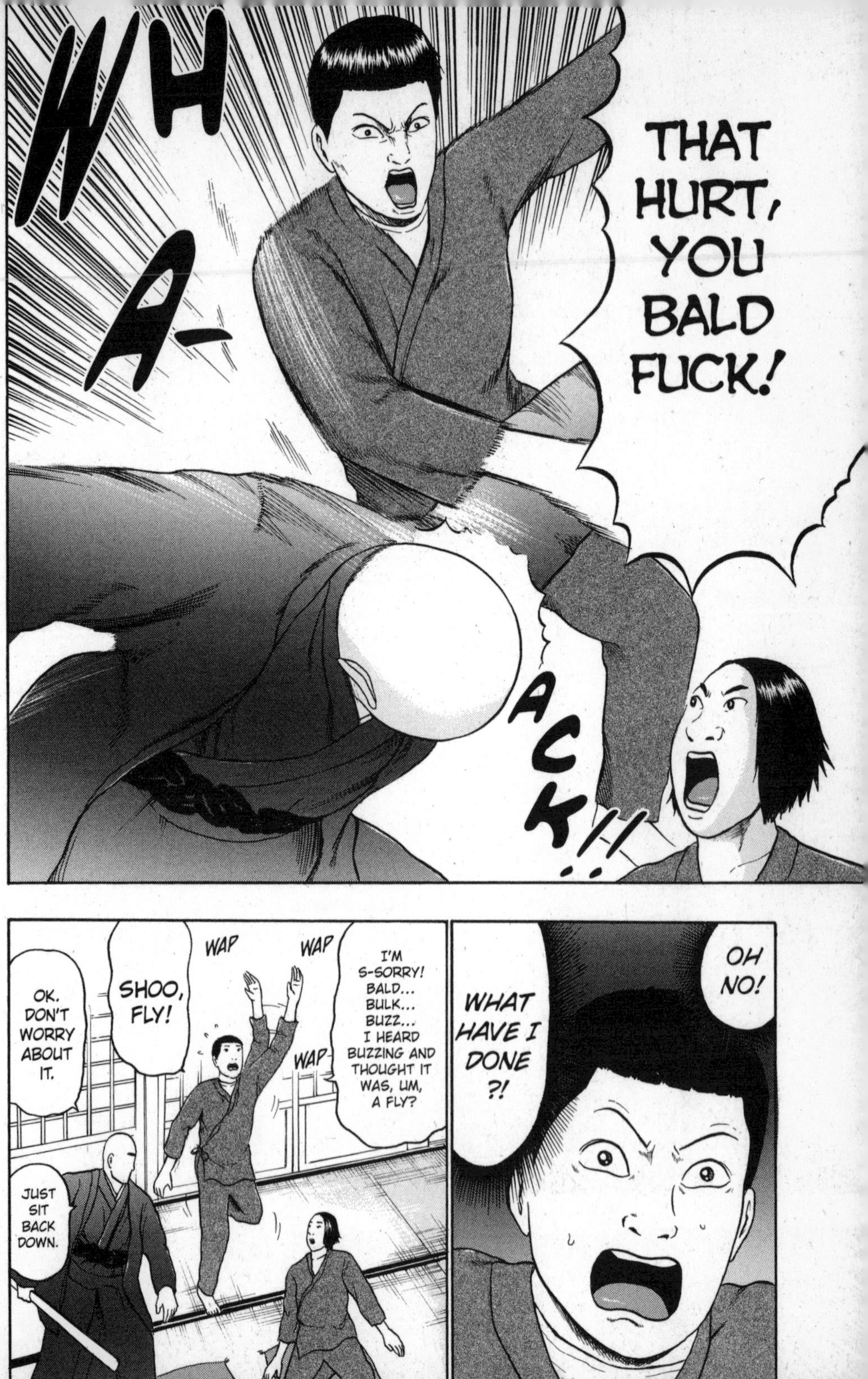
THAT HURT, YOU BALD FUCK!
WHA-
ACK!!
OH NO!
WHAT HAVE I DONE?!
I'M S-SORRY! BALD... BULK... BUZZ... I HEARD BUZZING AND THOUGHT IT WAS, UM, A FLY?
WAP
WAP
WAP
SHOO, FLY!
OK. DON'T WORRY ABOUT IT.
JUST SIT BACK DOWN.

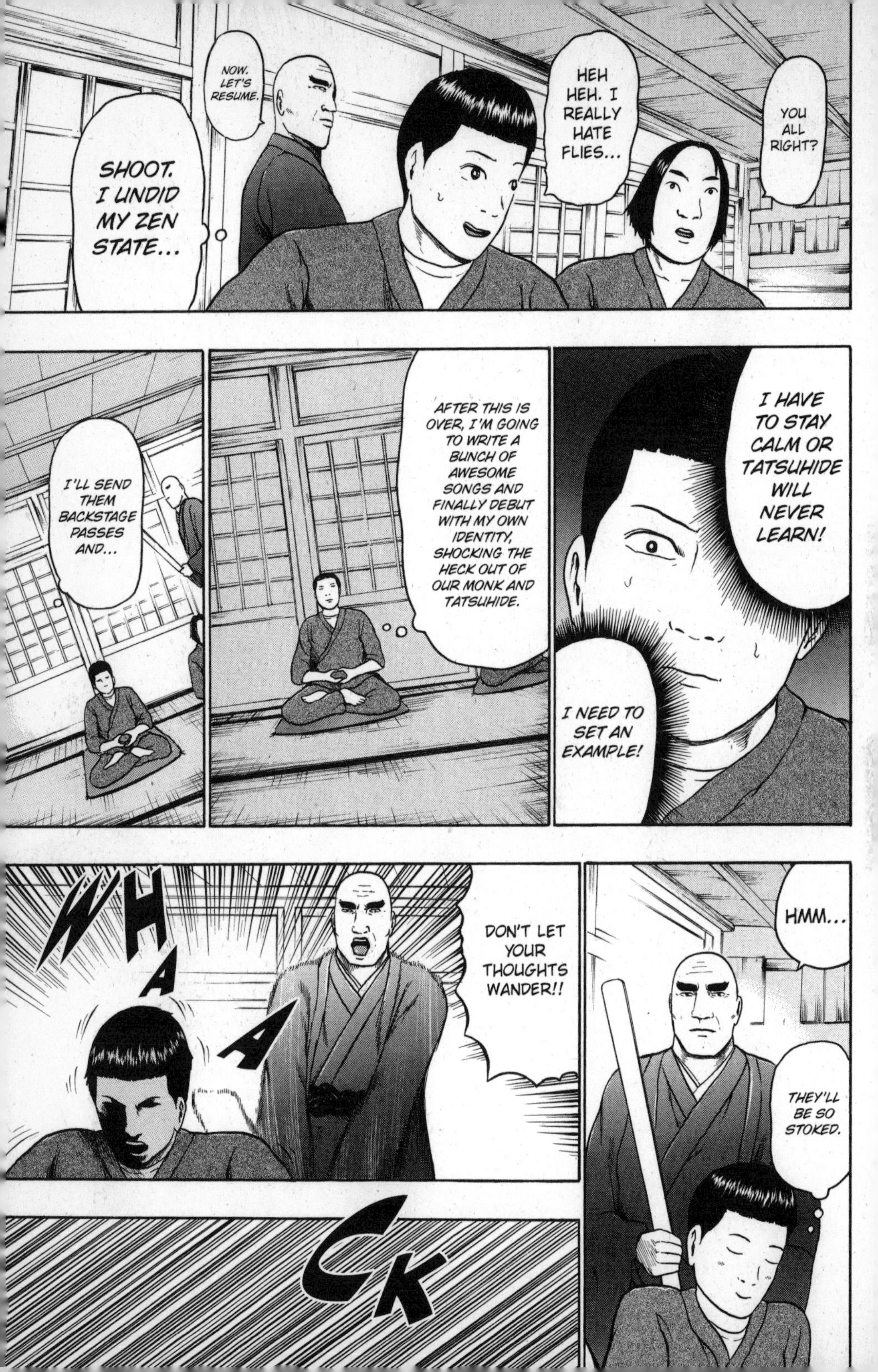
YOU ALL RIGHT?
HEH HEH. I REALLY HATE FLIES...
NOW. LET'S RESUME.
SHOOT. I UNDID MY ZEN STATE...
I HAVE TO STAY CALM OR TATSUHIDE WILL NEVER LEARN!
I NEED TO SET AN EXAMPLE!
AFTER THIS IS OVER, I'M GOING TO WRITE A BUNCH OF AWESOME SONGS AND FINALLY DEBUT WITH MY OWN IDENTITY, SHOCKING THE HECK OUT OF OUR MONK AND TATSUHIDE.
I'LL SEND THEM BACKSTAGE PASSES AND...
HMM...
THEY'LL BE SO STOKED.
DON'T LET YOUR THOUGHTS WANDER!!
WHAA
CK

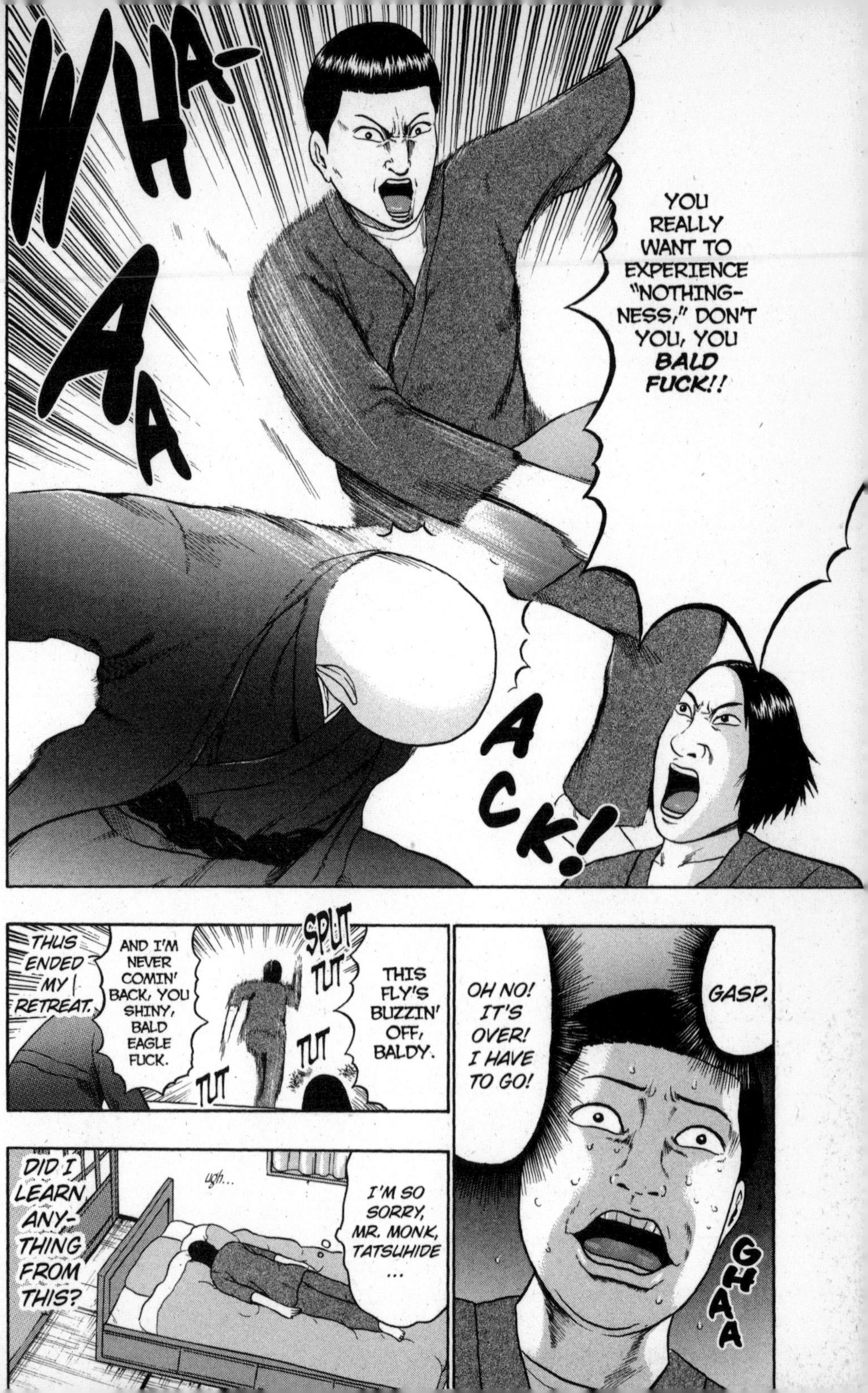

YOU REALLY WANT TO EXPERIENCE "NOTHING-NESS," DON'T YOU, YOU BALD FUCK!!
WHA-AAA
ACK!
GASP.
OH NO! IT'S OVER! I HAVE TO GO!
GHAA
SPLUT
TUT
THIS FLY'S BUZZIN' OFF, BALDY.
TUT
AND I'M NEVER COMIN' BACK, YOU SHINY, BALD EAGLE FUCK.
TUT
THUS ENDED MY RETREAT.
I'M SO SORRY, MR. MONK, TATSUHIDE ...
ugh...
DID I LEARN ANY-THING FROM THIS?

DMC LEXICON

🎭 MINI RETREAT

A Buddhist retreat in which one does not have to take the tonsure and go bald. Said to correct the wrongs in one's life, you meditate, genuflect, and assume a pure diet alongside a bald man. Said bald man will have much wisdom to impart. This has a way of making nervous people feel smaller. Especially people who are nervous about balding.

Usage: Is a Mini Retreat the balding equivalent of a comb over?

デトロイト・メタル・シティ
Detroit Metal City

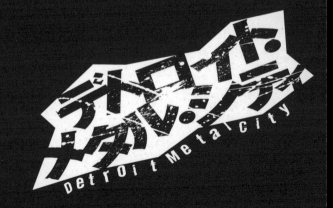

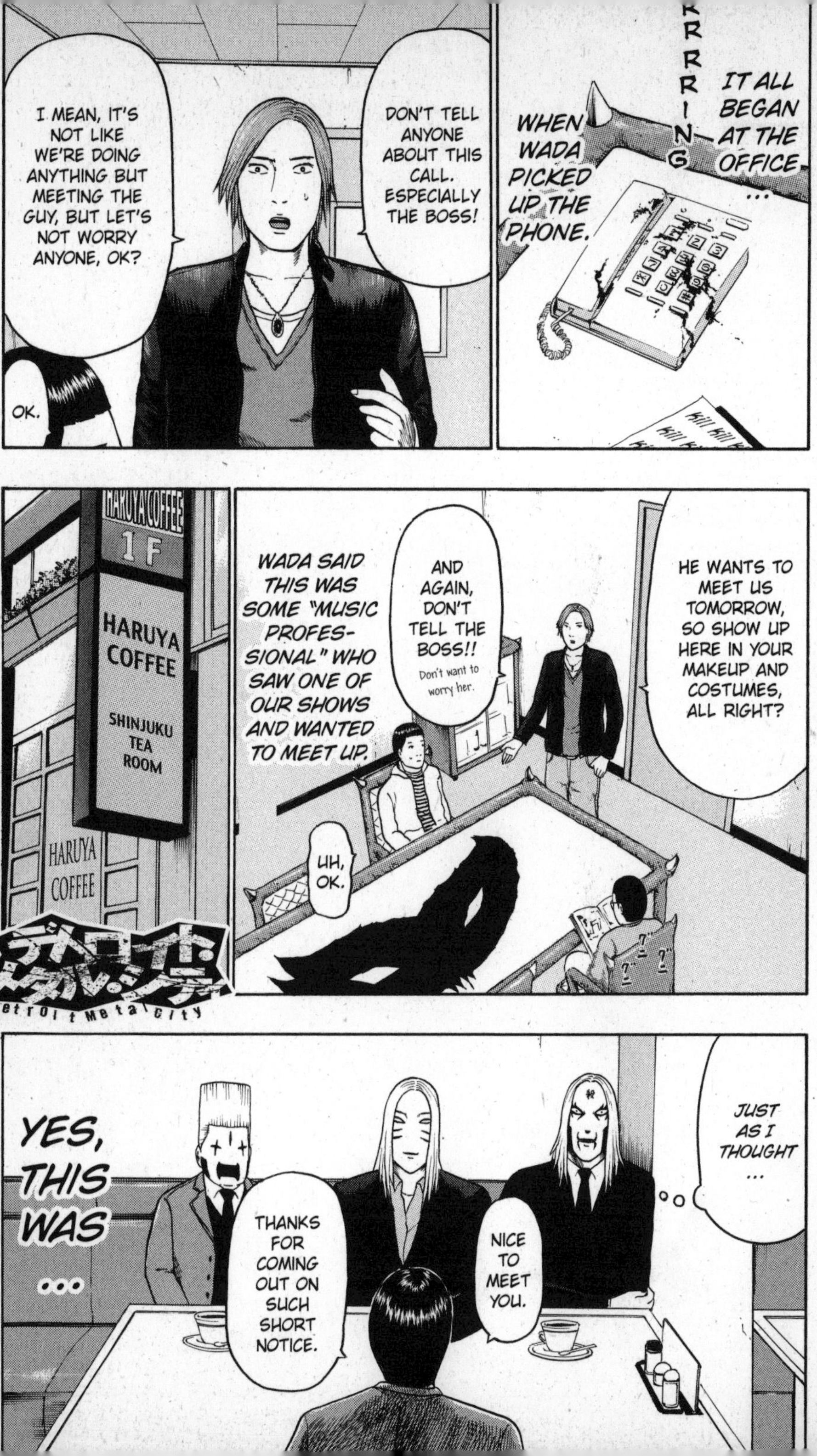
KRRRING
IT ALL BEGAN AT THE OFFICE...
WHEN WADA PICKED UP THE PHONE.
DON'T TELL ANYONE ABOUT THIS CALL. ESPECIALLY THE BOSS!
I MEAN, IT'S NOT LIKE WE'RE DOING ANYTHING BUT MEETING THE GUY, BUT LET'S NOT WORRY ANYONE, OK?
OK.
HE WANTS TO MEET US TOMORROW, SO SHOW UP HERE IN YOUR MAKEUP AND COSTUMES, ALL RIGHT?
AND AGAIN, DON'T TELL THE BOSS!!
Don't want to worry her.
WADA SAID THIS WAS SOME "MUSIC PROFES-SIONAL" WHO SAW ONE OF OUR SHOWS AND WANTED TO MEET UP.
UH, OK.
HARUYA COFFEE 1F
HARUYA COFFEE SHINJUKU TEA ROOM
HARUYA COFFEE
DetrOit MetaL city
JUST AS I THOUGHT...
NICE TO MEET YOU.
THANKS FOR COMING OUT ON SUCH SHORT NOTICE.
YES, THIS WAS...

TRACK 45 Hunting

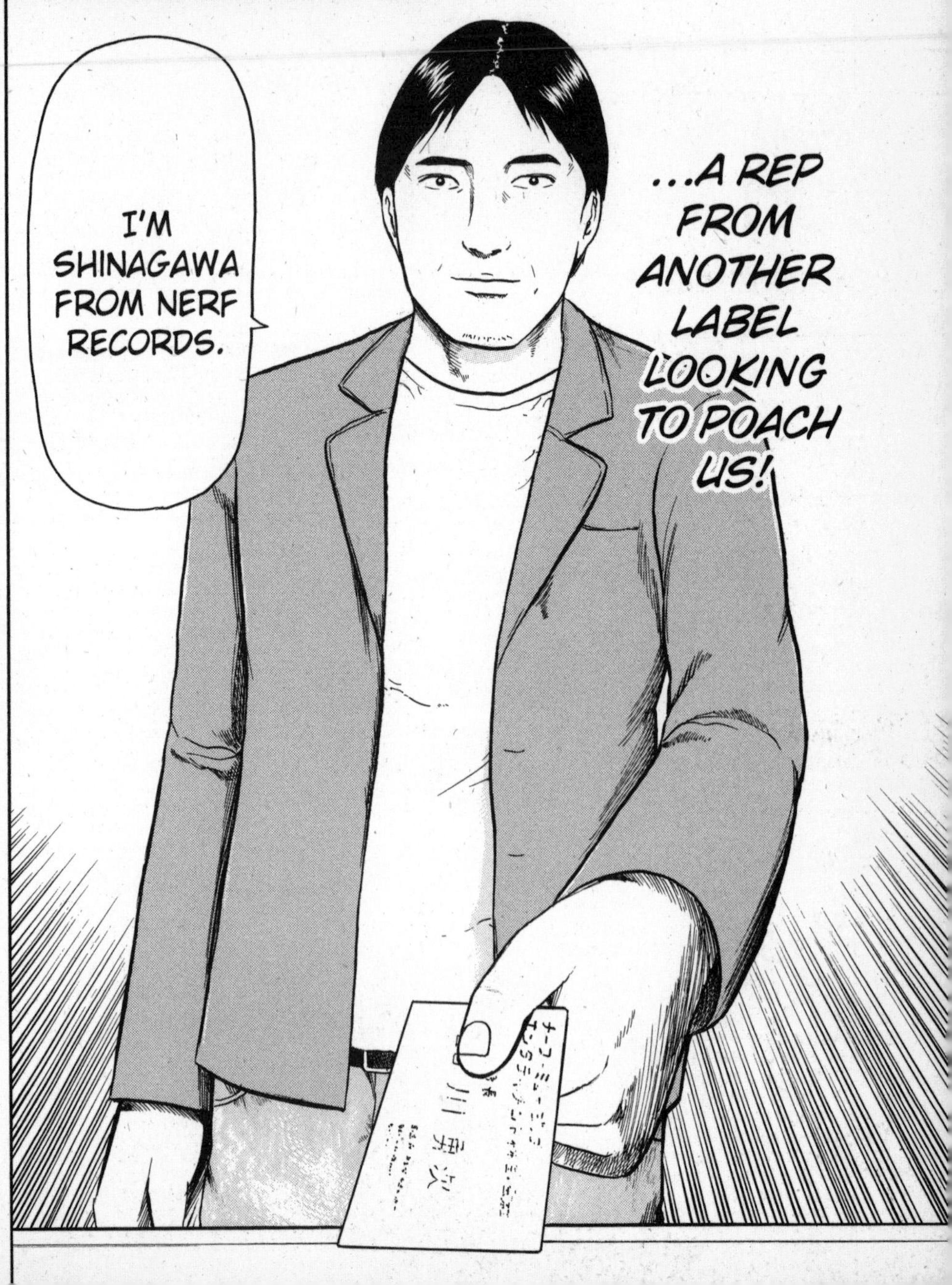
I'M SHINAGAWA FROM NERF RECORDS.
...A REP FROM ANOTHER LABEL LOOKING TO POACH US!

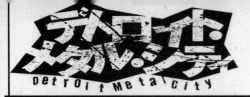

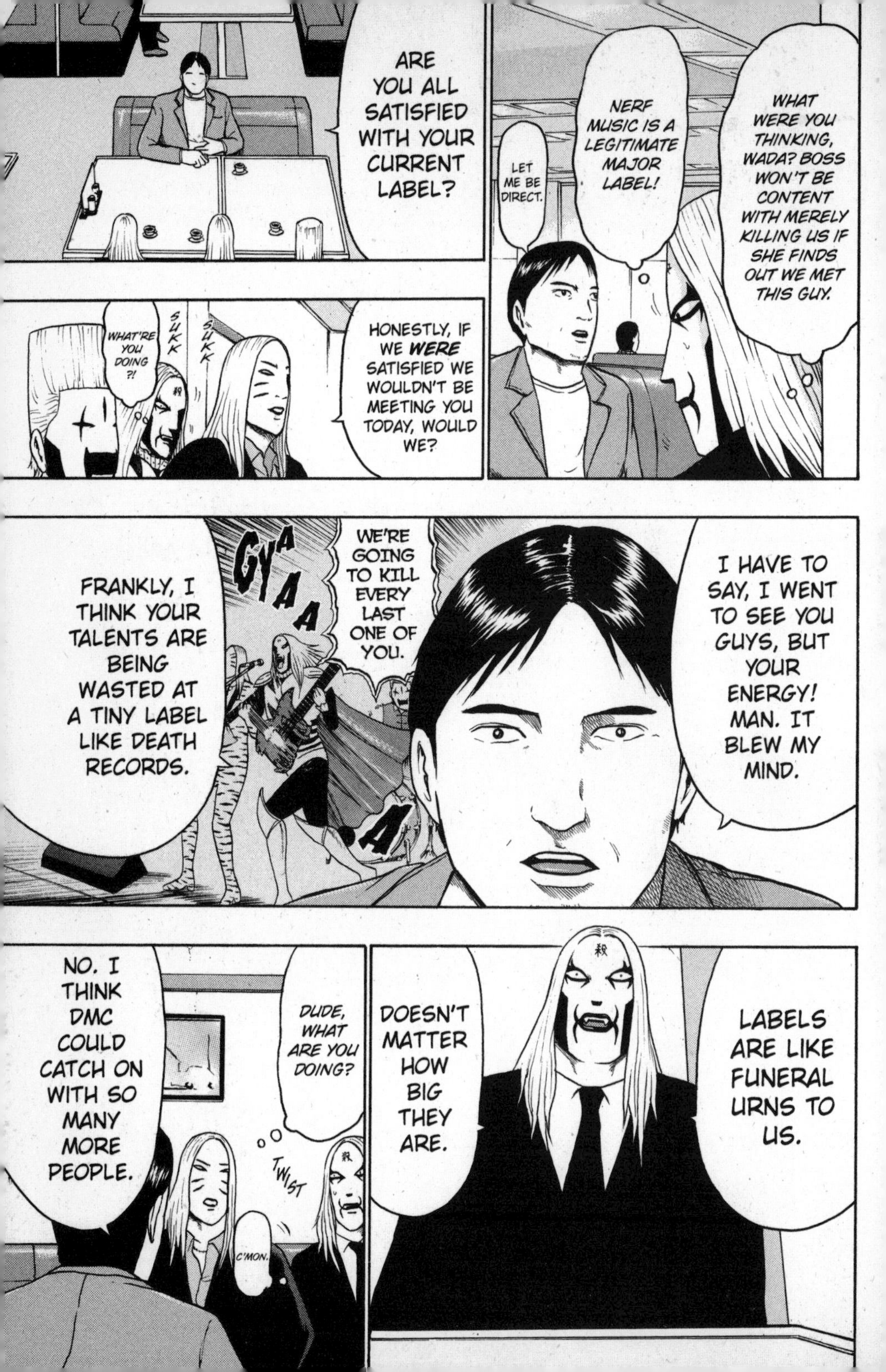
WHAT WERE YOU THINKING, WADA? BOSS WON'T BE CONTENT WITH MERELY KILLING US IF SHE FINDS OUT WE MET THIS GUY.
NERF MUSIC IS A LEGITIMATE MAJOR LABEL!
LET ME BE DIRECT.
ARE YOU ALL SATISFIED WITH YOUR CURRENT LABEL?
HONESTLY, IF WE *WERE* SATISFIED WE WOULDN'T BE MEETING YOU TODAY, WOULD WE?
SUKK
SUKK
WHAT'RE YOU DOING ?!
I HAVE TO SAY, I WENT TO SEE YOU GUYS, BUT YOUR ENERGY! MAN. IT BLEW MY MIND.
WE'RE GOING TO KILL EVERY LAST ONE OF YOU.
GYAAAA
FRANKLY, I THINK YOUR TALENTS ARE BEING WASTED AT A TINY LABEL LIKE DEATH RECORDS.
LABELS ARE LIKE FUNERAL URNS TO US.
DOESN'T MATTER HOW BIG THEY ARE.
DUDE, WHAT ARE YOU DOING?
TWIST
C'MON.
NO. I THINK DMC COULD CATCH ON WITH SO MANY MORE PEOPLE.

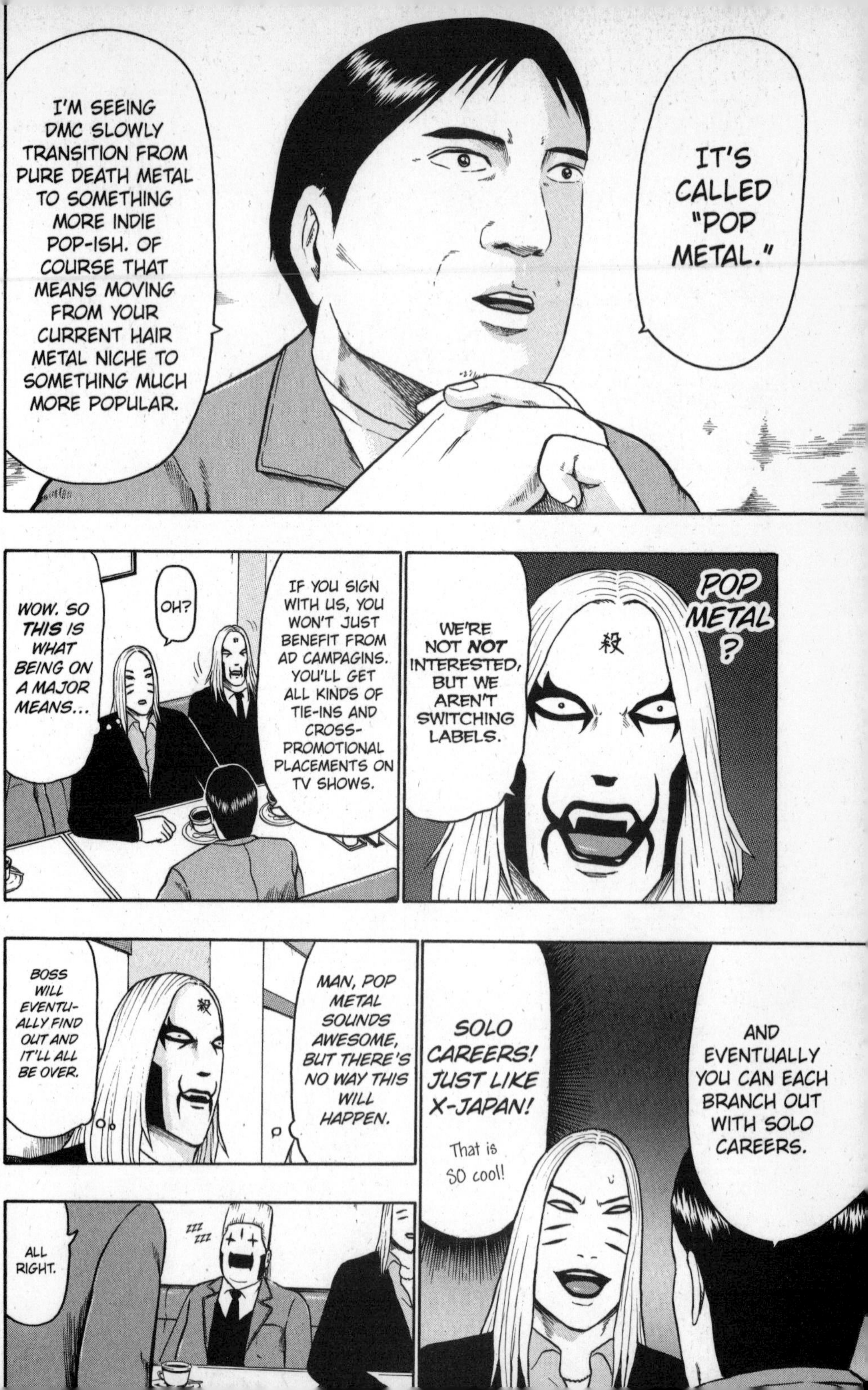

IT'S CALLED "POP METAL."
I'M SEEING DMC SLOWLY TRANSITION FROM PURE DEATH METAL TO SOMETHING MORE INDIE POP-ISH. OF COURSE THAT MEANS MOVING FROM YOUR CURRENT HAIR METAL NICHE TO SOMETHING MUCH MORE POPULAR.
POP METAL?
WE'RE NOT ***NOT*** INTERESTED, BUT WE AREN'T SWITCHING LABELS.
IF YOU SIGN WITH US, YOU WON'T JUST BENEFIT FROM AD CAMPAGINS. YOU'LL GET ALL KINDS OF TIE-INS AND CROSS-PROMOTIONAL PLACEMENTS ON TV SHOWS.
OH?
*WOW. SO **THIS** IS WHAT BEING ON A MAJOR MEANS...*
AND EVENTUALLY YOU CAN EACH BRANCH OUT WITH SOLO CAREERS.
SOLO CAREERS! JUST LIKE X-JAPAN!
That is SO cool!
MAN, POP METAL SOUNDS AWESOME, BUT THERE'S NO WAY THIS WILL HAPPEN.
BOSS WILL EVENTU-ALLY FIND OUT AND IT'LL ALL BE OVER.
ZZZ ZZZ
ALL RIGHT.

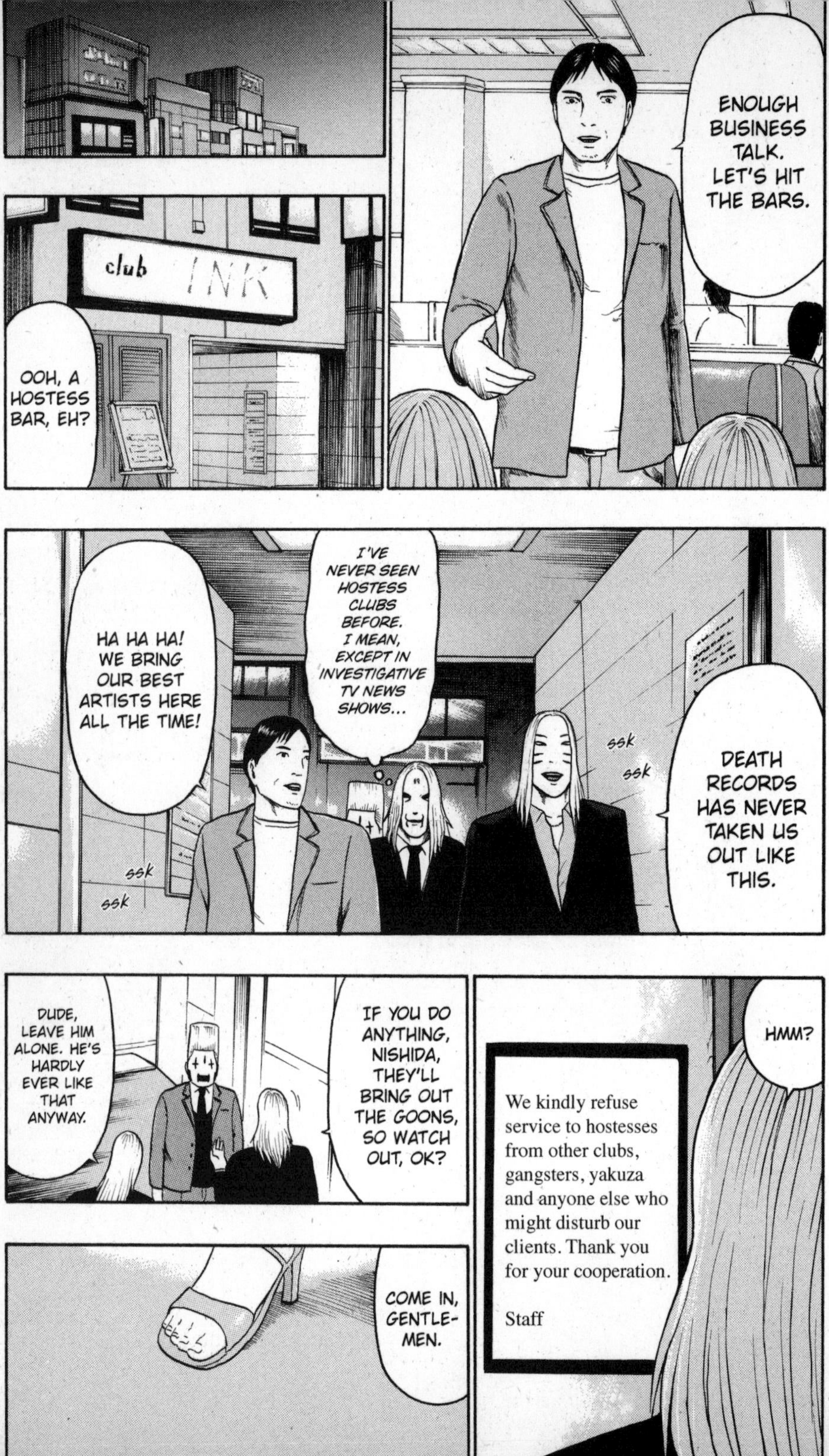
ENOUGH BUSINESS TALK. LET'S HIT THE BARS.
club INK
OOH, A HOSTESS BAR, EH?
DEATH RECORDS HAS NEVER TAKEN US OUT LIKE THIS.
ssk
ssk
I'VE NEVER SEEN HOSTESS CLUBS BEFORE. I MEAN, EXCEPT IN INVESTIGATIVE TV NEWS SHOWS...
HA HA HA! WE BRING OUR BEST ARTISTS HERE ALL THE TIME!
ssk
ssk
HMM?
We kindly refuse service to hostesses from other clubs, gangsters, yakuza and anyone else who might disturb our clients. Thank you for your cooperation.
Staff
IF YOU DO ANYTHING, NISHIDA, THEY'LL BRING OUT THE GOONS, SO WATCH OUT, OK?
DUDE, LEAVE HIM ALONE. HE'S HARDLY EVER LIKE THAT ANYWAY.
COME IN, GENTLE-MEN.

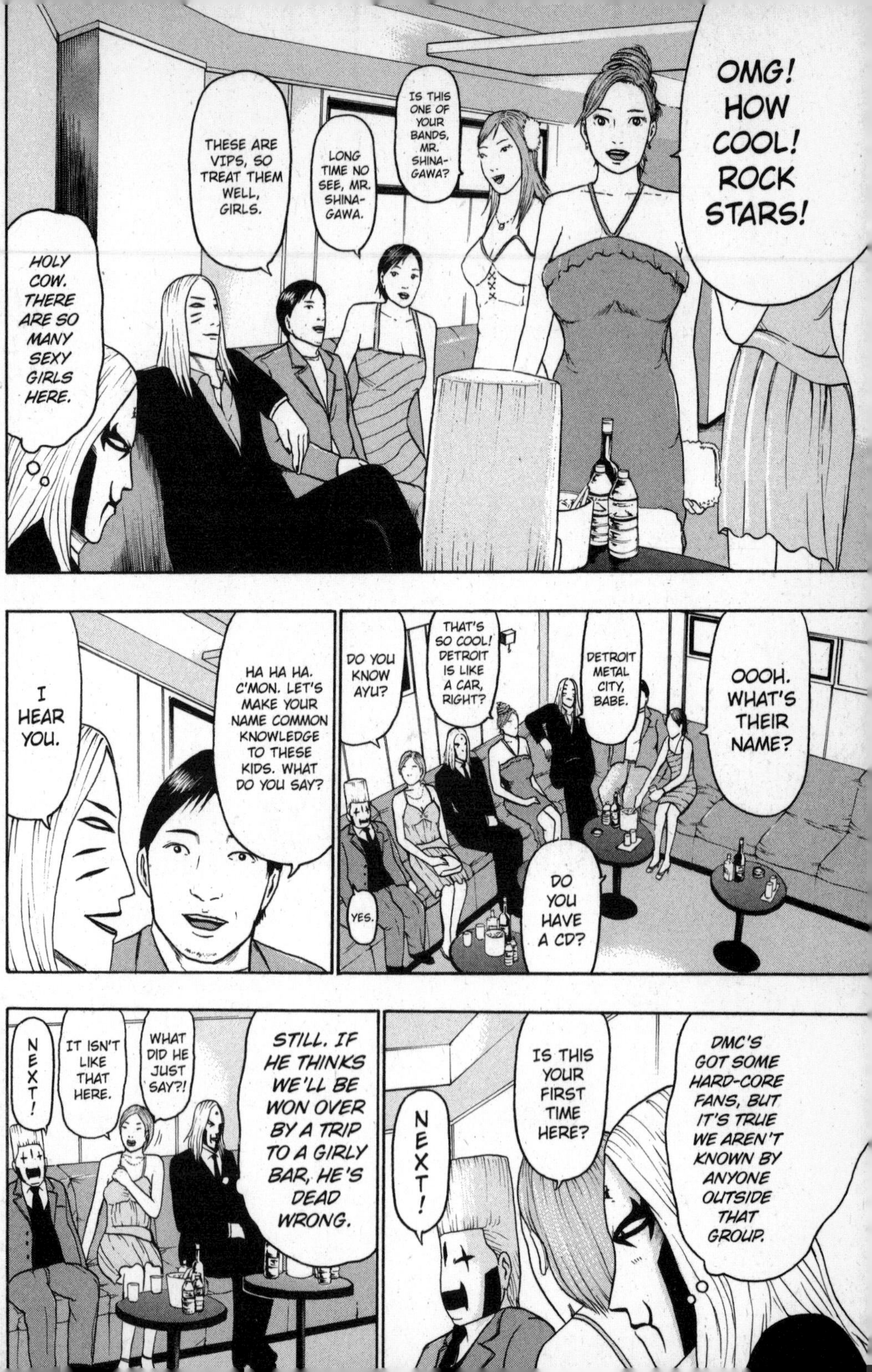
OMG! HOW COOL! ROCK STARS!
IS THIS ONE OF YOUR BANDS, MR. SHINAGAWA?
LONG TIME NO SEE, MR. SHINAGAWA.
THESE ARE VIPS, SO TREAT THEM WELL, GIRLS.
HOLY COW. THERE ARE SO MANY SEXY GIRLS HERE.
OOOH. WHAT'S THEIR NAME?
DETROIT METAL CITY, BABE.
THAT'S SO COOL! DETROIT IS LIKE A CAR, RIGHT?
DO YOU KNOW AYU?
DO YOU HAVE A CD?
YES.
HA HA HA. C'MON. LET'S MAKE YOUR NAME COMMON KNOWLEDGE TO THESE KIDS. WHAT DO YOU SAY?
I HEAR YOU.
DMC'S GOT SOME HARD-CORE FANS, BUT IT'S TRUE WE AREN'T KNOWN BY ANYONE OUTSIDE THAT GROUP.
IS THIS YOUR FIRST TIME HERE?
NEXT!
STILL. IF HE THINKS WE'LL BE WON OVER BY A TRIP TO A GIRLY BAR, HE'S DEAD WRONG.
WHAT DID HE JUST SAY?!
IT ISN'T LIKE THAT HERE.
NEXT!

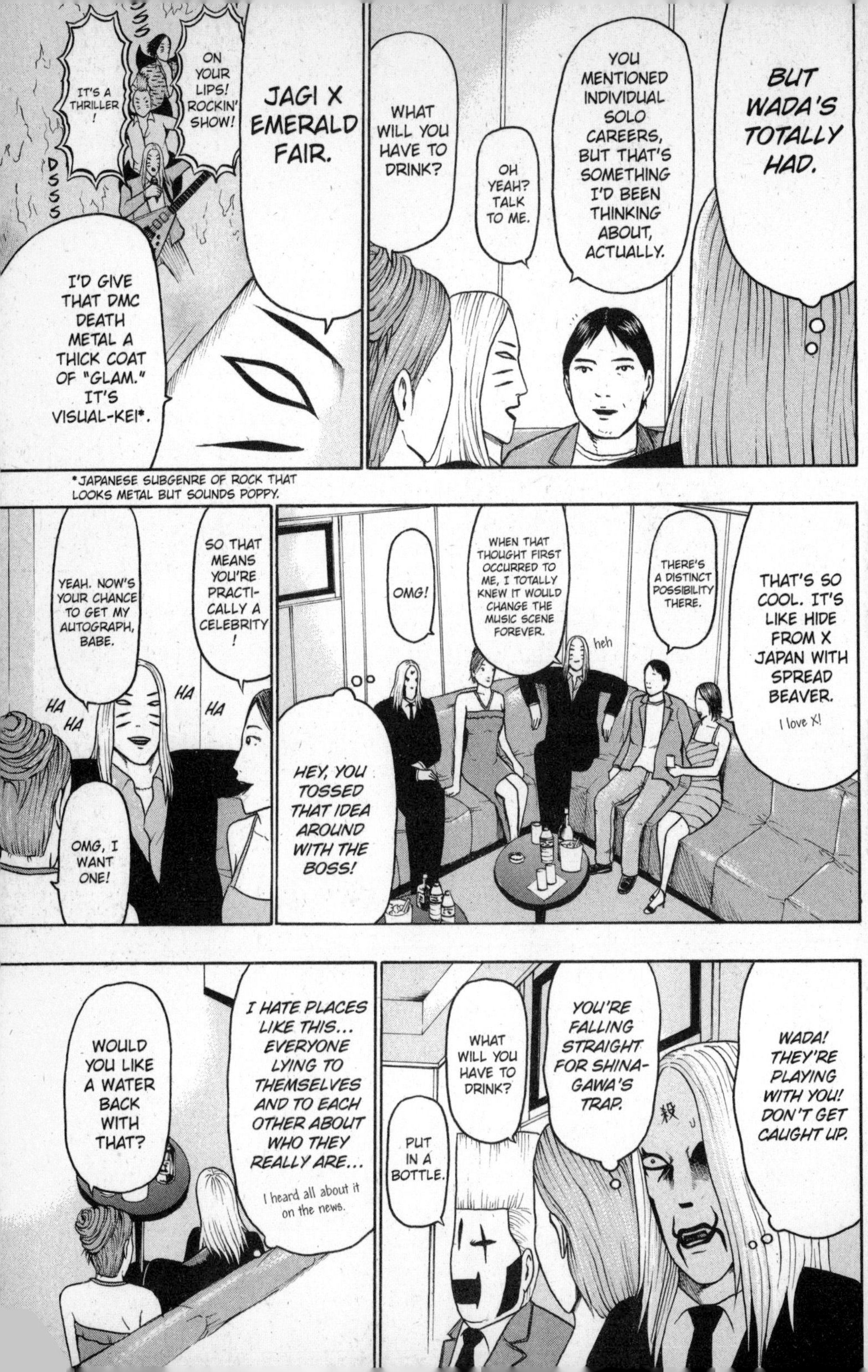
BUT WADA'S TOTALLY HAD.
YOU MENTIONED INDIVIDUAL SOLO CAREERS, BUT THAT'S SOMETHING I'D BEEN THINKING ABOUT, ACTUALLY.
OH YEAH? TALK TO ME.
WHAT WILL YOU HAVE TO DRINK?
JAGI X EMERALD FAIR.
ON YOUR LIPS! ROCKIN' SHOW!
IT'S A THRILLER!
DSSS
I'D GIVE THAT DMC DEATH METAL A THICK COAT OF "GLAM." IT'S VISUAL-KEI*.
*JAPANESE SUBGENRE OF ROCK THAT LOOKS METAL BUT SOUNDS POPPY.
THAT'S SO COOL. IT'S LIKE HIDE FROM X JAPAN WITH SPREAD BEAVER.
I love X!
THERE'S A DISTINCT POSSIBILITY THERE.
heh
WHEN THAT THOUGHT FIRST OCCURRED TO ME, I TOTALLY KNEW IT WOULD CHANGE THE MUSIC SCENE FOREVER.
OMG!
HEY, YOU TOSSED THAT IDEA AROUND WITH THE BOSS!
SO THAT MEANS YOU'RE PRACTICALLY A CELEBRITY!
YEAH. NOW'S YOUR CHANCE TO GET MY AUTOGRAPH, BABE.
HA HA HA HA
OMG, I WANT ONE!
WADA! THEY'RE PLAYING WITH YOU! DON'T GET CAUGHT UP.
殺
YOU'RE FALLING STRAIGHT FOR SHINAGAWA'S TRAP.
WHAT WILL YOU HAVE TO DRINK?
PUT IN A BOTTLE.
I HATE PLACES LIKE THIS... EVERYONE LYING TO THEMSELVES AND TO EACH OTHER ABOUT WHO THEY REALLY ARE...
I heard all about it on the news.
WOULD YOU LIKE A WATER BACK WITH THAT?

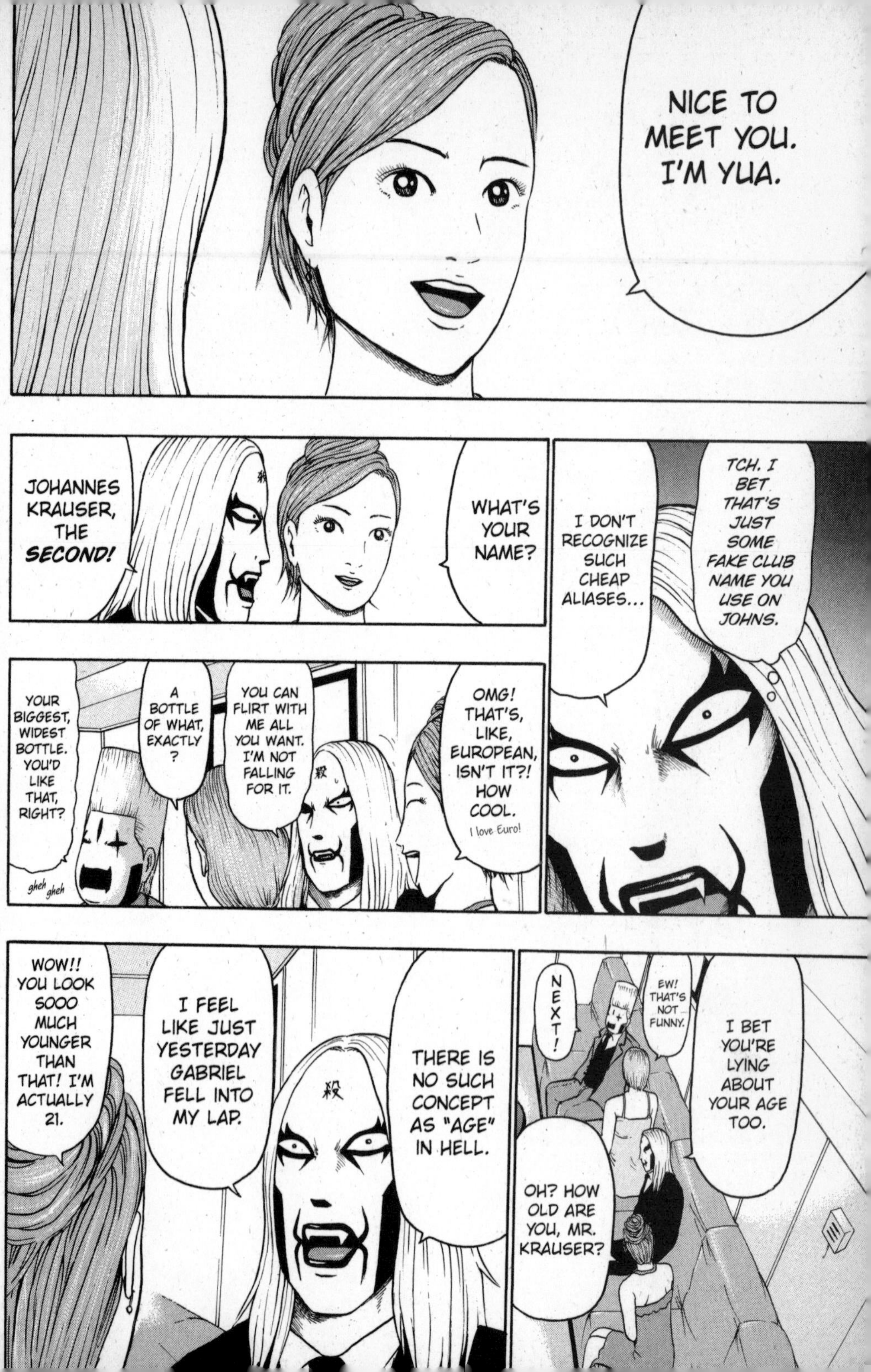
NICE TO MEET YOU. I'M YUA.
TCH. I BET THAT'S JUST SOME FAKE CLUB NAME YOU USE ON JOHNS.
I DON'T RECOGNIZE SUCH CHEAP ALIASES...
WHAT'S YOUR NAME?
JOHANNES KRAUSER, THE SECOND!
OMG! THAT'S, LIKE, EUROPEAN, ISN'T IT?! HOW COOL.
I love Euro!
YOU CAN FLIRT WITH ME ALL YOU WANT. I'M NOT FALLING FOR IT.
A BOTTLE OF WHAT, EXACTLY?
YOUR BIGGEST, WIDEST BOTTLE. YOU'D LIKE THAT, RIGHT?
gheh gheh
I BET YOU'RE LYING ABOUT YOUR AGE TOO.
EW! THAT'S NOT FUNNY.
NEXT!
OH? HOW OLD ARE YOU, MR. KRAUSER?
THERE IS NO SUCH CONCEPT AS "AGE" IN HELL.
I FEEL LIKE JUST YESTERDAY GABRIEL FELL INTO MY LAP.
WOW!! YOU LOOK SOOO MUCH YOUNGER THAN THAT! I'M ACTUALLY 21.

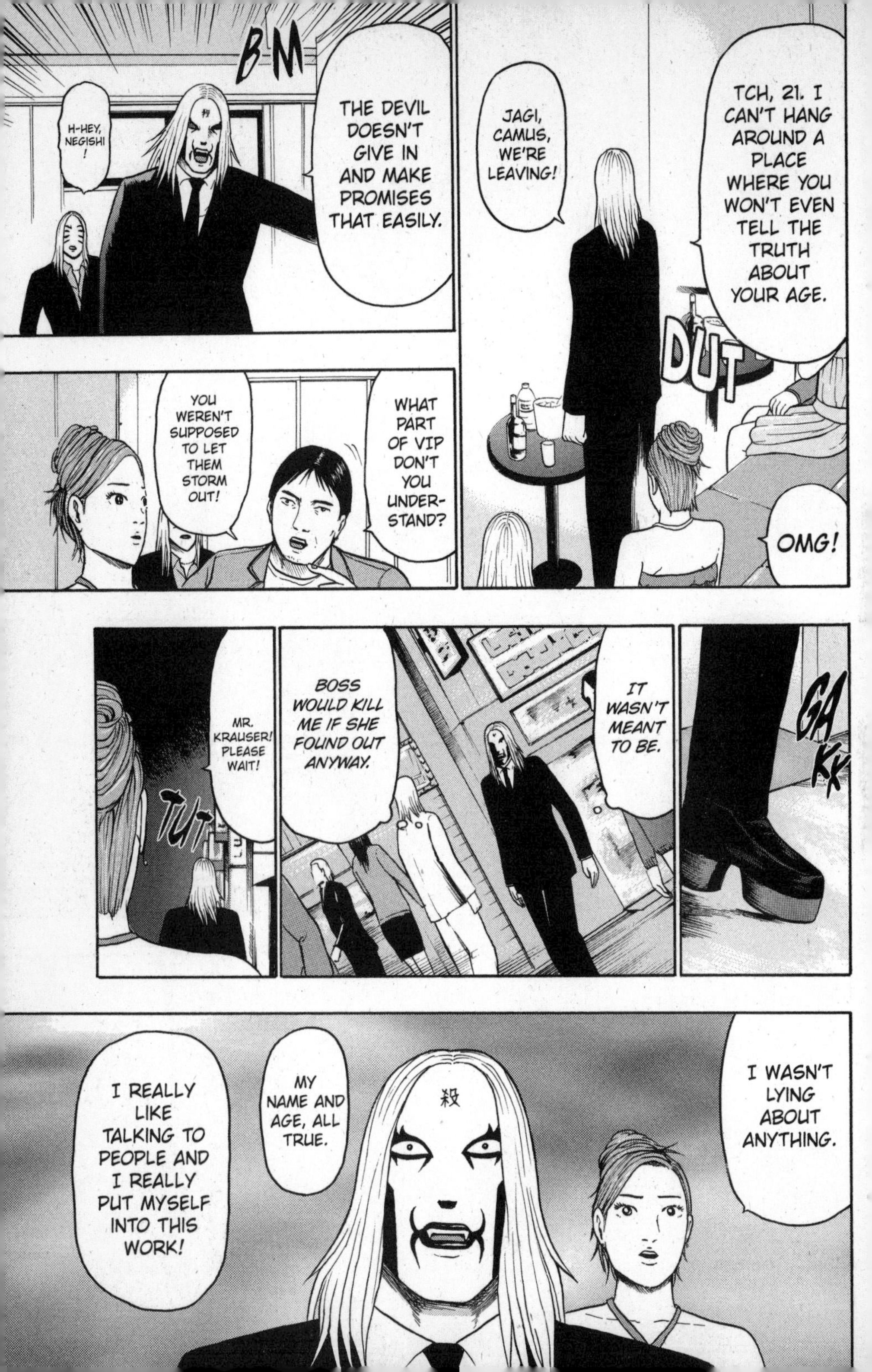
TCH, 21. I CAN'T HANG AROUND A PLACE WHERE YOU WON'T EVEN TELL THE TRUTH ABOUT YOUR AGE.
JAGI, CAMUS, WE'RE LEAVING!
DUT
OMG!
BM
THE DEVIL DOESN'T GIVE IN AND MAKE PROMISES THAT EASILY.
H-HEY, NEGISHI!
WHAT PART OF VIP DON'T YOU UNDER-STAND?
YOU WEREN'T SUPPOSED TO LET THEM STORM OUT!
GAKK
IT WASN'T MEANT TO BE.
BOSS WOULD KILL ME IF SHE FOUND OUT ANYWAY.
MR. KRAUSER! PLEASE WAIT!
TUT
I WASN'T LYING ABOUT ANYTHING.
MY NAME AND AGE, ALL TRUE.
I REALLY LIKE TALKING TO PEOPLE AND I REALLY PUT MYSELF INTO THIS WORK!

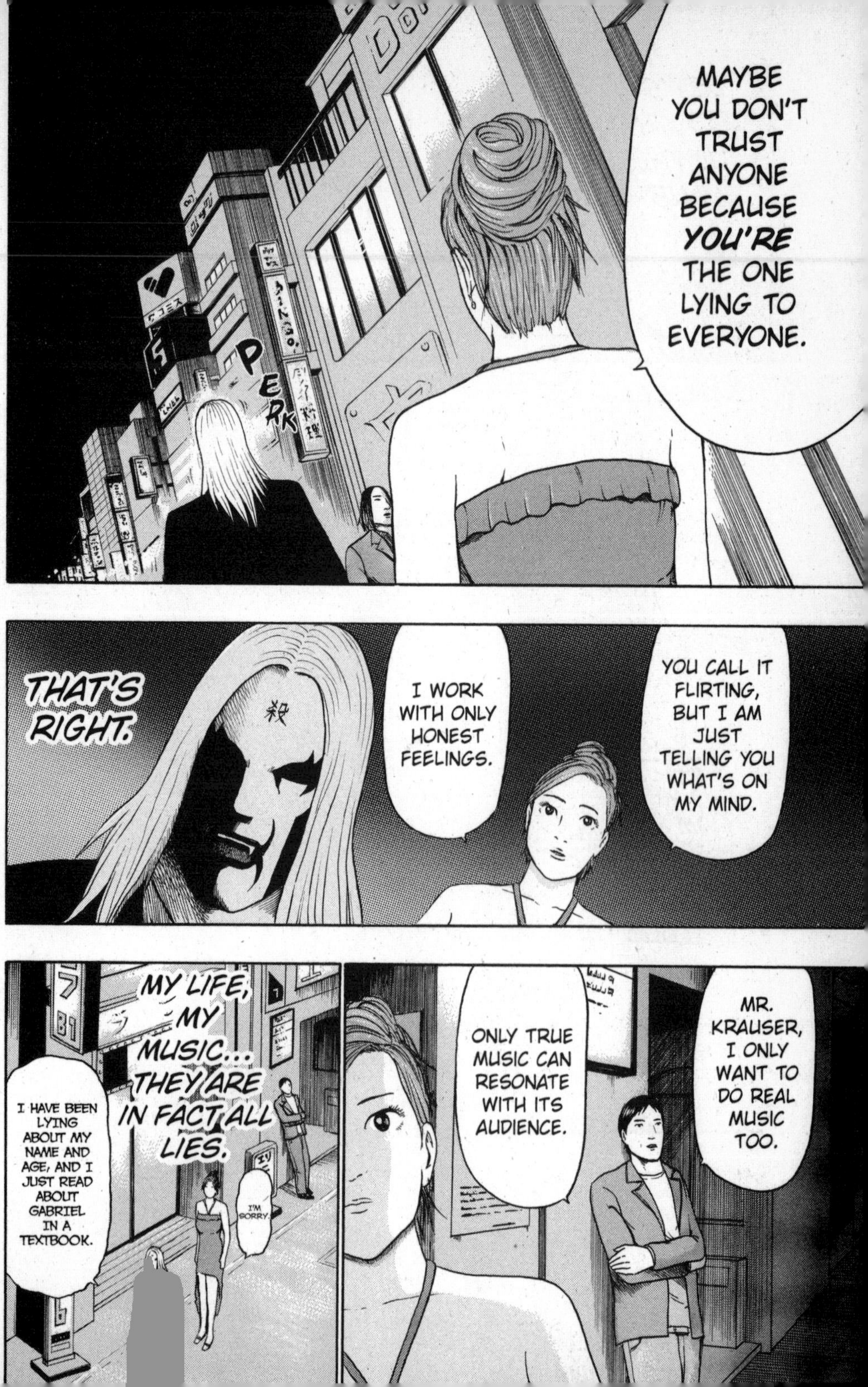
MAYBE YOU DON'T TRUST ANYONE BECAUSE *YOU'RE* THE ONE LYING TO EVERYONE.
PERK
YOU CALL IT FLIRTING, BUT I AM JUST TELLING YOU WHAT'S ON MY MIND.
I WORK WITH ONLY HONEST FEELINGS.
THAT'S RIGHT.
MR. KRAUSER, I ONLY WANT TO DO REAL MUSIC TOO.
ONLY TRUE MUSIC CAN RESONATE WITH ITS AUDIENCE.
MY LIFE, MY MUSIC... THEY ARE IN FACT ALL LIES.
I'M SORRY.
I HAVE BEEN LYING ABOUT MY NAME AND AGE, AND I JUST READ ABOUT GABRIEL IN A TEXTBOOK.

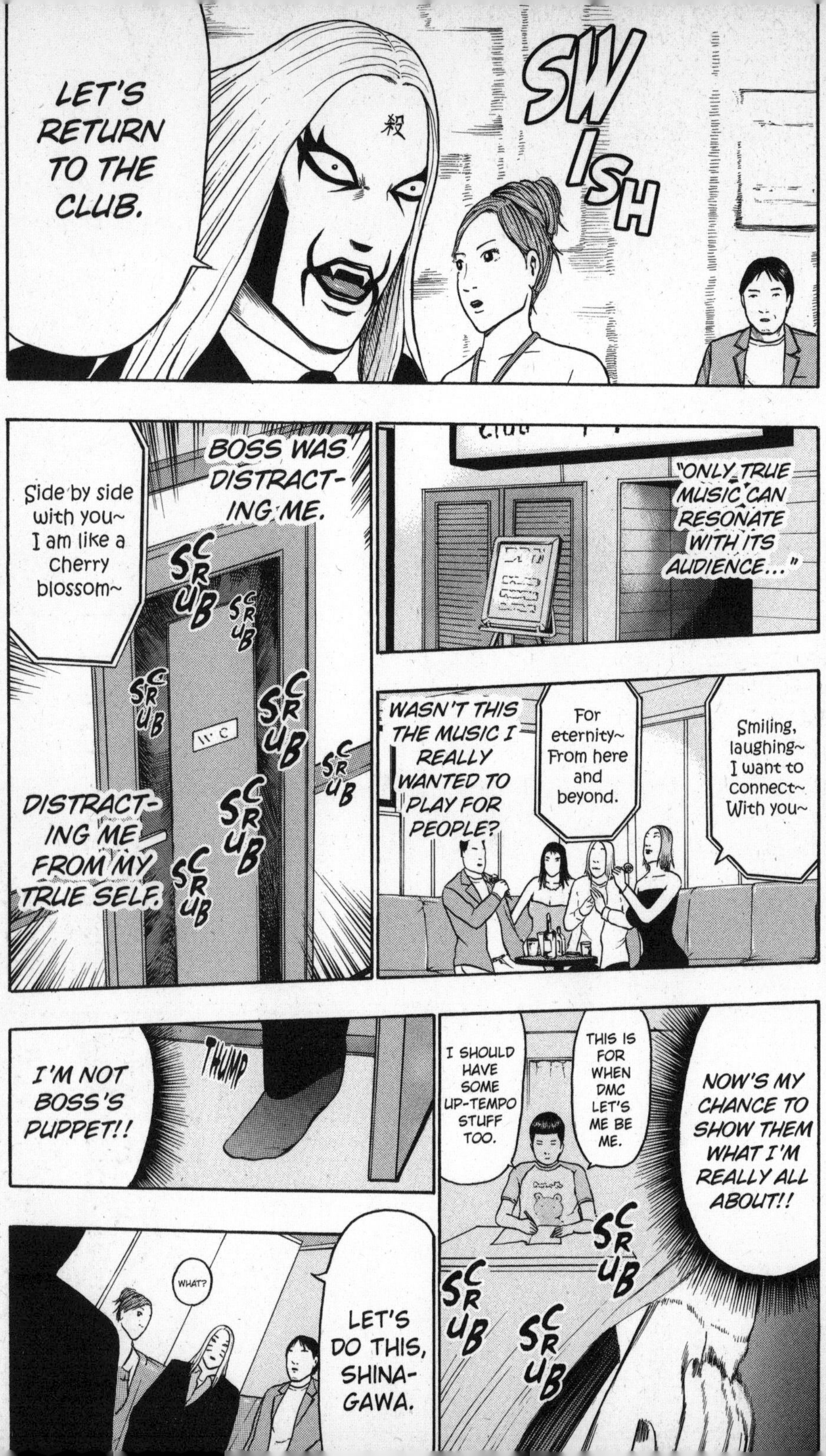
SWISH
LET'S RETURN TO THE CLUB.
"ONLY TRUE MUSIC CAN RESONATE WITH ITS AUDIENCE..."
Smiling, laughing~ I want to connect~ With you~
For eternity~ From here and beyond.
WASN'T THIS THE MUSIC I REALLY WANTED TO PLAY FOR PEOPLE?
BOSS WAS DISTRACTING ME.
Side by side with you~ I am like a cherry blossom~
SCRUB SCRUB SCRUB SCRUB SCRUB SCRUB SCRUB
W C
DISTRACTING ME FROM MY TRUE SELF.
NOW'S MY CHANCE TO SHOW THEM WHAT I'M REALLY ALL ABOUT!!
THIS IS FOR WHEN DMC LET'S ME BE ME.
I SHOULD HAVE SOME UP-TEMPO STUFF TOO.
SCRUB SCRUB SCRUB
THUMP
I'M NOT BOSS'S PUPPET!!
LET'S DO THIS, SHINAGAWA.
WHAT?

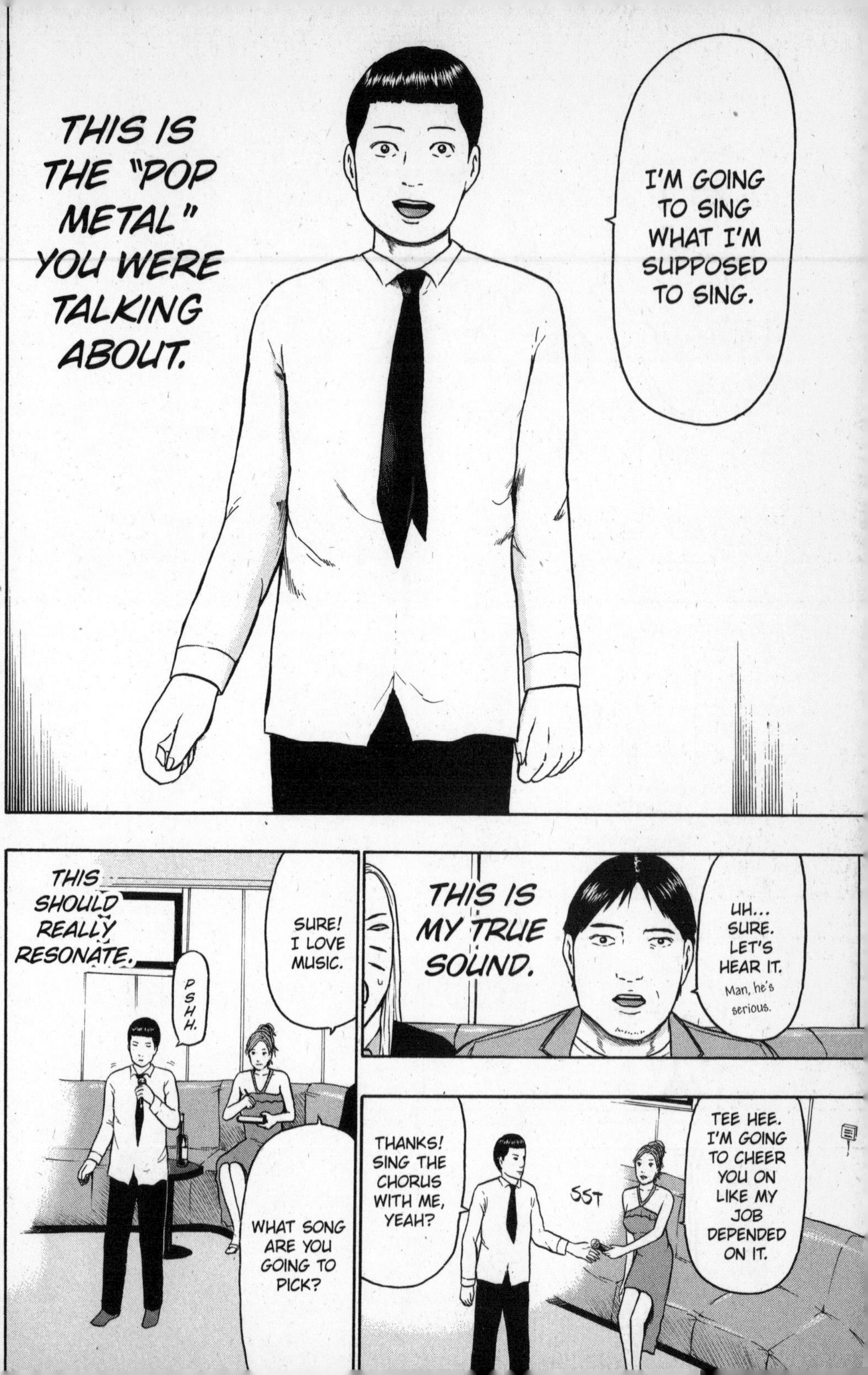
I'M GOING TO SING WHAT I'M SUPPOSED TO SING.
THIS IS THE "POP METAL" YOU WERE TALKING ABOUT.
UH... SURE. LET'S HEAR IT.
Man, he's serious.
THIS IS MY TRUE SOUND.
TEE HEE. I'M GOING TO CHEER YOU ON LIKE MY JOB DEPENDED ON IT.
SST
THANKS! SING THE CHORUS WITH ME, YEAH?
SURE! I LOVE MUSIC.
PSHH.
THIS SHOULD REALLY RESONATE.
WHAT SONG ARE YOU GOING TO PICK?

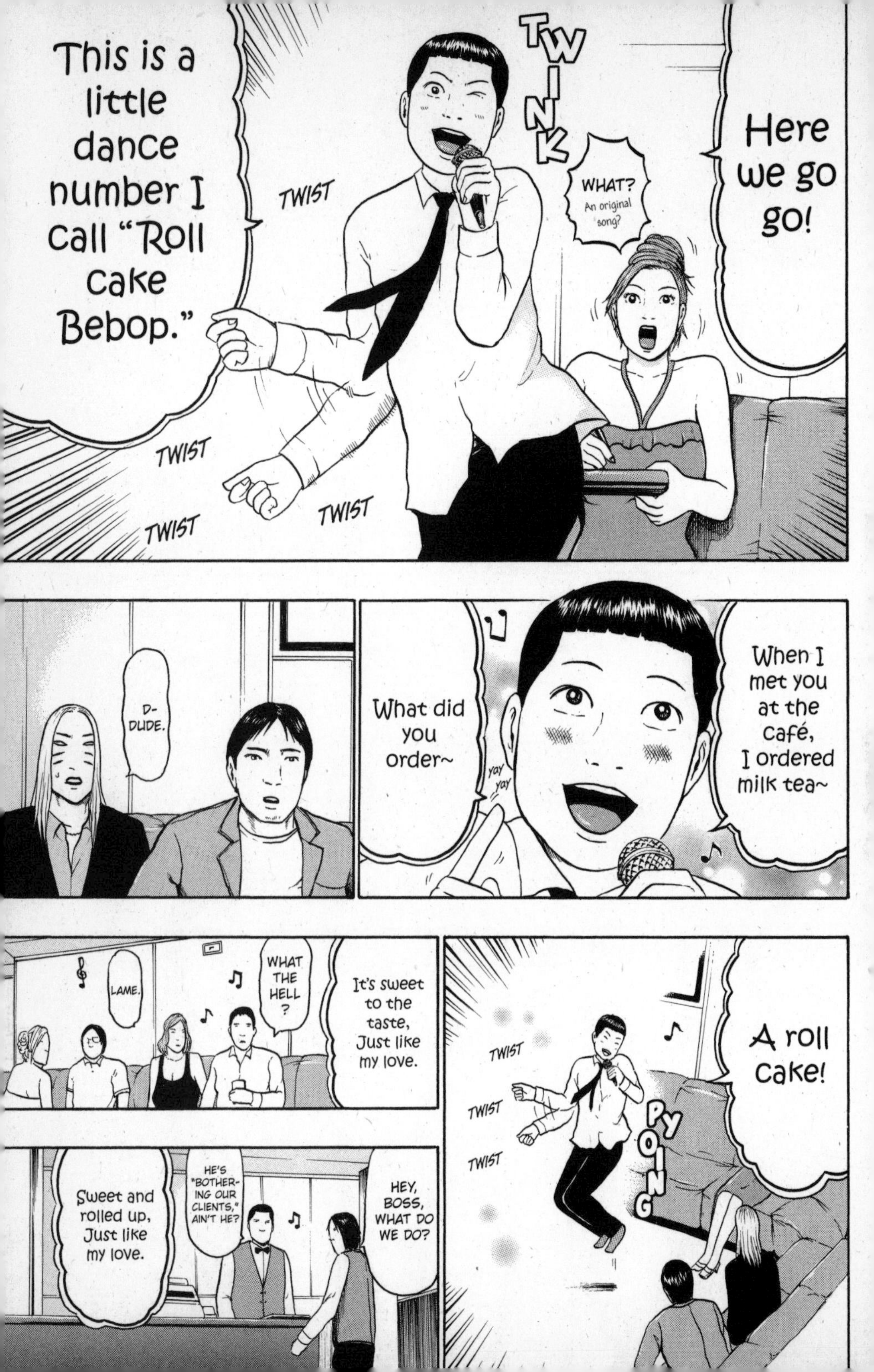
Here we go go!
TWINK
WHAT? An original song?
This is a little dance number I call "Roll cake Bebop."
TWIST
TWIST
TWIST
TWIST
When I met you at the café, I ordered milk tea~
What did you order~
yay yay
D-DUDE.
A roll cake!
PYOING
TWIST
TWIST
TWIST
It's sweet to the taste, Just like my love.
WHAT THE HELL?
LAME.
HEY, BOSS, WHAT DO WE DO?
HE'S "BOTHERING OUR CLIENTS," AIN'T HE?
Sweet and rolled up, Just like my love.

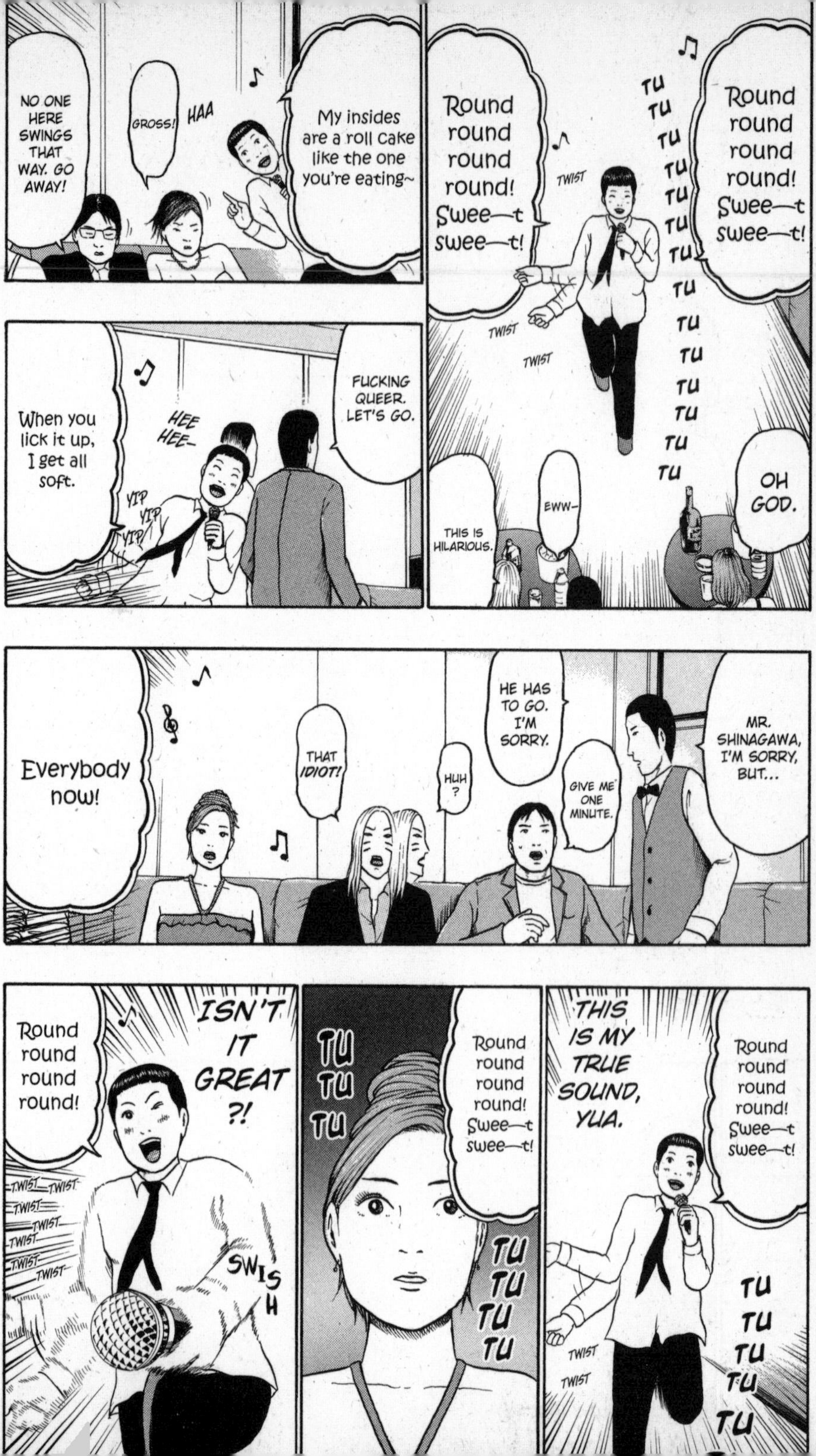

Round round round round! Swee—t swee—t!
TU TU TU TU TU TU TU TU TU TU TU TU TU TU
Round round round round! Swee—t swee—t!
TWIST
TWIST
TWIST
OH GOD.
EWW–
THIS IS HILARIOUS.
My insides are a roll cake like the one you're eating~
HAA
GROSS!
NO ONE HERE SWINGS THAT WAY. GO AWAY!
FUCKING QUEER. LET'S GO.
HEE HEE–
When you lick it up, I get all soft.
YIP YIP YIP
MR. SHINAGAWA, I'M SORRY, BUT...
HE HAS TO GO. I'M SORRY.
GIVE ME ONE MINUTE.
HUH?
THAT IDIOT!
Everybody now!
Round round round round! Swee—t swee—t!
THIS IS MY TRUE SOUND, YUA.
TU TU TU TU TU
TWIST
TWIST
Round round round round! Swee—t swee—t!
TU TU TU
TU TU TU TU
ISN'T IT GREAT?!
Round round round round!
TWIST TWIST TWIST TWIST TWIST TWIST TWIST
SWISH

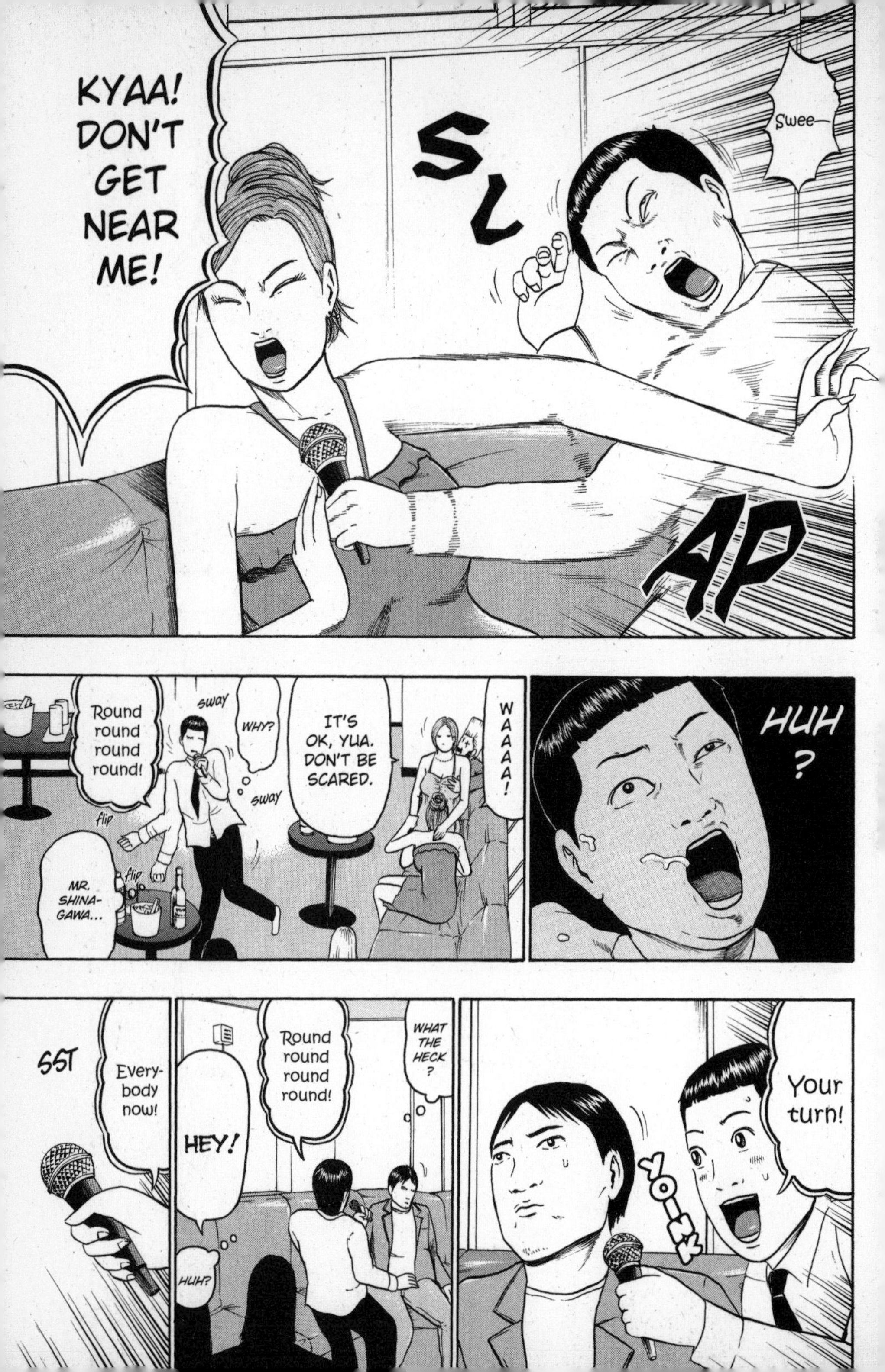
Swee—
SL
KYAA! DON'T GET NEAR ME!
AP
HUH?
WAAAAA!
IT'S OK, YUA. DON'T BE SCARED.
WHY?
sway
Round round round round!
sway
flip
MR. SHINA-GAWA...
flip
Your turn!
YOINK
WHAT THE HECK?
Round round round round!
HEY!
HUH?
Every-body now!
SST

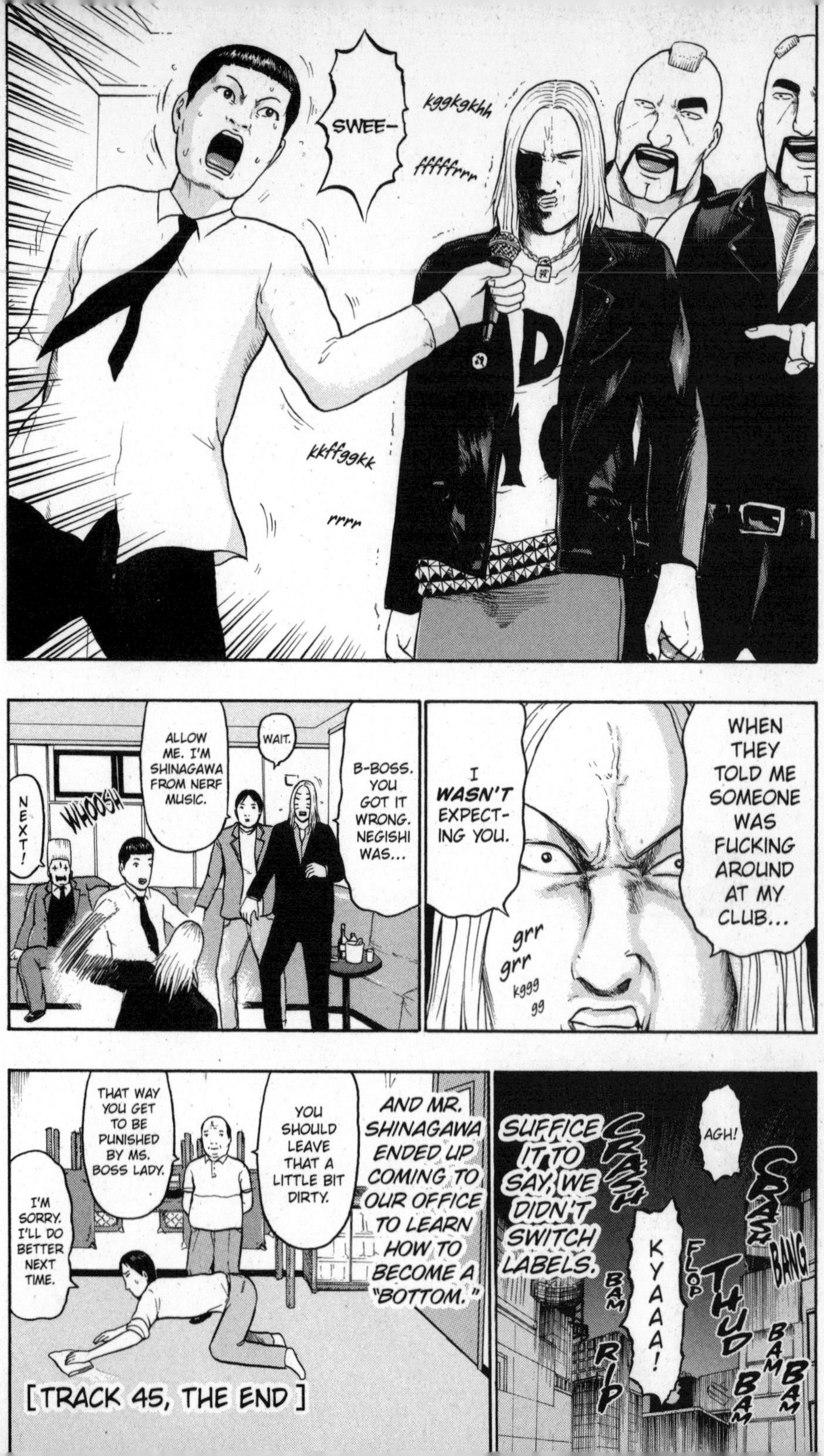
kggkgkhh
ffffrrr
SWEE-
kkffggkk
rrrr
WHEN THEY TOLD ME SOMEONE WAS FUCKING AROUND AT MY CLUB...
I WASN'T EXPECTING YOU.
grr grr
kggg gg
B-BOSS. YOU GOT IT WRONG. NEGISHI WAS...
WAIT.
ALLOW ME. I'M SHINAGAWA FROM NERF MUSIC.
WHOOSH
NEXT!
AGH!
CRASH
CRASH
BANG
SUFFICE IT TO SAY, WE DIDN'T SWITCH LABELS.
FLOP
THUD
KYAAA!
BAM
RIP
BAM
BAM
BAM
BAM
AND MR. SHINAGAWA ENDED UP COMING TO OUR OFFICE TO LEARN HOW TO BECOME A "BOTTOM."
YOU SHOULD LEAVE THAT A LITTLE BIT DIRTY.
THAT WAY YOU GET TO BE PUNISHED BY MS. BOSS LADY.
I'M SORRY. I'LL DO BETTER NEXT TIME.
[TRACK 45, THE END]

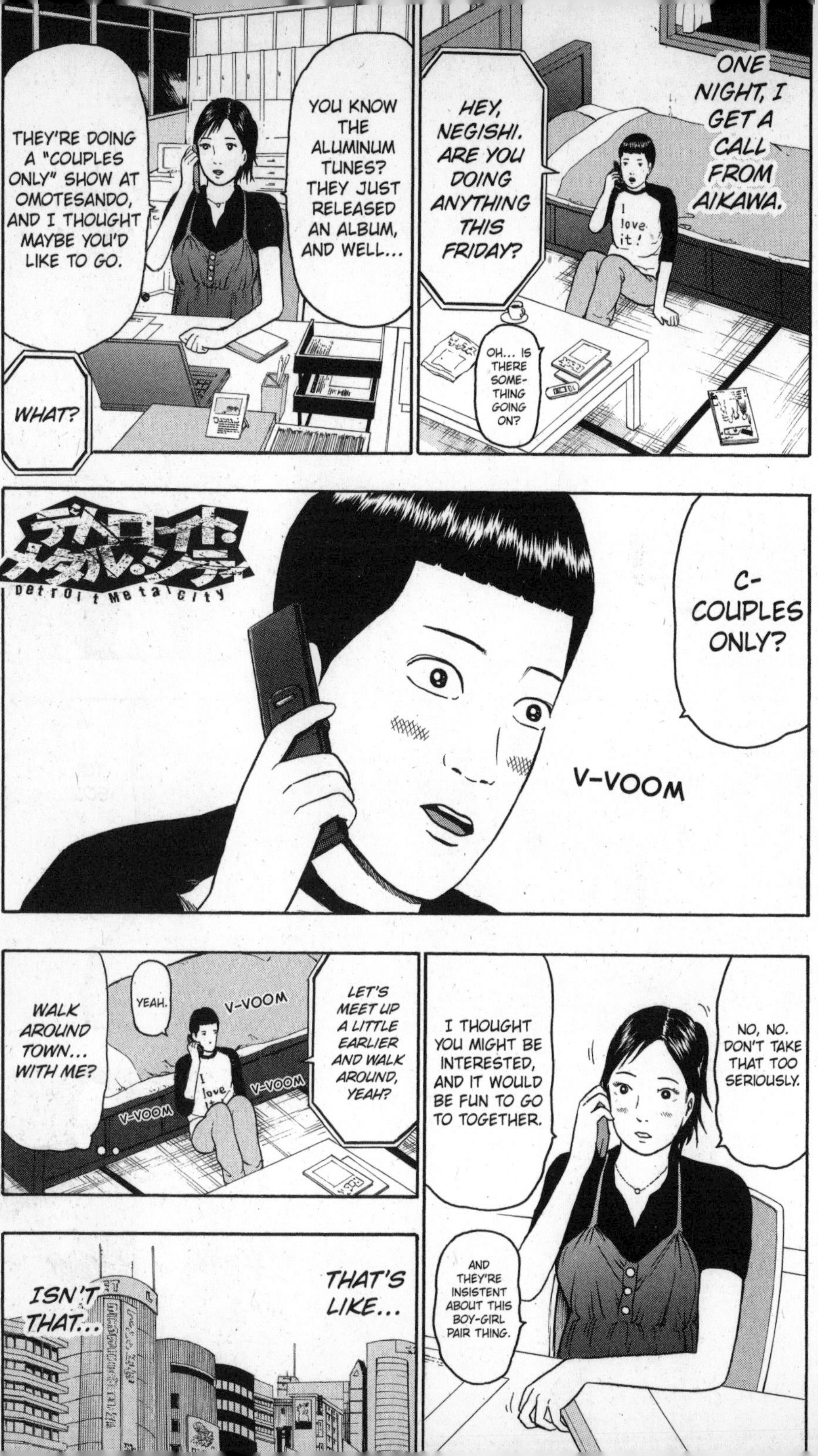
ONE NIGHT, I GET A CALL FROM AIKAWA.
HEY, NEGISHI. ARE YOU DOING ANYTHING THIS FRIDAY?
OH... IS THERE SOMETHING GOING ON?
YOU KNOW THE ALUMINUM TUNES? THEY JUST RELEASED AN ALBUM, AND WELL...
THEY'RE DOING A "COUPLES ONLY" SHOW AT OMOTESANDO, AND I THOUGHT MAYBE YOU'D LIKE TO GO.
WHAT?
C-COUPLES ONLY?
V-VOOM
NO, NO. DON'T TAKE THAT TOO SERIOUSLY.
I THOUGHT YOU MIGHT BE INTERESTED, AND IT WOULD BE FUN TO GO TO TOGETHER.
AND THEY'RE INSISTENT ABOUT THIS BOY-GIRL PAIR THING.
LET'S MEET UP A LITTLE EARLIER AND WALK AROUND, YEAH?
V-VOOM
YEAH.
V-VOOM
V-VOOM
WALK AROUND TOWN... WITH ME?
THAT'S LIKE...
ISN'T THAT...

TRACK 46 Fortune-Telling

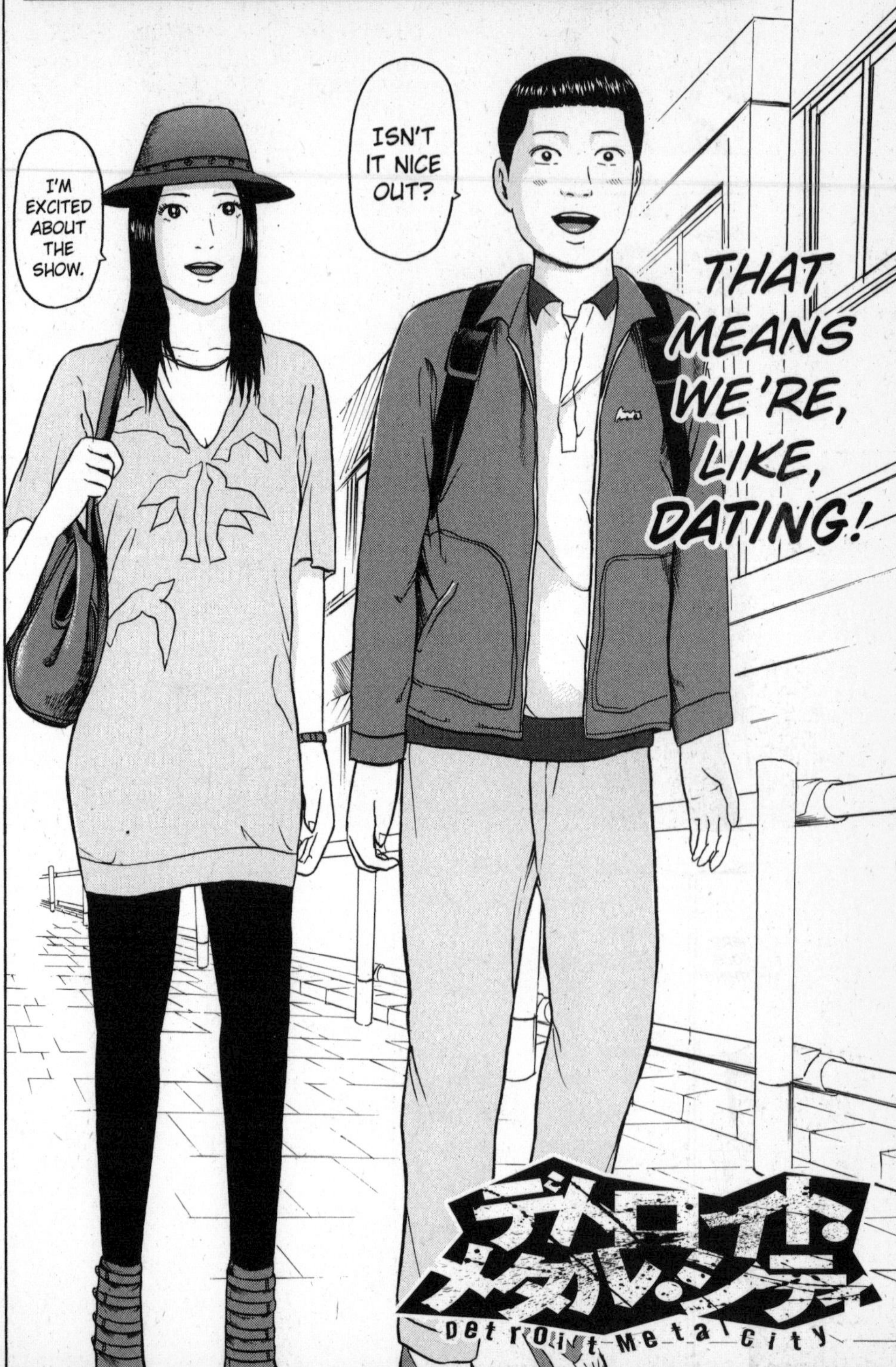
ISN'T IT NICE OUT?
I'M EXCITED ABOUT THE SHOW.
THAT MEANS WE'RE, LIKE, DATING!
Detroit Metal City

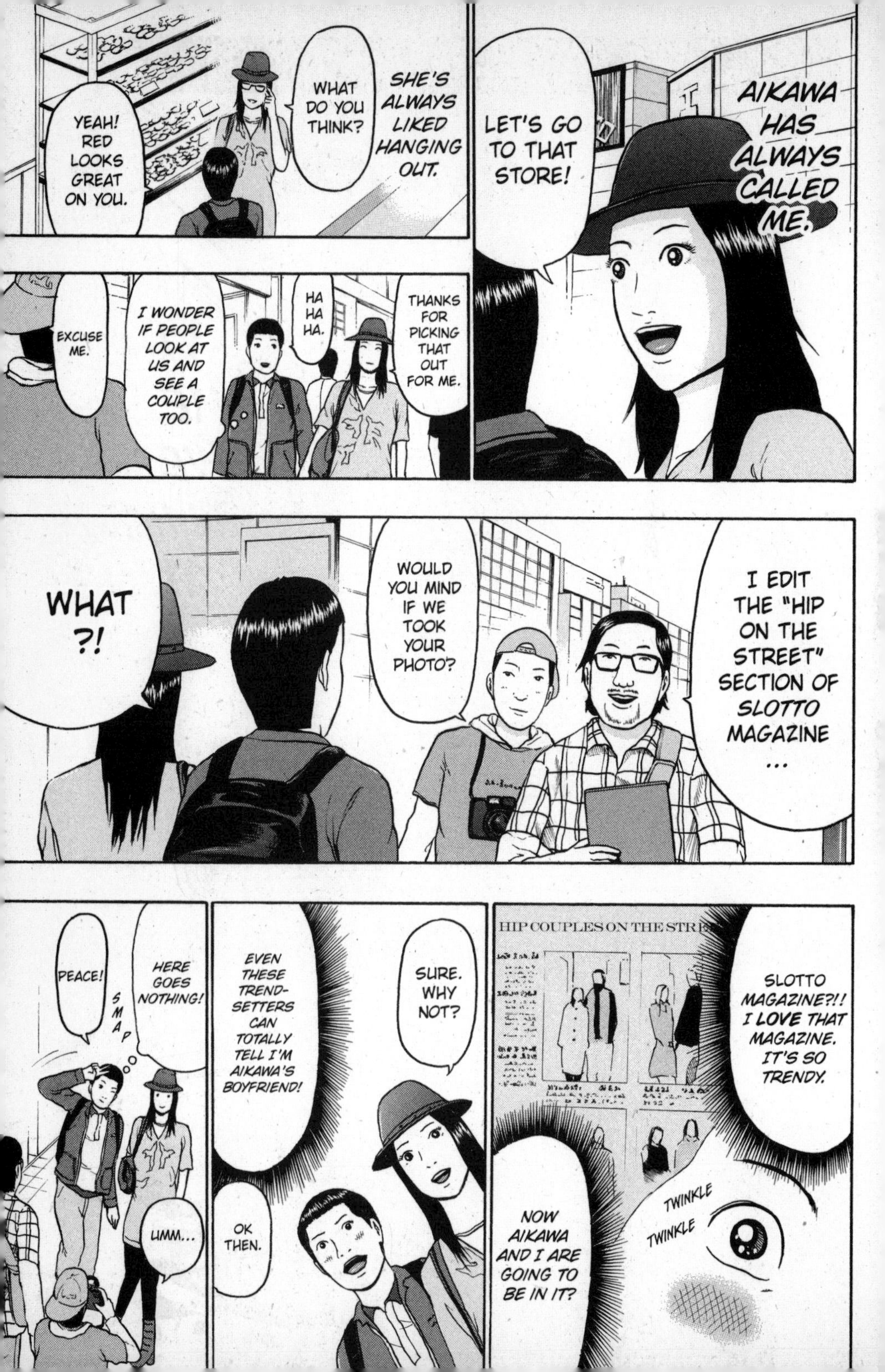
AIKAWA HAS ALWAYS CALLED ME.
LET'S GO TO THAT STORE!
SHE'S ALWAYS LIKED HANGING OUT.
WHAT DO YOU THINK?
YEAH! RED LOOKS GREAT ON YOU.
THANKS FOR PICKING THAT OUT FOR ME.
HA HA HA.
I WONDER IF PEOPLE LOOK AT US AND SEE A COUPLE TOO.
EXCUSE ME.
I EDIT THE "HIP ON THE STREET" SECTION OF SLOTTO MAGAZINE ...
WOULD YOU MIND IF WE TOOK YOUR PHOTO?
WHAT ?!
HIP COUPLES ON THE STRE
SLOTTO MAGAZINE?!! I LOVE THAT MAGAZINE. IT'S SO TRENDY.
TWINKLE
TWINKLE
NOW AIKAWA AND I ARE GOING TO BE IN IT?
SURE. WHY NOT?
EVEN THESE TREND-SETTERS CAN TOTALLY TELL I'M AIKAWA'S BOYFRIEND!
OK THEN.
HERE GOES NOTHING!
PEACE!
SMAP
UMM...

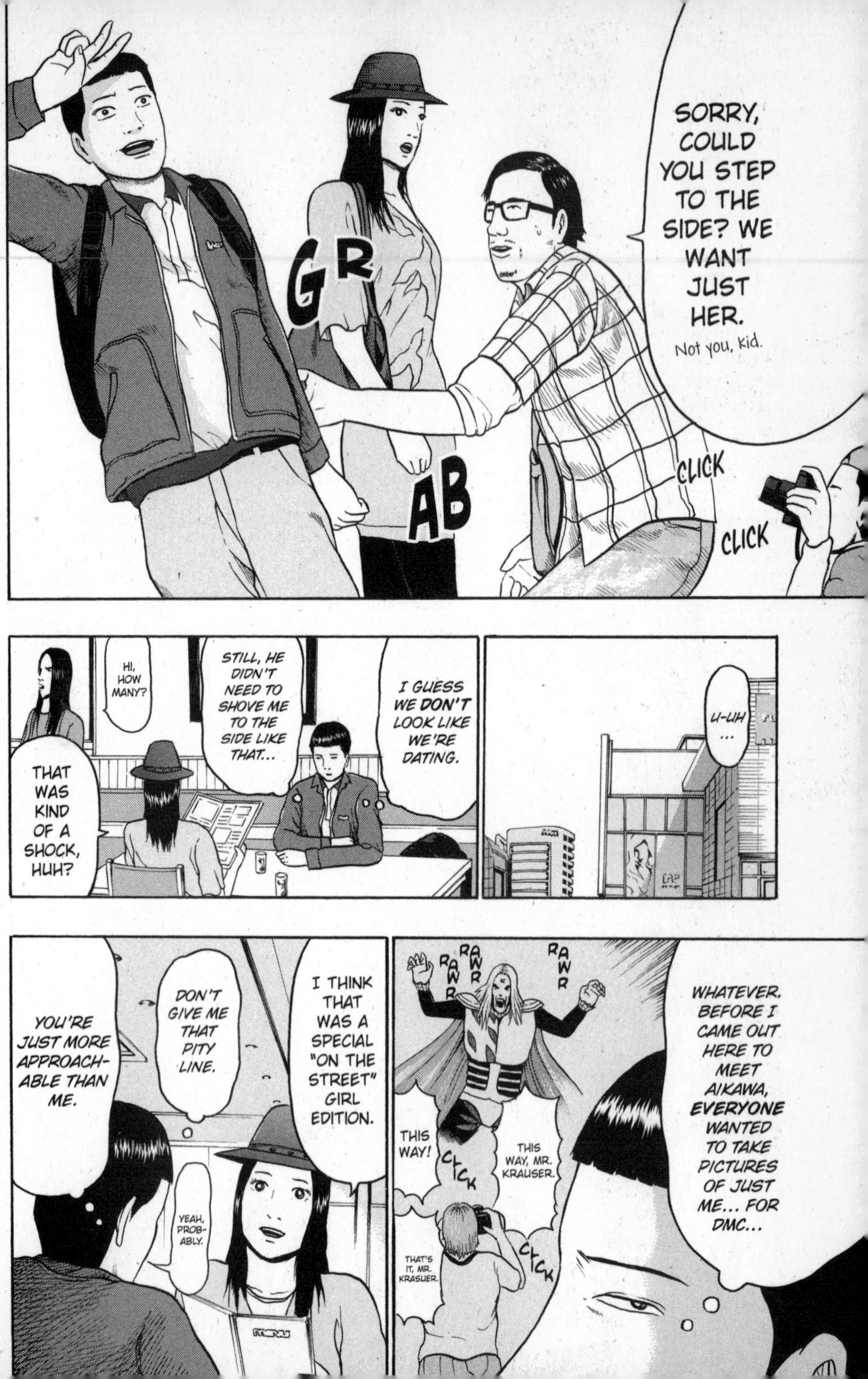
SORRY, COULD YOU STEP TO THE SIDE? WE WANT JUST HER.
Not you, kid.
GRAB
CLICK
CLICK
U-UH...
I GUESS WE DON'T LOOK LIKE WE'RE DATING.
STILL, HE DIDN'T NEED TO SHOVE ME TO THE SIDE LIKE THAT...
HI, HOW MANY?
THAT WAS KIND OF A SHOCK, HUH?
WHATEVER. BEFORE I CAME OUT HERE TO MEET AIKAWA, EVERYONE WANTED TO TAKE PICTURES OF JUST ME... FOR DMC...
RAWR
RAWR
RAWR
RAWR
THIS WAY, MR. KRAUSER.
THIS WAY!
CLICK
CLICK
THAT'S IT, MR. KRASUER.
I THINK THAT WAS A SPECIAL "ON THE STREET" GIRL EDITION.
DON'T GIVE ME THAT PITY LINE.
YOU'RE JUST MORE APPROACHABLE THAN ME.
YEAH, PROBABLY.

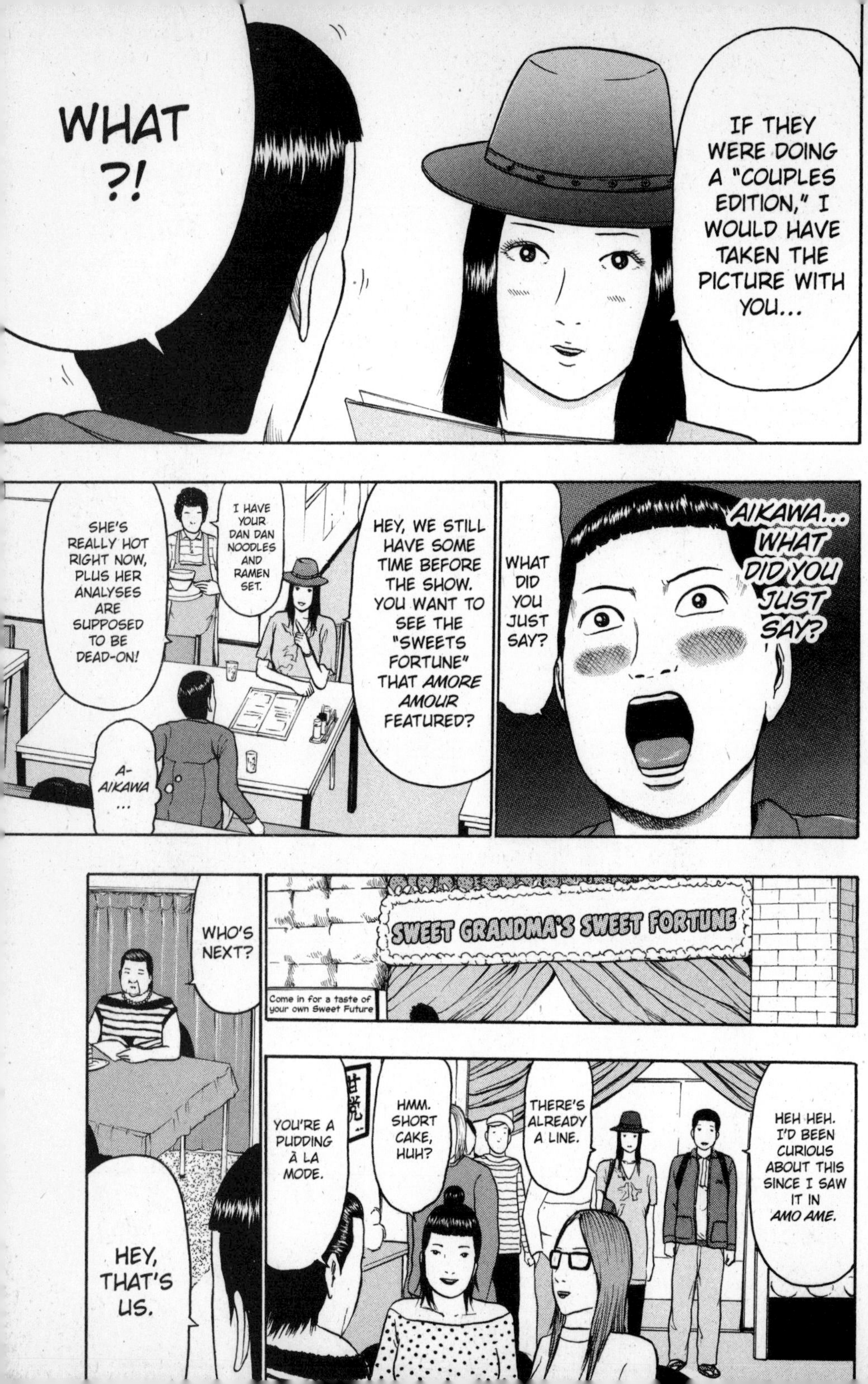
IF THEY WERE DOING A "COUPLES EDITION," I WOULD HAVE TAKEN THE PICTURE WITH YOU...
WHAT ?!
AIKAWA... WHAT DID YOU JUST SAY?
WHAT DID YOU JUST SAY?
HEY, WE STILL HAVE SOME TIME BEFORE THE SHOW. YOU WANT TO SEE THE "SWEETS FORTUNE" THAT *AMORE AMOUR* FEATURED?
I HAVE YOUR DAN DAN NOODLES AND RAMEN SET.
SHE'S REALLY HOT RIGHT NOW, PLUS HER ANALYSES ARE SUPPOSED TO BE DEAD-ON!
A- AIKAWA ...
SWEET GRANDMA'S SWEET FORTUNE
Come in for a taste of your own Sweet Future
HEH HEH. I'D BEEN CURIOUS ABOUT THIS SINCE I SAW IT IN *AMO AME.*
THERE'S ALREADY A LINE.
HMM. SHORT CAKE, HUH?
YOU'RE A PUDDING À LA MODE.
WHO'S NEXT?
HEY, THAT'S US.

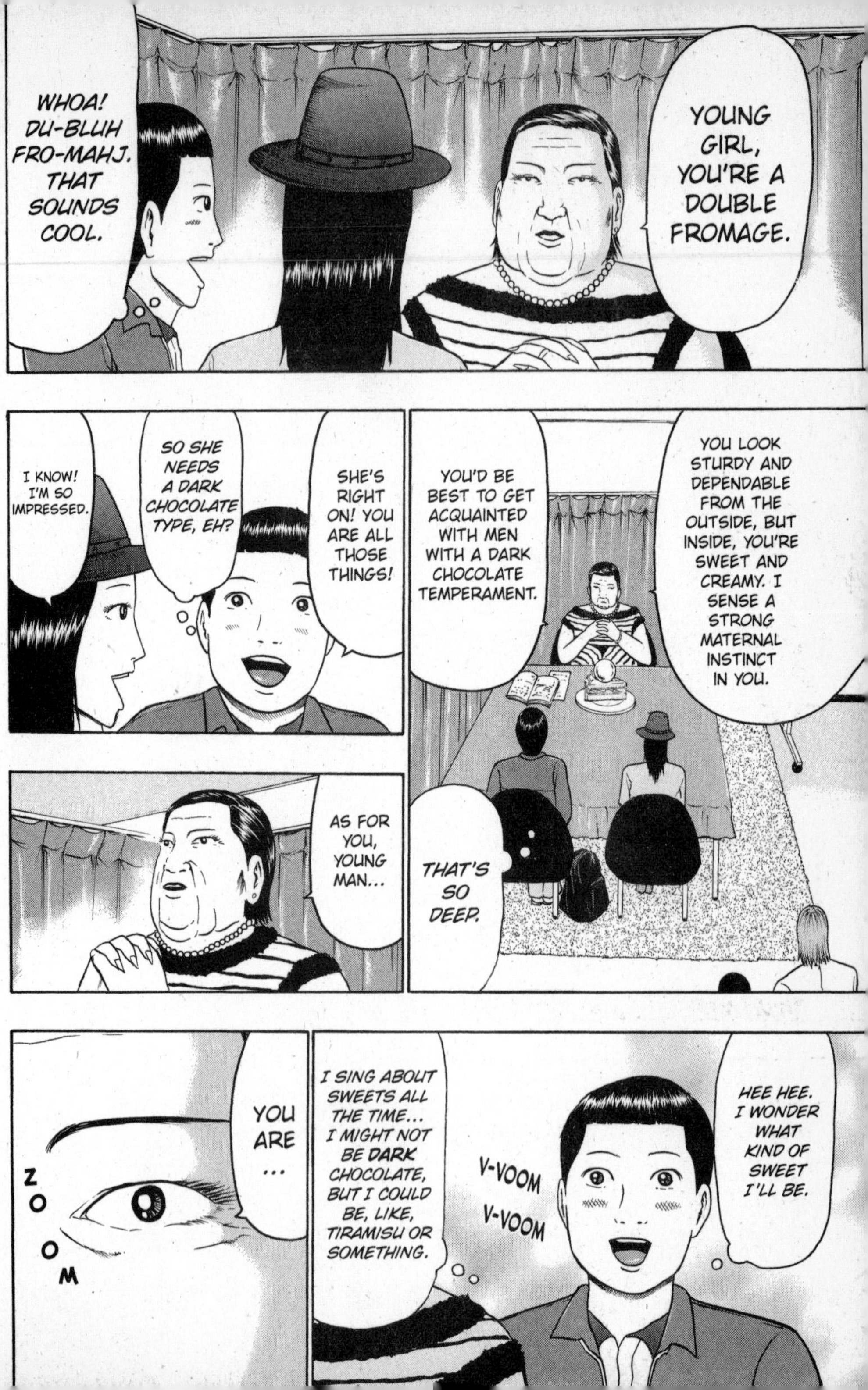
YOUNG GIRL, YOU'RE A DOUBLE FROMAGE.
WHOA! DU-BLUH FRO-MAHJ. THAT SOUNDS COOL.
YOU LOOK STURDY AND DEPENDABLE FROM THE OUTSIDE, BUT INSIDE, YOU'RE SWEET AND CREAMY. I SENSE A STRONG MATERNAL INSTINCT IN YOU.
YOU'D BE BEST TO GET ACQUAINTED WITH MEN WITH A DARK CHOCOLATE TEMPERAMENT.
THAT'S SO DEEP.
SHE'S RIGHT ON! YOU ARE ALL THOSE THINGS!
SO SHE NEEDS A DARK CHOCOLATE TYPE, EH?
I KNOW! I'M SO IMPRESSED.
AS FOR YOU, YOUNG MAN...
HEE HEE. I WONDER WHAT KIND OF SWEET I'LL BE.
V-VOOM
V-VOOM
I SING ABOUT SWEETS ALL THE TIME... I MIGHT NOT BE DARK CHOCOLATE, BUT I COULD BE, LIKE, TIRAMISU OR SOMETHING.
YOU ARE ...
ZOOOM

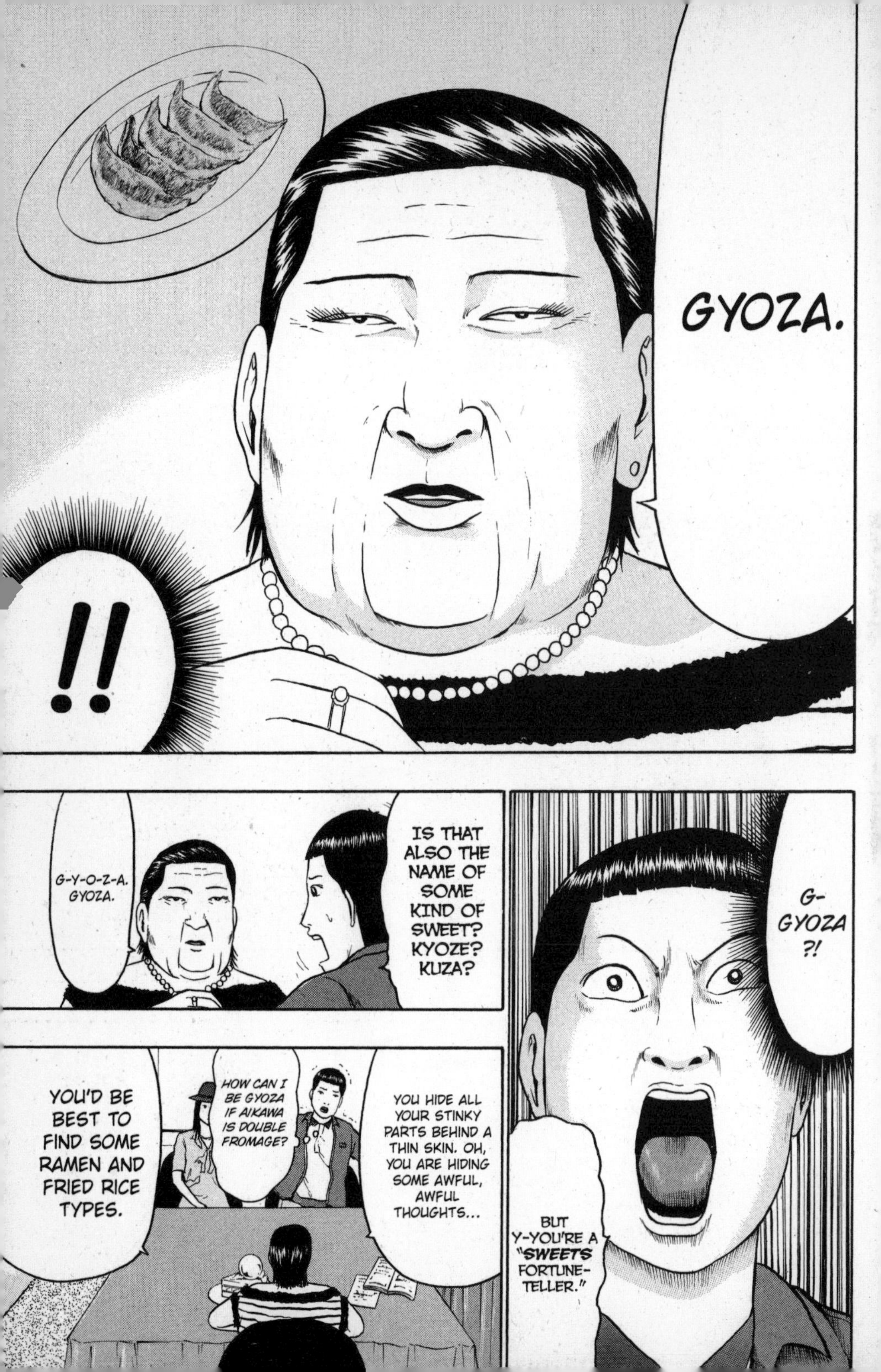
GYOZA.
!!
G-GYOZA?!
BUT Y-YOU'RE A "SWEETS FORTUNE-TELLER."
IS THAT ALSO THE NAME OF SOME KIND OF SWEET? KYOZE? KUZA?
G-Y-O-Z-A. GYOZA.
YOU HIDE ALL YOUR STINKY PARTS BEHIND A THIN SKIN. OH, YOU ARE HIDING SOME AWFUL, AWFUL THOUGHTS...
HOW CAN I BE GYOZA IF AIKAWA IS DOUBLE FROMAGE?
YOU'D BE BEST TO FIND SOME RAMEN AND FRIED RICE TYPES.

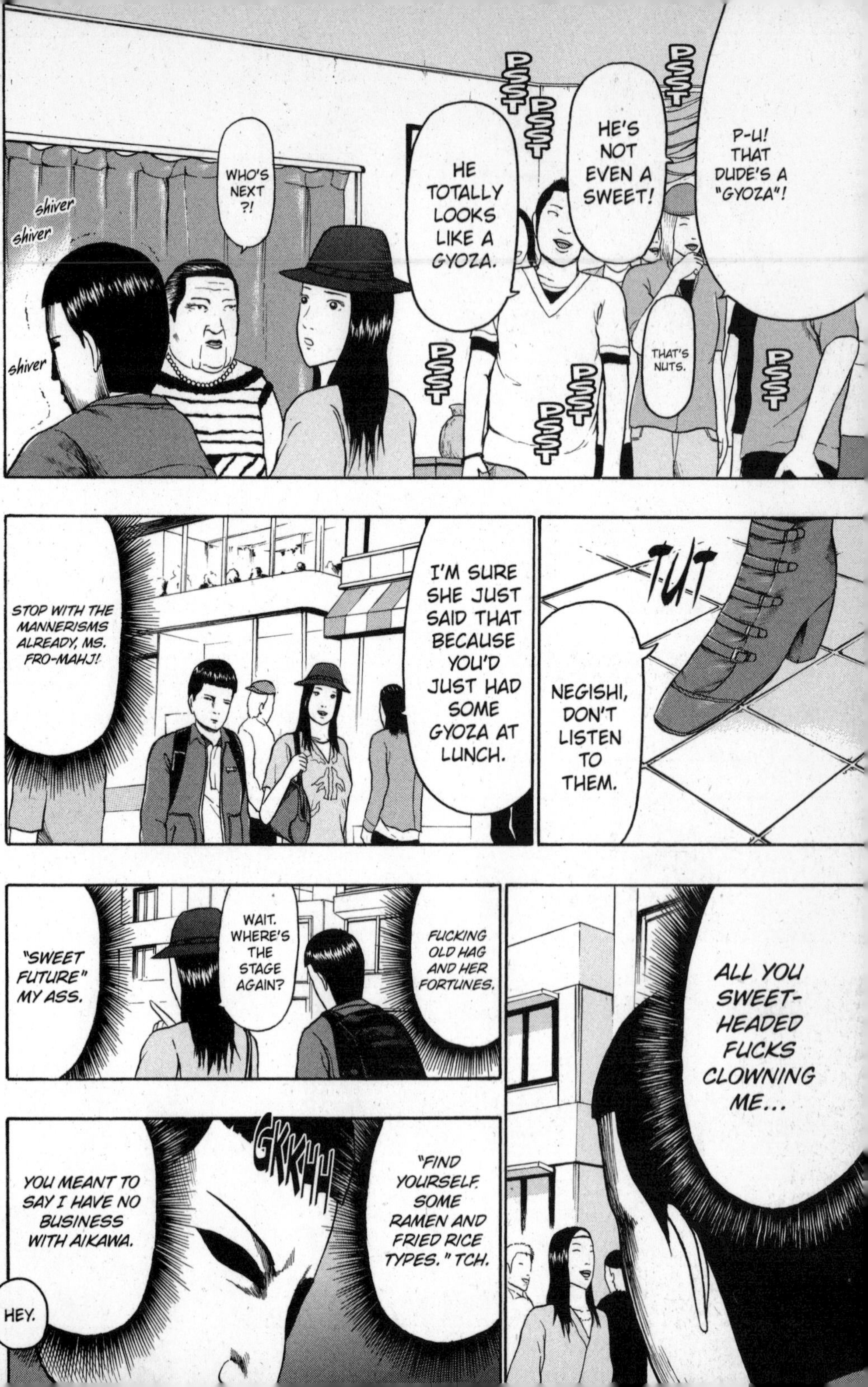
P-U! THAT DUDE'S A "GYOZA"!
PSST
HE'S NOT EVEN A SWEET!
PSST
THAT'S NUTS.
PSST PSST
PSST
PSST PSST
HE TOTALLY LOOKS LIKE A GYOZA.
PSST
WHO'S NEXT ?!
shiver shiver
shiver
TUT
NEGISHI, DON'T LISTEN TO THEM.
I'M SURE SHE JUST SAID THAT BECAUSE YOU'D JUST HAD SOME GYOZA AT LUNCH.
STOP WITH THE MANNERISMS ALREADY, MS. FRO-MAHJ!
ALL YOU SWEET-HEADED FUCKS CLOWNING ME...
FUCKING OLD HAG AND HER FORTUNES.
WAIT. WHERE'S THE STAGE AGAIN?
"SWEET FUTURE" MY ASS.
GKKHH
"FIND YOURSELF. SOME RAMEN AND FRIED RICE TYPES." TCH.
YOU MEANT TO SAY I HAVE NO BUSINESS WITH AIKAWA.
HEY.

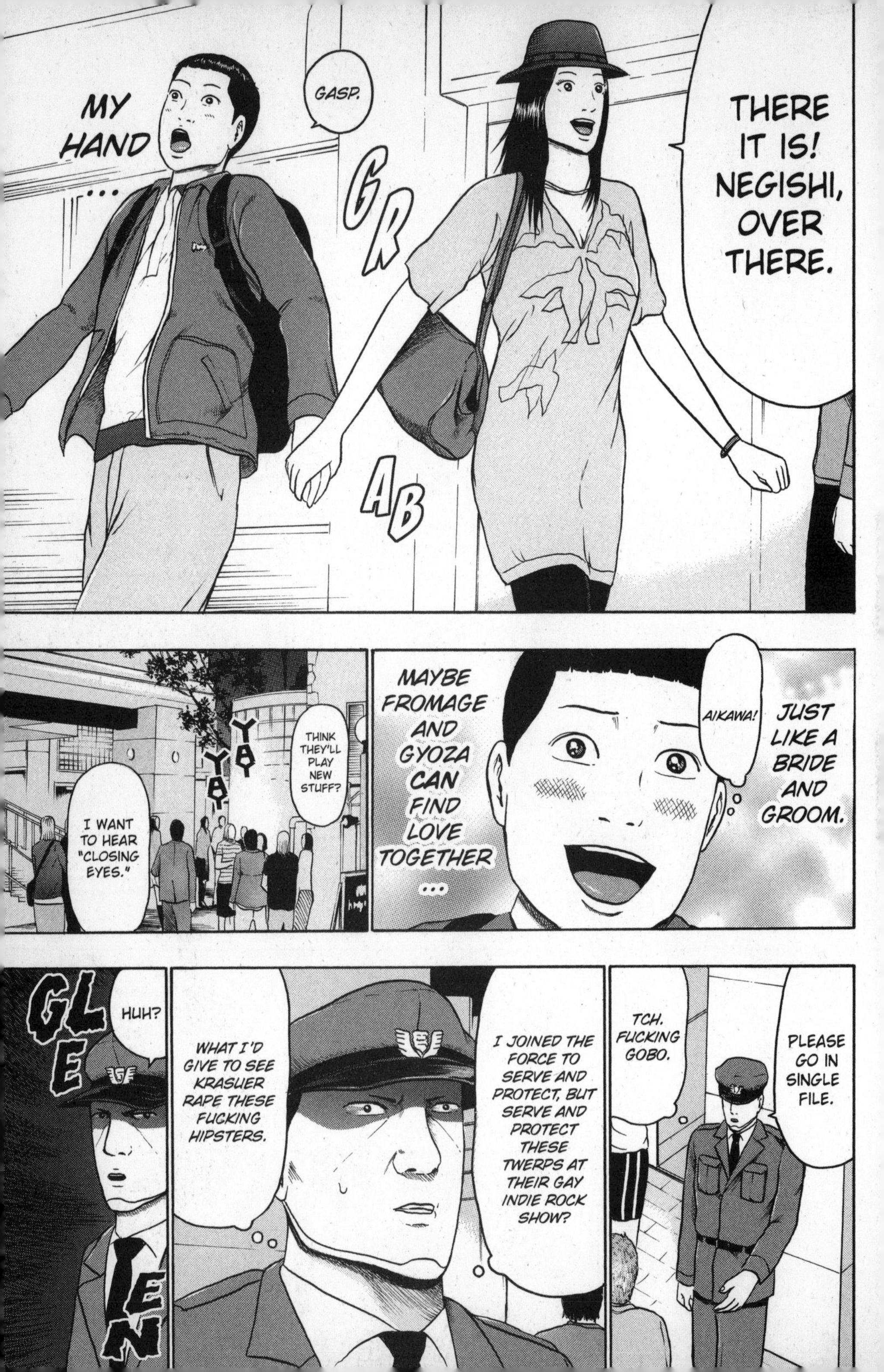
THERE IT IS! NEGISHI, OVER THERE.
GR
AB
GASP.
MY HAND ...
AIKAWA!
JUST LIKE A BRIDE AND GROOM.
MAYBE FROMAGE AND GYOZA CAN FIND LOVE TOGETHER ...
YAY
YAY
THINK THEY'LL PLAY NEW STUFF?
I WANT TO HEAR "CLOSING EYES."
PLEASE GO IN SINGLE FILE.
TCH. FUCKING GOBO.
I JOINED THE FORCE TO SERVE AND PROTECT, BUT SERVE AND PROTECT THESE TWERPS AT THEIR GAY INDIE ROCK SHOW?
WHAT I'D GIVE TO SEE KRASUER RAPE THESE FUCKING HIPSTERS.
HUH?
GLE
EN

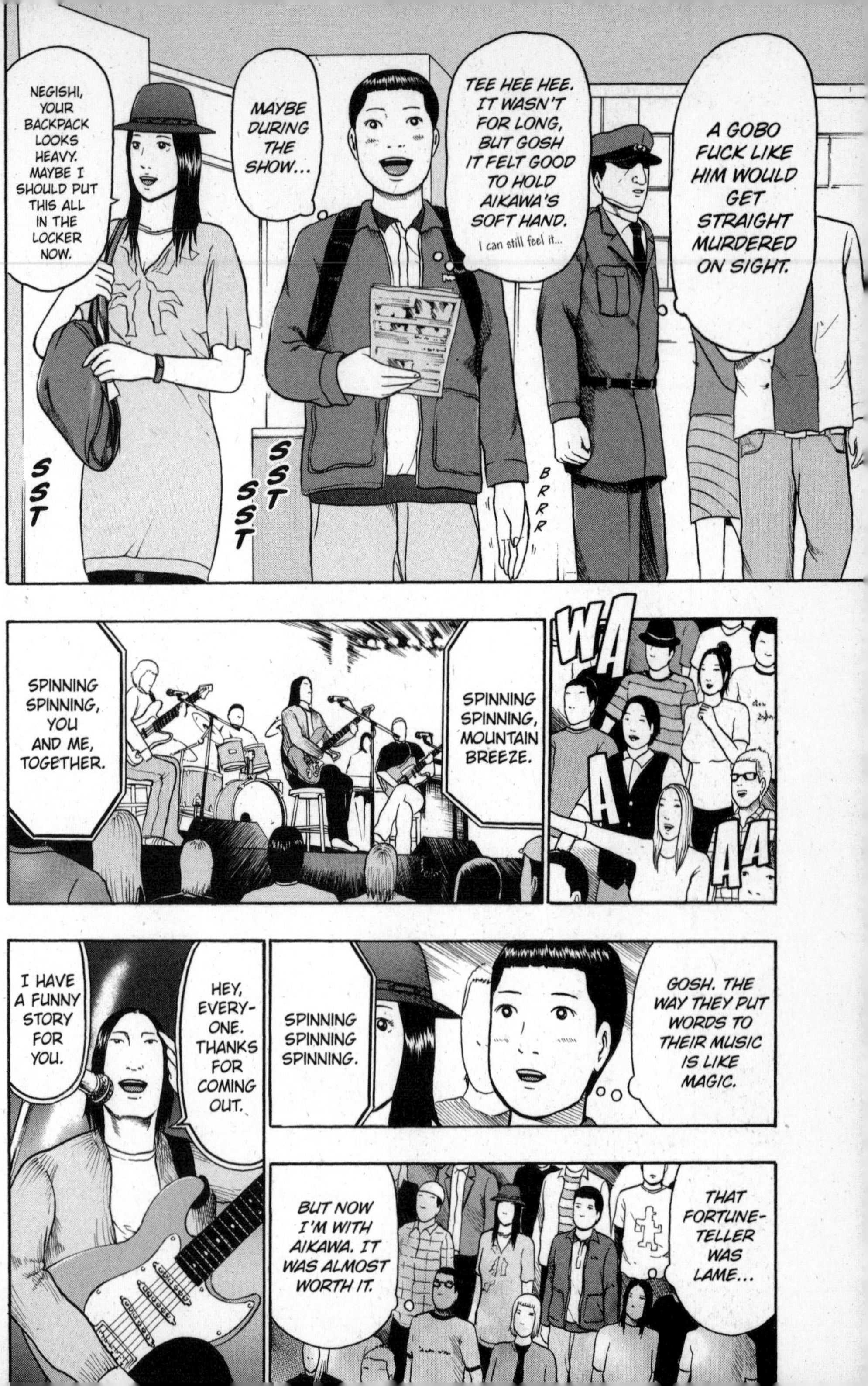
A GOBO FUCK LIKE HIM WOULD GET STRAIGHT MURDERED ON SIGHT.
TEE HEE HEE. IT WASN'T FOR LONG, BUT GOSH IT FELT GOOD TO HOLD AIKAWA'S SOFT HAND.
I can still feel it...
BRRR
MAYBE DURING THE SHOW...
SST SST
SST
NEGISHI, YOUR BACKPACK LOOKS HEAVY. MAYBE I SHOULD PUT THIS ALL IN THE LOCKER NOW.
SST
WAAAA
SPINNING SPINNING, MOUNTAIN BREEZE.
SPINNING SPINNING, YOU AND ME, TOGETHER.
GOSH. THE WAY THEY PUT WORDS TO THEIR MUSIC IS LIKE MAGIC.
SPINNING SPINNING SPINNING.
THAT FORTUNE-TELLER WAS LAME...
BUT NOW I'M WITH AIKAWA. IT WAS ALMOST WORTH IT.
HEY, EVERYONE. THANKS FOR COMING OUT.
I HAVE A FUNNY STORY FOR YOU.

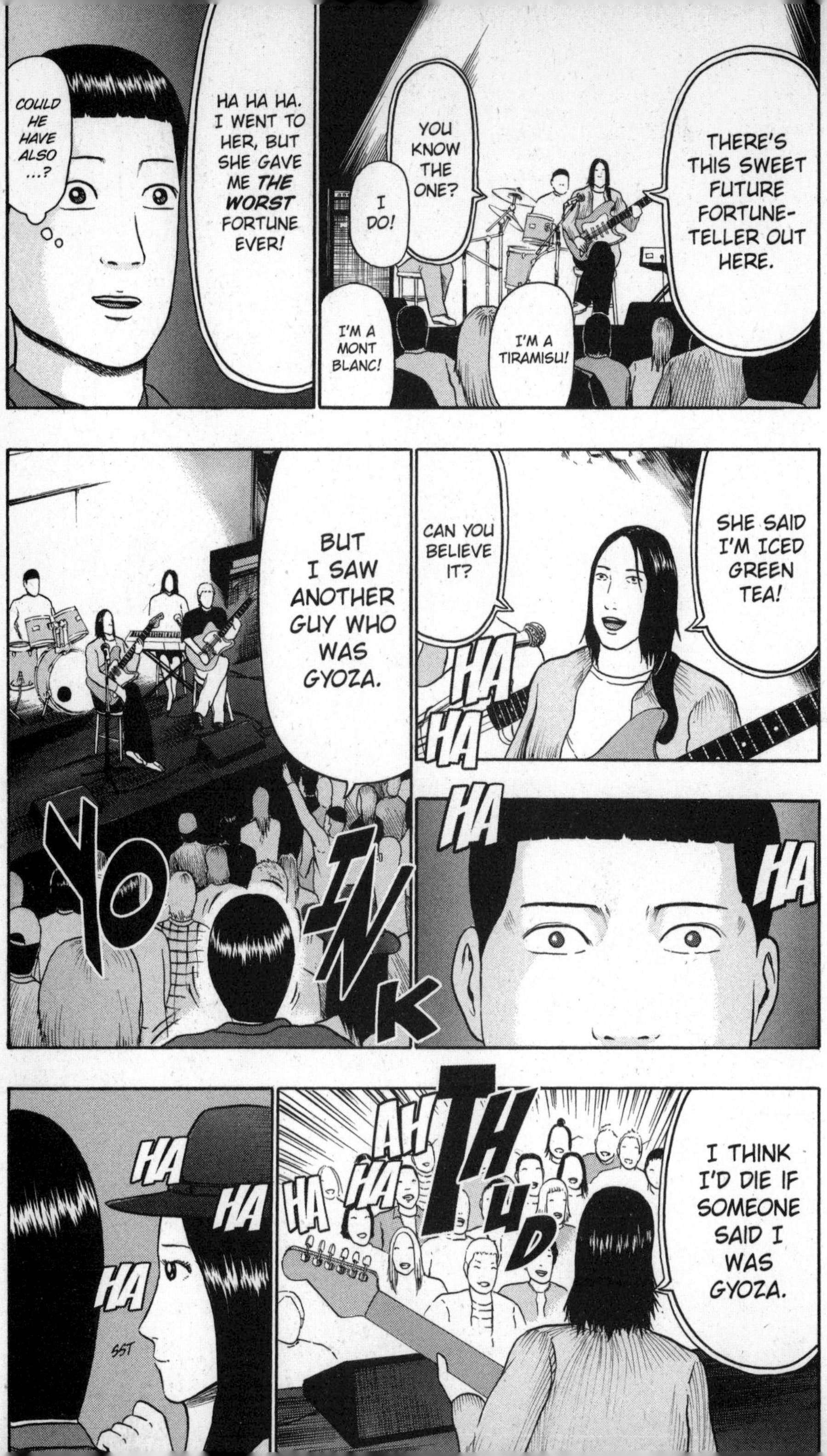
THERE'S THIS SWEET FUTURE FORTUNE-TELLER OUT HERE.
YOU KNOW THE ONE?
I DO!
I'M A TIRAMISU!
I'M A MONT BLANC!
HA HA HA. I WENT TO HER, BUT SHE GAVE ME *THE WORST* FORTUNE EVER!
COULD HE HAVE ALSO ...?
SHE SAID I'M ICED GREEN TEA!
CAN YOU BELIEVE IT?
HA HA
HA HA
BUT I SAW ANOTHER GUY WHO WAS GYOZA.
YOINK
I THINK I'D DIE IF SOMEONE SAID I WAS GYOZA.
THUD
AH HA HA HA
HA HA HA
SST

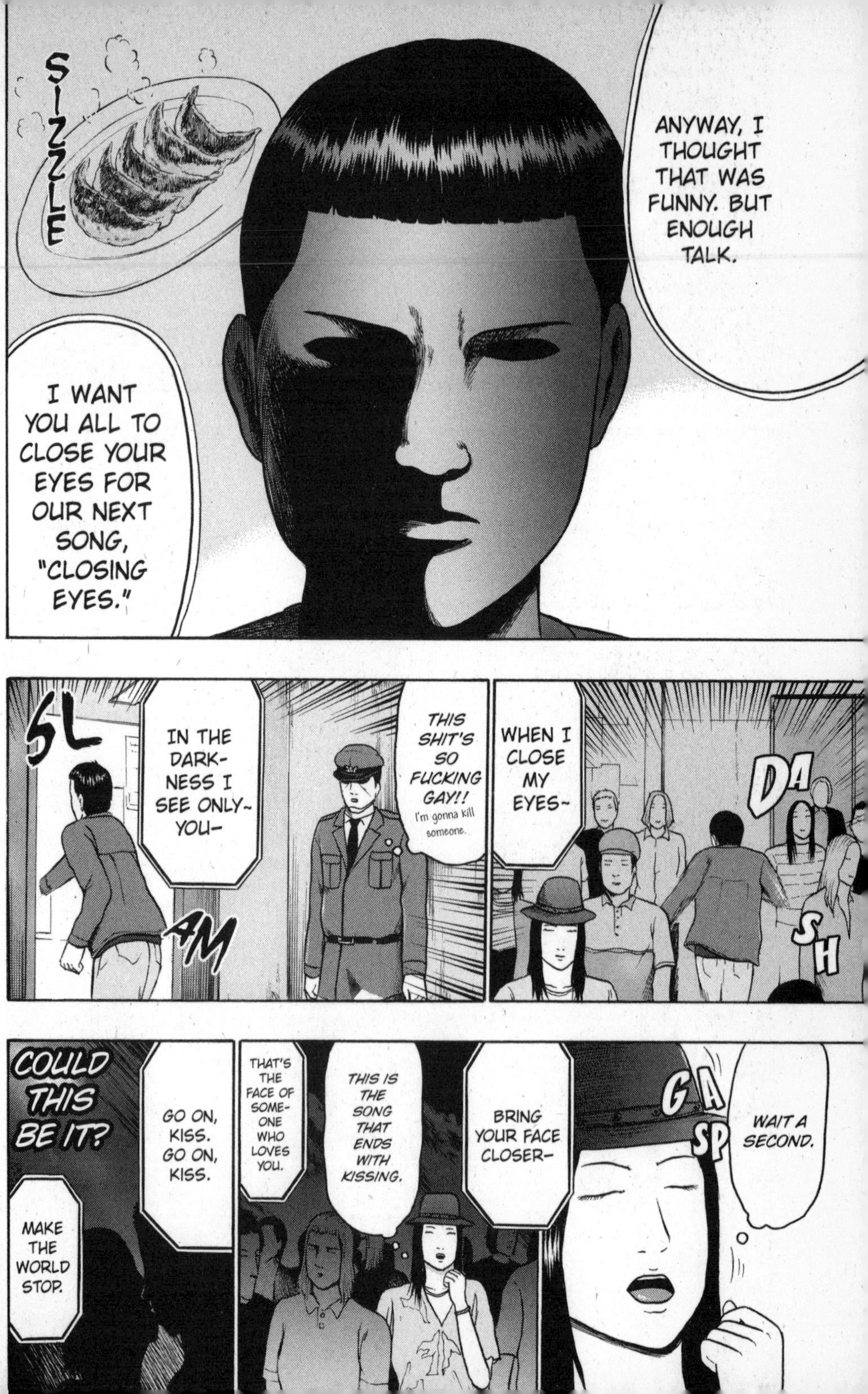
ANYWAY, I THOUGHT THAT WAS FUNNY. BUT ENOUGH TALK.
SIZZLE
I WANT YOU ALL TO CLOSE YOUR EYES FOR OUR NEXT SONG, "CLOSING EYES."
DASH
WHEN I CLOSE MY EYES~
THIS SHIT'S SO FUCKING GAY!!
I'm gonna kill someone.
SLAM
IN THE DARKNESS I SEE ONLY~ YOU~
WAIT A SECOND.
GASP
BRING YOUR FACE CLOSER~
THIS IS THE SONG THAT ENDS WITH KISSING.
THAT'S THE FACE OF SOMEONE WHO LOVES YOU.
GO ON, KISS. GO ON, KISS.
COULD THIS BE IT?
MAKE THE WORLD STOP.

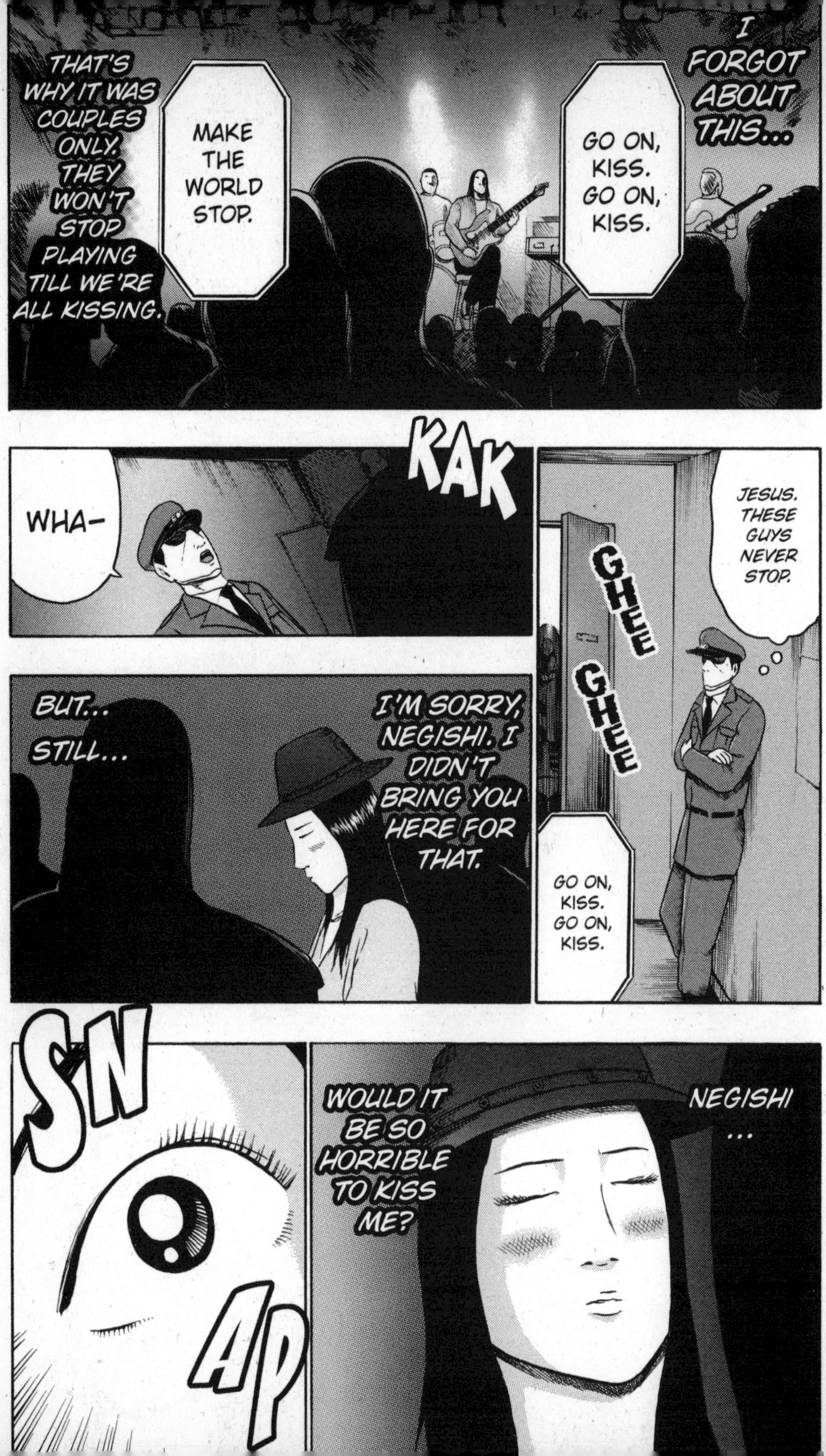
I FORGOT ABOUT THIS...
GO ON, KISS. GO ON, KISS.
MAKE THE WORLD STOP.
THAT'S WHY IT WAS COUPLES ONLY. THEY WON'T STOP PLAYING TILL WE'RE ALL KISSING.
JESUS. THESE GUYS NEVER STOP.
GHEE
GHEE
GO ON, KISS. GO ON, KISS.
KAK
WHA-
I'M SORRY, NEGISHI. I DIDN'T BRING YOU HERE FOR THAT.
BUT... STILL...
NEGISHI ...
WOULD IT BE SO HORRIBLE TO KISS ME?
SN
AP

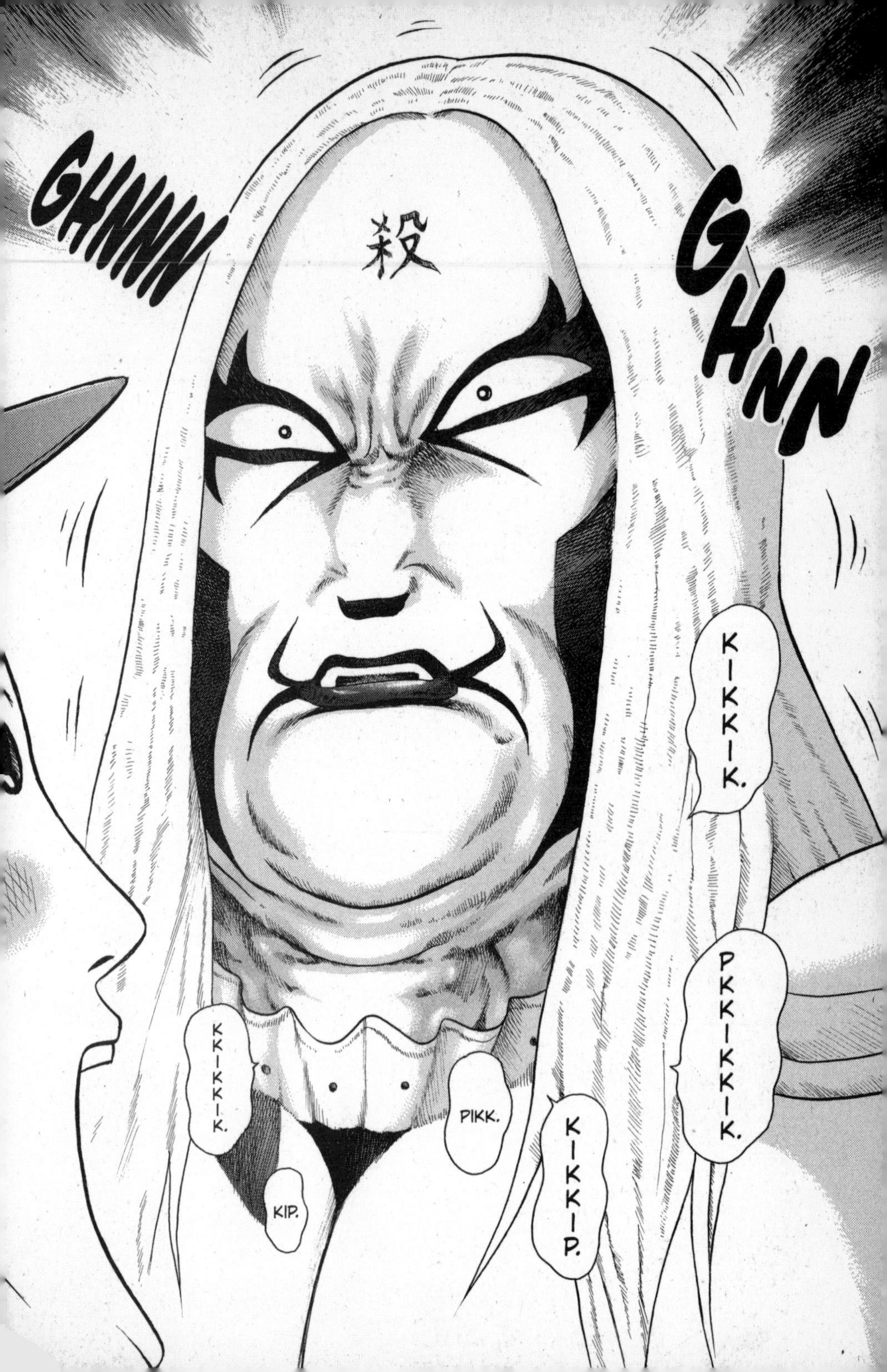
GHNN
殺
GHNNN
KIKKIK.
PKKIKKIK.
KIKKIP.
PIKK.
KKIKKIK.
KIP.

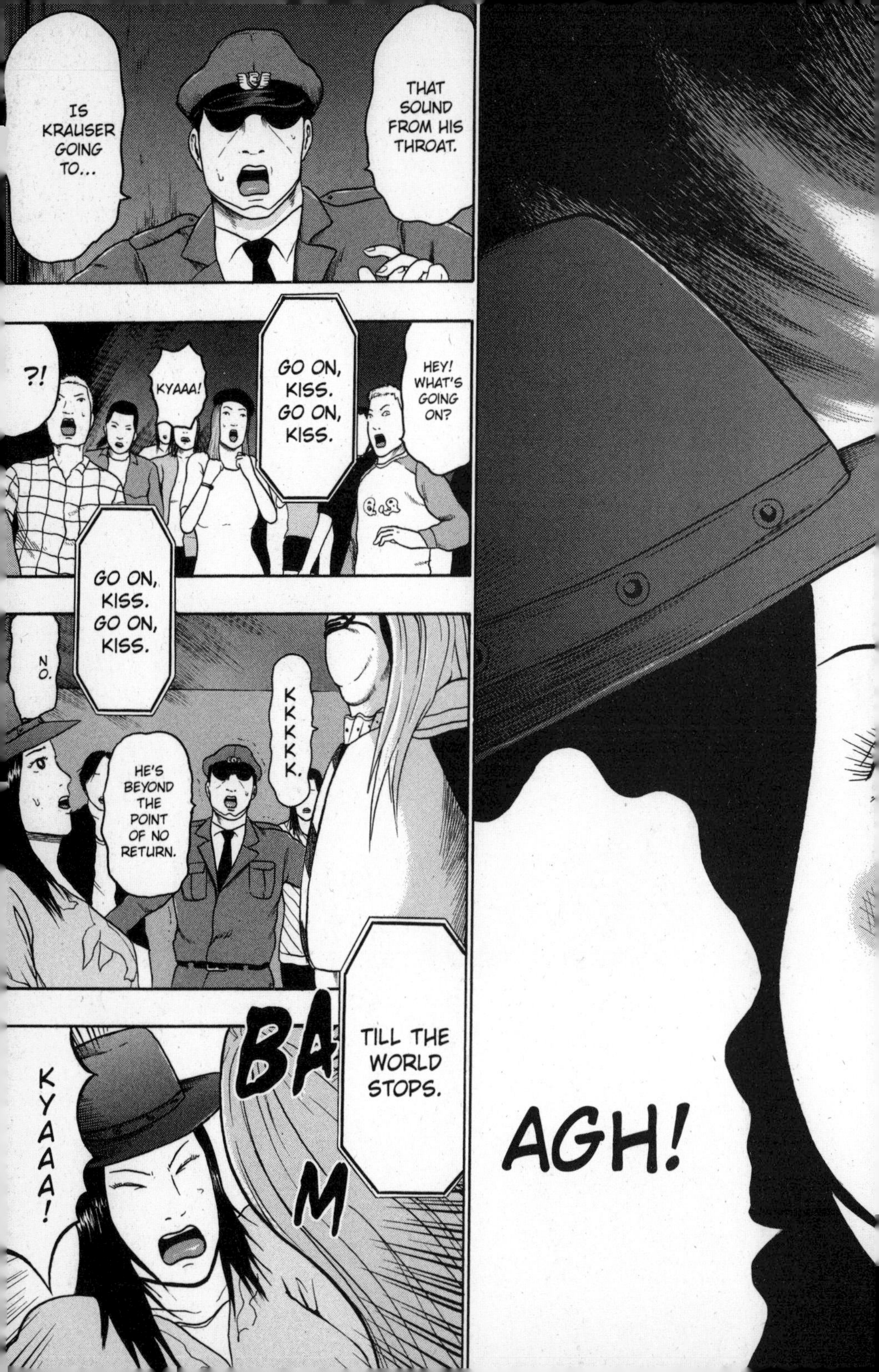
AGH!
THAT SOUND FROM HIS THROAT.
IS KRAUSER GOING TO...
HEY! WHAT'S GOING ON?
GO ON, KISS. GO ON, KISS.
KYAAA!
?!
GO ON, KISS. GO ON, KISS.
KKKKK.
HE'S BEYOND THE POINT OF NO RETURN.
NO.
TILL THE WORLD STOPS.
BAM
KYAAAA!

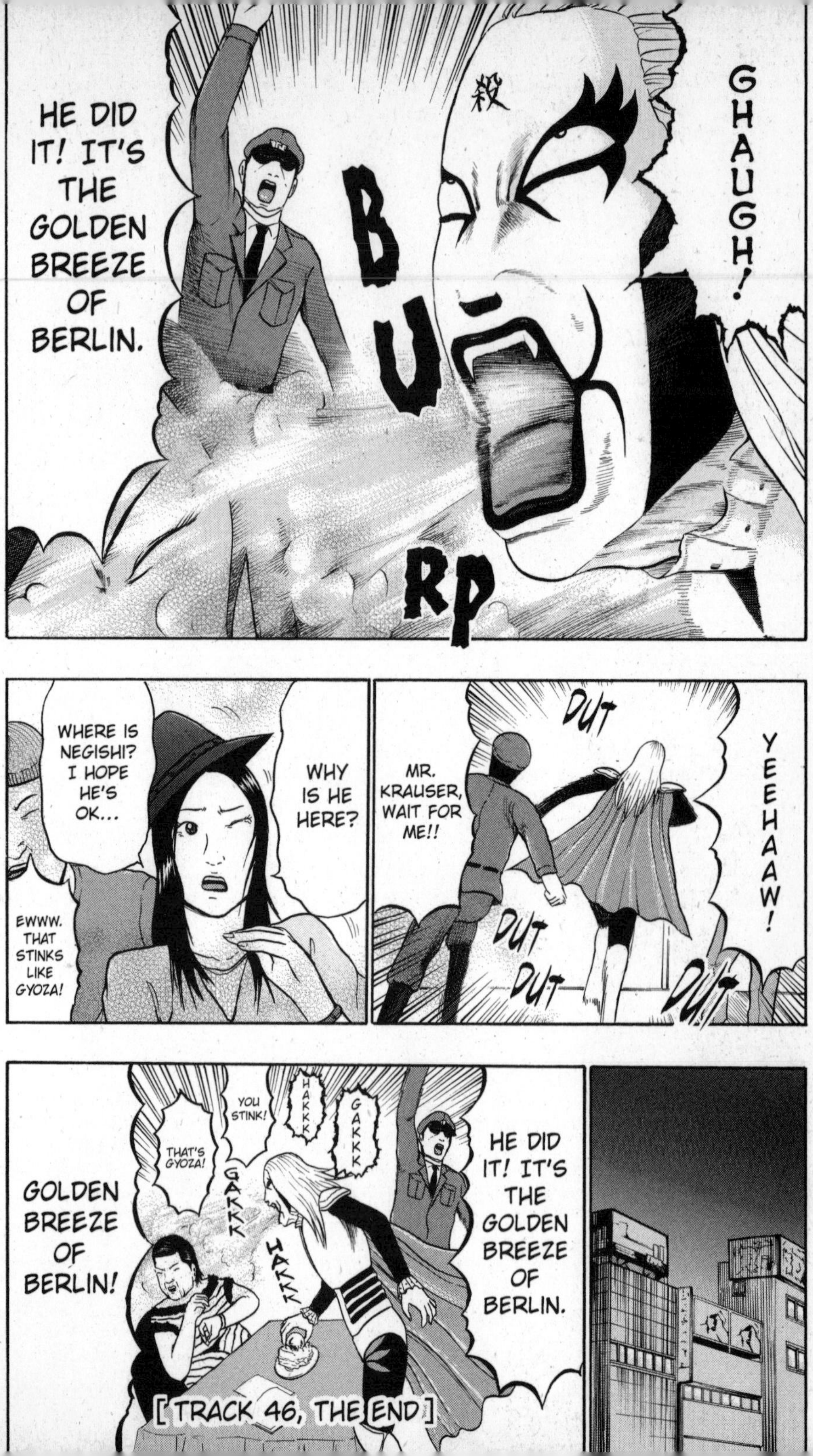

GHAUGH!
BURP
HE DID IT! IT'S THE GOLDEN BREEZE OF BERLIN.
YEEHAAAW!
DUT
MR. KRAUSER, WAIT FOR ME!!
DUT
DUT
DUT
DUT
WHY IS HE HERE?
WHERE IS NEGISHI? I HOPE HE'S OK...
EWWW. THAT STINKS LIKE GYOZA!
HE DID IT! IT'S THE GOLDEN BREEZE OF BERLIN.
GAKKK
HAKKK
YOU STINK!
THAT'S GYOZA!
GAKKK
HAKKK
GOLDEN BREEZE OF BERLIN!
[TRACK 46, THE END]

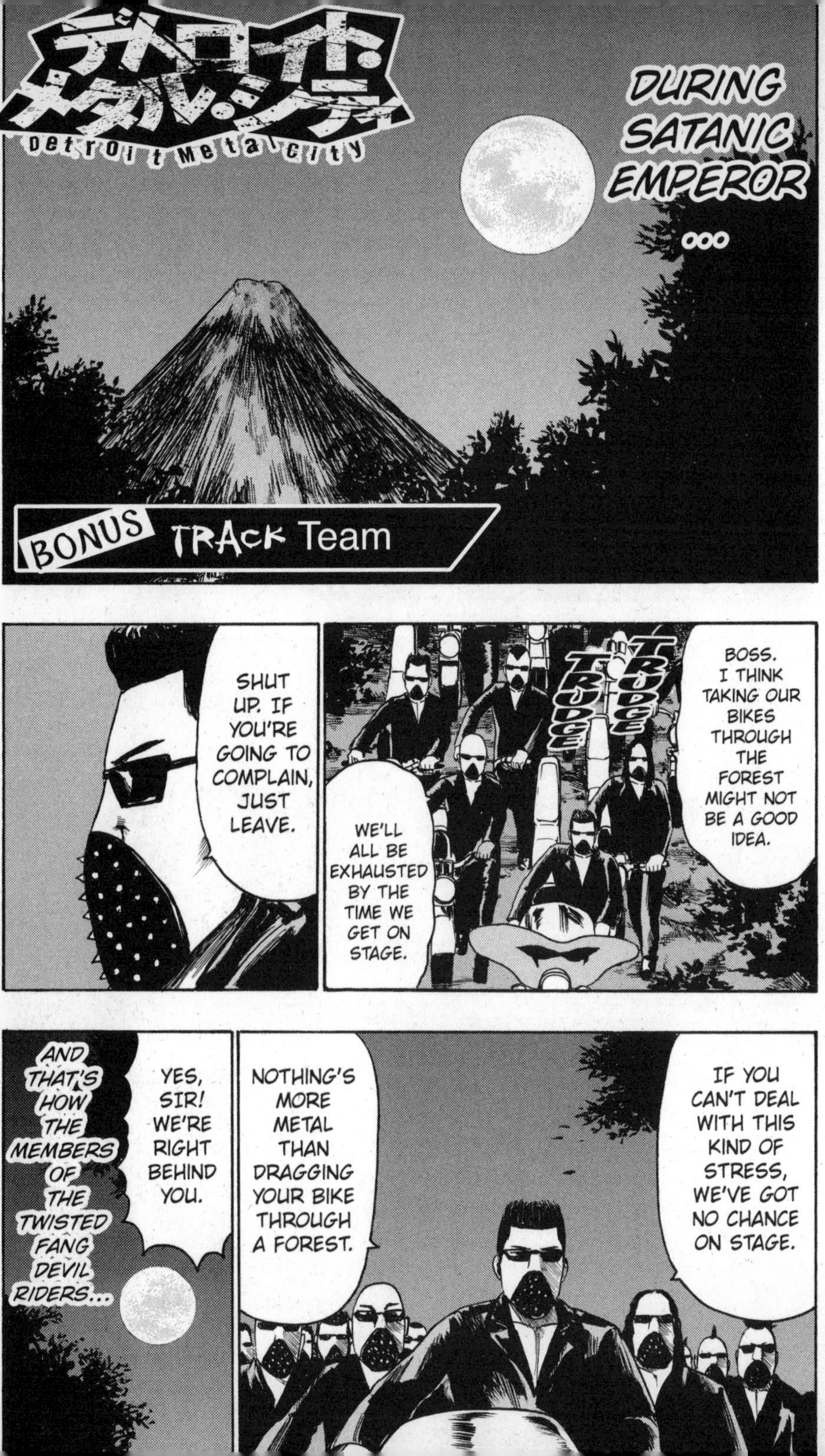
Detroit Metal City
DURING SATANIC EMPEROR...
BONUS TRACK Team
TRUDGE TRUDGE
BOSS. I THINK TAKING OUR BIKES THROUGH THE FOREST MIGHT NOT BE A GOOD IDEA.
WE'LL ALL BE EXHAUSTED BY THE TIME WE GET ON STAGE.
SHUT UP. IF YOU'RE GOING TO COMPLAIN, JUST LEAVE.
IF YOU CAN'T DEAL WITH THIS KIND OF STRESS, WE'VE GOT NO CHANCE ON STAGE.
NOTHING'S MORE METAL THAN DRAGGING YOUR BIKE THROUGH A FOREST.
YES, SIR! WE'RE RIGHT BEHIND YOU.
AND THAT'S HOW THE MEMBERS OF THE TWISTED FANG DEVIL RIDERS...

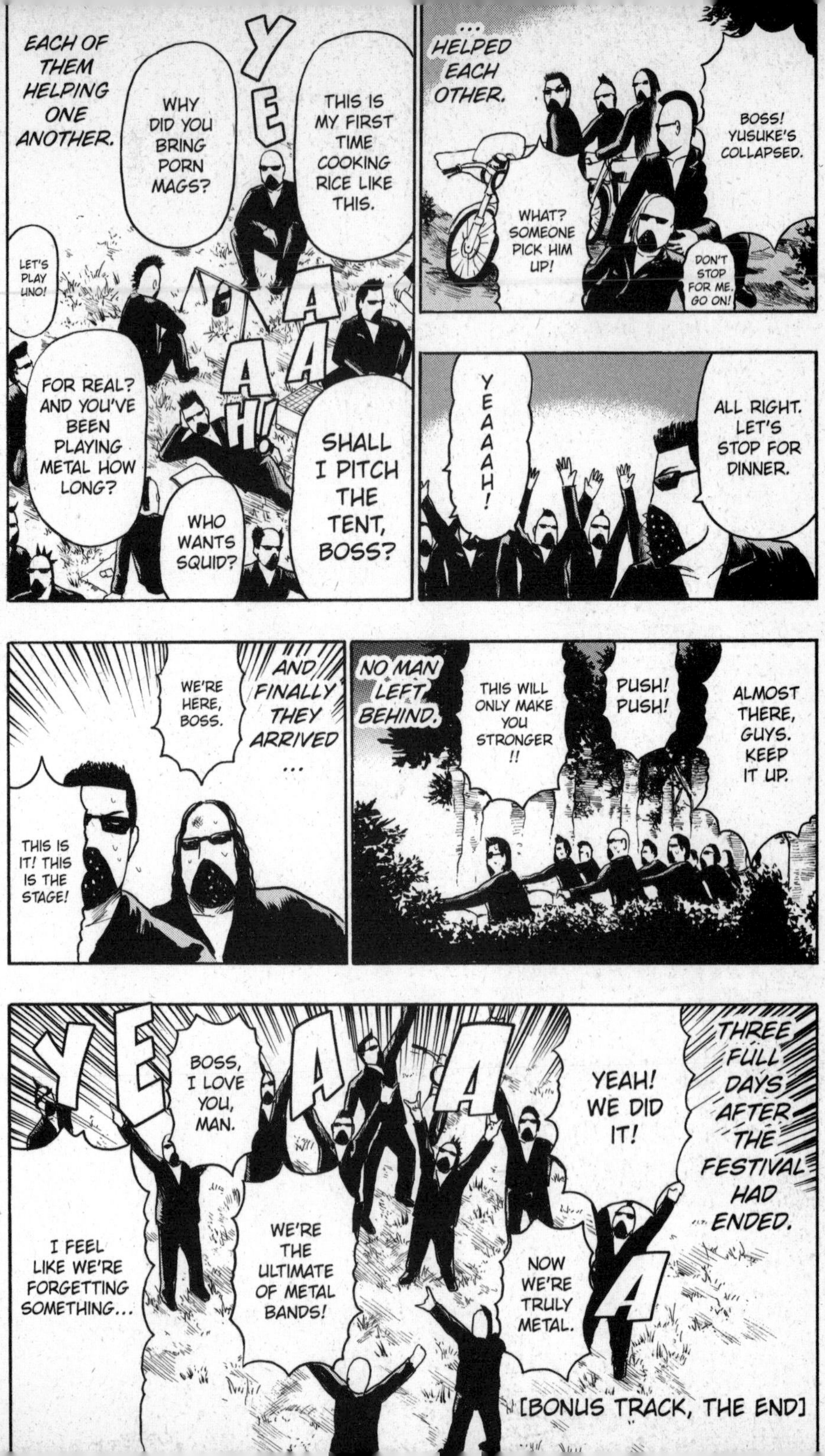

... HELPED EACH OTHER.
BOSS! YUSUKE'S COLLAPSED.
WHAT? SOMEONE PICK HIM UP!
DON'T STOP FOR ME. GO ON!
ALL RIGHT. LET'S STOP FOR DINNER.
YEAAAAH!
EACH OF THEM HELPING ONE ANOTHER.
YEAAAH!
THIS IS MY FIRST TIME COOKING RICE LIKE THIS.
WHY DID YOU BRING PORN MAGS?
LET'S PLAY UNO!
SHALL I PITCH THE TENT, BOSS?
FOR REAL? AND YOU'VE BEEN PLAYING METAL HOW LONG?
WHO WANTS SQUID?
NO MAN LEFT BEHIND.
ALMOST THERE, GUYS. KEEP IT UP.
PUSH! PUSH!
THIS WILL ONLY MAKE YOU STRONGER !!
AND FINALLY THEY ARRIVED ...
WE'RE HERE, BOSS.
THIS IS IT! THIS IS THE STAGE!
THREE FULL DAYS AFTER THE FESTIVAL HAD ENDED.
YEAAAA
YEAH! WE DID IT!
BOSS, I LOVE YOU, MAN.
NOW WE'RE TRULY METAL.
WE'RE THE ULTIMATE OF METAL BANDS!
I FEEL LIKE WE'RE FORGETTING SOMETHING...
[BONUS TRACK, THE END]

Detroit Metal City

VOLUME 4

STORY AND ART BY KIMINORI WAKASUGI
VIZ SIGNATURE EDITION

ENGLISH ADAPTATION Annus Itchii
TOUCH-UP ART & LETTERING John Hunt
DESIGN Courtney Utt
EDITOR Kit Fox

VP, PRODUCTION Alvin Lu
VP, SALES & PRODUCT MARKETING Gonzalo Ferreyra
VP, CREATIVE Linda Espinosa
PUBLISHER Hyoe Narita

Published by VIZ Media, LLC
P.O. Box 77010
San Francisco, CA 94107

10 9 8 7 6 5 4 3 2 1
First printing, March 2010

VIZ SIGNATURE
{ www.vizsignature.com }

VIZ media
{ www.viz.com }

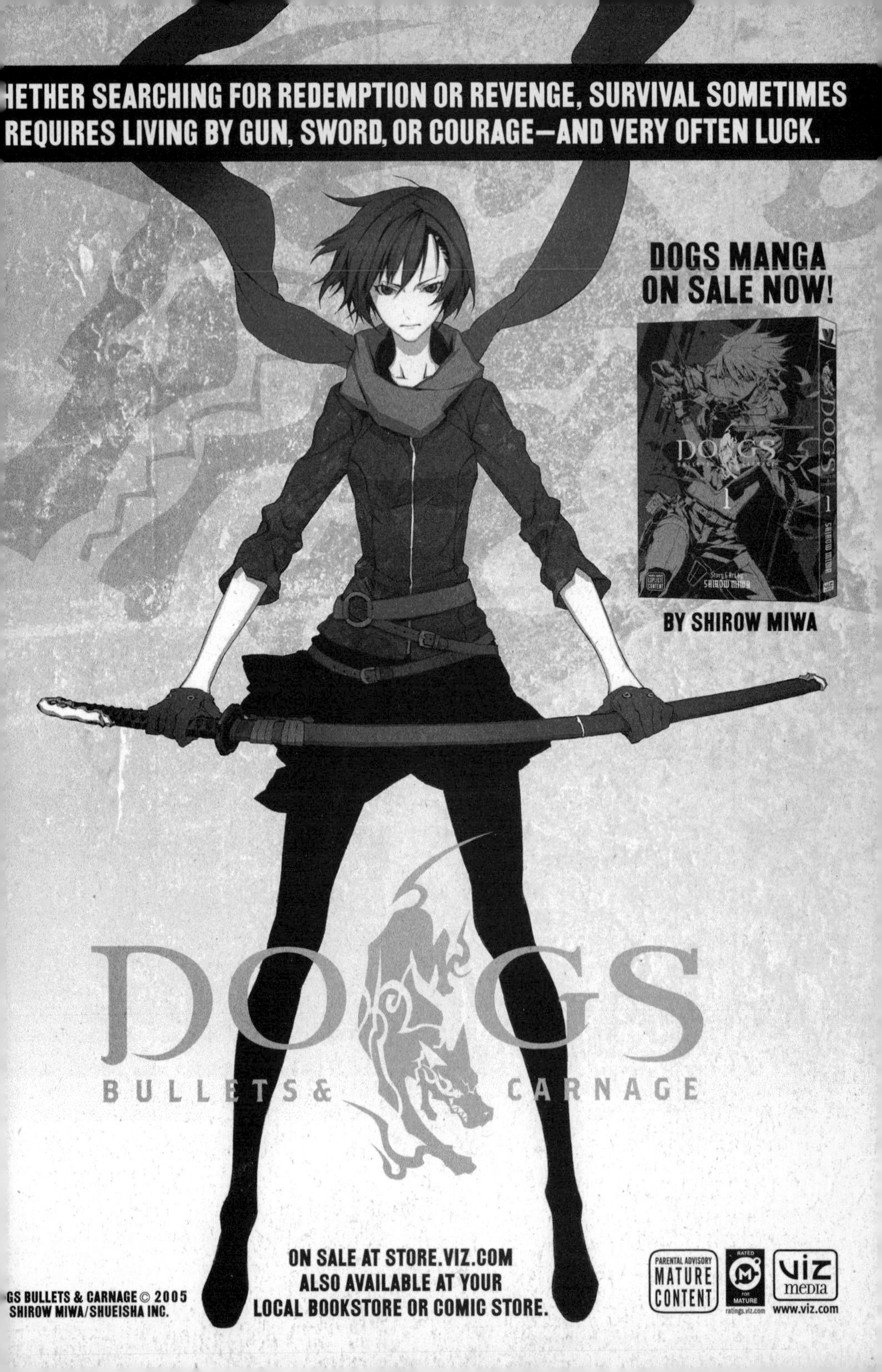

HETHER SEARCHING FOR REDEMPTION OR REVENGE, SURVIVAL SOMETIMES REQUIRES LIVING BY GUN, SWORD, OR COURAGE—AND VERY OFTEN LUCK.
DOGS MANGA ON SALE NOW!
BY SHIROW MIWA
DOGS
BULLETS & CARNAGE
ON SALE AT STORE.VIZ.COM
ALSO AVAILABLE AT YOUR
LOCAL BOOKSTORE OR COMIC STORE.
GS BULLETS & CARNAGE © 2005
SHIROW MIWA/SHUEISHA INC.
PARENTAL ADVISORY
MATURE CONTENT
RATED M FOR MATURE
ratings.viz.com
viz media
www.viz.com

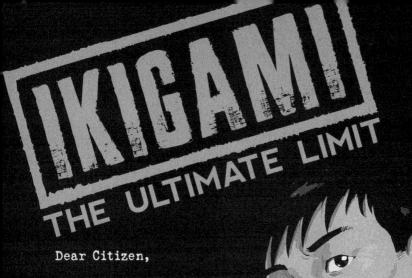

Hey! You're Reading in the Wrong Direction!

This is the **end** of this graphic novel!

To properly enjoy this VIZ graphic novel, please turn it around and begin reading from **right to left.** Unlike English, Japanese is read right to left, so Japanese comics are read in reverse order from the way English comics are typically read.

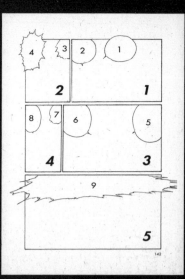

Follow the action this way

This book has been printed in the original Japanese format in order to preserve the orientation of the original artwork. Have fun with it!